Labour History and the Economy in Iran

Labour History and the Economy in Iran

Workers, Entrepreneurs and the State

Edited by
Mary Yoshinari and Serhan Afacan

I.B.TAURIS
LONDON • NEW YORK • OXFORD • NEW DELHI • SYDNEY

I.B. TAURIS
Bloomsbury Publishing Plc, 50 Bedford Square, London, WC1B 3DP, UK
Bloomsbury Publishing Inc, 1385 Broadway, New York, NY 10018, USA
Bloomsbury Publishing Ireland, 29 Earlsfort Terrace, Dublin 2, D02 AY28, Ireland

BLOOMSBURY, I.B. TAURIS and the I.B. Tauris logo are trademarks of Bloomsbury Publishing Plc

First published in Great Britain 2025

Series design: Adriana Brioso
Cover image: Hassan Saeli Kordehdeh working late in the lumbermill, c. 1965. Family album.

A catalogue record for this book is available from the British Library.

A catalog record for this book is available from the Library of Congress.

ISBN: HB: 978-0-7556-5259-4
ePDF: 978-0-7556-5262-4
eBook: 978-0-7556-5263-1

Typeset by Deanta Global Publishing Services, Chennai, India

Contents

List of figures vii
List of tables viii
List of contributors ix
Acknowledgements xii
Note on transliteration xiii

Part I Introduction and historiography 1

1 Introduction and overview 3
2 Evolution of labour historiography in Iran: From 'old' to 'new' labour history scholarship *Touraj Atabaki* 9

Part II The agency of workers, guilds and merchants 33

3 The convergence of the guilds and craftsmen with the labour movement in Iran, 1918–23 *Hojjat Fallah Tootkar* 35
4 The Economy Movement, an Iranian merchants' organization in response to the crisis in Iran-Soviet trade relations (1921–7) *Soheila Torabi Farsani* 55
5 Growth or bread: Craftsmen's reactions to industrialization policies under Reza Shah *Serhan Afacan* 71

Part III Economic development and the state 91

6 Iran's quest for economic autonomy: Foreign trade, banking, companies and industry, 1921–46 *Mary Yoshinari* 93
7 The political economy of social policy developments in Iran, 1920s–70s *Reza Omidi* 115
8 The Commercial Bank of Iran: The first private bank, from establishment to merger *Ali Tatari* 137
9 The role of workers and the state in Iranian mining, 1920s–50s *Abdolreza Alamdar* 161

Part IV Statistics versus family memoirs of labour and industry 179

10 Workforce, working conditions and labour relations in urban Iran: 1950s–60s *Willem Floor* 181
11 Recollections of the Risbaf (Carding) Complex in Qom *Ali Gheissari* 201
12 The private sector during the post-war era: The destiny of an entrepreneurial family *Ali Asghar Saeidi* 223
13 A pious lumbermill worker in Rasht and the impact of labour laws, 1920s–70s *Majid Saeli Kordehdeh* 245

Index 267

Figures

6.1	All registered companies in Iran, 1932–41	98
6.2	Registered joint-stock companies in provinces and Tehran, 1932–41	99
6.3	Gol Bangiz, glassware entrepreneur, Tehran, *c.* 1936	101
6.4	New registered companies in Tehran and their capital (millions of rials), 1946–8	104
8.1	Mostafa Tajaddod, *c.* 1968	140
8.2	Commercial Bank of Iran, *c.* 1968	144
8.3	Commercial Bank's net profits, term deposits and branches/kiosks, 1950–76	145
10.1	Khatunabad brickworkers, 1956	187
10.2	Khatunabad brickworkers on strike, 1957	191
11.1	Members of the Tehran Chamber of Commerce, 1935	202
11.2	Haj Mirza Ali Gheissarieh, Farvardin 1315 (March–April 1936)	204
11.3	Risbaf Factory Complex in Qom, 1938	205
11.4	Front from right to left: Prime Minister Ali Amini, while visiting Qom Risbaf Factory, and Morteza Gheissari, member of the board of directors, 1 Dey 1340 (22 December 1961)	206
11.5	Eid al-Fitr prayer, near the Risbaf Factory in Qom, 4 September 1978	212
12.1	Left to right: Haj Seyyed Mohammad Ladjevardian, *c.* 1940; Ahmad Ladjevardi, Haj Seyyed Akbar Ladjevardian, Ghassem and Habib Ladjevardi, *c.* 2005; Haj Seyyed Mahmoud Ladjevardi, *c.* 1975	225
13.1	Left to right: Hassan Saeli Kordehdeh with his co-workers, *c.* 1965	250
13.2	Hassan Saeli Kordehdeh, *c.* 1965	251
13.3	Left: Hassan Saeli Kordehdeh working late in the lumbermill, *c.* 1965	252
13.4	Centre: Hassan Saeli Kordehdeh, visiting his former co-workers, *c.* 1991	258

Tables

3.1	Iranian Trade Unions and Their Members, *c.* 1922	36
6.1	Iranian Companies and Their Statistics, 1940/1	97
8.1	Commercial Bank's Foreign Exchange Transactions, 1956–9	148
9.1	Number of Requests for Issuance of Discovery Licence for Group Two Mines, 1940–65	170
10.1	Workforce in Iran, 1921–76 (Thousands)	182
10.2	Non-Agricultural Workforce, 1955	183

Contributors

Serhan Afacan is Professor of History in the Institute of Middle East and Islamic Countries at Marmara University, Istanbul, Turkey. His publications include 'Men of Mission: Turkey's Ambassadors to Iran in the Early Republican Period (1922–1938)', in *Comparativ* (2023); 'Workers as Petitioners: Discursive Practices of Iranian Textile Workers, 1906–1941', in *Cihannüma* (2020); 'Revisiting Labour Activism in Iran: Some Notes on the Vatan Factory Strike in 1931', in *International Labour and Working-Class History* (2018); and 'Foreign Goods Native Consumption: Popular Reactions to Foreign Economic Domination and the Grassroots Perceptions of Economic Development in Iran', in *Iran and the Middle East: Transnational Encounters and Social History* (2015).

Abdolreza Alamdar is an independent researcher, specializing in sociology. Previously, he was affiliated with the Centre for Iranian Studies at SOAS University of London. His research interests include Iran's labour, mining and commodity history and memory studies. His most recent publication is 'From Worker-Peasant to Reluctant Revolutionary Industrial Worker in the Establishment of Iran's Copper Industry: The Sarcheshmeh Copper Mine, 1960s–1970s', in *Iranian Studies* (2023). Other notable works include 'The Establishment of Iran's Copper Mining Industry: The Downfall of Anaconda and Selection Trust in the 1960s–70s', in *Born with a Copper Spoon: A Global History of Copper, 1830–1980* (2022).

Touraj Atabaki is Senior Research Fellow at the International Institute of Social History and Professor Emeritus of Social History of the Middle East and Central Asia at Leiden University. His forthcoming publications are *Social History of the Iranian Oil Industry* and *Fallen in the Whirlwind: Life and Time of Iranian Migrant Labour and Political Activists during the Soviet Great Purge* (English translation co-authored with Lana Ravandi-Fadai of the original Russian version, published in 2020). Atabaki's articles on the social history of workers and the labouring poor in West and Central Asia have appeared in *International Labor and Working-Class History*, *Iranian Studies* and *Studies in History*.

Hojjat Fallah Tootkar is Professor of History in the Faculty of Literature and Humanity Sciences at Imam Khomeini International University, Qazvin, Iran. His notable publications include *Sattar Khan* (1399/2020); *The Historiography of Doctor Ali Shariati* (1396/2017); *Guilds: From the Iranian Constitutional Revolution to the Overthrow of the Qajar Dynasty (1285–1304 [1906–1925])* (1395/2016); and *The Life, Works and Historiographical Thoughts of Doctor Abdolhadi Haeri* (1395/2016). His research findings on the Tehran Union of Guilds, women's education and the constitutional movement in Talesh have been published in the Iranian academic journals, *Faslnameh-ye Farhang-e Mardom*, *Faslnameh-ye Olum-e Ejtemaei* and *Tarikhnameh-e Iran bad az Eslam*.

Willem Floor, independent scholar, has published a number of books and articles on the socio-economic history of Iran. His most recent book is *History of Glass & Ceramics in Iran, 1500–1925* (2023). His notable publications with a research focus on modern Iranian history include *Guilds, Merchants and Ulama in Nineteenth-Century Iran* (2009); *Labor & Industry in Iran, 1850–1941* (2009); *Textile Imports into Qajar Iran: Russia versus Great Britain, The Battle for Market Domination* (2009); *Agriculture in Qajar Iran* (2003); *Traditional Crafts in Qajar Iran, 1800–1925* (2003); *Labour Unions, Law and Conditions in Iran (1900–1941)* (1985); and *Industrialization in Iran, 1900–1941* (1984).

Ali Gheissari is Professor of History at the University of San Diego, United States. He has written extensively on the intellectual history and politics of modern Iran and on modern philosophy and social theory. His recent publications include '*Fruits of the Gardens*: Ethics, Metaphysics, and Textual Pleasures in late Qajar Iran', in *Journal of Persianate Studies* (2024); 'Resāle, Maqāle, and Ketāb: An Overview of Persian Expository and Analytical Prose', in *A History of Persian Literature* (2021); and 'Iran's Dialectic of the Enlightenment: Constitutional Experience, Transregional Connections, and Conflicting Narratives of Modernity', in *Iran's Constitutional Revolution of 1906 and Narratives of the Enlightenment* (2016).

Reza Omidi, Social Policy and Development Studies Expert, has been Professor in the Department of Social Planning at the University of Tehran, Iran. His notable publications include 'The Ups and Downs of Social Policy in Iran: 1300–1380 [1921–2001]', in *Goftogu* (1397/2018); 'Conflict Analysis in Social Policy: Examining the Process of Drafting the Law on the Structure of the Comprehensive Welfare and Social Security System', in *Motalaat va Taqiqat-e Ejtemaei dar Iran* (1398/2019); and two chapters (co-authored with Pooya Alaedini), 'Development of Iran's Social Welfare Institutions' and 'Education Policy in Iran: Developments over the Past Four Decades', in *Social Policy in Iran: Main Components and Institutions* (2022).

Ali A. Saeidi is Associate Professor of Economic Sociology and Social Policy at the Faculty of Social Sciences, University of Tehran, Iran. From 2022 to 2023, he has been visiting research fellow at the Middle East Centre of the London School of Economics. He has published five biographies on the leading Iranian businessmen and technocrats of the 1950s–70s. His most recent publications include 'Governing by Partnership: The Role of Abdolhossein Nikpour and the Chambers of Commerce in Iran's National Economy' (co-authored with Mary Yoshinari), in *Middle Eastern Studies* (2023); and 'Challenges for Family Capitalism during the Pahlavi Period: 1941–1979', in *Iran Namag* (2020).

Majid Saeli Kordehdeh is Senior Expert in Public Relations and International Affairs and Expert in Information and the Website of the Parliamentary Library of Iran. He has authored two books, *A Comparative Study of the Political Context of the Electoral Laws and Rules of the Iranian Parliament from 1906 to 1996* (1999) and *The Islamic Revolutionary Council of Iran from December 1978 to July 1980* (2003). He also has been invited to present two papers at Tokyo University of Foreign Studies, Japan, in 2009 and 2012 – most recently, 'The Authenticity and Importance of Parliamentary Debates in the Contemporary Historiography of Iran'.

Ali Tatari is Senior Researcher at the Library, Museum and Document Center of the Iranian Parliament, Tehran, Iran. He is also a historian, book editor, university lecturer and dissertation referee in the fields of economic and legislative history and has conducted extensive research on behalf of the Chambers of Commerce, Industries, Mines and Agriculture of Tehran and Iran. His most recent notable publications include *The Story of the House of the Private Sector: The Tehran Chamber of Commerce According to Historical Documents* (1401/2022) and *133 Years of the Tehran Chamber of Commerce from the Qajar Period to the Present Day* (1395/2017).

Soheila Torabi Farsani is Professor in the Department of History at Islamic Azad University, Najafabad Branch, Isfahan, Iran. Her recent notable publications include 'The Chamber of Commerce and Internal Conflicts among Merchants of Bushehr in the Early 1950s', in *Iran Namag* (2021); *Iranian Women in Transition from Tradition to Modernity* (1497/2018); *From the Council of Merchants' Representatives to the Iranian Chamber of Commerce: The Genesis and Evolution of the Chamber of Iran from the Beginning until the Islamic Revolution (1263–1357 SH)* (1392/2013); and 'Merchants, Class Identification Process and Constitutionalism', in *Iran's Constitutional Revolution: Popular Politics, Cultural Transformations and Transnational Connections* (2010).

Mary Yoshinari is an independent researcher and former Social Sciences and Humanities Research Council of Canada (SSHRC) postdoctoral fellow. Her recent publications include 'Governing by Partnership: The Role of Abdolhossein Nikpour and the Chambers of Commerce in Iran's National Economy' (co-authored with Ali A. Saeidi), in *Middle Eastern Studies* (2023); and 'From the Imperial Periphery to the Boundaries of Power: Soviet Diplomatic Officials in 1930s Iran', in *Russians in Iran: Diplomacy and Power in the Qajar Era and Beyond* (2018). Her forthcoming book, *Iran's Modern Economic History, 1921–1946*, re-evaluates the development of the Iranian economy in national and global contexts – including the role of local actors.

Acknowledgements

We are very grateful for the assistance of Ms Berrin Çalışkan in the preparation of this volume. Also, we would like to thank Mr Majid Saeli Kordehdeh and Dr Ali Asghar Saeidi for helping us locate various issues of Iranian newspapers on short notice. Likewise, our many thanks to Dr Soheila Torabi Farsani for advising us on certain translation matters.

Note on transliteration

Persian words have been transliterated according to the Iranian Studies scheme with modifications for popular names and digital publication, including the citations.

Part I

Introduction and historiography

1

Introduction and overview

Labour and the economy have been, and continue to be, among the paramount concerns of any society, including that of Iran. By the same token, these two interrelated topics are pivotal in understanding Iran's modern history. During the Qajar period, and even earlier, economic power was deemed a fundamental element of just governance and maintaining the societal order. Moreover, diligent labour was extolled, with employers instructed and encouraged to promptly remunerate their workers upon the completion of their tasks. However, adhering to these principles within the framework of the modern economic system has proven to be more complicated. Iran's path towards modernization since the late nineteenth century can be viewed as an endeavour to increase not only its military and political strength but also its economic power and wealth.

While Iran's economic decline had commenced decades earlier, foreign domination began to take root in the mid-nineteenth century. Iran's increasing integration into the global economic system, accompanied by an influx of imported goods and a downturn in its craft industries, created further economic, social and political problems, ultimately alienating various segments of Iranian society from the Qajar state. This predicament led to the Constitutional Revolution of 1905–6, which was seen by many Iranians as an essential step towards political progress, economic reform and national prosperity. This movement was part of a revolutionary trend that arose simultaneously in other old eastern empires, that is, the Ottoman domains and Imperial Russia. Unfortunately, a combination of internal and external factors hindered the realization of these aspirations to a great extent. Instead, Reza Khan's gradual ascent to power from 1921 onwards resulted in the Pahlavi dynasty's establishment in 1925. Here, it may be said that Iran's unstable economic situation was a major catalyst for these political developments.

Throughout the 1920s–70s, Iran underwent a series of profound transformations. During Reza Shah's reign (1925–41), economic policies were geared towards achieving self-sufficiency with an emphasis on establishing modern economic institutions, infrastructure, factories and companies. To some extent, these policies were influenced by contemporaneous developments in neighbouring countries, especially Turkey and the Soviet Union, as well as European models, such as Germany. Conversely, far less attention was given to the welfare of workers, both within the burgeoning mechanized factories and elsewhere. Moreover, Reza Shah's authoritarian regime systematically suppressed trade unions and collective labour action, particularly during the 1930s.

With Mohammad Reza Shah's return to power (1953–79), Iran intensified its participation in the global market and ultimately emerged as a significant world oil exporter. While trade unions and political parties operated relatively freely from late 1941 to mid-1953, the autocratic nature of his rule increasingly restricted the right to freedom of association during the post-war period.

While certain aspects of Iran's economic and labour history in the twentieth century are well known, many others remain understudied. Hence, this edited volume aims to contribute to the extant historiography by gathering twelve labour and economic historians to shed light on some of these underexplored dimensions. This idea emerged from the editors' lengthy and productive discussions on modern Iranian history and its historiographical turns. For over a decade, both of us have been immersed in the study of our respective subfields, whose questions share similar and interconnected roots. We agreed that bringing together a unique and geographically diverse group of scholars who have considerable expertise on modern Iran's economic and labour history would yield new and more comprehensive answers. This book is the product of our concerted and collective effort. It comprises twelve chapters that encompass a wide range of subjects about Iran's labour and economic history, each drawing from a varied and distinct set of primary sources.

To a greater or lesser extent, most contributors have utilized Iranian newspapers, such as *Ettelaat* and *Keyhan*, from the National Library and Archives of Iran and the Library, Museum and Document Center of the Iranian Parliament. The similarities end there, however. Hojjat Fallah Tootkar has examined a wide selection of workers' newspapers, such as *Haqiqat*, whereas Serhan Afacan has focused on craftsmen's petitions. In addition, Abdolreza Alamdar has studied telegraphs and letters from workers and government officials, and Soheila Torabi Farsani has analysed the correspondence of merchants lobbying the government and police reports on their activities. She also has drawn upon the Amin al-Zarb Archives. On the other hand, Reza Omidi has conducted research at the Planning and Budget Organization of Iran, and Ali Tatari has accessed the resources of the Central Bank of Iran's Monetary and Banking Research Institute.

Soviet documents from Russian state archives have provided new perspectives in Mary Yoshinari's work, along with British sources, also utilized by Serhan Afacan and Abdolreza Alamdar. Conversely, Willem Floor has made ample use of overlooked Iranian periodicals published in English, such as *Echo Reports* and *Iran Almanac and Book of Facts*. These archival methodologies may be contrasted with the oral history and recollections of Ali Gheissari, Ali Asghar Saeidi and Majid Saeli Kordehdeh. In terms of historiography, Touraj Atabaki has reviewed an impressive range of sources in his labour history compendium. Here, it may be noted that pioneering books, such as Habib Ladjevardi's *Labor Unions and Autocracy in Iran*, which is insightfully discussed by Dr Atabaki, are highly relevant for both labour and economic history. As discussed in Chapter 12, Dr Ladjevardi came from a prominent entrepreneurial family.

Still, it may be asked why labour and economic history have been combined in this edited volume. In response to this question, firstly, we would like to point out that each of these chapters raises issues that are relevant to both of these subfields. For example, in Chapter 10, Dr Gheissari's narrative of the Qom Risbaf Complex not only describes factory workers' facilities and working conditions but also paints fascinating portraits of other staff (e.g. steward, groundskeeper and accountant) who worked for his grandfather. Moreover, in Chapter 13, Mr Saeli Kordehdeh's biographical sketch of his father's working life also sheds light on the mindset of provincial urban employers, while corroborating Dr Floor's findings about the inefficacy of Iranian labour laws. Both have a lot to say about family economics and the cost of living, too.

Secondly, this volume explores family relations within the context of the household and the workplace. While Chapter 10 refers to 'the law' of the Iranian father's word, Chapter 13 reveals that such a patriarchal power dynamic could be overturned by the Iranian mother and her daughter in order to improve their living conditions. The recollections of Mr Saeli Kordehdeh and Dr Gheissari, who both spent their childhood years in the family workshop/factory milieu, may be compared, as well. Furthermore, the division of family labour is analysed by Dr Floor and Dr Saeidi at the lower and upper levels of the socio-economic ladder, that is, the brick production line and the corporate management team, including Behpush's Director, Lily Ladjevardian. As seen in Chapter 6, Gol Bangiz also operated a glassworks enterprise in the 1930s. Likewise, the education of Iranian girls and women has been considered from two different angles: Chapter 10 presents state statistics, whereas Chapters 12 and 13 provide accounts of informal opportunities for night schooling and adult literacy classes offered by the private sector.

Thirdly, taken collectively and comparatively, these chapters can generate further discussion about class identity, socio-economic position and agency in Iran. While Iranian guilds, merchants, craftsmen, miners and brick workers were all advocating for their economic rights in various ways, what were the similarities and differences in their strategies and modes of action? Further to this, considering the vast array of strategies of resistance, rebellion and calls for reforms, for example, strikes, protests, sanctuary, boycotts, bazaar closures, petitions, manifestos, telegrams and novels and poems, did any or all of these groups of economic actors express shared and/or intrinsic sociocultural traits related to being an Iranian – or a global citizen? One reoccurring theme, especially in Chapters 3, 12 and 13, is the importance of personal and professional ethics.

Fourthly, another point that can be made is that Chapters 7 and 9, which both have a greater emphasis on the state's role in policymaking, treat labour and economic history in fairly equal measure. Reza Omidi's innovative study of the evolution of welfare policies and Abdolreza Alamdar's in-depth analysis of mining expansion both demonstrate in distinctive ways how such policies were shaped by political changes in Iran from the interwar to the post-war periods, while highlighting the pivotal role of leftist and labour movements' activism, especially during the 'interregnum' of 1941–53. In addition, both chapters show how external factors, such as the United States and Great Britain, were involved – for better or worse – in these transformations.

Fifthly, this volume assesses Iran's economic development from multiple angles, including its drivers, results and societal impacts. For example, Chapters 6 and 8 link the economic nationalism and anti-colonialism of the interwar and post-war periods, illustrating how the National Bank's efforts to counter British dominance paved the way for the Commercial Bank's purchase of the Imperial Bank's buildings in 1952. Yet, the state bank's governor, Abol Hassan Ebtehaj, had tried to prevent the establishment of the country's first private bank. Moreover, Chapter 9 describes how, in response to the dispute with the Anglo-Iranian Oil Company, Iranian mining development intensified under the government of Prime Minister Mohammad Mossadegh. However, Dr Omidi has noted in Chapter 7 that Iran's social welfare policymaking was challenged by a sudden rise in oil revenues and rapid industrialization during the 1960s.

While the state had to assume a leading role in the mining sector, Dr Tatari, Dr Gheissari and Dr Saeidi conclude in Chapters 8, 11 and 12 that the opposite was true in private sector banking and the textile industry, where local entrepreneurs, such as Mostafa Tajaddod, Haj Mirza Ali Gheissarieh and the Ladjevardis and Ladjevardians exhibited drive, business acumen and philanthropy. Another interesting commonality is how religion could be intertwined with business practices – that is, banking at the Hajj, the clergy's significant investment in the Qom Carding Factory and the production of velvet prayer rugs in Kashan. On the other hand, Dr Floor maintains a dim view of Iranian entrepreneurs in Chapter 10, asserting that the government was in many respects unable to break the parasitic and exploitative bonds of landlord-peasant relations.

This volume also offers three distinctive perspectives on industrialization, specifically in the textile sector. In Chapter 4, Dr Afacan draws attention to the negative economic effects of the modern textile factory system on Iranian craftsmen in the 1930s, whereas in Chapter 11, Dr Gheissari describes the Qom Carding Factory's origins, including the securing of investment, allocation of land, architectural design and installing of machinery and power generators, which supplied electricity to the city of Qom. Conversely, in Chapter 12, Dr Saeidi explains how the Behshahr Industrial Group expanded and diversified its operations during the post-war years but was ultimately a victim of the revolutionary fervour that nationalized the private sector.

Apart from showing how workers, entrepreneurs, merchants and state officials attempted to negotiate their respective positions within Iran's developing economy, there are various levels of dialogue between these chapters. For instance, Chapters 4 and 6 discuss similar topics and time periods, albeit using different frameworks. While Dr Torabi Farsani takes a decidedly microhistorical approach, squarely focused on the Iranian merchants who joined the 'Economy Movement', including their activities, supporters and achievements, Dr Yoshinari provides a broader geographical and chronological view of Iran's foreign trade with the Soviet Union. Consequently, these local and global historical perspectives, which attest to the benefit of archival research in both Iranian and foreign archives, are even more insightful when read in tandem.

Lastly, in response to Dr Atabaki's call for new perspectives in Iranian labour and working class history that transcend a singular view aligned with the history of the socialist movement, this volume rethinks the trope of the leftist unionized worker versus the capitalist employer/state. For example, Dr Fallah Tootkar shows in Chapter 3 that some Iranian guilds (including tradesmen), craftsmen, labour unions and merchants supported the editors of leftist newspapers in the early 1920s; likewise, the pro-labour and socialist faction of the Fourth Majles was led by Qajar prince Soleiman Mirza Eskandari. Yet, by the following decade, as explained in Chapter 4, Iranian craftsmen were facing an uphill battle against the state's economic modernization programme. Chapters 13 and 10 also illustrate that uneducated lower-class labourers could express astute political views and organize effective strikes among themselves without the leadership of leftist intellectuals. Rather, in Chapter 9, we see the reverse: the labour action of the Zirab coal miners and their families inspired the writings and activism of leftist social critic Jalal Al-e Ahmad.

Overall, this volume presents a number of new perspectives on the relationship between workers, entrepreneurs and the state during a transformative period in the modern history of Iran. Although various facets of the Iranian economy are explored in detail, this topic does not outweigh the people who were involved with it in numerous ways. Furthermore, a major aim of our book is to raise the profile of various actors across the political and socio-economic spectrum of modern Iranian history, thereby challenging the notion of monolithic top-down power relations. Thus, we invite the reader to explore these themes in more detail in the chapters that follow.

2

Evolution of labour historiography in Iran

From 'old' to 'new' labour history scholarship

Touraj Atabaki

Iran's political fragmentation and economic decline, which started with the fall of the Safavid Empire in the early eighteenth century, coincided with the dawn of the era of global industrialization and integration (1750–1900), and endured for nearly a century, casting a long shadow over the country's development. With the establishment of the Qajar Empire (1796–1925), Persia embarked on a path towards reclaiming the territorial and political coherence reminiscent of the Safavid era. However, this newly constituted empire quickly found its territorial integrity under constant threat in an era when emerging colonial powers aggressively sought to expand their territorial dominions. For Persia, the Treaties of Golestan (1813) and Turkmenchay (1828), which resulted from protracted military conflicts with the Tsarist Empire, marked a turning point. These treaties not only entailed the complete relinquishment of its territorial holdings in the Caucasus but also initiated a gradual yet profound transformation in its political and socio-economic landscape. As the twentieth century dawned, Persia found itself ensnared in semi-colonial status, subject to the interests and machinations of Britain and Tsarist Russia, as the two dominant powers, which regarded Persia as their own sphere of influence. In response to this semi-colonial subjugation, a series of revolutions took place in Persia.

The initial revolution, known as the Constitutional Revolution (1905–9), brought about profound transformations in the socio-economic and sociocultural fabric of the nation. Its primary objective was the restructuring of the political landscape, the abolition of the monarchical regime, the establishment of the rule of law and the imposition of accountability in the exercise of both political and economic power. During this period, a foundational principle emerged, asserting a limited equality among citizens before the law, which initially extended only to male citizens. Additionally, the revolution aimed to modernize Persian society by fostering the industrialization of the nation's economy. However, the path of the Constitutional Revolution was fraught with formidable challenges. Initially, the absence of a strong central state hindered its progress. Subsequently, it encountered resistance and coercion from Tsarist Russia.

The outbreak of the First World War further complicated matters, casting additional obstacles in its path.

The discovery of petroleum reserves in southern Persia in 1908 coincided with the Constitutional Revolution and significantly elevated the geopolitical importance of the nation. Oil, in this context, emerged as a strategically significant commodity, shaped not merely by geological processes but also by intricate social and economic factors. On a global scale, oil capitalism emerged as the pre-eminent economic system, supplanting the financial capitalism that had predominated during the preceding century. This ascendancy of oil capitalism endured throughout the twentieth century, exerting a pervasive and enduring influence on global affairs.

The pivotal role played by Persian oil during the First World War profoundly reshaped Persia's trajectory throughout the twentieth century. Two notable coups d'état in 1921 and 1953, as well as the seismic reverberations of the second revolution in 1979, are all intrinsically linked, either directly or indirectly, to oil. The coup d'état of 1921 heralded the dawn of the Pahlavi dynasty's reign (1925–79), instigating a sweeping panoply of authoritarian political and economic modernization policies throughout Persia. This transformational epoch bore testament to the ruling regime's earnest efforts to accommodate certain demands of constitutionalists, albeit with a conspicuous exception – the elusive avoidance of autocracy.

In the realm of economic history pertaining to modern Persia, a prevailing consensus emerges, one that delineates the Constitutional Revolution and the eruption of the First World War as the decisive junctures marking the culmination of early capitalist development within Persia. These pivotal events, in tandem, cast a long shadow, cleaving the fifty-four-year epoch of Pahlavi rule that ensued into two distinct phases: a formative period characterized by the emergence of industrial capitalism (1925–63), followed by an era of burgeoning capitalist relations of production, led by the developmental state (1963–78).

History and historiography of the working class and labouring poor

The historical exploration of labour in Iran traces its origins back to the nineteenth century, predominantly revolving around the sphere of industrial labour. Research endeavours in this field have been extensive, yet studies on the history of agricultural labour have remained notably scarce. Ann Lambton's two pioneering works in this regard have greatly impacted our understanding of land tenure dynamics in Iran.[1] However, as the years rolled on, the subject of agricultural labour largely faded from scholarly view, save for the efforts of Farhad Kazemi and Ervand Abrahamian, who examined the non-revolutionary peasantry in modern Iran.[2] In subsequent years, Kazemi embarked on a comparative study, culminating in a compelling examination that delved into the revolutionary peasantry of Iran, Iraq and Turkey. This edited volume explored the complex relationship between peasants and politics in the Middle East.[3] In the same volume, Ahmad Ashraf's chapter carved out a path towards deeper insights into agrarian relations, both in the pre-revolutionary and post-revolutionary epochs. It presented an invaluable opportunity for discerning the complex class composition that underpinned the events of the Iranian Revolution of 1978–9.[4]

Studies of guilds and guild-based labour should also be mentioned. One of the earliest works on this subject, written by Mir Abolqasem Fendereski,[5] briefly describes the positions of artisans and craftsmen in Safavid Persia and the interdependency of the townsmen who worked as members of a certain guild. Also, in his PhD dissertation, Mehdi Keyvani provides a survey of all available sources on guilds.[6] Following this broad literature survey, Keyvani studies the social, political, cultural and religious functions of each guild and examines their relations with merchants and the state in late-seventeenth- and early-eighteenth-century Persia. However, while the position of guild masters has been described in Keyvani's study, what is missing in his work and similar studies is the position of apprentices or labourers working in the guilds during this period. Willem Floor's two studies are major contributions towards filling this gap.[7] Moreover, Kuznetsova's work on guilds could be considered another exception, since she draws on Russian, Armenian and Georgian sources and conveys a picture of the labourer (whom she refers to as 'muzdvar' [*mozdur*], meaning 'one who is paid, a hired worker or labourer') in eighteenth- and nineteenth-century Persia.[8]

As for Persia's industrial working class, one can trace its origins back to the latter half of the nineteenth century, having roots beyond political boundaries. The migration of the labouring poor from Persia in search of employment opportunities commenced in this period. During this era, a substantial exodus of Persian labourers began, seeking livelihoods abroad. Their destinations of choice included Imperial Russia, India, the Ottoman Empire and northern and western Africa. Among these destinations, Tsarist Russia, characterized by its burgeoning economy during the late nineteenth century, emerged as a magnet for a considerable number of Iranian workers, primarily hailing from the central and northern provinces of Persia.

By the time of the Russian Revolution of 1917, the population of Persian migrant workers in Russia had swelled to unprecedented numbers. These labourers predominantly worked in Baku's oil and mining industries, in addition to their involvement in the construction of roads and railroads. Their labour was instrumental in shaping the southern territories of the Russian Empire, the Caucasus and Central Asia, contributing significantly to the economic dynamism of Tsarist Russia during this period.

The annals of scholarly inquiry into Persian migrant workers owe a debt to Soviet historians, who can be rightfully credited as pioneers in illuminating this crucial facet of history. Drawing upon the abundant archival resources of the Tsarist administration in the Caucasus, historians such as Belova and Strigunov undertook the task of documenting the experiences and journeys of Persian migrant labourers within the Caucasus region. Their scholarly endeavours yielded a wealth of empirical data, furnishing scholars with an unparalleled and detailed account of the lives and labour of Persian migrants in this pivotal region.[9]

Building upon the foundational work of these Soviet historians, Hassan Hakimian emerged as a figure in the study of Persian labour migration. He employed a comprehensive analytical framework, anchored within the broader context of the

Persian political economy during the late nineteenth and early twentieth centuries. Hakimian's scholarship brought into focus the complex interplay between labour migration and the economic dynamics of Persia during this transformative period, shedding light on the manifold factors that propelled labourers from Persia to southern Russia. His work not only enriched our understanding of the historical backdrop but also underscored the intrinsic connections between labour mobility and the broader socio-economic landscape of Persia during this era.[10]

As the twentieth century dawned, the contours of industrialization began to take shape within the territorial boundaries of Persia, setting the stage for the emergence of industrial workers. This process of industrialization, though gradual, marked a significant transition for the country. It unfolded within the context of Persia's limited integration into the global economy and the prevalence of relatively low customs duties, averaging around 4–5 per cent, on imported manufactured goods. These economic dynamics unfolded alongside a series of pivotal political transformations that would shape the trajectory of the nation.[11]

Following in the footsteps of the early Soviet labour historians, Abdullaev made a notable contribution to the field of labour history in 1963 with the publication of his book on Iran's industrialization and the emergence of the Iranian working class during the late nineteenth and early twentieth centuries. Abdullaev's analytical framework, characterized by a strain of Soviet essentialism, bore the imprint of historical materialism as perceived through the lens of the Soviet-Stalinist perspective.[12] However, one should not underestimate the substantial contribution made by Abdullaev's work. His meticulous examination of historical facts and statistical data added significant value to the understanding of the formation of the Iranian working class. Abdullaev's scholarly endeavours continue to shed light on the historical evolution of labour and industrialization in Iran, offering valuable insights that remain relevant to the study of labour history.

Floor stands out as another historian who has dedicated his scholarship to the study of Persia's working class in the late nineteenth century. While Abdullaev's work draws heavily from Tsarist Russian accounts and statistical data, Floor's historiography is informed by European travellers' accounts, coupled with diplomatic sources, primarily of British origin. These diverse sources, each with their distinct vantage points, converge to shape Floor's nuanced understanding of the historical narrative.

However, it is noteworthy that these two scholarly endeavours share a common limitation: the conspicuous absence of Persian sources, notably, documents carefully archived in central and local repositories, including the invaluable petitions of labourers submitted to the shah, local authorities and various institutions. Also, the interpretive lenses through which Abdullaev and Floor view labour in Persia during this epoch diverge significantly. In Abdullaev's narrative, the formation of the working class and the evolution of its collective consciousness are inextricably intertwined with the unfolding of capitalism, replete with the crucible of class conflict and class struggle. Conversely, Floor portrays a starkly different reality. Here, labour is depicted not as a coherent class entity but rather as a cluster within the larger framework of the ruled populace (*ro'āyā*). In this framework, labour is portrayed as lacking agency and control over its own destiny, bereft of the ability to steer the course of its development or determine the pace at which progress unfolds.[13]

The global and regional movements advocating for social progress, modernization and the ultimate goal of constitutionalism had been steadily evolving since the mid-nineteenth century. This historical trajectory reached its zenith with a series of transformative revolutions that unfolded in Tsarist Russia (1906), Persia (1905–9) and Ottoman Turkey (1908). Within these constitutional movements, a core group of radical political activists emerged, whose interpretation of constitutionalism transcended the mere empowerment of individual autonomy, critical thinking and human agency, by extending to the establishment of a unified legal system.[14]

These activists, firmly rooted in a resolute social democratic ethos, were to some extent affiliated with the Second International of Socialist and Labour Parties (1889–1916). Prior to the Constitutional Revolution in Persia, these Iranian social democrats had already laid the groundwork for their political aspirations by forming the Social Democratic Party (Ferqeh-ye Ejtemaiyun-e Ammiyun). Following the success of the revolution, they transitioned to the next phase of their political journey, founding the Democrat Party of Iran (Hezb-e Demokrat-e Iran), and commenced their political activities within the Iranian Parliament.[15]

The outbreak of the First World War, compounded by the Russian Revolution, infused an additional layer of radicalism into these Iranian social democrats. Their transformation culminated in June 1920, after strenuous efforts and a tumultuous path, with the establishment of the Communist Party of Iran (Hezb-e Komunist-e Iran). This marked a significant turning point in the ideological landscape of Iran, where socialist and communist ideals gained a foothold and began to shape the political discourse, leaving an enduring legacy that would influence the nation's trajectory in the years to come.[16]

With the establishment of the Communist Party of Iran, an organization aligned with the Third International, commonly known as the Comintern, a new paradigm emerged within the realm of labour studies and labour historiography on Persia. This paradigm was fundamentally reshaped by the tenets of Marxism-Leninism, leading to a re-evaluation of late-nineteenth- and early-twentieth-century Persian history through the prism of class dynamics and class conflict. This ideological shift emphasized the pivotal role of the Iranian working class in the context of modern Persian history, infusing it with agency and historical significance.

One of the luminaries contributing to this evolving historiography was Avetis Sultanzadeh, a co-founder of the Communist Party of Iran and an active member of the early Comintern. In his inaugural scholarly work, *Sovremennaia Persiia* (Contemporary Persia), published in 1922, Sultanzadeh drew upon extensive fieldwork to present a comprehensive analysis of Persia's agrarian economy.[17] Furthermore, he scrutinized the trajectory of capitalism's development within the country. In this work, he also elucidated the social status of both agrarian and urban labourers, offering critical insights into their roles within the Persian economy since the late nineteenth century.[18]

In a subsequent book published in 1925, Sultanzadeh continued to explore the evolution of the Iranian working class. He adeptly linked this transformation to the unfolding political developments in Persia after the First World War, particularly in the context of the ascendancy of Reza Khan. In his analysis, Sultanzadeh praised Reza Khan as a representative of the 'nationalist bourgeoisie', a perspective that aligned with the Comintern and Soviet viewpoint regarding Iran and its neighbouring nation, Turkey, during this historical juncture.[19] Sultanzadeh's scholarly contributions stand as significant landmarks in the development of labour studies and labour historiography in Persia. His works not only shed light on the intricate interplay of class dynamics but also serve as a testament to the ideological currents that shaped the discourse surrounding Iran's sociopolitical landscape during this transformative era.

After the formation of the Tudeh Party of Iran in 1941, along with other leftist parties and organizations, efforts began to collect the recollections of labour activists who had witnessed the earliest attempts to initiate the labour movement. These endeavors gradually laid the groundwork for compiling a comprehensive history of the labour movement. Initially, the primary focus of these efforts was on organized labour. An illustrative example of such historical scholarship is Shokrollah Mani's account of unionization endeavours in Iran, which, to this day, has remained an invaluable resource.[20]

However, it was during the 1960s and 1970s that a distinct shift occurred in the historiography of labour and the working class in Iran. This transformation was underscored by the influential narratives of political activists and scholars who drew from sources like Mani's work and other materials derived from the Communist Party of Iran and the Comintern archive. These Tudeh Party historians, conducting their research in exile, embarked on the compilation of studies that sought to illuminate the history of communist and working-class movements in Iran.[21]

What sets these studies apart is the unique perspective of Tudeh Party historians concerning labour history. For these political activists, labour history was intrinsically tied to the history of factory-based organized labour, with a strong affiliation to the communist movement. In this context, Ardashes (Ardeshir) Avanesiyan, a prominent member of both the Communist Party and, later, the Tudeh Party, emphasized this association by attributing the establishment and shaping of the foundations of Iranian workers' unions to the central role of the Communist Party.[22]

Two decades after the publication of E. P. Thompson's *The Making of the English Working Class*,[23] Iranian historiography was significantly influenced by his groundbreaking contributions, largely through the scholarship of Ervand Abrahamian. This initial engagement with Thompson's ideas occurred in the 1980s, marked by Abrahamian's studies and the release of his work, *Iran Between Two Revolutions*.[24]

In this intellectual milieu, shaped by the influence of Thompson's neo-Marxist paradigm, Abrahamian charted an unexplored course. He expanded the intellectual horizon, contending that class dynamics must be comprehended within the expansive framework of hegemonic culture. These class dynamics, he argued, engaged in intricate social contests with other segments of society, thereby elucidating Iran's transformative historical narrative.

In the 1980s, it was not solely the cadre of Iranian Marxist activists who found themselves grappling with the enigmatic aftermath of the revolution. Scholarly circles within the Marxist tradition, too, commenced a profound reckoning. They embarked on an introspective journey, challenging the essentialist and teleological narratives proffered by more rudimentary iterations of historical materialism. These scholars grappled with the task of deciphering the complex social foundations underpinning the Islamic Revolution of 1978–9, which ushered the politically active clergy into ascendancy.

In the late 1980s, Touraj Atabaki, as a disciple of Abrahamian, revisited the labour movement in Iran during the Second World War and evaluated Avanesiyan's stance on the close association between labour unions and political parties. In his scholarship, Atabaki critically examined how the early formation of the Comintern and Stalinist labour historiography tended to conflate the roles of the party and the union.[25] He argued that this perspective had contributed to an oversimplified understanding of the labour movement, often neglecting independent unions not aligned with political parties. Moreover, Atabaki contended that within this particular school of historiography, there was a selective amnesia leading to the disregard of independent unions that operated autonomously, without political party affiliations. This critique challenged the prevailing notion that unions in Iran were invariably linked to political parties, shedding light on a more diverse and nuanced landscape of labour organizations.[26]

In a collaborative study focused on the labour movement preceding the Second World War, Jalil Mahmoudi and Nasser Saeidi echoed Atabaki's perspective, questioning the previously established narrative that fused unions and political parties together. Their scholarship reinforced the notion that a more variegated labour history existed in Iran, one that included independent unions operating beyond the purview of political parties.[27]

In Habib Ladjevardi's seminal work, *Labor Unions and Autocracy in Iran*,[28] while the temporal focal point is confined to the years 1941–53, in his introductory and concluding remarks, the author extends his analytical gaze to encompass the Constitutional Revolution and the twilight of the Pahlavi epoch. Ladjevardi's inquiry is dedicated to the trajectory of labour activism, with a conspicuous delimitation of its scope to organized labour, primarily during episodes marked by heightened and adversarial forms of engagement.

Within the annals of Ladjevardi's scholarship, regrettably, there is a conspicuous absence of coverage on unorganized labour or alternative manifestations of labour protest, such as petitioning or other peaceful modes of dissent. Nevertheless, it would be remiss to undervalue the two conspicuous accomplishments embedded within Ladjevardi's oeuvre. Firstly, he adopts a distinctive methodology by refraining from treating the labour movement as a subservient appendage to the political landscape, instead endowing it with a notably independent agency. Secondly, his research repertoire draws upon a wealth of diverse sources, both Persian and non-Persian, with particular reliance on diplomatic narratives culled from American and British archives. Noteworthy in its omission, however, are the substantive sources originating from Soviet archives, which regrettably remain beyond the purview of Ladjevardi's investigation.

In the realm of Iranian labour history preceding the Second World War, the 1980s witnessed the emergence of two important books on the 1900–41 period: Farhang Ghassemi's study of Iranian trade unionism[29] and Willem Floor's *Labour Unions, Law and Conditions in Iran*.[30] Both of these scholarly contributions stood out for their conspicuous departure from Marxist ideological underpinnings. As elucidated by the titles of these scholarly works, the focal point of analysis for both authors remained firmly entrenched within the domain of organized labour and their multifarious activities. Nonetheless, a significant point of divergence between Ghassemi's approach and that of Floor lies in their respective conceptualizations of worker agency within the labour movement.

Ghassemi, while acknowledging the intricate web of political affiliations entwining the labour movement, notably in its symbiotic relationships with social democratic, socialist and communist political groups and parties, presents a nuanced perspective on the notion of labour agency. In his analysis of the historical backdrop against which labour activists emerged, Ghassemi proffers instances that might be characterized as manifestations of indigenous initiatives within this burgeoning movement.

Conversely, Floor approaches the autonomy of labour agency with a degree of scepticism. He posits that 'the trade unions were started and led by men whose material and cultural background made them members of the middle class'.[31] He also argues that workers in general lacked the time, energy, understanding and capability of organizing labour activities. Thus, members of Iran's Marxist intelligentsia 'considered labour problems as being an integral part of the socio-economic and political system in which imperialism and capitalism were the moving forces'.[32] This perspective appears to cast a shadow of doubt upon the notion of independent labour agency, emphasizing instead the influence of middle-class origins and orientations upon the leadership and direction of the labour unions.

Nonetheless, it would be wrong to disregard the contributions of Floor's scholarship. Floor adeptly harnesses a wealth of material to construct a vivid portrayal of the working and living conditions of labourers in Iran. His research encompasses important facets, such as the cost of living, wages, hygiene and nutrition, working hours and workplace safety. Also, Floor's comprehensive narrative extends to include an exhaustive examination of labour regulations and legislation in Iran throughout the initial four decades of the twentieth century. In doing so, he unfurls a meticulously crafted tapestry that intricately weaves together the legal frameworks and regulatory mechanisms governing labour and employment during this pivotal era.

E. P. Thompson's impact on Iranian labour historiography

In a 2013 article commemorating the fiftieth anniversary of the publication of *The Making of the English Working Class*, Abrahamian underscored Thompson's enduring legacy. He emphasized that Thompson's approach was characterized by a deliberate avoidance of grand theoretical frameworks, sweeping generalizations and overly abstract distinctions. Instead, Thompson's distinctive appeal lay in his commitment to immersing himself, and by extension, fellow historians, in the rich tapestry of the past. He advocated for the examination of empirical data and historical evidence as the primary foundation for drawing broader conclusions and insights. Thompson's continuing influence, as Abrahamian noted, resides in his dedication to a rigorous and thorough engagement with historical materials before embarking on the journey of crafting overarching narratives and interpretations.[33]

The recognition of unorganized labour agency, in all its temporal and contextual manifestations, has occupied a central place in the extensive contemplation and discourse on global labour history at the International Institute of Social History. Marcel van der Linden's specific contribution, through his incisive critique of the structuralist approach to labour history, has been central to the shift from the traditional 'old labour history' paradigm, characterized by its focus on institutional and organized labour movements, to a more inclusive and diverse historiographical paradigm.[34] This new paradigm broadens the scope to include unorganized labour, informal sectors and non-Western perspectives, thereby enriching an understanding of labour history in a global context.

In 2003, Atabaki and van der Linden undertook the editorial stewardship of an issue of the *International Review of Social History* titled 'Twentieth Century Iran: History from Below'. This volume featured three articles delving into the intricate tapestry of Iran's twentieth-century working-class history. Kaveh Ehsani's contribution to this volume merits particular attention. Ehsani embarked on an exploration of the multifaceted roles played by labourers, migrants, women and modest functionaries in the evolution and configuration of Abadan, an oil-refining city in Iran, over the course of the twentieth century.[35] Of paramount significance in Ehsani's work is his deliberate avoidance of narrowing his focus solely to the labour force within Abadan's oil industry. Instead, he illuminates the threads of resistance woven by Abadan's inhabitants at large, as they grappled with the task of redefining the urban landscape of the company town and asserting their stake in its transformation.

The second article within this compendium, authored by Touraj Atabaki, explores the transnational dimensions of working-class formation. By unearthing documents from diverse repositories, including Tsarist Russian, Soviet and Iranian archives, Atabaki delves into the history of the everyday lives of Iran's labouring poor and working class, who resided on the peripheries of the Tsarist Empire in the prelude to the 1917 Russian Revolution.[36] His scrutiny centres on the quotidian experiences of migrant labourers and the inclusive culture they created within the towns to which they migrated. Atabaki's work sheds light on the kaleidoscope of identities embraced by these migrant workers, encompassing class, ethnicity, language and political allegiances. Moreover, he examines how, amidst a complex political milieu, certain identities could ascend in prominence over others.

Lastly, Willem Floor's contribution to this compilation focuses on the world of labour within the brick kilns of south Tehran.[37] In his study, Floor underscores the dire and deplorable working and living conditions endured by these labourers, who straddled the boundaries between urbanization and transient rural life, representing one of the most impoverished segments of Iran's labouring class. He also delves into the realm of labour activism among the brick kiln workers, conducting a comparative analysis of six strikes that unfolded between July 1953 and April 1979. Through this analysis, Floor unveils the narratives of struggle and resistance that underscored the lives of these labourers, shedding light on their quest for improved working conditions and a modicum of dignity within the workplace.

Taken together, these three studies represent an important addition to the historiography of Iran's working class, offering a multifaceted exploration of their experiences, identities and struggles throughout the twentieth century.

Social history of labour in the Iranian oil industry

In the year 2010, a noteworthy research initiative was launched at the International Institute of Social History, marking a significant contribution to the broader field of global labour history.[38] This project was dedicated to the comprehensive exploration of the social history of labour within the Iranian oil industry. With the resolute aim to craft a rigorous empirical and qualitative study spanning the entirety of the oil industry's 100-year history (from 1908 to 2018), the researchers harnessed the theoretical and analytical frameworks provided by the evolving discipline of new labour history. The project's focus extended to five principal areas of inquiry, each offering critical insights into the dynamics of labour and the working class within the Iranian oil industry: composition of the labour force; process of labour formation; labour relations; labour migration, mobility and integration; living conditions/quality of life.

Indeed, this research project culminated in a substantial body of work, including PhD dissertations,[39] articles and books. Collectively, these scholarly outputs represent a dedicated and rigorous effort to untangle the intricate web of labour history within the Iranian oil industry. By employing the analytical tools and methodologies of the new labour history, the researchers aimed to illuminate the multifaceted dimensions of this historical narrative.

In the autumn of 2013, the journal *International Labor and Working-Class History* featured a special section dedicated to the social history of Iranian oil workers.[40] This collection included an essay by Touraj Atabaki, which probed into the formation of the working class within the Iranian oil industry.[41] Within his essay, Atabaki examined the nascent stages of the oil industry's labour force, which predominantly comprised individuals drawn from the ranks of tribal communities and village-based labouring populations. These workers, upon their recruitment, were subjected to the stringent labour discipline inherent in an advanced industrial economy. Over time, this process played a pivotal role in shaping the early clusters of what would become Iran's modern working class. Atabaki's analysis ventured into the realm of workers' consciousness, echoing the arguments put forth by Zachary Lockman.[42] Both scholars contended that the process of working-class formation transcended mere material conditions; it was equally a discursive endeavour. This perspective challenged the conventional structuralist and objectivist definitions of the worker and the working class.

Atabaki's narrative postulated that, following their lengthy journey of recruitment and adaptation to a novel labour discipline, the individuals labouring within the Iranian oil industry emerged with a newfound sense of self-identity. They began to view themselves as a distinct collective with a shared social identity. This evolving self-image was characterized by an iconic vision of group solidarity, one that united individuals through the cultural negotiations and contestations of their daily lives.

Maral Jefroudi, another contributor to this special section, presented a compelling study focused on the 'Long Sixties' era in the Iranian oil industry.[43] During this period, the Iranian government initiated top-down economic and social reforms while concurrently erecting formidable barriers to independent trade unionism. Jefroudi's article challenges the prevailing narrative within Iranian historiography, which often characterizes this era as marked by state repression or structural limitations within the working class that ostensibly hindered workers from embarking on collective radical actions.

Contrary to this prevailing view, Jefroudi puts forth the argument that the actions of workers during this period were shaped by both objective and subjective factors inherent to their class. Rather than pursuing confrontational actions that might have antagonized the government or jeopardized the benefits they had gained through social reforms, workers engaged in forms of collective action that aligned with their interests. In essence, they sought to safeguard their acquired benefits without directly challenging the state's authority. Furthermore, Jefroudi contends that it is essential to situate and qualitatively analyse workers' repertoires of collective action in a broader context. She posits that these actions should not be measured against an idealized or rigid notion of radical activism but instead be understood within the specific sociopolitical and economic context of the time.

Peyman Jafari's study in the same special issue focuses on the experiences of oil workers during the 1970s, a critical decade that culminated in the Iranian Revolution of 1978–9.[44] His contribution to the historiography of oil workers and their role in the revolution offers an examination of the institutional, socio-economic, political and cultural conditions that prevailed among Iranian oil workers in the years leading up to this transformative period. Moreover, Jafari examines the underlying factors that elucidate their active participation in the Iranian Revolution. In his research, Jafari challenges the prevailing notion of a 'labour aristocracy', often ascribed to the oil workers. Instead, he undertakes a nuanced exploration of the mechanisms that contributed to the establishment of systems of control, conflict and consent within the oil industry.

Other publications within the 'Social History of Labour in the Iranian Oil Industry' have focused on labour migration, mobility and transregional integration. Notably, the agency of Indian migrant workers within the Iranian oil industry during the first half of the twentieth century emerged as a central theme in these studies. These investigations scrutinized various aspects, including the ethno-religious identities of these Indian workers, the recruitment processes that brought them to Iran, the conditions of their employment, the terms of their contracts and the experiences they encountered once they had secured employment within the industry.[45] Atabaki's article stands as a major contribution to this exploration, shedding light on the multifaceted dimensions of Indian labourers' roles within the Iranian oil industry.

Additionally, a separate study conducted by Atabaki and Ehsani probed the concept of the transregional integration of labour during the First World War.[46] This research centred on the global transition from coal to oil as the dominant energy source during the conflict, which, in turn, laid the foundation for the emergence of a new politico-economic regime known as Fordism. This regime was characterized by mass industrial production and consumption, all underpinned by scientific labour management.

Amidst the array of conferences that transpired in conjunction with the 'Social History of Labour in the Iranian Oil Industry', held under the auspices of the International Institute of Social History, one conspicuous symposium bore the appellation 'Working for Oil in a Global Context'. The scholarly fruit of this academic assembly, enriched by the participation of researchers hailing from both the northern and southern hemispheres, materialized into *Working for Oil: Comparative Social Histories of Labor in the Global Oil Industry*, edited by Touraj Atabaki, Elisabetta Bini and Kaveh Ehsani. This edited volume traverses the expansive terrain of labour history, spanning from Colombia to Nigeria, and from the United States to Finland and India.[47]

Mattin Biglari is another scholar whose research has contributed towards a nuanced examination of Iran's oil industry through the lens of social history.[48] His PhD dissertation has elucidated the complex transformation of the Iranian labour force in the oil-refining sector between 1933 and 1951. This specific period encompassed the consequential renewal of Iran's oil agreement with the Anglo-Persian Oil Company in 1933, leading up to the epoch-making nationalization of this industrial titan in 1951. Subsequently, Biglari has embarked upon a sustained scholarly journey, further delving into various facets of the oil industry's social history, disseminating his research findings in a significant number of published articles.[49]

Unveiling multifaceted labour dynamics across varied commodities

Serhan Afacan's doctoral research on the social history of labour within the Iranian textile industry, spanning from the inception of the Constitutional Revolution to the conclusion of Reza Shah's reign in 1941, holds considerable significance within the field.[50] Several noteworthy aspects stand out in his work on labourers' petitions, providing valuable insights into the voices and grievances of the working class during this pivotal period. By drawing upon these primary sources, Afacan adds depth and authenticity to his exploration of labour history.

Moving beyond traditional and formal organized labour and collective labour action, Afacan's research broadens the conceptualization of labour itself. He transcends the boundaries of conventional definitions by acknowledging the diverse forms of labour and work arrangements that existed during this era. Throughout his study, Afacan considers various facets of workers' lives beyond their experiences at the worksite. This holistic approach encompasses such aspects as their social, cultural and economic circumstances, offering a well-rounded portrayal of the working class during this period. In essence, his research breaks new ground in the social history of labour through the restoration of craft workers' agency and extensive exploration of their lives, contributing to a more nuanced perspective on the multifaceted experiences of the Iranian working class during this transformative period.[51]

Copper, a vital commodity, stands as an exemplar for which labour agency assumes a profound significance, in both its extraction and subsequent production. The exploration of the complex network of workers and employees within Iran's copper industry serves as the central focus of Abdolreza Alamdar's doctoral dissertation.[52] In this scholarly endeavour, Alamdar demonstrates an assiduous commitment to delineating the pivotal role played by labour in the evolutionary narrative of copper production, particularly within the vicinity of Sarcheshmeh, situated near the city of Kerman in south-eastern Iran. The scope of his historical inquiry commences with the inception of copper's discovery in this locale and carefully tracks subsequent developments until the seismic events that heralded the Revolution of 1978–9.

Through his scholarly inquiries, Alamdar ventures to challenge the prevailing metanarrative, a dominant historical discourse which asserts that the labourers toiling within the confines of the mines were at the vanguard of the Iranian Revolution of 1978–9. In addition to his groundbreaking work on the copper mining and refining sector, Alamdar's academic journey has encompassed a continuing exploration of the social history of labour within the context of diverse Iranian commodities, including pistachio nuts, thereby enriching the scholarly landscape with multifaceted insights into the narratives of toil and production.[53]

The 'old' historiographical discourse surrounding labour, in bygone eras, exhibited a notable deficiency in its acknowledgement of intersectionality, particularly in relation to gender identity, as additional layers interwoven with the broader construct of class identity. This phenomenon is particularly salient within societies marked by a measure of gender segregation, such as Iran, primarily propelled by religious doctrines and justifications. The heightened focus on elucidating the intricacies of gender dynamics within the realm of labour agency has, in more recent decades, arisen as an outcome of the diligent scholarly pursuits and contributions that define the burgeoning field of 'new' labour history.

Valentine Moghadam's contribution to Iranian historiography, particularly within the realm of social history, is notable for her emphasis on the often-overlooked gender components within the historical narrative. Her work delves into women's economic participation across what she terms Iran's 'long twentieth century'.[54] Moghadam's research highlights the significant role played by Iranian peasant and working-class women as a substantial reservoir of cheap and unpaid labour. This predicament parallels the marginalized status often experienced by child labourers during this period. By drawing attention to this issue, she sheds light on the economic contributions of women, who have been frequently relegated to the periphery of historical accounts. Furthermore, Moghadam's classification of labour goes beyond the conventional boundaries, bringing domestic labour, servitude and prostitution to the forefront. These forms of labour, often rendered invisible or overlooked in traditional historiography, are central to her analysis. However, she acknowledges that even in her study, these critical aspects of history may not receive the comprehensive attention they deserve.

The extent of workers' participation and their impact on the Revolution of 1978–9, as well as the gains they accrued from this transformative event, remain subjects of active investigation within the domain of 'new' labour history research. Asef Bayat emerges as a pioneering figure in the study of Iranian labour history during this revolutionary period and its aftermath. His research involved extensive fieldwork conducted among workers in Tehran and the city of Tabriz, located in north-western Iran, spanning from 1980 to 1981.[55] Bayat's study not only scrutinized industrial relations within Iran but also provided a unique perspective by revisiting post-revolutionary Iran through the lens of its workers.

What distinguishes Bayat's work is its focus on the experiences and perspectives of the working class during this tumultuous period. His interviewees were active participants in the revolutionary upheaval that led to the downfall of the monarchy. Subsequently, they were instrumental in establishing councils (*showrāhā*) to exercise partial and temporary control over workplaces, particularly in large factories. Moreover, Bayat introduced a novel perspective into Iranian labour historiography. He demonstrated that the domain of labour history is not confined solely to labour researchers. Instead, it encompasses a broader spectrum of disciplines and stakeholders, including social historians, political scientists, leftist activists and even religious (Islamic) authorities. This recognition underscores the multifaceted and interdisciplinary nature of labour history and the diverse voices and perspectives that contribute to the understanding of working-class experiences and behaviours.[56]

Ahmad Ashraf's academic analysis of Iranian working-class agency during the same period also stands out as a noteworthy contribution to the field of Iranian labour history. His study, characterized by a meticulous methodology and employing both quantitative and qualitative approaches, delves into the intricate dynamics of economic changes and developments that Iran underwent during the 1970s and the initial phases of the post-revolutionary era.[57]

Ashraf's research goes beyond a surface examination of events and circumstances; it delves deep into the underlying economic transformations that defined this period. This approach allows for a comprehensive understanding of how economic shifts shaped the sociopolitical landscape for the Iranian working class. Crucially, Ashraf's study challenges prevailing notions regarding the revolutionary disposition of Iran's working class. By subjecting the revolutionary makeup of this class to rigorous analysis, he prompts a re-evaluation of established narratives. This critical assessment invites a more nuanced understanding of the multifaceted nature of working-class agency during this tumultuous period.

Fakhreddin Azimi's work stands out in a distinctive genre, offering readers an insightful portrayal of the Iranian labouring poor throughout the twentieth century.[58] This unique perspective is conveyed through an interview with Amir, a truck driver born in 1921, and his family. Amir's narrative paints a vivid picture of the everyday life experienced by the labouring poor in Iran during various crucial periods. Amir Agha's recollections span from the interwar era through the tumultuous years of the Second World War, when Iran found itself occupied by the Allied Forces. His account provides invaluable insights into the challenges, struggles and resilience of the Iranian working class during this time of international and domestic upheaval. Furthermore, Amir Agha's assessment of the political movements and parties in the post-war period, leading up to the 1978–9 Revolution, adds a layer of historical depth to his narrative. This first-hand perspective offers a unique glimpse into the social and political changes that Iran underwent throughout the twentieth century, as seen through the eyes of a working-class individual.

Haideh Moghissi and Saeed Rahnema's study delves into the complex history of the Iranian working class during the post-revolutionary period.[59] Their research encompasses a comprehensive review of the evolution of the Iranian working-class movement throughout the twentieth century, ultimately leading to the post-1978–9 Revolution era. The authors' analysis extends to the configuration of the working populace, offering insights into their composition in terms of employment, occupation and gender during the mid-1990s. This detailed examination of the labour force provides a nuanced understanding of the socio-economic dynamics at play within Iran during this time.

In addition to their analysis of the composition of the Iranian working class, Moghissi and Rahnema examine the labour policies enacted by the Islamic government since its inception. They explore the government's 'contentious preoccupations' with labour policy, shedding light on its approach to labour relations, workers' rights and the broader implications for the working class. Crucially, the authors also investigate the resistance encountered by the Islamic government's labour policies from both the independent working-class movement and the civil society movement at large. This exploration offers insights into the ongoing struggles and tensions within Iranian society in the post-revolutionary period.

Peyman Jafari has made significant contributions to the historiography of post-revolutionary labour activism and the civil rights movement in Iran through two distinct studies. In the first study, Jafari explores the dynamic transformations in workers' socio-economic conditions and labour activism across four distinct periods in Iranian history. These periods include the Iran-Iraq War (1980–8), the era of economic reconstruction under Ali Akbar Hashemi Rafsanjani (1989–97), the reforms implemented during Mohammad Khatami's presidency (1997–2005) and the neo-populist policies of Mahmoud Ahmadinejad (2005–13).[60]

In his second study, Jafari places these transformations within the more expansive context of class re-formation.[61] He argues that labour activism in Iran has become increasingly interconnected with wider civil society movements and their demands. This integration extends beyond labour-related issues and encompasses broader concerns related to democratization, women's rights and ecological sustainability. Jafari's analysis highlights the complex and multifaceted nature of civil society activism in contemporary Iran and underscores the interconnectedness of various social and political movements.

A comprehensive survey of research within the realm of Iranian working-class and labouring poor history would be incomplete without acknowledgement of the documentary publications authored by Cosroe Chaqueri. These volumes serve as invaluable assets for scholars and researchers in these specialized fields.[62] Although Chaqueri's principal emphasis has been on socialist and communist movements in Iran, his compilation of reprinted documents constitutes a substantial and indispensable resource for social historians and other scholars with an interest in contemporary Iranian history.

These documents, spanning from the early twentieth century to the period leading up to the 1978–9 Revolution, draw from a wide range of archives, including the national and diplomatic archives of the United States, Britain, Germany and France. Additionally, Chaqueri incorporates materials from the former Marx-Engels-Lenin Institute in Moscow, further enriching the diversity of sources. His collection also features leaflets and pamphlets published by various political groups and parties, providing insights into the multifaceted landscape of political and labour activism in Iran.

Conclusion

In conclusion, the historiography of labour and the working class in Iran has undergone significant transformations over the course of almost 100 years. These transformations have been characterized by the adoption of new theoretical and methodological approaches that align with the broader field of global labour history. For much of this century-long journey, Iranian labour historiography had been closely associated with the history of the socialist movement. This association, however, did not fully embrace the evolving theoretical and methodological advancements emerging within the field. Instead, it often adhered to essentialist and teleological narratives, motivated by a desire to revisit the past.

As a result, the historiography of labour in Iran remained constrained for a considerable period, failing to explore new trajectories that would encompass the diverse identities and experiences of workers beyond the conventional categories. Workers, in this conventional view, were predominantly characterized as urban, non-migrant, organized, factory-based, free, salaried and Muslim males. Yet, the evolution of labour historiography in Iran has not been static. Over time, it has confronted and adapted to new challenges. One such challenge has been the imperative to trace the multiple identities of the working class. This shift in perspective has called upon historians of Iranian labour and the working class to expand their horizons, acknowledging the varied and intersecting identities that shape workers' experiences in Iran.

However, the overarching conclusion drawn from these observations is that the field of labour studies in Iran remains in its nascent stages and has not yet comprehensively explored all relevant dimensions. Notably, certain areas have received relatively scant attention, such as domestic work and the plight of domestic workers. Similarly, the historical examination of poverty, when linked with the history of the impoverished labouring poor, holds the potential to illuminate the intricacies of the everyday lives of the marginalized in Iran. Within this context, it is essential to acknowledge the commendable efforts of Mohammad Maljoo, whose research on the lifestyles of the impoverished has contributed to an enhanced understanding of the social history of poverty in Iran. Furthermore, his work sheds light on the government's responses to these challenges, providing valuable insights into the solutions implemented in addressing the predicaments faced by the underprivileged.[63]

In this journey of transformation, Iranian labour historiography has transcended its earlier limitations and ventured into more nuanced and inclusive terrain. It has embraced the complexities of labour history, recognizing the rich tapestry of identities, struggles and aspirations that define the working class in Iran. As a result, contemporary scholarship in this field offers a more comprehensive and empathetic understanding of the Iranian working class and its place within the broader historical narrative.

Notes

1 Ann Lambton, *Landlord and Peasant in Persia: A Study of Land Tenure and Land Revenue Administration* (London: Oxford University Press, 1953); idem, *The Persian Land Reform, 1962–1966* (Oxford: Clarendon Press, 1969).
2 Farhad Kazemi and Ervand Abrahamian, 'The Nonrevolutionary Peasantry of Modern Iran', *Iranian Studies* 11, no. 1–4 (1978): 259–304.
3 Farhad Kazemi, 'Peasant Uprisings in Twentieth-Century Iran, Iraq, and Turkey', in *Peasants and Politics in the Modern Middle East*, eds. Farhad Kazemi and John Waterbury (Miami: Florida International University Press, 1991), 101–24.
4 Ahmad Ashraf, 'State and Agrarian Relations Before and After the Iranian Revolution, 1960–1990', in *Peasants and Politics*, 277–311.
5 Mir Abolqasem Fendereski, *Resaleh-ye Sanaeyeh* (Qom: Bustan-e Ketab, 1387/2008).
6 Mehdi Keyvani, *Artisans and Guild Life in the Later Safavid Period: Contributions to the Social-Economic History of Persia* (Berlin: Klaus Schwarz Verlag, 1982).
7 Willem Floor, 'The Guilds in Iran – an Overview from the Earliest Beginnings till 1972', *Zeitschrift der Deutschen Morgenländischen Gesellschaft* 125, no. 1 (1975): 99–116; idem, *Guilds, Merchants, and Ulama in Nineteenth Century Iran* (Washington, DC: Mage, 2009).
8 N. A. Kuznetsova, 'Materialy k kharakterstike remeslennogo provizvodstva v iranskom gorode XVIII–nachala XIX veka', in *The Economic History of Iran: 1800–1914*, ed. Charles Issawi (Chicago: University of Chicago Press, 1971), 285–92.
9 N. K. Belova, 'Ob otkhodnichestve iz Severo-Zapadnogo Irana v kontse XIX–nachale XX veka', *Voprosyistorii*, no. 10 (1956): 112–21; I. V. Strigunov, *Iz istorii formirovaniia bakinskogo proletariata, 70–90-e gody XIX v* (Baku: Akademii Nauk Azerbaidzhanskoi SSR, 1960).
10 Hassan Hakimian, 'Wage Labor and Migration: Persian Workers in Southern Russia, 1880–1914', *International Journal of Middle East Studies* 17, no. 4 (1985): 443–62.
11 Julian Bharier, *Economic Development in Iran 1900–1970* (London: Oxford University Press, 1971), 171.
12 Zakir Zul'fugarovich Abdullaev, *Promyshlennost' i zarozhdenie rabochego klassa Irana v kontse XIX-nachale XX vv* (Baku: Akademii Nauk Azerbaidzhanskoi SSR, 1963).
13 Ibid., 21.
14 Ali Gheissari, 'Constitutional Rights and the Development of Civil Law in Iran, 1907–1941', in *Iran's Constitutional Revolution: Popular Politics, Cultural Transformations and Transnational Connections*, eds. H. E. Chehabi and Vanessa Martin (London: I.B. Tauris, 2010), 69–79, 72.
15 For the history of early social democratic organizations, see Abdolhossein Agahi, 'Piramun-e Nakhostin Ashenayi-ye Iraniyan ba Marksism', *Donya*, no. 3 (1341/1962): 105–9.
16 For the development of the early socialist movement in Iran, see Touraj Atabaki, 'Missing Labour in the Metanarratives of Practicing Modernity in Iran: Labour Agency in Refashioning the Discourse of Social Development', in *Interventions: The*

Impact of Labour Movements on Social and Cultural Development, eds. David Mayer and Jürgen Mittag (Leipzig: AVA, 2013), 171–95.
17 For the early Soviet-constructed school of oriental and Iranian studies, see Touraj Atabaki and Lana Ravandi-Fadai, 'Iranshenasi-ye Sorkh', *Iran Nameh* 30, no. 2 (2015): 174–90.
18 Avetis Sultanzadeh, *Sovremennaia Persiia* (Moscow: n.p., 1922).
19 Avetis Sultanzadeh, *Persiia* (Moscow: Gosudarstvennoe Izdatel'stvo, 1925), 49–53.
20 Shokrollah Mani, *Tarikhcheh-ye Nahzat-e Kargari dar Iran* (Tehran: Taban, 1325/1946).
21 Ali Shamideh, *Rabochee i profsoiuznoe dvizhenie v Irane posle Vtoroi Mirovoi voiny, 1946–1953 gg* (Baku: Akademii Nauk Azerbaidzhanskoi SSR, 1965); idem, *Rabochee i profsoiuznoe dvizhenie v Irane, 1941–1946* (Baku: Akademii Nauk Azerbaidzhanskoi SSR, 1961); Abdolsamad Kambakhsh, 'Nazari beh Panjah Sal Faaliyyat-e Hezb-e Tabaqeh-ye Kargar dar Iran', *Donya*, no. 2 (1349/1970): 2–15; Ardeshir Avanesiyan, *Safahati Chand az Jonbesh-e Kargari va Komunisti-ye Iran dar Dowran-e Avval-e Saltanat-e Reza Shah (1922–1933)* (Leipzig: Tudeh Party of Iran, 1358/1979); Abdolhossein Agahi, '60 Sal az Tarikh-e Tasis-e Hezb-e Komunist-e Iran Gozasht', *Donya*, no. 3 (1980): 30–63; Mehdi Keyvani, *Haftad Sal-e Jonbesh-e Sandikayi dar Iran* (Tehran: Tudeh Party of Iran, 1359/1980), 28–41.
22 Avanesiyan, *Safahati*, 7.
23 Edward Palmer Thompson, *The Making of the English Working Class* (London: Victor Gollancz, 1963).
24 Ervand Abrahamian, *Iran Between Two Revolutions* (Princeton: Princeton University Press, 1983).
25 Touraj Atabaki, 'L'Organisation syndicale ouvrière en Iran, de 1941 à 1946', *Soual* 8 (1988): 35–60.
26 Touraj Atabaki, 'The Comintern, the Soviet Union and Labour Militancy in Interwar Iran', in *Iranian-Russian Encounters: Empires and Revolutions since 1800*, ed. Stephanie Cronin (London: Routledge, 2013), 298–323.
27 Jalil Mahmoudi and Nasser Saeidi, *Showq-e Yek Khiz-e Boland: Nakhostin Ettehadiyyehha-ye Kargari dar Iran, 1285–1320* (Tehran: Qatreh, 1381/2002).
28 Habib Ladjevardi, *Labor Unions and Autocracy in Iran* (New York: Syracuse University Press, 1985).
29 Farhang Ghassemi, *Sandikalism dar Iran: Mobarezat va Sharayet-e Kar va Zendegi-ye Zahmatkeshan, 1284–1320* (Paris: Bonyad-e Mossadegh, 1985).
30 Willem Floor, *Labour Unions, Law and Conditions in Iran (1900–1941)* (Durham: University of Durham, 1985).
31 Ibid., 2.
32 Ibid.
33 Ervand Abrahamian, 'Voice of the Discontented', *History Workshop Journal* 76, no. 1 (2013): 256–8.
34 Marcel van der Linden, 'Labour History: The Old, the New and the Global', *African Studies* 66, no. 2–3 (2007): 169.
35 Kaveh Ehsani, 'Social Engineering and the Contradictions of Modernization in Khuzestan's Company Towns: A Look at Abadan and Masjed-Soleyman', *International Review of Social History* 48, no. 3 (2003): 361–99.
36 Touraj Atabaki, 'Disgruntled Guests: Iranian Subaltern on the Margins of the Tsarist Empire', *International Review of Social History* 48, no. 3 (2003): 401–26.
37 Willem Floor, 'The Brickworkers of Khatunabad: A Striking Record (1953–1979)', *International Review of Social History* 48, no. 3 (2003): 427–55.

38 'Global Labour History', IISH, accessed 21 April 2024, https://socialhistory.org/en/research/global-labour-history.

39 Robabeh Motaghedi, 'Tasir-e Sanat-e Naft bar Tahavvol-e Hayat-e Ejtemaei dar Forudestan-e Manateq-e Naft Khiz-e Jonub-e Iran, 1287–1304' (PhD diss., Alzahra University, 1392/2013); Kaveh Ehsani, 'The Social History of Labor in the Iranian Oil Industry: The Built Environment and the Making of the Industrial Working Class (1908–1941)' (PhD diss., Leiden University, 2014); Maral Jefroudi, 'If I Deserve It, It Should Be Paid to Me. A Social History of Labour in the Iranian Oil Industry 1951–1973' (PhD diss., Leiden University, 2017); Peyman Jafari, 'Oil, Labour and Revolution in Iran: A Social History of Labour in the Iranian Oil Industry, 1973–1983' (PhD diss., Leiden University, 2018).

40 Touraj Atabaki, 'Writing the Social History of Labor in the Iranian Oil Industry', *International Labor and Working-Class History*, no. 84 (2013): 154–8.

41 Touraj Atabaki, 'From *Amaleh* (Labor) to *Kargar* (Worker): Recruitment, Work Discipline and Making of the Working Class in the Persian/Iranian Oil Industry', *International Labor and Working-Class History*, no. 84 (2013): 159–75.

42 For this argument see Zachary Lockman, 'Imagining the Working Class: Culture, Nationalism, and Class Formation in Egypt, 1899–1914', *Poetics Today* 15, no. 2 (1994): 158–9.

43 Maral Jefroudi, 'Revisiting "the Long Night" of Iranian Workers: Labor Activism in the Iranian Oil Industry in the 1960s', *International Labor and Working-Class History* 84 (2013): 176–94.

44 Peyman Jafari, 'Reasons to Revolt: Iranian Oil Workers in the 1970s', *International Labor and Working-Class History* 84 (2013): 195–217.

45 Touraj Atabaki, 'Far from Home, But at Home: Indian Migrant Workers in the Iranian Oil Industry', *Studies in History* 31, no. 1 (2015): 85–114.

46 Touraj Atabaki and Kaveh Ehsani, 'Oil and Beyond: Expanding British Imperial Aspirations, Emerging Oil Capitalism, and the Challenge of Social Questions in the First World War', in *The World During the First World War*, eds. Helmut Bley and Anorthe Kremers (Essen: Klartext, 2014), 261–87.

47 Touraj Atabaki, Elisabetta Bini and Kaveh Ehsani, eds, *Working for Oil: Comparative Social Histories of Labor in the Global Oil Industry* (New York: Palgrave Macmillan, 2018).

48 Mattin Biglari, 'Refining Knowledge: Expertise, Labour and Everyday Life in the Iranian Oil Industry, c. 1933-51' (PhD diss., SOAS University of London, 2020).

49 Mattin Biglari, 'Making Oil Men: Expertise, Discipline and Subjectivity in the Anglo-Iranian Oil Company's Training Schemes', in *Life Worlds of Middle Eastern Oil: Histories and Ethnographies of Black Gold*, eds. Nelida Fuccaro and Mandana Limbert (Edinburgh: Edinburgh University Press, 2023), 221–48; idem and Rowena Abdul Razak, 'Resource Imperialism and Resistance: Labour, Security and Social Reproduction after Iranian Oil Nationalisation', *Journal of Energy History*, no. 9 (2023), energyhistory.eu/en/node/325.

50 Serhan Afacan, 'State, Society, and Labour in Iran, 1906–1941: A Social History of Iranian Industrialization and Labour with Reference to the Textile Industry' (PhD diss., Leiden University, 2015).

51 Based on his PhD dissertation, Afacan published two articles: 'Revisiting Labor Activism in Iran: Some Notes on the Vatan Factory Strike in 1931', *International Labor and Working-Class History* 93 (2018): 201–20; 'Workers as Petitioners: Discursive Practices of Iranian Textile Workers, 1906–1941', *Cihannüma* 6, no. 2 (2020): 157–77.

52 Abdolreza Alamdar, 'The State, Entrepreneur, and Labour in the Establishment of the Iranian Copper Mining Industry: The Sarcheshmeh Copper Mine, 1966–1979' (PhD diss., Leiden University, 2019).
53 Abdolreza Alamdar, 'From Worker-Peasant to Reluctant Revolutionary Industrial Worker in the Establishment of Iran's Copper Industry: The Sarcheshmeh Copper Mine, 1960s–1970s', *Iranian Studies* 56, no. 2 (2023): 321–43.
54 Valentine M. Moghadam, 'Hidden from History? Women Workers in Modern Iran', *Iranian Studies* 33, no. 3–4 (2000): 377–401.
55 Asef Bayat, *Workers and Revolution in Iran: A Third World Experience of Workers' Control* (London: Zed Books, 1987). See also Valentine Moghadam, 'Industrial Development, Culture and Working-Class Politics: A Case Study of Tabriz Industrial Workers in the Iranian Revolution', *International Sociology* 2, no. 2 (1987): 151–75. Moghadam has argued that the late conversion of Tabriz's working class to revolutionary protest was due to their relatively privileged status.
56 Asef Bayat, 'Historiography, Class, and Iranian Workers', in *Workers and Working Classes in the Middle East: Struggles, Histories, Historiographies*, ed. Zachary Lockman (Albany: State University of New York Press, 1994), 165–210, at 165.
57 Ahmad Ashraf, 'Kalbod-Shekafi-ye Enqelab: Naqsh-e Kargaran-e Sanati dar Enqelab-e Iran', *Goftogu*, no. 55 (1389/2010): 55–123.
58 Fakhreddin Azimi, 'Amir Agha: An Iranian Worker', in *Struggle and Survival in the Modern Middle East*, ed. Edmund Burke, III (Berkeley: University of California Press, 1993), 290–304.
59 Haideh Moghissi and Saeed Rahnema, 'The Working Class and the Islamic State in Iran', in *Iranian-Russian Encounters*, 280–301.
60 Peyman Jafari, 'Rupture and Revolt in Iran', *International Socialism*, no. 124 (2009): 95–163.
61 Sina Moradi (pseudonym), 'Labour Activism and Democracy in Iran', Working Paper 22 (The Hague: Humanist Institute for Cooperation with Developing Countries, July 2013).
62 Cosroe Chaqueri, ed., *The Condition of the Working Class in Iran: A Documentary History*, 4 vols (Tehran: Antidote, 1368/1989–1370/1991).
63 Mohammad Maljoo, *Khiz-e Kham. Keshakesh-e Mostamandan va Divansalaran az 1309 ta 1320 dar Iran* (Tehran: Cheshmeh, 1402/2023).

Bibliography

Abdullaev, Zakir Zul'fugarovich. *Promyshlennost' i zarozhdenie rabochego klassa Irana v kontse XIX–nachale XX vv*. Baku: Akademii Nauk Azerbaidzhanskoi SSR, 1963.
Abrahamian, Ervand. *Iran Between Two Revolutions*. Princeton: Princeton University Press, 1983.
Abrahamian, Ervand. 'Voice of the Discontented'. *History Workshop Journal* 76, no. 1 (2013): 256–8.
Afacan, Serhan. 'Revisiting Labor Activism in Iran: Some Notes on the Vatan Factory Strike in 1931'. *International Labor and Working-Class History* 93 (2018): 201–20.
Afacan, Serhan. 'State, Society, and Labour in Iran, 1906–1941: A Social History of Iranian Industrialization and Labour with Reference to the Textile Industry'. PhD diss., Leiden University, 2015.

Afacan, Serhan. 'Workers as Petitioners: Discursive Practices of Iranian Textile Workers, 1906–1941'. *Cihannüma* 6, no. 2 (2020): 157–77.
Agahi, Abdolhossein. '60 Sāl az Tārikh-e Tāsis-e Hezb-e Komunist-e Irān Gozasht'. *Donya,* no. 3 (1359/1980): 30–63.
Agahi, Abdolhossein. 'Pirāmun-e Nakhostin Āshenāyi-ye Irāniyān bā Mārksism'. *Donya,* no. 3 (1341/1962): 105–9.
Alamdar, Abdolreza. 'From Worker-Peasant to Reluctant Revolutionary Industrial Worker in the Establishment of Iran's Copper Industry: The Sarcheshmeh Copper Mine, 1960s–1970s'. *Iranian Studies* 56, no. 2 (2023): 321–43.
Alamdar, Abdolreza. 'The State, Entrepreneur, and Labour in the Establishment of the Iranian Copper Mining Industry: The Sarcheshmeh Copper Mine, 1966–1979'. PhD diss., Leiden University, 2019.
Ashraf, Ahmad. 'Kālbod-Shekāfi-ye Enqelāb: Naqsh-e Kārgarān-e San'ati dar Enqelāb-e Irān'. *Goftogu,* no. 55 (1389/2010): 55–123.
Ashraf, Ahmad. 'State and Agrarian Relations Before and After the Iranian Revolution, 1960–1990'. In *Peasants and Politics in the Modern Middle East,* edited by Farhad Kazemi and John Waterbury, 277–311. Miami: Florida International University Press, 1991.
Atabaki, Touraj. 'Disgruntled Guests: Iranian Subaltern on the Margins of the Tsarist Empire'. *International Review of Social History* 48, no. 3 (2003): 401–26.
Atabaki, Touraj. 'Far from Home, But at Home: Indian Migrant Workers in the Iranian Oil Industry'. *Studies in History* 31, no. 1 (2015): 85–114.
Atabaki, Touraj. 'From 'Amaleh (Labor) to *Kargar* (Worker): Recruitment, Work Discipline and Making of the Working Class in the Persian/Iranian Oil Industry'. *International Labor and Working-Class History,* no. 84 (2013): 159–75.
Atabaki, Touraj. 'L'Organisation syndicale ouvrière en Iran, de 1941 à 1946'. *Soual* 8 (1988): 35–60.
Atabaki, Touraj. 'Missing Labour in the Metanarratives of Practicing Modernity in Iran: Labour Agency in Refashioning the Discourse of Social Development'. In *Interventions: The Impact of Labour Movements on Social and Cultural Development,* edited by David Mayer and Jürgen Mittag, 171–95. Leipzig: AVA, 2013.
Atabaki, Touraj. 'The Comintern, the Soviet Union and Labour Militancy in Interwar Iran'. In *Iranian-Russian Encounters: Empires and Revolutions since 1800,* edited by Stephanie Cronin, 298–323. London: Routledge, 2013.
Atabaki, Touraj. 'Writing the Social History of Labor in the Iranian Oil Industry'. *International Labor and Working-Class History,* no. 84 (2013): 154–8.
Atabaki, Touraj, Elisabetta Bini and Kaveh Ehsani, eds. *Working for Oil: Comparative Social Histories of Labor in the Global Oil Industry.* New York: Palgrave Macmillan, 2018.
Atabaki, Touraj and Kaveh Ehsani. 'Oil and Beyond: Expanding British Imperial Aspirations, Emerging Oil Capitalism, and the Challenge of Social Questions in the First World War'. In *The World During the First World War,* edited by Helmut Bley and Anorthe Kremers, 261–87. Essen: Klartext, 2014.
Atabaki, Touraj and Lana Ravandi-Fadai. 'Irānshenāsi-ye Sorkh'. *Iran Nameh* 30, no. 2 (2015): 174–90.
Avanesiyan, Ardeshir. *Safahāti-ye Chand az Jonbesh-e Kārgari va Komunisti-ye Irān dar Dowrān-e Avval-e Saltanat-e Rezā Shāh (1922–1933).* Leipzig: Tudeh Party of Iran, 1358/1979.
Azimi, Fakhreddin. 'Amir Agha: An Iranian Worker'. In *Struggle and Survival in the Modern Middle East,* edited by Edmund Burke, III, 290–304. Berkeley: University of California Press, 1993.

Bayat, Asef. 'Historiography, Class, and Iranian Workers'. In *Workers and Working Classes in the Middle East: Struggles, Histories, Historiographies*, edited by Zachary Lockman, 165–210. Albany: State University of New York Press, 1994.
Bayat, Asef. *Workers and Revolution in Iran: A Third World Experience of Workers' Control.* London: Zed Books, 1987.
Belova, N. K. 'Ob otkhodnichestve iz Severo-Zapadnogo Irana v kontse XIX–nachale XX veka'. *Voprosy istorii*, no. 10 (1956): 112–21.
Bharier, Julian. *Economic Development in Iran, 1900–1970*. London: Oxford University Press, 1971.
Biglari, Mattin. 'Making Oil Men: Expertise, Discipline and Subjectivity in the Anglo-Iranian Oil Company's Training Schemes'. In *Life Worlds of Middle Eastern Oil: Histories and Ethnographies of Black Gold*, edited by Nelida Fuccaro and Mandana Limbert, 221–48. Edinburgh: Edinburgh University Press, 2023.
Biglari, Mattin. 'Refining Knowledge: Expertise, Labour and Everyday Life in the Iranian Oil Industry, c. 1933–51'. PhD diss., SOAS University of London, 2020.
Biglari, Mattin and Rowena Abdul Razak. 'Resource Imperialism and Resistance: Labour, Security and Social Reproduction after Iranian Oil Nationalisation'. *Journal of Energy History*, no. 9 (2023), energyhistory.eu/en/node/325.
Chaqueri, Cosroe, ed. *The Condition of the Working Class in Iran: A Documentary History.* 4 vols. Tehran: Antidote, 1368/1989–1370/1991.
Ehsani, Kaveh. 'Social Engineering and the Contradictions of Modernization in Khuzestan's Company Towns: A Look at Abadan and Masjed-Soleyman'. *International Review of Social History* 48, no. 3 (2003): 361–99.
Ehsani, Kaveh. 'The Social History of Labor in the Iranian Oil Industry: The Built Environment and the Making of the Industrial Working Class (1908–1941)'. PhD diss., Leiden University, 2014.
Fendereski, Mir Abolqasem. *Resāleh-ye Sanā ʾyeh*. Qom: Bustan-e Ketab, 1387/2008.
Floor, Willem. *Guilds, Merchants, and Ulama in Nineteenth Century Iran*. Washington, DC: Mage, 2009.
Floor, Willem. *Labour Unions, Law and Conditions in Iran (1900–1941)*. Durham: University of Durham, 1985.
Floor, Willem. 'The Brickworkers of Khatunabad: A Striking Record (1953–1979)'. *International Review of Social History* 48, no. 3 (2003): 427–55.
Floor, Willem. 'The Guilds in Iran – an Overview from the Earliest Beginnings till 1972'. *Zeitschrift der Deutschen Morgenländischen Gesellschaft* 125, no. 1 (1975): 99–116.
Ghassemi, Farhang. *Sandikālism dar Irān: Mobārezāt va Sharāyet-e Kār va Zendegi-ye Zahmatkeshān, 1284–1320*. Paris: Bonyad-e Mossadegh, 1985.
Gheissari, Ali. 'Constitutional Rights and the Development of Civil Law in Iran, 1907–1941'. In *Iran's Constitutional Revolution: Popular Politics, Cultural Transformations and Transnational Connections*, edited by H. E. Chehabi and Vanessa Martin, 69–79. London: I.B. Tauris, 2010.
Hakimian, Hassan. 'Wage Labor and Migration: Persian Workers in Southern Russia, 1880–1914'. *International Journal of Middle East Studies* 17, no. 4 (1985): 443–62.
Jafari, Peyman. 'Oil, Labour and Revolution in Iran: A Social History of Labour in the Iranian Oil Industry, 1973–1983'. PhD diss., Leiden University, 2018.
Jafari, Peyman. 'Reasons to Revolt: Iranian Oil Workers in the 1970s'. *International Labor and Working-Class History* 84 (2013): 195–217.
Jafari, Peyman. 'Rupture and Revolt in Iran'. *International Socialism*, no. 124 (2009): 95–163.

Jefroudi, Maral. 'If I Deserve It, It Should Be Paid to Me: A Social History of Labour in the Iranian Oil Industry, 1951–1973'. PhD diss., Leiden University, 2017.
Jefroudi, Maral. 'Revisiting "the Long Night" of Iranian Workers: Labor Activism in the Iranian Oil Industry in the 1960s'. *International Labor and Working-Class History* 84 (2013): 176–94.
Kambakhsh, Abdolsamad. 'Nazari beh Panjāh Sāl Faʿāliyyat-e Hezb-e Tabaqeh-ye Kārgar dar Irān'. *Donya*, no. 2 (1349/1970): 2–15.
Kazemi, Farhad. 'Peasant Uprisings in Twentieth-Century Iran, Iraq, and Turkey'. In *Peasants and Politics in the Modern Middle East*, edited by Farhad Kazemi and John Waterbury, 101–24. Miami: Florida International University Press, 1991.
Kazemi, Farhad and Ervand Abrahamian. 'The Nonrevolutionary Peasantry of Modern Iran'. *Iranian Studies* 11, no. 1–4 (1978): 259–304.
Keyvani, Mehdi. *Artisans and Guild Life in the Later Safavid Period: Contributions to the Social-Economic History of Persia*. Berlin: Klaus Schwarz Verlag, 1982.
Keyvani, Mehdi. *Haftād SālnJonbesh-e Sandikāyi dar Irān*. Tehran: Tudeh Party of Iran, 1359/1980.
Kuznetsova, N. A. 'Materialy k kharakteristike remeslennogo proizvodstva v iranskom gorode XVIII–nachala XIX veka'. In *The Economic History of Iran, 1800–1914*, edited by Charles Issawi, 285–92. Chicago: University of Chicago Press, 1971.
Ladjevardi, Habib. *Labor Unions and Autocracy in Iran*. New York: Syracuse University Press, 1985.
Lambton, Ann. *Landlord and Peasant in Persia: A Study of Land Tenure and Land Revenue Administration*. London: Oxford University Press, 1953.
Lambton, Ann. *The Persian Land Reform, 1962–1966*. Oxford: Clarendon Press, 1969.
Lockman, Zachary. 'Imagining the Working Class: Culture, Nationalism, and Class Formation in Egypt, 1899–1914'. *Poetics Today* 15, no. 2 (1994): 157–90.
Mahmoudi, Jalil and Nasser Saeidi. *Showq-e Yek Khiz-e Boland: Nakhostin Ettehādiyyehhā-ye Kārgari dar Irān, 1285–1320*. Tehran: Qatreh, 1381/2002.
Maljoo, Mohammad. *Khiz-e Khām: Keshākesh-e Mostamandān va Divānsālārān az 1309 tā 1320 dar Irān*. Tehran: Cheshmeh, 1402/2023.
Mani, Shokrollah. *Tārikhcheh-ye Nahzat-e Kārgari dar Irān*. Tehran: Taban, 1325/1946.
Moghadam, Valentine M. 'Hidden from History? Women Workers in Modern Iran'. *Iranian Studies* 33, no. 3–4 (2000): 377–401.
Moghadam, Valentine M. 'Industrial Development, Culture and Working-Class Politics: A Case Study of Tabriz Industrial Workers in the Iranian Revolution'. *International Sociology* 2, no. 2 (1987): 151–75.
Moghissi, Haideh and Saeed Rahnema. 'The Working Class and the Islamic State in Iran'. In *Iranian-Russian Encounters: Empires and Revolutions since 1800*, edited by Stephanie Cronin, 280–301. London: Routledge, 2013.
Moradi, Sina (pseudonym). 'Labour Activism and Democracy in Iran'. Working Paper 22. The Hague: Humanist Institute for Cooperation with Developing Countries, July 2013.
Motaghedi, Robabeh. 'Taʾsir-e Sanʿat-e Naft bar Tahavvol-e Hayāt-e Ejtemāʿi dar Forudestān-e Manāteq-e Naft-e Khiz-e Jonub-e Irān, 1287–1304'. PhD diss., Alzahra University, 1392/2013.
Shamideh, Ali. *Rabochee i profsoiuznoe dvizhenie v Irane, 1941–1946*. Baku: Akademii Nauk Azerbaidzhanskoi SSR, 1961.
Shamideh, Ali. *Rabochee i profsoiuznoe dvizhenie v Irane posle Vtoroi Mirovoi voiny, 1946–1953 gg*. Baku: Akademii Nauk Azerbaidzhanskoi SSR, 1965.

Strigunov, I. V. *Iz istorii formirovaniia bakinskogo proletariata, 70–90-e gody XIX v.* Baku: Akademii Nauk Azerbaidzhanskoi SSR, 1960.
Sultanzadeh, Avetis. *Persiia.* Moscow: Gosudarstvennoe Izdatel'stvo, 1925.
Sultanzadeh, Avetis. *Sovremennaia Persiia.* Moscow: n.p., 1922.
Thompson, Edward Palmer. *The Making of the English Working Class.* London: Victor Gollancz, 1963.
Van der Linden, Marcel. 'Labour History: The Old, the New and the Global'. *African Studies* 66, no. 2–3 (2007): 169–80.

Part II

The agency of workers, guilds and merchants

3

The convergence of the guilds and craftsmen with the labour movement in Iran, 1918–23

Hojjat Fallah Tootkar

Iranian workers were active from the period of the First National Consultative Assembly (the Majles or Parliament) onwards.[1] At that time, workers at printing houses conducted their activities as 'the Typesetters' Association' (Anjoman-e Ajza-ye Mabuat-e Hurufi) along with other guild associations, which was the first attempt to form the labour movement's identity.[2] From that time onwards, the printing house workers organized for collective action on numerous occasions. During the Second Majles, they started publishing the newspaper *Ettefaq-e Kargaran* (Workers' Unity) and went on strike for a week to claim their rights.[3]

Moreover, in support of the consolidation of the constitutional system, tramway workers established their own association during the First Majles. There also are references in the sources to the protests of workers in municipal services, such as road construction.

With the inception of the First World War, this social struggle faded away. However, once the war was over, especially after the October Revolution of 1917 and with its subsequent political and ideological impact on Iran, the intellectual ground was prepared for the sociopolitical agitation of workers.

The chaotic economic situation of the country and the famine of 1918/9 (1297 SH), during which, in the words of Avetis Mikhailian, widely known as Sultanzadeh, 'hundreds and thousands of people perished from hunger and constantly rising food prices posed a life-threatening hunger to the masses, workers and toilers', laid the socio-economic ground for protests.[4] It was in this context that the printing workers in Tehran acted as pioneers and established their trade union. The workers elected Seyyed Mohammad Dehgan, the in-house editor of *Haqiqat* newspaper, as head of their union and Ebrahim Nahid, the typesetter (*safheh-band*) of the Rowshani Printing House, as its secretary.[5] In 1918 (1297 SH), they organized a widespread strike, which is said to have lasted for fourteen days.[6] This strike brought various achievements for the printing workers, such as regulating the relations between workers and employers, and introducing eight hours of work per day, as well as securing better sanitary conditions at the printing houses.[7]

This successful movement of the printing workers impressed workers and craftsmen employed in other industries, who considered establishing their own unions. Here, the Printing Workers' Union, particularly Mohammad Dehgan, played a role. *Haqiqat*, whose first issue appeared in January 1922 (Dey 1300), accelerated this movement.

In his report, while referring to the miserable situation of the weaving workers, whose number was about a thousand in 1921/2 (1300), Shokrollah Mani noted that these people were mostly seasonal workers, whose workplace remained open for only half of the year and remained idle for the other six months. As a result, weaving workers endured very bad conditions. In describing the background of the establishment of the Weaving Workers' Union, he recalled that these workers became excited about the advantages of forming a union, as explained by Ahmad Lame, a member of the Printing Workers' Union, and embarked upon establishing their own with his and Dehgan's support. They also elected Mani as the head of their union.[8] This union went on a full-day strike on 4 May 1922 (13 Ordibehesht 1301) because 'the owners of the textile factories had wanted to reduce the workers' wages by an *abbāsi* [equal to four *shāhis*; both units of local coinage]. Eventually, the factory owners had to reverse their decision, and the strikers then went back to work the following Saturday.'[9] The textile workers also elected three of their colleagues for membership in the United Council of Workers (Showra-ye Mottahedeh-ye Kargaran).

With the establishment of trade unions in the capital, the General Council of United Workers of Tehran (Showra-ye Omumi-ye Mottahedeh-ye Kargaran-e Tehran) was established in late 1921 (1300) under Dehgan's supervision.[10] Each trade union had three representatives on the General Council.[11] The number of trade unions and their members were listed in a 1922 (1301) report (see Table 3.1) sent by Dehgan to the Moscow-based Profintern (Red International of Labour Unions).[12]

The composition of the unions within the Tehran General Council is worthy of consideration. Unions of bakers, tailors, shoemakers, shop apprentices and sugar makers generally had an artisanal tradition. In fact, out of approximately 8,000 workers who were members of the Council, about 7,450 had artisanal origins.

Apart from the list of trade unions, it appears from Dehgan's report that other workers and craftsmen also started to form unions during this period. Drapers' shop

Table 3.1 Iranian Trade Unions and Their Members, *c.* 1922

Name of Union	Number of Members (German Translation)	Number of Members (French Translation)
Bakers	3,000	3,000
Tailors	2,000	2,000
Shoemakers	1,800	1,800
Post and telegraph workers	90–350	270
Sugar makers	90–350	300
Printing house workers	90–350	350
Shop apprentices	90–350	350
Employees of trading houses	90–350	350
Gold embroidery workers	--	150
Total	7,250–8,550	8,570

Source: Cosroe Chaqueri, *Asnad-e Tarikhi-ye Jonbesh-e Kargari, Sosiyal Demokrasi va Komunisti-ye Iran*, vol. 6 (Tehran: Elm, 1358/1979), 114.

workers formed their own union, and in a meeting on the evening of 3 June 1922 (12 Khordad 1301), they elected the following representatives: Ala al-Din Taqavi, Seyyed Hossein Jalilzadeh, Seyyed Habibollah Torki, Mirza Kuchek Zarrin Qalam, Seyyed Javad Taheri, Mirza Gholam Hossein Nazemzadeh, Mirza Mohammad Hossein Tehrani, Seyyed Kuchek Amanollahi and Mirza Hadi Khorram.[13] This report indicated that the union had been formed at least a year before the election was held.

Cigarette shop workers also formed a union. *Eqtesad-e Iran* mentioned its formation on 3 August 1922 (11 Mordad 1301): 'Cigarette shop workers held a general meeting with the attendance of 113 workers and elected, with a majority of votes, Karim Aqa, Mirza Ali Akbar and Abbas Khan to the membership of the General Union.' The employers of these workers threatened to fire those who joined the union in order to discourage them from its membership.[14] Thus, they fired five workers who were members of the union. But due to the union's resistance and protest, 'The owners of the shops admitted their mistakes and reinstated them with full apologies'.[15]

The Construction Workers' Union was among other labour organizations formed at this time. Its prominent representatives included: 'Ostad Mohammad Bana, Aqa Seyyed Mehdi, Aqa Molla Mohammad, Ostad Mohammad Ebrahim and Ostad Abdol Hossein'.[16] Within this trade union, which was one of the most active, disagreements arose. Hence, its members held a meeting in late May 1923 (early Khordad 1302) in order to reach an agreement on certain issues, including professional conduct, work ethics, working conditions and even the proper way of raising their children. An outstanding example of the mentality and behaviour of workers and craftsmen of this period, this programme, which was the written pledge of the Union of Construction Workers and signed by the aforementioned representatives, speaks of their high and broad level of understanding about trade union matters, their children's education, both boys and girls, the seriousness of work, support for domestic production and industry and the observation of religious customs.

In his report, Shokrollah Mani also mentions the names of labour union representatives in the General Council of United Workers. Apart from those mentioned earlier, public baths workers also had a union and their representative in this council was Reza Paberahneh. Others that were members of the General Council included: the Ministry of Post and Telegraph Employees Union, the Pharmaceutical Workers' Union, the Municipal Workers' Union (Street Sweepers), the Teachers' Union and the Government Departments' Union. The General Council of United Workers had about thirty to forty members.[17]

Although the General Council of United Workers in Tehran did not follow the ideology of the Communist Party of Iran (CPI) and denied any connection with Bolshevism,[18] the CPI's activities played a decisive role in increasing the workers' class consciousness. Conversely, the social composition of the labour unions, which mainly arose from the previous guild-artisanal organizations, was such that they had an extensive connection with religion and its institutions. They showed particular enthusiasm for holding religious festivals and ceremonies. For example, printing press workers, whose modern labour organization was the General Council's most knowledgeable member, had a special dedication to holding religious gatherings. During the Muharram month of 1923 (1342 AH), they gathered in the mosque of the late Aqa Sheikh Abdol Hossein to listen to the preacher, who was supposed 'to discuss and expound on the current situation and Islamic truths'.[19] This certainly was not a tactical move, nor did it mean that the General Council of United Workers had no link with the CPI or was not influenced by it. Because, in the approved programme of the First Congress of the Communist Party of Iran, it was stated that CPI activists should not be hostile to the religious feelings of the people, since taking an anti-religious stand would only work to the advantage of the class enemies of the workers and toilers. All of this is mentioned because, from the author's point of view, any historiography about the labour movement of this era that does not refer to the CPI's efforts to create a history and identity for the independent movement of the working class is an obvious distortion. For instance, Parviz (Seyyed Jafar Pishevari), a CPI activist, was one of the principal columnists of *Haqiqat*.

The activities of guilds and tradesmen in this period are closely related to the labour movement. This period starts with the coup d'état launched by Seyyed Zia al-Din Tabatabaei and Reza Khan on 22 February 1921 (3 Esfand 1299). After the coup and seizure of power, Seyyed Zia immediately ordered the arrest of a large number of statesmen, landholders and guild leaders, such as Haj Mohammad Taqi Bonakdar and Haj Seyyed Mohammad Eslambolchi. He issued a manifesto that led to the entrapment (*eqfāl*) of a number of CPI veterans and such intellectuals as Mirzadeh Eshghi and Aref Qazvini. In this document, dated 27 February 1921 (8 Esfand 1299), Seyyed Zia severely criticized the statesmen and politicians who had obscured the promises of freedom and law in order 'to establish the rudimentary lawless policy of personal gain and unbridled feudal principles of the Middle Ages'.[20] He also remarked that during the fifteen years that had passed since the Constitutional Revolution, several hundred nobles and notables had inherited the country and 'sucked the blood of the people and the nation like leeches'. He believed that the time had come for which 'the lifespan of this class [had] passed'. Addressing his compatriots, while pointing out the need for change in the entire state of affairs, he noted:

> It is necessary to consider the value of the labour and toil of the workers and the farmers, and to end the cycle of their desolation and misery. To achieve this goal, the first step that should be taken is the distribution of the royal lands [*khālesajāt*] and state lands among the farmers, as well as the making of laws to benefit the farmer more than the feudal landlord. Transactions between the landlord and the farmer will be adjusted, and the means for the latter's health and livelihood will be provided.

Seyyed Zia also mentioned the expansion of education and training, the elimination of hardship and the high cost of living and other measures to improve people's lives.

However, in the author's opinion, this entire discourse was the demagoguery of the representatives of the ruling class, that is, the bourgeois-landholding class – used to prevent the spread of the influence of Marxist ideas and the Jangali Movement. That he explicitly talks about adjusting landlord-farmer relations instead of abolishing those of landlord and peasant indicates that Seyyed Zia, a prime minister linked to imperialism, understood the interests of the Iranian bourgeois/landholding class better than they did. This, naturally, has been seen in European history, too. Louis Bonaparte in France was much the same. Of course, Seyyed Zia could not play the role of an Iranian Louis Bonaparte due to his apparent history of relations with British imperialism, the opposition of nobles to him and the lack of an instrument of domination. Reza Khan (Sardar-e Sepah or Commander of the Army) was fit for this role and issued the statement 'I rule' after the coup d'état. As it turned out, Zia's Cabinet did not last long, and Ahmad Qavam (al-Saltaneh) came to power after him on 4 June 1921 (14 Khordad 1300). One of the most challenging issues for Qavam's Cabinet (the first lasted until 17 January 1922/27 Dey 1300) was the massive strike of teachers for their unpaid wages.

Sultanzadeh believed that, unlike the labour unions that only had an economic function, the Teachers' Union had a political function as well.[21] Labour unions and trade organizations supported the teachers' strike. In response to the disparaging words of Abdol Hossein Teymurtash (Sardar Moazzam Khorasani), who said that he 'would not exchange the rotting bones of a soldier for twenty teachers', *Haqiqat* reacted sharply:

> Make no mistake; we also consider the soldier to be holy. The soldiers are our brothers of yesterday with whom we used to study in school. Tomorrow it is our turn to sacrifice ourselves on the patriotic fronts. You follow the trail of your comrades, and we will not sell the rotten bones of one teacher to a hundred people from the likes of you, mister.[22]

It was in such a context that with the efforts of the socialist faction led by Soleiman Mirza Eskandari in the Parliament, Qavam's government finally fell, to be replaced by Mirza Hassan Khan Pirnia (Moshir al-Dowleh), who formed his cabinet on 22 January 1922 (2 Bahman 1300) and stayed in power until 13 June 1922 (22 Khordad 1301). After the formation of Moshir al-Dowleh's Cabinet, Ahmad Shah planned to leave for Europe.[23] This issue aroused the concern of some of the heads of the trades and guilds. As a protest, these leaders organized the closing of the bazaar and expressed their dissatisfaction with the Shah's imminent departure from the country.[24] However, Ahmad Shah did not pay much attention to this expression of regret and left for Europe. By 22 February 1922 (3 Esfand 1300), the press had started to criticize Seyyed Zia as the agent of 'the black coup'. This angered Reza Khan, and in a very harsh statement that addressed the newspaper editors, he reminded them that he was 'the real cause of the coup'.[25] He also threatened these editors and beat up some of them.[26]

As a result, some newspaper editors, including Mohammad Farrokhi Yazdi, the editor of *Tufan*, sought sanctuary in the Soviet embassy.[27] Farrokhi and his friends were supported by the labour unions and a group of guilds and craftsmen. Also, in protest against Reza Khan's threats, a group of newspaper editors went to the Majles to seek sanctuary.[28] *Haqiqat* published an article entitled 'Preserving Freedom is the Duty of the Nation' and emphasized the necessity of restoring the constitution and abolishing military rule.[29] *Haqiqat* reminded the Minister of War that 'the army should serve the interests of the nation'. While supporting the national army, this newspaper noted that its leader should not be against freedom but should work for 'the unity of the worker-cultivator and the army' against 'the rotten aristocracy'.[30] These statements show how *Haqiqat* failed to perceive the true nature of Reza Khan, who was in charge of the army at this time.

Farrokhi and the other newspaper editors stayed in the Soviet embassy for quite a long time. Meanwhile, an essay was published in his defence by merchants and tradesmen in Tehran, portraying him as 'a virtuous and sensible Iranian who is attentive to the matters of his country'.[31] They also supported his sanctuary and praised his attention to public freedom and the safeguarding of the constitution. They noted that Farrokhi and the other editors only 'want the implementation of the constitution, and nothing else'. As a further show of solidarity, they added: 'Therefore, we, the undersigned, consider Mr Farrokhi to be the rightful one, and we agree with him.'

This essay was signed by eighty-two businessmen and tradesmen from the Tehran Bazaar. However, none of the following merchants' and heads of guilds' names appeared on the document: Haj Mohammad Hossein Amin al-Zarb, Mirza Mohammad Moein al-Tojjar Bushehri, Haj Mohammad Taqi Bonakdar, Haj Mohammad Hossein Razzaz, Haj Seyyed Mohammad Eslambolchi, Ali Akbar Saatsaz and Haj Sheikh Abdol Hossein Kharazi. In fact, not only were they not upset about the violation of the constitution by the closing of the press, they also sought to impose further restrictions on it and shut down even more publications. *Haqiqat* referred to these guild heads, for example, Bonakdar, Kharazi and Razzaz, as 'the peddlers [*dowreh-ye gardhā*]', adding: 'the entire nation is fully aware of their disposition, [and] along with some wretched apprentices, who are their underlings . . . [they] went to the Council of Ministers to complain about the contents of the freedom-seeking press.'[32] Pishevari, the chief columnist of *Haqiqat*, opined, 'This type of demagoguery and corruption will never work today.'[33]

The aforementioned newspaper editors, who remained in the sanctuary of the Majles, published a statement to inform the nation about their struggle against the military regime and advocacy for the implementation of the constitution: 'Compatriots, the intolerable oppression and adversity of the reactionaries and daily policies of the police state have compelled us to finally make our own rules by having a sit-in.'[34] They added that they had taken refuge, 'In pursuance of the objective and obtaining our national rights, we only and solely rely on the National Consultative Assembly and the most sacred of all buildings, which is filled with the blood of the youth and martyrs of the path of freedom'. In their declaration, they mentioned that the purpose of their sit-in was not based on personal objectives but rather 'collective aspirations' and the demand for trampled rights and the implementation of the constitution. They reminded the reader that the government and the Majles 'must officially announce how and under what principles the government of Iran is administered, and whichever form is introduced, we must be treated according to its rules, standards and regulations, and they must safeguard our national dignity'.

The Committee of Sanctuary-Claiming Newspaper Editors also published a statement with the signatures of Farrokhi, Hossein Falsafi and Mirza Mostowfi Khan Derakhshan, who were the editors of *Tufan*, *Hayat* and *Tanbih-e Derakhshan*, respectively. At the end of their letter, entitled 'A Warning to the Fourth Majles', while denouncing the legal plan of the jury of the press in the Majles, they thoroughly criticized the deputies:

> The Fourth Majles! Did they not whip the editor of the newspaper in front of you and you sat quietly? The Fourth Majles! Did they not, despite your presence, issue a death sentence without trial, and you pretended not to see it? The Fourth Majles! Has not martial law been maintained in the capital, where you show off, while you were busy approving the pension to be paid to the deposed Shah?[35]

The newspaper editors' sanctuary continued in the Soviet embassy and the Majles, while War Minister Reza Khan, regardless of such protests, as well as those of some guilds, craftsmen and labour unions, sought to consolidate his power. Meanwhile, a large group of intellectuals from the guilds and craftsmen wrote a letter in support of the sanctuary seekers in the Soviet embassy, in which they said, 'the nation supports the implementation of the constitution . . . [and] reforms', and it 'hates reaction and cannot spend too much [time] on this deliberation and be patient'.[36] At the end of this declaration, they emphasized: 'We consider Farrokhi, who took sanctuary at the embassy of the labour government of Russia, to be freedom-seeking and righteous, and we know that he pursues the same goal.' Further to these protests, a group of tradesmen and workers gathered in Baharestan Square in Tehran, where the Majles was, and still is, located to demand the implementation of the constitution in late April 1922 (early Ordibehesht 1301).[37]

On 2 May 1922 (11 Ordibehesht 1301), workers and craftsmen held a rally to celebrate International Workers' Day and declared it a holiday. In this regard, *Haqiqat* wrote in an editorial entitled 'May 1st' that 'on the first day of the month, workers and farmers, nationalists, merchants, tradesmen and other guilds' stop work and 'conduct social demonstrations, political meetings and ethical conferences'.[38]

Workers and craftsmen not only commemorated May Day in 1922 but also continued to support the struggle of intellectuals for the restoration of the constitution. However, Reza Khan did not pay attention to these protests and continued to violate the constitution. He asked Prime Minister Mirza Hassan Khan Moshir al-Dowleh to authorize the banning of *Haqiqat*, but the latter deemed this request to be illegal. This issue was one of the main reasons for Moshir al-Dowleh's resignation.[39] But surprisingly, this issue, which was raised at that time, was denied by the newspaper itself. Despite criticizing his conduct, *Haqiqat*, as a newspaper that reflected the views of labour unions, suffered from the same delusion towards Reza Khan that the CPI suffered by following the Soviet Union. In an editorial entitled 'The Reason for the Cabinet's Resignation', *Haqiqat* upheld Reza Khan's denial of the claims that he was involved in Moshir al-Dowleh's resignation and had disregarded the constitution, writing, 'Sardar-e Sepah has . . . stated that he has always wanted to uphold the law by acting in accordance with the will of the nation . . . and everyone knows that he is not afraid of anybody and does not like flattery and lying.'[40]

Haqiqat went even further, claiming: 'Why should we not write and say that the aristocratic and anti-freedom aspect of Mr. Moshir al-Dowleh caused his cabinet's downfall?' The newspaper then alleged that he was opposed to the freedom of the press. Conversely, while criticizing 'some of Sardar-e Sepah's measures against freedom', the *Haqiqat* editorialist considered this issue to be 'slander and libel' against him and claimed that the reason for such attitudes was that 'he is not an aristocrat, does not have serfs, does not have land and does not have a title'. This superficial and formalist view that reduced Reza Khan's class nature to his personal traits and individual characteristics – which, of course, did not have any roots in reality – laid the ground for several years of the silencing of labour unions during his rise to power. They so mistakenly pinned their hopes on Reza Khan that they preferred this soldier and former member of the Cossack Brigade, who now, in concord with the imperialist policy of Great Britain, stepped into the power arena, over a statesman, like Moshir al-Dowleh.

The Workers' Union, which exerted influence over workers, craftsmen and a group of tradesmen, increasingly undermined the power of guild leaders, including Bonakdar and Kharazi. This came to such a point that these leaders decided to fight back against the labour unions by gathering their supporters. *Haqiqat* mentioned this issue in an article entitled 'The Peddlers Again' and wrote that the supporters of Bonakdar and Kharazi attacked 'comrade Mirza Gholam Hossein, the representative of the drapers' house'.[41]

The activism of the Workers' Union engendered self-awareness in the workers and apprentices of the shops. This issue became the basis of conflict and confrontation between the apprentices and the heads of the guilds. In mid-June 1922 (late Khordad 1301), *Haqiqat* reported on a confrontation between bakery apprentices and workers and their employers. In the context of increasing conflicts within the guild hierarchy, the representatives of the trades and guilds went to the Majles in late June (early Tir 1301) to complain about this issue in connection with the excessive surcharges desired by shop owners.[42]

After the fall of Moshir al-Dowleh's Cabinet, Qavam al-Saltaneh came to power on 18 June 1922 (27 Khordad 1301) to remain there until mid-January 1923 (late Dey 1301). This time, by forming a cabinet in the foreign policy arena, he aimed to sign contracts with American oil companies and draw the Americans into the Iranian political scene. This policy was met with criticism from intellectuals and the leftist press, such as *Eqtesad-e Iran*.[43] In the domain of domestic affairs, Qavam followed a two-step programme. According to the first step, the bill presented by the press jury to the Majles for approval was to create legal restrictions upon the independent and free press. The second step, on the other hand, would prevent Reza Khan from gaining power. To advance the first step of his programme, Qavam decided to ban newspapers, such as *Eqtesad-e Iran*, which were critical of the government's foreign policy. He launched his plan, but this caused a massive reaction from the labour movement. The Union of Printing and Textile Workers launched strikes. Of course, the issue of low wages was also instrumental in the strike of the textile workers. The unfair distribution of state orders also played a role in the printing workers' strike. But for whatever reason they started, the strikes coincided with the suspension of *Eqtesad-e Iran*, which ultimately resumed its publication.[44] This newspaper was suspended after the thirtieth issue was published on Wednesday 30 August 1922 (7 Shahrivar 1301) and resumed its publication with the thirty-first issue on Thursday 14 September 1922 (22 Shahrivar 1301). In the same issue of the newspaper, the lifting of the suspension was deemed to be 'one of the national conquests on the road to implementing the country's constitution'.[45] The independent press continued to fight against the jury bill and referred to it as 'the negation of freedom law'.[46]

Reza Khan, who had established military regimes in Tehran and several provinces, such as Azerbaijan, and extensively intervened in the affairs of other ministries, infuriated some Fourth Majles deputies. By his order, the revenues of the Indirect Tax Department and the income of the General Department of State Lands of the Country and the Food Taxes of Tehran, which were collected from the people, were handed over to the Ministry of War without being deposited into the General Treasury. Apart from this, the restrictions put on the press and the beating of Mirza Hashem Khan Mohit Mafi, the editor of *Vatan* newspaper, who had opposed the Ministry of War's measures, compelled the deputies to act.[47] Thus, in a session on 5 October 1922 (12 Mehr 1301), Mirza Mohsen Motamed al-Tojjar, the deputy of Tabriz, and Seyyed Hassan Modarres, the deputy of Tehran, criticized the Minister of War. After criticizing Reza Khan's greed, Modarres concluded: 'My opinion about the war minister is that his merits outweigh his defects. We should try to eliminate his flaws and increase his useful qualities for the benefit of the country.'[48]

In his lengthy speech, Motamed al-Tojjar, while expressing the goals and ideals of constitutionalism, objected to the silence of the deputies in the face of lawbreaking. He reminded them that people had complained about the silence of the Majles and its deputies, adding: 'They, without any legal authorization, close newspapers, and arrest, imprison, exile, manhandle and beat their editors. Why? Because they criticized the excessive oppression and abuse, the selection of incompetent people for government jobs, the embezzlement and thousands of other misdeeds, and showed government officials the right path.'[49] He also criticized the Ministry of War, stating: 'In the constitution, the deeds are divided and each minister is responsible for his work. Is this being observed here?' Motamed al-Tojjar, while calling this situation dangerous, noted that the Majles should 'summon the government, the current leaders and officials as soon as possible to make them observe the constitutional laws of the country, and to make each of the ministers seriously engage in reforms in their respective departments and scopes of authority'.

Motamed al-Tojjar also called for the removal of military regimes from the capital and other regions and urged ministers to engage in reforms, adding: 'The government should be warned and forced to strictly observe the country's constitution and to monitor the implementation of the laws approved by the Majles.' He also thoroughly criticized the country's chaotic situation, a major part of which was the by-product of the War Minister's measures, and lastly, he proposed that a delegation be appointed by the Majles 'to discuss the current situation of the country with the interior ministers and to propose a solution'.

We have no information about the reactions of the General Council of United Workers, individual labour unions, guilds and craftsmen to these developments. But the leftist *Eqtesad-e Iran*, while defending the deputies' critiques against the 'great minister [*vazir-e mo'azzam*]', wrote that 'with the ruling military regimes, another government came into existence within the ministries of finance, justice and domestic affairs of the current government. Suddenly, a desire to achieve one's goal with the assistance of naive people, even if there is any lawlessness, is perceived to be a military dictatorship.'[50]

Reza Khan was outraged by the speeches of Motamed al-Tojjar and Modarres and issued his feigned resignation to the military commanders. In reaction to this development, military units marched in front of the Majles to show their displeasure with the speeches of the two deputies. Mohammad Taqi Bahar (Malek al-Shoara) wrote about this incident: 'the route of all these units was specifically determined to pass by the door of Baharestan.'[51] From the provinces, the military commanders of the army transmitted threatening telegrams to the capital and asked Crown Prince Mohammad Hassan Mirza to reappoint Reza Khan to the Ministry of War. Eventually, they convinced the latter to withdraw his resignation. Afterwards, he attended the Majles while in session and announced the abolition of martial law. Mirza Hossein Khan Pirnia (Motamen al-Molk), the speaker of the Majles, also thanked him on behalf of the deputies, for his services in the creation of security within the country.[52]

After this incident, *Eqtesad-e Iran* continued its fight against Qavam and noted that although Reza Khan's military dictatorship had ceased to exist, instead 'Qavam al-Saltaneh is pursuing a personal dictatorship in the political arena'.[53] Soleiman Mirza and his associates in the Majles, contrary to Modarres and his circle, were pursuing the impeachment of Qavam and the fall of his cabinet. As it turned out, the conflict between the pro- and anti-Qavam deputies was taken outside of the Majles as Tehran became the scene of the ongoing quarrel between the two factions. The supporters of Qavam's Cabinet and a group of his followers gathered in Tehran's Jameh Mosque. The leaders of this gathering, who were the aforementioned guild heads, Bonakdar, Razzaz and Kharazi, fought with Soleiman Mirza and his associates. They then shut down the Tehran Bazaar for several days starting from 20 October 1922 (27 Mehr 1301) and gathered in the Majles to chant slogans against Soleiman Mirza and Qavam's other opponents. In response to these acts, the General Council of United Workers of Tehran published a statement against the supporters of Qavam's Cabinet entitled 'The Games of Conspiracy and Intrigue Have Not Yet Ended; They Still Go On'. They reminded the reader that Qavam's supporters in the Majles 'are wearing the hat of demagoguery . . . and shout "Oh Islam, oh Shariah," and have decided to make the nation distrustful and cynical about a righteous, sincere and pious deputy like Soleiman Mirza, who has never been deceived by foreigners'.

With reference to the Jameh Mosque gathering, *Eqtesad-e Iran* recalled, 'Scholars of Islam and honourable preachers, who were wholly unaware of the incident, were implicated, and in the name of religion, they were taken out of their homes and forced into the Jameh Mosque to help the reactionaries.'[54] The Workers' Union also believed that the curtain of deceit would be lifted, and 'the truth of the matter will be revealed to the scholars and clerics and the motley deceptive policies of Qavam al-Saltaneh will be exposed'. The workers pointed out to Qavam's supporters that their accusations of irreligion were in fact true of them:

> Unlike you, the freedom-seekers are Muslim, and they are supporters of Islam and Muslims. You want to implement [British statesman William Ewart] Gladstone's [imperialist] commands by throwing your turbans on the ground [an expression of one's displeasure] and a thousand other methods, and in the name of Islam, you erase Islam. However, unlike you, the freedom-seekers want to show the truth of Islam to the people and you deceptive traitors.

The workers also pointed out to the people of Iran that 'this is not a war between Islam and atheism, but rather, a war between freedom and reactionism, [since] Qavam's supporters want to suffocate the freedom-seekers in the name of Islam'. While protesting the closure of the Tehran Bazaar, which, they noted, had deprived them of their livelihood, they expressed 'hope that this damage inflicted on us by the intrigues of Qavam al-Saltaneh will soon be compensated by him'. Moreover, they noted that the bazaar was not closed by 'the shop owners' but, rather, 'as a result of the pressure of a handful of mean-spirited demagogues'. While supporting the minority of Majles deputies led by Soleiman Mirza, the workers demanded the punishment of the newspapers that wrote articles against religion. At the end of their statement, these slogans were written: 'Long live Islam, long live the religion of Mohammad, long live the freedom-seekers, long live the self-sacrificing minority, long live Soleiman Mirza, long live the other righteous deputies, long live the workers of the world, death to the devilish reactionaries, may the villainous traitors be destroyed and extinct.'

But the fact was that the pro-Qavam faction and deputies such as Modarres were not only influential among the heads of the guilds but also had supporters among the labour unions. This issue caused conflict and physical clashes among the workers. Shokrollah Mani wrote in his report: 'Several representatives (of the General Council of United Workers) had links with the late Modarres and other reactionary deputies of the Majles. The conflict between reaction and freedom impacted the workers' population and created animosity and discord among the General representatives.'[55] Mani added, 'the late Modarres and his associates, with the help of the government, gathered some ruffians and illiterate folks from the fruit vendors of the squares in five neighborhoods of Tehran and a group of reactionary tradesmen from the bazaar, and organized them against *Haqiqat* newspaper', then attacks were planned and they attacked the Workers' Union and their cultural and press activities.[56]

Nonetheless, the efforts of Soleiman Mirza and the Socialist Party faction of the Majles, along with several other deputies, prepared the ground for the fall of Qavam's government, which was replaced by the Cabinet of Mostowfi al-Mamalek (Mirza Hassan Ashtiani) on 15 February 1923 (25 Bahman 1301). Under Mostowfi, whose government stayed in power until 15 June 1923 (24 Khordad 1302), the atmosphere of electoral competition of the Fifth Majles gradually emerged. Workers and craftsmen also rose up and joined the fray. The left-wing political parties as well as the labour and guild organizations of Tehran and other cities were determined to elect representatives to the Majles who would help advance their goals.

In a statement published in April 1923 (Farvardin 1302), the Union of Pharmaceutical Workers of Tehran addressed the labourers and workers of Iran in general, and Tehran, in particular. While enumerating the characteristics of the current age, they regarded its main feature to be the struggle between capitalists and workers and considered the way to liberate the proletariat (*zahmatkeshān*) to be 'taking the reins of the Majles in their hands and giving deputy seats to their own kind'.[57] The pharmaceutical workers, fearing the impact of propaganda from the candidates opposed to labour aspirations, warned the workers and labourers: 'Do not be deceived by those parasites of the aristocracy and do not take an axe in your own hand to uproot yourself.' They also considered the workers to be the agents of the country's development and the increase in its wealth:

'Labour comrades! Your country will not develop, except by your own hands, wealth will not be produced in the country, except by your efforts, and independence will not endure, unless by your self-sacrifice.'

During this period, through the advocacy of *Kar* newspaper, labour and craft unions put their effort into revealing the true face of those they considered to be anti-labour, such as Seyyed Zia al-Din, Qavam and Modarres, and only endorsed 'Prince Soleiman Mirza and his good comrades'.[58] Workers and craftsmen also commemorated 2 May 1923 (11 Ordibehesht 1302), like the previous year, by taking the day off work. Moreover, their unions defended Mostowfi's government, which *Kar* deemed 'the National Cabinet', and condemned its opponents and called Modarres 'the leader of the reactionaries'. Modarres and his associates attempted to bring Qavam back to power.[59] However, not only did these efforts fail, but Qavam also was exiled to Europe after a plot was revealed, whereby he and several others allegedly had planned to assassinate Reza Khan. Yet, Bahar asserted that this plot was a sham.[60]

Meanwhile, the Construction Workers' Union of Tehran planned to hold a memorial service on Friday, 16 June 1923 (25 Khordad 1302) to honour the memory of Seyyed Hossein Kezazi,[61] a former deputy from Kermanshah, who had been shot dead on the evening of 6 June (15 Khordad). But evidently, this event was cancelled due to the prohibition of such gatherings, since the union stated that 'the reactionaries have banned assemblies, and prevented speeches, conferences and meetings. Hence, the council decided to hold a complete recitation of the Quran for Martyr Kezazi today in the Shah Mosque. [But] with these constant pressures, it has been postponed to a suitable day.'[62] Nevertheless, guilds, craftsmen, workers and various segments of Iranian society participated in other protests. For example, due to events that had taken place in Iraq, leading to the exile of Shia ulema in Iran, an assembly was held in the Shah Mosque, where a petition against 'British oppression' was penned with about 2,000 signatures and sent to the League of Nations.[63] Apart from such political activism, guilds and craftsmen went on strike for economic issues. In one case, Shoemakers' Guild members protested the high rents of shops, which the owners periodically raised. On 17 September 1923 (25 Shahrivar 1302), they stopped work, and more than 300 shoemakers from Tehran went to the Ministry of Justice, where 'They were complaining about the shop owners, and were told by the Prime Minister to convey their demands and declarations by electing two representatives'.[64]

By this time, Mostowfi had been replaced by Moshir al-Dowleh, who returned to power on 15 June 1923 (24 Khordad 1302). However, the latter's cabinet did not last either because of Reza Khan's greed for further power. Eventually, Ahmad Shah issued an order for Reza Khan to form a cabinet and left for Europe, never to return. On 28 October 1923 (5 Aban 1302), Reza Khan formed his cabinet and appointed Soleiman Mirza Eskandari, the leader of the Socialist Party, as Minister of Education, while some of his associates were appointed to the following positions: Mirza Qasim Khan (Sur-e Esrafil), Ministry of the Interior; Amanollah Khan Ardalan (Ezz al-Mamalek), Ministry of Public Works and Commerce; Khodayar Khan Amir Lashkar, Ministry of Post and Telegraph. In this way, Reza Khan sought the support of the Socialist Party and labour unions. Two days after forming the Cabinet, he announced his government's plan to the people: 'I have never believed in uttering a series of splendid words devoid of truth and pompous statements that were not followed by action. I have always believed that the truth can be told through valid actions rather than words.'[65] In this declaration, he summarized his programme in two articles: 'Protecting the rights of the country and the enforcement of law'. In a second declaration announced days later, on 13 November 1923 (21 Aban 1302), he named the destructive factors in the country:

> During periods of decline, two series of misfortunes will always befall the nation and the country, either of which, if there is no immediate foresight and urgent prevention of contingency, can sufficiently destabilize the foundation of the national character of every nation, and drive them to the furthest degree of disintegration: 1. Disruption of order and lack of internal security. 2. Anarchical ideas and fragmentation of beliefs and morals.

Farrokhi's *Tufan* believed that while the reading of this declaration's provisions was worthy of reverence, they could only be implemented by a government that 'refrains from enforcing foreign ideas'.[66]

Reza Khan believed that due to the efforts of the last few years, the first problem had been eliminated, but the second problem, anarchical ideas, was still under consideration. He believed that the reason for this was the dependency 'on foreign principles'. To eliminate the fragmentation of beliefs, the first step he took was to interfere in the election process of the Fifth Majles. In this way, the names of the deputies that came out of the ballot boxes were chosen in line with his instructions. Previously, Reza Khan had expressed his disappointment with the Fourth Majles in negotiations with Sir Percy Loraine, the British ambassador in Tehran, adding that he had to wait until its term was over, and 'at that time, care should be taken to elect the right parliament'.[67] Although such figures as Seyyed Hassan Modarres, Mohammad Mossadegh, Moshir al-Dowleh, Motamen al-Molk, Mostowfi al-Mamalek and several other pro-constitutionalist and independent statesmen were elected in Tehran, the election results in the counties and the provinces were of a different order. According to Bahar: 'The Ministry of War won the provinces and the influence of the commanders of the army corrupted the elections.'[68] Yahya Dowlatabadi also believed that Reza Khan wanted 'the Majles deputies to be those who agreed with his personal policies'.[69]

The Fifth Majles opened on 12 February 1924 (22 Bahman 1302) with the speech of Crown Prince Mohammad Hassan Mirza. This assembly was full of Reza Khan's supporters due to the intervention of his army commanders in the elections. At this time, whispers of republicanism were being proposed. These rumours aimed at attracting support for Reza Khan from the labour unions, the Socialist Party, the Soviet Union and pro-republican intellectual groups. His supporters in the Majles were determined to resolve the issue of converting the monarchy into a republic by the spring of 1924 (the beginning of 1303). In a telegraph sent on 23 February (3 Esfand) to Ahmad Khan Amir Ahmadi, the western army commander, Prime Minister Reza Khan said: 'The subject of the republic is a national affair and should be implemented upon the insistence of the nation and the government.' Accordingly, he instructed that merchants and guilds, journalists and clerics in western Iran should be encouraged to 'pressure the National Consultative Assembly and the government with one slogan [*āhang*] from the entire western region through your deputies and give full authority to the same Majles deputies to change the constitution, converting the regime of the country to a republic'.[70]

This manufactured discourse was, of course, heard from all of the provinces. *Golshan*, a pro-Reza Khan newspaper, published 'pro-republican telegrams from the provinces' which 'earnestly wanted the conversion of the monarchy into a republic'.[71] The same newspaper also reported the closure of the Tehran Bazaar and the request of guildsmen and merchants for the abolishment of the monarchy.

In the Fifth Majles, the majority belonged to the Tajaddod (Renewal or Modernity) Party, which was an enthusiastic supporter of Reza Khan. In addition, fourteen deputies from the Socialist Party were supporters of his policies. There also was a small minority, whose spokesman was Modarres.[72] Alongside these groups were a number of individual and independent deputies, such as Mossadegh, Moshir al-Dowleh, Mostowfi al-Mamalek, Motamen al-Molk, Seyyed Hassan Taqizadeh, Yahya Dowlatabadi and Hossein Ala. The parliamentary minority led by Modarres was aware of the majority's goal of raising the issue of proclaiming a republic. Thus, the minority decided to oppose the credentials of the majority deputies in order to eliminate the base of support for the republican proposal. Intent on this task, Modarres determined that, by delaying the verification of the deputies' credentials, the proposal of 'the republican bill' would be blocked in the Majles.

Seyyed Mohammad Tadayon, the spokesman for Reza Khan's supporters and the Tajaddod Party, criticized Modarres's scheme and thus proposed that the Majles should deal with the vital parliamentary issues. The parliamentary majority sent a delegation to the palace to request the departure of the Crown Prince until the establishment of the republic. In mid-March (late Esfand), groups organized in Tehran and marched in support of a republican government. Some labour unions, such as the Union of Drapers' Shop Workers, also published declarations in defence of Reza Khan's republic. On the other hand, Modarres's attempt to block the formation of a republic angered a pro-republican deputy named Ehya al-Saltaneh Bahrami, who slapped him on the ear in the hallway of the Majles.[73] This incident enraged the guilds and bazaaris in the Tehran Bazaar and increased their opposition to the republican plan. Thus, the pro-Modarres guild leaders closed the bazaar. A large group of bazaaris also entered Baharestan Square and the courtyard of the Majles on 23 March 1923 (2 Farvardin 1302), where they chanted: 'Death to the republic and long live Ahmad Shah; we want the religion of the Prophet, not a republic'.[74]

At this point, the military forces, along with Reza Khan, entered the courtyard of the Majles and beat and cursed the protesters. Objecting to his presence, Motamen al-Molk, the speaker of the Majles, asked: 'What are you doing here?'[75] Reza Khan replied that he had come to maintain order. Then Motamen al-Molk reminded him of his responsibility to maintain order at the Majles. This may have been the last encounter of a powerful Majles speaker with a dictator during the Constitutional era. Hence, Reza Khan had to apologize to him. In order to find a way out of this impasse and to restore his prestige, Reza Khan went to Qom under the pretext of seeing off the emigrant ulema. After meeting with prominent scholars in Qom – Abdol Karim Haeri Yazdi, Seyyed Abol Hassan Esfahani and Mirza Hossein Naini – he issued a declaration to 'the general public' recommending 'the suspension of the topic of the republic'. A declaration also was issued by the grand ayatollahs in favour of abandoning the issue of the republic and supporting Reza Khan.[76] However, the minority group of deputies in the Majles persisted in fighting with him. This time, Reza Khan resigned in his usual manner and retreated to Bumehen, a small town near Tehran. After his resignation, the commanders of the armies threatened the Majles and demanded his quick return. Pro-Reza Khan newspapers also joined this campaign. Finally, the Majles sent a delegation to Bumehen and invited him back to Tehran.[77] Upon his return to the capital, he was welcomed by the Printing Workers' Union.[78]

After his return, Reza Khan removed Soleiman Mirza Eskandari, Khodayar Khan Amir Lashkar and Ezz al-Mamalek Ardalan from their cabinet posts. Thus, according to Sultanzadeh, he threw off the mantle of republicanism.[79] Afterwards, he gradually adopted a stricter policy against trade/labour unions and suppressed them in order to put an end to their political activism. Moreover, the pro-Reza Khan newspaper *Qanun*, based on its denial of any class struggle, existence of conflicting relations between capitalists and workers or division of society into classes, considered such issues to be evidence of the imposition of European historical realities upon Iranian society. Such an argument was meant to justify Reza Khan's repressive policies.[80]

Henceforth, we no longer encounter any overt manifestations of political opposition from the labour/trade unions. Newspaper reports on their activism were confined to guild-related issues. For example, in a protest to the press, one of the shoemakers considered the advertisement of foreign-sewn shoes to be the reason for the bankruptcy of the shoe industry and asked the Majles deputies 'to think about the circumstances of a handful of Tehrani tradesmen, and to consider how foreign goods made nearly half of Iran's population poor and destitute'.[81] Further to this, because of the economic losses caused by the importation of American shoes, the representatives of the shoemakers' workshop in Tehran sought sanctuary in the office of the Cabinet.[82]

The guilds supported Reza Khan's efforts to promote the country's carpet-weaving industry.[83] They also participated in the meetings of the Economic Council held in Takiyeh Dowlat and presented proposals, especially to prevent the import of luxury goods.[84] In the summer of 1925 (1304), guilds and craftsmen had to deal with broken and perforated coinage. To solve this problem, guilds and merchants wrote to the Economic Council and Prime Minister Reza Khan.[85] Of course, the same problem affected tradesmen in other cities, and sometimes they used it to their advantage to increase profits. For instance, they used to 'deduct five *shahi* for every two *qirans* [20 shahis equalled one qiran] that had a black spot'. The Tehran municipality also placed all of the guilds' transactions under its supervision through the Department of Foodstuffs and Guilds, although it set prices in consultation with the guild heads.[86] During this period, the government presented a plan 'to change the guild taxes',[87] which, after some time, was approved by the Sixth Majles on 12 December 1926 (20 Azar 1305).[88]

Conclusion

After the end of the First World War and the ideological reverberations of the October Revolution, transformations in political groups and gradually in guilds and craftsmen emerged in Iran. The First Congress of the Communist Party of Iran was held in Anzali in July 1920 (Tir 1299). Subsequently, the Communist Party recognized craftsmen as revolutionary allies of the working class. Therefore, activity among craftsmen and tradesmen became one of the party's propaganda goals. Over time, the activities of this party expanded in Tehran and other cities, such as Tabriz. The Workers' Party was formed in Tabriz and began to attract craftsmen and tradesmen. In Tehran, the General Council of United Workers was established, with most of its members being craftsmen. This led to craftsmen playing a supporting role in the labour movement and being influenced by the teachings of class struggle. This situation further weakened the old guild structure, increasing conflicts among the guild ranks, which consisted of masters, journeymen, apprentices and errand boys. It goes without saying that political movements opposed to the Tehran Workers' Union had the support of some guild groups.

The establishment of the Trade Union Association and the formation of the new General Council of United Workers in Tehran and various provinces marked a new era for the activities of guilds and craftsmen. However, starting from 1924 (1303), when Reza Khan discarded the mantle of republicanism, the widespread suppression of labour and trade unions commenced. With the beginning of Reza Shah's rule, guilds and craftsmen no longer played an effective role in trade union organizations. Due to the dependence of their leaders on the Pahlavi regime, these organizations were unable to maintain an independent existence. This outcome was one of the obstacles to the realization of democracy in Iran. Consequently, a nineteen-year period full of highs and lows in the activism of guilds and craftsmen in the sociopolitical domain began with a desire for change during the Constitutional Revolution but ultimately concluded with submission to a centralized, absolute regime that did not tolerate any independent institutions.

Notes

1 For the full text of this chapter, see Hojjat Fallah Tootkar, *Asnaf az Enqelab-e Mashrutiyyat-e Iran ta Enqeraz-e Qajariyye, 1285–1304* (Tehran: Rasanesh-e Novin; Ketab-e Sadra, 1394/2015), 386–408, 421–5 and 429–30.
2 In this regard, see *Sobh-e Sadeq*, no. 51 (24 Rabi al-Thani 1325/6 June 1907): 2–3.
3 There are two issues of *Ettefaq-e Kargaran*. Concerning the workers' strike, see also *Iran-e Now* 1, no. 230 (12 Jamadi al-Sani 1328/21 June 1910): 2; no. 237 (22 Jamadi al-Sani 1328/1 July 1910): 3.
4 Cosroe Chaqueri, *Asnad-e Tarikhi-ye Jonbesh-e Kargari, Sosiyal Demokrasi va Komunisti-ye Iran: Asar-e Avetis Soltanzadeh*, vol. 4 (Florence: Mazdak, 1993), 100.
5 Shokrollah Mani, *Tarikhcheh-ye Nahzat-e Kargari dar Iran* (Tehran: Taban, 1358/1979), 12. Concerning Seyyed Mohammad Dehgan's life, see Rahim Rais Niya, *Akherin Sangar-e Azadi: Majmueh-ye Maqalat-e Mir Jafar Pishevari dar Ruznameh-ye Haqiqat, Organ-e Ettehadiyyeh-ye Omumi-ye Kargaran-e Iran 1300–1301* (Tehran: Shirazeh, 1378/1999), 363–75.
6 Jalil Mahmoudi and Nasser Saeidi, *Showq-e Yek Khiz-e Boland: Nokhostin Ettehadiyyeh-ye Kargari dar Iran, 1285–1320* (Tehran: Qatreh, 1381/2002), 131;

Cosroe Chaqueri, *Asnad-e Tarikhi-ye Jonbesh-e Kargari, Sosiyal Demokrasi va Komunisti-ye Iran*, vol. 6 (Tehran: Elm, 1358/1979), 114.
7 Chaqueri, *Asnad-e Tarikhi*, vol. 4, 100; idem, *Asnad-e Tarikhi*, vol. 6, 114.
8 Mani, *Tarikhcheh*, 8–9.
9 *Haqiqat*, no. 69 (10 Ordibehesht 1301/1 May 1922): 3.
10 Mahmoudi and Saeidi, *Showq*, 142.
11 Mani, *Tarikhcheh*, 9.
12 Chaqueri, *Asnad-e Tarikhi*, vol. 6, 114.
13 *Haqiqat*, no. 98 (25 Khordad 1301/16 June 1922): 2.
14 *Eqtesad-e Iran* 3, no. 31 (22 Shahrivar 1301/14 September 1922): 2.
15 *Eqtesad-e Iran* 3, no. 41 (5 Mehr 1301/28 September 1922): 2.
16 *Kar* 1, no. 33 (17 Khordad 1302/8 June 1923): 2.
17 Mani, *Tarikhcheh*, 9–11.
18 *Haqiqat*, no. 29 (4 Esfand 1300/23 February 1922): 1.
19 *Kar* 1, no. 93 (14 Shahrivar 1302/6 September 1923): 2.
20 For the complete text of Seyyed Zia's manifesto, see Hossein Makki, *Tarikh-e Bist Saleh-ye Iran: Kudeta-ye 1299*, vol. 1 (Tehran: Elmi, 1323/1944), 125–9.
21 Chaqueri, *Asnad-e Tarikhi*, vol. 4, 101.
22 *Haqiqat* 1, no. 7 (21 Dey 1300/11 January 1922): 2.
23 Abdollah Mostowfi, *Sharh-e Zendegani-ye Man: Tarikh-e Ejtemaei va Edari-ye Dowreh-ye Qajariyyeh*, vol. 3 (Tehran: Zavvar, 1371/1992), 469.
24 'Tatil-e Bazar', *Haqiqat*, no. 12 (4 Bahman 1300/24 January 1922): 1.
25 Mohammad Taqi Bahar, *Tarikh-e Mokhtasar-e Ahzab-e Siyasi-ye Iran: Enqeraz-e Qajariyyeh*, vol. 1 (Tehran: Amir Kabir, 1379/2000), 185–8.
26 Mostowfi, *Sharh-e Zendegani*, 497–9.
27 Ibid., 498.
28 Ibid., 499, 501–2.
29 *Haqiqat*, no. 49 (8 Farvardin 1301/29 March 1922): 1; *Haqiqat*, no. 50 (9 Farvardin 1301/30 March 1922): 1; *Haqiqat*, no. 51 (10 Farvardin 1301/31 March 1922): 1.
30 *Haqiqat*, no. 54 (16 Farvardin 1301/6 April 1922): 1.
31 Ibid., 2.
32 *Haqiqat*, no. 55 (17 Farvardin 1301/7 April 1922): 2.
33 *Haqiqat*, no. 65 (3 Ordibehesht 1301/24 April 1922): 1.
34 Ibid., 2.
35 Ibid.
36 Ibid., 3.
37 *Haqiqat*, no. 69 (7 Ordibehesht 1301/28 April 1922): 3.
38 *Haqiqat*, no. 70 (8 Ordibehesht 1301/29 April 1922): 2.
39 Mostowfi, *Sharh-e Zendegani*, 503.
40 *Haqiqat*, no. 78 (22 Ordibehesht 1301/13 May 1922): 1.
41 *Haqiqat*, no. 101 (29 Khordad 1301/20 June 1922): 2; *Haqiqat*, no. 104 (2 Tir 1301/24 June 1922): 2.
42 *Haqiqat*, no. 104, 1.
43 *Eqtesad-e Iran* 3, no. 2 (28 Tir 1301/20 July 1922): 1.
44 *Eqtesad-e Iran* 3, no. 34 (26 Shahrivar 1301/18 September 1922): 2.
45 *Eqtesad-e Iran* 3, no. 31 (22 Shahrivar 1301/14 September 1922): 1.
46 *Eqtesad-e Iran* 3, no. 33 (25 Shahrivar 1301/17 September 1922): 1.
47 Bahar, *Tarikh*, vol. 1, 228.

48 *Surat-e Mozakerat-e Majles-e Showra-ye Melli: Dowreh-ye Chaharom* (Tehran: Ruznameh-ye Rasmi-ye Keshvar-e Iran, 1330/1951), 1162–3.
49 For the complete text of Motamed al-Tojjar's speech, see Bahar, *Tarikh*, vol. 1, 229; *Surat-e Mozakerat-e Majles*, 1161–2.
50 *Eqtesad-e Iran* 3, no. 49 (16 Mehr 1301/9 October 1922): 1.
51 Bahar, *Tarikh*, vol. 1, 237.
52 Ibid., 240–2.
53 *Eqtesad-e Iran* 3, no. 56 (26 Mehr 1301/19 October 1922): 1.
54 *Eqtesad-e Iran* 3, no. 58 (28 Mehr 1301/21 October 1922): 1–2.
55 Mani, *Tarikhcheh*, 15. Also, concerning the influence of Modarres among some guilds, see Ali Abolhassani (Monzer), 'Mosahebeh ba Hossein Shah Hosseini, Farzand-e Marhum-e Haj Sheikh Zain al-Abedin Shah Hosseini dar Mowred-e Marhum-e Haj Sheikh Hossein Lankarani', *Tarikh-e Moaser-e Iran* 4, no. 13–14 (Spring and Summer 1379/2000): 291.
56 Mani, *Tarikhcheh*, 16.
57 *Kar* 1, no. 15 (27 Farvardin 1302/17 April 1923): 4.
58 *Kar* 1, no. 27 (31 Ordibehesht 1302/22 May 1923): 1; *Kar* 1, no. 36 (21 Khordad 1302/12 June 1923): 1.
59 *Kar* 1, no. 37 (23 Khordad 1302/14 June 1923): 1; *Kar* 1, no. 38 (24 Khordad 1302/15 June 1923): 1.
60 Mohammad Taqi Bahar, *Tarikh-e Mokhtasar-e Ahzab-e Siyasi-ye Iran: Enqeraz-e Qajariyyeh*, vol. 2 (Tehran: Amir Kabir, 1379/2000), 31–3.
61 *Kar* 1, no. 38: 2.
62 *Kar* 1, no. 39 (25 Khordad 1302/16 June 1923): 1.
63 *Kar* 1, no. 68 (26 Shahrivar 1302/18 September 1923): 1; Bahar, *Tarikh*, vol. 1, 352–60.
64 Ibid.
65 Mostowfi, *Sharh-e Zendegani*, 570.
66 *Tufan* 2, no. 32 (20 Aban 1302/12 November 1923): 1.
67 Mansoureh Ettehadieh (Nezam-Mafi), *Majles va Entekhabat az Mashruteh ta Payan-e Qajariyyeh* (Tehran: Nashr-e Tarikh-e Iran, 1375/1996), 72.
68 Bahar, *Tarikh*, vol. 2, 27.
69 Yahya Dowlatabadi, *Hayat-e Yahya*, vol. 4 (Tehran: Attar; Ferdowsi, 1371/1992), 304.
70 Farhad Rostami, *Pahlaviha: Khandan-e Pahlavi beh Revayat-e Asnad*, vol. 1 (Tehran: Moasseseh-ye Motaleat-e Tarikh-e Moaser-e Iran, 1378/1999), 104.
71 *Golshan* 7, no. 57 (29 Esfand 1302/20 March 1924): 2.
72 Concerning the political party factions of the Fifth Majles, see Bahar, *Tarikh*, vol. 2, 27–8, 58.
73 Bahar, *Tarikh*, vol. 2, 36.
74 Bahar talks about the role of such heads of guilds as Abd al-Hossein Kharrazi in mobilizing the bazaris: Bahar, *Tarikh*, vol. 2, 45–7.
75 Bahar, *Tarikh*, vol. 2, 48.
76 Mostowfi, *Sharh-e Zendegani*, 601–2.
77 Hossein Makki, *Tarikh-e Bist Saleh-ye Iran: Moqaddamat-e Taghyir-e Saltanat*, vol. 2 (Tehran: Elmi, 1324/1945), 522–4; Bahar, *Tarikh*, vol. 2, 76–7.
78 Willem Floor, *Ettehadiyyehha-ye Kargari va Qanun-e Kar dar Iran*, trans. Abolqasem Sari (Tehran: Tus, 1371/1992), 36.
79 Avetis Sultanzadeh, *Enkeshaf-e Eqtesadi-ye Iran va Amperiyalism-e Engelestan*, trans. F. Kusha (Tehran: Maziyar, 1383/2004), 36.
80 *Qanun* 4, no. 4 (26 Aban 1303/17 November 1924): 1.

81 Ibid., 4; *Qanun* 4, no. 6 (2 Azar 1303/23 November 1924): 4.
82 *Qanun* 4, no. 10 (13 Azar 1303/4 December 1924): 1.
83 *Fekr-e Azadi* 3, no. 22 (28 Bahman 1303/17 February 1925): 170.
84 *Qanun* 4, no. 35 (30 Tir 1304/21 July 1925): 1.
85 *Qanun* 4, no. 40 (25 Mordad 1304/16 August 1925): 2.
86 *Qanun* 4, no. 38 (18 Mordad 1304/9 August 1925): 1.
87 *Fekr-e Azadi* 3, no. 10 (27 Azar 1303/18 December 1924): 73.
88 Reza Mokhtari Esfahani, *Asnadi az Anjomanha-ye Baladi, Tojjar va Asnaf (1300–1320 HS)*, vol. 1 (Tehran: Vezarat-e Farhang va Ershad-e Eslami, 1380/2001), 152–7.

Bibliography

Archives and libraries

National Library and Archives of Iran, Tehran

Primary sources

Surat-e Mozākerāt-e Majles-e Showrā-ye Melli: Dowreh-ye Chaharom. Tehran: Ruznameh-ye Rasmi-ye Keshvar-e Iran, 1330 (1951).

Periodicals

Eqtesād-e Irān
Ettefaq-e Kārgarān
Fekr-e Azadi
Golshan
Haqiqat
Irān-e Now
Kār
Qānun
Sobh-e Sādeq
Tufān

Secondary sources

Abolhassani (Monzer), Ali. 'Mosāhebeh bā Hossein Shāh Hosseini, Farzand-e Marhum-e Hāj Sheikh Zain al-Abedin Shāh Hosseini dar Mowred-e Marhum-e Hāj Sheikh Hossein Lankarāni'. *Tarikh-e Moaser-e Iran* 4, no. 13–14 (Spring and Summer 1379/2000): 285–342.
Bahar, Mohammad Taqi. *Tārikh-e Mokhtasar-e Ahzāb-e Siyāsi-ye Irān: Enqerāz-e Qājāriyyeh*. Vol. 1 and 2. Tehran: Amir Kabir, 1379 (2000).
Chaqueri, Cosroe. *Asnād-e Tārikhi-ye Jonbesh-e Kārgari, Sosiyāl Demokrāsi va Komunisti-ye Irān: Āsār-e Āvetis Soltānzādeh*. Vol. 4. Florence: Mazdak, 1993.
Chaqueri, Cosroe. *Asnād-e Tārikhi-ye Jonbesh-e Kārgari, Sosiyāl Demokrāsi va Komunisti-ye Irān*. Vol. 6. Tehran: Elm, 1358 (1979).

Dowlatabadi, Yahya. *Hayāt-e Yahya*. Vol. 4. Tehran: Attar; Ferdowsi, 1371 (1992).
Esfahani, Reza Mokhtari. *Asnādi az Anjomanhā-ye Baladi, Tojjār va Asnāf (1300–1320 HS)*. Vol. 1. Tehran: Vezarat-e Farhang va Ershad-e Eslami, 1380 (2001).
Ettehadieh (Nezam-Mafi), Mansoureh. *Majles va Entekhābāt az Mashruteh tā Pāyān-e Qājāriyyeh*. Tehran: Nashr-e Tarikh-e Iran, 1375 (1996).
Floor, Willem. *Ettehādiyyehhā-ye Kārgari va Qānun-e Kār dar Irān*. Translated by Abolqasem Sari. Tehran: Tus, 1371 (1992).
Mahmoudi, Jalil and Nasser Saeidi. *Showq-e Yek Khiz-e Boland: Nokhostin Ettehādiyyeh-ye Kārgari dar Iran, 1285–1320*. Tehran: Qatreh, 1381 (2002).
Makki, Hossein. *Tārikh-e Bist Sāleh-ye Irān: Kudetā-ye 1299*. Vol. 1. Tehran: Elmi, 1323 (1944).
Makki, Hossein. *Tārikh-e Bist Sāleh-ye Irān: Moqaddamāt-e Taghyir-e Saltanat*. Vol. 2. Tehran: Elmi, 1324 (1945).
Mani, Shokrollah. *Tārikhcheh-ye Nahzat-e Kārgari dar Irān*. Tehran: Taban, 1358 (1979).
Mostowfi, Abdollah. *Sharh-e Zendegāni-ye Man: Tārikh-e Ejtemāʿi va Edāri-ye Dowreh-ye Qājāriyyeh*. Vol. 3. Tehran: Zavvar, 1371 (1992).
Rais Niya, Rahim. *Ākherin Sangar-e Āzādi: Majmuʿeh-ye Maqālāt-e Mir Jafar Pishevari dar Ruznameh-ye Haqiqat, Orgān-e Ettehādiyyeh-ye ʿOmumi-ye Kārgarān-e Irān 1300–1301*. Tehran: Shirazeh, 1378 (1999).
Rostami, Farhad. *Pahlavihā: Khāndān-e Pahlavi beh Revāyat-e Asnād*. Vol. 1. Tehran: Moasseseh-ye Motaleat-e Tarikh-e Moaser-e Iran, 1378 (1999).
Sultanzadeh, Avetis. *Enkeshāf-e Eqtesādi-ye Irān va Amperiyālism-e Engelestān*. Translated by F. Kusha. Tehran: Maziyar, 1383 (2004).
Tootkar, Hojjat Fallah. *Asnāf az Enqelāb-e Mashrutiyyat-e Irān tā Enqerāz-e Qājāriyye, 1285–1304*. Tehran: Rasanesh-e Novin; Ketab-e Sadra, 1394 (2015).

4

The Economy Movement, an Iranian merchants' organization in response to the crisis in Iran-Soviet trade relations (1921–7)

Soheila Torabi Farsani

Introduction

In the first half of the nineteenth century, Iran's exports to the Russian Empire did not include industrial manufactures and were mainly agricultural products, such as silk, cotton, rice and dried fruit.[1] These commodities were mostly produced in the northern parts of the country. The most important issues pertaining to Iranian commerce at this time could be summarized in a few statements, namely the insecurity of commercial capital, in the sense that there were no laws enacted by state or civil bodies respecting private ownership of capital, and the non-existence of proper roads to connect cities and towns across the vast expanse of the country. Of course, not to mention, the highway men and bandits who robbed commercial caravans on a regular basis.

There also were irregularities in the functioning of the customs offices, whose proceedings were more often dependent on the common law and the occasional *farmān* (decree) of Fath-Ali Shah Qajar. Tariffs were sometimes calculated on the basis of the price of goods, or their weight, or the number of beasts of burden carrying the goods, as there were not any defined and respected laws and regulations through which to proceed with the functioning of the customs offices in Iran. Accordingly, there was escalating financial corruption, bribery and collusion between merchants and the governor-general of the area. On top of the customs tariffs, there were other taxes, such as road tolls, and other tolls and levies to be paid once the goods reached a town on the way, as well as a poll tax and countless other arbitrary taxes, all of which the merchants had to comply with.[2]

In that era, two very important military and political events took place in the shape of the two wars that broke out between Iran and the Russian Empire. These military clashes led, ultimately, to the ratification of the Golestan Treaty in 1813 and the Turkmenchay Treaty in 1828. These treaties included clauses pertaining to commercial affairs, which not only regulated customs tariffs in order to increase the importation of foreign goods, Russian ones in particular, but also provided a foundation for most commercial constraints on the part of Iranian merchants in the years to come.

In the eighth clause of the Golestan Treaty, the freedom of bilateral trade had been strongly stressed.[3] In the ninth clause, the amount of customs tariffs on commodities owned by Russian merchants had been set at 500 dinars for every toman's worth of merchandise, which came out to a levy of 5 per cent. Moreover, it could only be charged once and for all at the entrance to one city. The Turkmenchay Treaty also stressed and repeated that Russian subjects would only be charged a 5 per cent tariff on their goods, and that, too, only at the customs offices situated on the borders. On the other hand, Iranian merchants still had to pay, on top of whatever customs tariffs were required, road tolls and a number of other taxes and levies. This made it quite impossible for Iranian merchants to fairly compete with their Russian counterparts.[4]

Towards the end of the nineteenth century and up to the outbreak of the Constitutional Revolution of 1905, Russia's leverage and political power in Iran greatly increased. With the annulment of the Tobacco Régie concession in 1890, which was seen as a failure on the part of the British, Russia took the upper hand in the Iranian political and economic arena. In northern parts of Iran, where Russia in effect enjoyed a monopoly in commercial affairs, it built gravel roads in order to facilitate the transfer of goods. In addition, the financial transactions of Russian merchants were conducted and administered by the Russian Discount and Loans Bank of Persia and Credit (Bank-e Esteqrazi). Thus, during the two decades prior to the outbreak of the Constitutional Movement, trading transactions between Iran and Russia rapidly increased, and, by the same token, transactions with Britain decreased. The amount of trade between Iran and Russia rose from nine million roubles in 1875 to 94 million roubles in 1914.[5] During these years, the bulk of Iran's exports to Russia consisted of agricultural commodities, such as cotton, rice, wool, hides, leather and hand-woven carpets.[6]

Merchants' associations

The increase in the volume of Iran's commercial transactions from the second half of the nineteenth century onwards, together with the state concessions allotted to Russia and Britain, as well as the integration of the Iranian economy into the world economy, which resulted in the influx of foreign capital, triggered a set of events that prompted Iranian merchants to establish a more coherent form of associations amongst themselves. Although there were social-hierarchical estates within the bazaar, where the big merchants formed the highest rank, and there used to be an official head merchant (*ra'is al-tojjār*), the new situation that the merchants found themselves confronting brought about the dire need for the establishment of new associations on a modern footing, other than the traditional guilds, so that more decisive measures could be taken to tackle their problems.

Accordingly, in 1883, Mirza Hassan Amin al-Zarb petitioned for royal assent to form the Association of Merchants' Representatives (Majles-e Vokala-ye Tojjar) in a letter to Nasser al-Din Shah.[7] This Association, ultimately, proved to be the first modern collective organization of the merchants, whose purpose was to enable them to exploit economic and political concessions. Iranian merchants had, by now, attained a mutual understanding of the need for collective action in the face of the onslaught of foreign capital and felt that state support was a necessity. On top of this, the lack of supportive state legal codes and the encroachment on the part of governors in the provinces made merchants even more inclined to form a non-governmental association. In effect, this modern association took the place of their traditional guild system with its head merchant, as the new association was more unified and covered many more issues faced by the merchants. After the end of the First World War, as the situation had required, a session was convened by the merchants based in the capital city, Tehran, at the residence of Haj Mohammad Jafar Tajer Khameneh on 13 July 1919, in order to elect the members of the administrative committee of the Merchants' Union (Ettehadiyyeh-ye Tojjar) and also to ratify its regulatory bylaws.[8] Meanwhile, due to the victory of the Constitutional Movement and establishment of the Majles (National Consultative Assembly or Iranian Parliament), and the sheer presence of merchants in the Majles, the previous merchants' association ceased its activities.

General trends in Iranian commerce

After the victory of the Constitutional Revolution, the Russian Empire was still a major commercial partner, whose trade with Iran comprised a very considerable volume. Customs General's statistics show that in the years 1906 up to 1912, Iran's exports to Russia surpassed its imports from that country. The considerable volume of trade between the two countries attested to the fact that conducting commerce with Russia was of great importance in the eyes of Iranian merchants. In spite of all this, during the 1908/9 period, there was a decrease of 20 per cent in the volume of imported Russian commodities into Iran. The following year, 1910/11, also witnessed a further decrease in the volume of Russian imports, amounting to a drop of three more percentage points.[9] The first incidence of a decrease in the volume of imports from Russia to Iran was primarily due to the 1908 World Economic Crisis, and also the internal crisis in Iran that ensued as a result of the chaos created after the victory of the Constitutional Revolution, which had led to political instability in the country. The second incidence of a decrease in commercial transactions between the two countries was due to the skirmishes of the central government with various pretenders to the throne in northern and western parts of Iran and also the presence of Russian troops in parts of northern Iran. These parts of the country faced such an emergency situation that the commercial activities of Russian merchants in the region were curtailed.

The reason why trade between Iran and Russia boasted such a high volume could mainly be attributed to the fact that the two countries shared a long border with dense population centres on both sides of the frontier. Also, what made trade so lucrative was the permission on the part of the Russians that granted Iranian merchants free transit for their commodities through Russia on to Europe. On top of this, Russia had provided such benefits as discounts on customs duties for the importation of Russian goods into Iran. On the list of Iranian goods for exportation to Russia, cotton had taken the place of raw silk in the aftermath of the infestation of silkworms in 1863. The agricultural regions of Mazandaran, Astarabad, (modern Gorgan), Semnan, Shahrud, Damghan, Isfahan, Kashan, Qom, Qazvin and Nishapur were all under cotton cultivation, and Mazandaran alone provided 26 per cent of all cotton exported to Russia.[10] Prior to the outbreak of the First World War, the most important Iranian goods exported to Russia were cotton, dried fruits and nuts (*khoshkbār*), rice, hand-woven carpets, hides and livestock.[11]

During the First World War, the balance of trade between Iran and Russia dropped by 18 per cent. Although Iranian exports to Russia before the war were on the increase, during the war years, they decreased by approximately 13 per cent, and imports from Russia dropped by 21 per cent. On the other hand, despite the impact of the Great War and the subsequent decrease in the balance of trade between the two countries, Iran's exports to Russia constituted nearly 66 per cent of its total volume of exports, and imports from Russia amounted to 56 per cent of all its imports. Thus, the statistics clearly show that, despite the existence of an apparent commercial crisis, Russia still happened to rank as the best trade partner of Iran. Furthermore, Russia had imposed a ban on European commodities to be transited through Russian territory into Iran and, at the same time, maintained duty relief on certain Russian goods, in order to encourage their exportation to Iran.[12]

Just before the Russian Revolution of 1917, in the Iranian solar year corresponding to 1915/16, Iran's imports from Russia had made up 57 per cent of all its imports, and its exports to the same country comprised 71 per cent of all its exports. The following year, corresponding to 1916/17, Iran's exports to Russia rose by almost 12 per cent. While Iran's imports from Russia constituted 46 per cent of all its imports, its exports to that country amounted to 69 per cent of all its exports. Thus, although Iran's total exports to Russia and trade balance with that country both decreased by a small margin, this trade balance still represented 57 per cent of all Iranian foreign trade.[13] In the year corresponding to 1917/18, which witnessed the outbreak of revolution in Russia, Iran's trade balance with Russia dropped to 33 per cent of all Iranian commercial transactions and thus decreased by 49 per cent compared to the previous year. Imports from Russia also dropped by 53 per cent and exports to the same country decreased by 46 per cent, compared to the previous year.[14]

However, during the following year, corresponding to 1918/19, the trade crisis escalated to the extent that it could be regarded as a trade collapse. The trade balance between Iran and Russia decreased by a total of 87 per cent; imports from Russia dropped by 91 per cent and exports to that country decreased by 82 per cent. This, in effect, amounted to total bankruptcy on the part of Iranian merchants doing business with Russia. The trade balance with Russia, which, before the Great War, accounted for 60 per cent of all Iranian foreign trade, abruptly dropped to a mere 12 per cent. At the same time, Iran's imports from Russia dropped from 55 per cent to a negligible 7 per cent of its total import volume, and its exports to that country dropped from 66 per cent to only 20 per cent.[15] It is worth mentioning that the decrease in the volume of trade between the two countries was partly due to a ban, on the part of Iran, prohibiting the exportation of food staples to Russia. This situation, without a doubt, amounted to a catastrophe for Iranian merchants doing business in the northern parts of the country. Furthermore, the catastrophic economic situation in Russia, the sociopolitical chaos created by the regime change in that country and, in particular, the declaration of independence by some ethnic regions of the former Russian Empire led to various bans being imposed by successor states on the export of commodities from their regions, which eventually resulted in the total severance of commercial dealings with many Russian ports. All and all, these successive events caused Iranian merchants, particularly in the northern parts of the country, to become greatly discontented and led to their collective uprising in a series of protests.

Crisis in trade relations between Iran and the Soviet Union

Commercial relations between Iran and its northern neighbour had witnessed significant growth, especially during the two decades leading up to the Constitutional Revolution. However, with the occurrence of the Russian Revolution, the Jangali Movement in the northern province of Gilan and military incidents in this region, trade in this part of the country completely collapsed. Although the Soviet government's diplomatic representative declared the annulment of all treaties and concessions between Iran and the former Russian Empire upon entering Tehran in 1918, the Iranian government was unable to take full advantage of this opportunity. In 1921, a comprehensive agreement was concluded between the two countries, which included bilateral trade and allowed for the transit of Iranian goods through Soviet territory. Customs duties were established according to the Treaty of 'Most Favoured Nations' (Dowal-e Kamelat al-Vedad).[16] However, the text of the agreement only referred to exports from the Soviet Union,[17] and Iranian envoy Moshaver al-Mamalek, who was responsible for its conclusion, did not realize this issue.[18] The ambiguities of this agreement were to be resolved at a later date through negotiations with the Soviet Union's embassy in Tehran.

The Soviet government placed its foreign trade exclusively in the hands of several authorized state trade organizations and imposed restrictions that hindered Iranian merchants' ability to do business and, on some occasions, confiscated their commercial properties. The transit of Iranian goods through the Soviet Union to Europe was prohibited, except during the limited periods of the annual Baku and Nizhny Novgorod trade fairs. Thus, the free exchange of goods became impossible.[19] These state commercial organizations were mainly responsible for exporting sugar, flour, chinaware and textiles to Iran.[20] Two of these organizations, Vneshtorg and Tsentrosoyuz, were authorized to export goods from the Soviet Union, which was prohibited for others. They also enjoyed a 10 per cent customs exemption, free use of ships and railways and had the customs general in their favour and urban transportation under their control,[21] effectively placing the trade of northern Iran in the hands of the Soviet government as a whole. The pricing system by which Iranian export goods were valued was determined by the Soviet government's designated trade organizations. Iranian exports of cotton were valued at a low price. The buying and selling of cotton was monopolized by the Soviet government, and Iran could not transport cotton through Soviet territory. The National Trade Commissariat of the Soviet Union had complete control over the assessment of the quality of goods and transportation arrangements[22] and demanded visas from Iranian merchants to pass through Soviet customs.[23] Several Iranian merchants were even detained in Moscow and Baku on one occasion for dealing in foreign currencies.[24]

Formation of the Economy Movement

'The Economy Movement' (Nahzat-e Eqtesad) was an organization established by Iranian merchants in order to combat the trade crisis that had arisen as a result of the 1917 Russian Revolution. This name was written above all their announcements, letters and statements throughout the country. The use of the word 'movement' (*nahzat*) was indicative of organization, coherence and protest. It expressed a nationwide anger in order to 'save us from economic death', as stated in the Iranian merchants' declarations. These merchants also declared: 'What should we do?', 'The homeland is in danger' and 'We must remove the attire of servitude'.[25] Their statements were imbued with a nationalistic tone that drew a line between Iranians and foreigners. Therefore, they employed the term 'foreign goods' (*kālāhā-ye khāreji*) when referring to financial investments from other countries. One of the characteristics of Iran's commercial capitalism in these years was the use of nationalistic concepts and elements. The pioneers of the Economy Movement were merchants mainly from the province of Gilan; thus, contrary to the usual way in which merchants would protest, this movement did not commence from Tehran because the northern regions had suffered the most from the new trade situation created by the Soviet Union.

The policy of the Economy Movement, as stated by the merchants of Gilan, concentrated on the following points: they demanded a balance between imports and exports and reciprocal treatment with the Soviet government and requested that the Iranian government put a ban on the entry of luxury goods into the country and put an end to the activities of Soviet trade organizations in Iran until the conclusion of an honourable trade treaty with the Soviet government. They also advocated for a policy of not participating in the Baku trade fair. Should the Iranian government choose not to support the demands put forward by the merchants, all Iranian citizens would have no other choice but to forcibly prevent the entry of Soviet goods into the northern ports of Iran. Those who would act in opposition to these demands would be sanctioned by the general public and declared to be traitors, and, therefore, would be ostracized by Iranian society.[26]

This local movement began in the north of the country, as stated before, but its notable and important feature was its rapid amalgamation into a united, cohesive and nationwide commercial association by the name of the League of Merchants' Union (Heyat-e Ettehadiyyeh-ye Tojjar). After the end of the First World War, on 12 Rabi al-Awwal 1338 (4 December 1919), under the leadership of Mohammad Hossein Amin al-Zarb, the association was established with the approval of its charter.[27] Despite the communication limitations at that time, it was able to manage a united and cohesive network of merchants throughout the country. Although the hope inspired by the constitutional victory had created optimism in the minds of the merchants that there would be a response to their demands, the government's inability to manage the country's affairs and post-constitutional and post-war crises necessitated the strengthening of collective organizations, resulting in the establishment of the Merchants' Union.

This time, the Merchants' Union issued statements, telegrams and letters with similar titles, such as 'the Economy Movement'. The Gilan Economy Movement also was associated with all the merchants of the central parts of the country and other provinces in written correspondence and telegrams. Merchants in most cities of the country presented their views as 'the Economy Movement'. Gilan, Hamadan, Qazvin, Khorasan, Tabriz, Shiraz, Isfahan and Tehran were among the regions that issued statements on this subject. The main principles of the Gilan merchants' policy were approved by all cities, but each added other items based on their own demands and presented their analysis of the dire economic conditions in the country. The reason for this unanimity and cooperation was the fundamental economic crisis throughout the country that had affected merchants nationwide, although northern merchants were more directly involved.

Impact of the Economy Movement on other cities, 1927–30

The Hamadan Merchants' Union emphasized the necessity of industrialization and strengthening textile, spinning and sugar factories. They described the economic situation for merchants, shopkeepers and artisans as sitting at an 'empty table without food', where 'images of food' instead of 'actual food' were served. They viewed increasing unemployment, cash shortages and import growth as serious problems for the country's economy.[28] Their solutions included increasing exports, improving the quality of agricultural and livestock products, strengthening the carpet-weaving industry, improving transportation infrastructure and establishing railways.[29]

In Qazvin, sixty-four merchants initially gathered and authorized the formation of a local Economy Movement. They held meetings once or twice a week, rotating the location among the merchants' homes. Approximately 270 individuals attended one of these meetings.[30] The Qazvin police department reported a gathering of 3,000 merchants and shopkeepers at Qazvin Shah Mosque, where statements from the Economy Movements of Tabriz, Tehran and Gilan were read out to the people present. Telegrams sent by the Economy Movement to Reza Shah, the Parliament, and the prime minister were read aloud.[31] The merchants adopted a tone and choice of words similar in style to the rhetoric of the Soviet Union itself, with tropes comparing Soviet commercial institutions to 'greedy capitalists of imperialist countries'.[32] The tone of these reports reflected a degree of trust and collaboration with the government, and it was said that the gathering of merchants and shopkeepers would conclude with police protection and in an orderly way.[33]

Merchants in Khorasan also formed the Khorasan Economy Movement in support of their fellow merchants. They mentioned the Soviet trading houses scattered throughout the country that imported their goods to Iran like a flood, but in return, Iranian goods were not permitted to be exported to the Soviet Union. The limited amount of Iranian exports that were allowed by the Soviets had to be purchased at their desired price. The merchants telegraphed the government, the Parliament and the Ministry of Commerce, asking them not to accept any commercial treaties without considering the demands and consultations with merchants' representatives.[34]

In Tabriz, a group of Muslim and Christian merchants held meetings and elected a twelve-member board of directors for the formation of the Tabriz Economy Movement. Telegraphs and guidelines also were issued for smaller cities. Telegraphs were exchanged between Tabriz and the Economy Movements of Marand, Urmia, Khoy and Astara.[35] They declared their agreement with the goals and demands of the Economy Movement in other cities and telegraphed the government and the Parliament. Similarly, a telegraph was sent from Mashhad to Tabriz, requesting them to send telegraphs to the Parliament and the government and then forward their telegraph to other cities. From Shiraz, too, there was news to the effect that the market had been closed, and merchants and shopkeepers had gathered and held a meeting at the home of a prominent merchant, Malek al-Tojjar, in order to convey the merchants' demands to the government.[36]

In Isfahan, merchants also issued a statement and declared their support for the Economy Movement in other cities. Isfahan merchants emphasized their previous experience in promoting Iranian goods through the Islamiyeh Company. Other issues that the Economy Movement advocated and referred to included: the formation of cooperative companies, the establishment of factories, agricultural reforms, mining development and increasing the production of goods, such as carpets, cotton, silk, wool, leather and similar items.[37] They also addressed the women of the country, urging them to refrain from using foreign goods, even though they may have been cheaper, and to opt for more expensive Iranian products.[38] The distinguishing factor in the Isfahan statement, compared to those of other cities, was their emphasis on the use of Iranian goods.

In Tehran, as well, merchants formed the capital's Economy Movement and joined forces with their counterparts across the country. In addition to agreeing with the Gilan Economy Movement's statement, they considered closing the borders to imports as a way to save the economy from destruction, which was a reaction to the Soviet Union's economic policy, but, in general, they defended the freedom of trade.[39] Furthermore, they raised various issues in their meetings, such as collecting the poor around the city, passing a law on petroleum extraction and establishing a national bank, which were among the demands in their petitions given to the government.[40]

The establishment of Economy Movement Leagues all over the country was an indication of Iranian merchants' efforts to demonstrate unity and collective cohesion, while strengthening intra-group structures and reaching a stage where individual interests were secured through collective solidarity. The declaration of united action for combating the onslaught of foreign capital and increasing exports, an inclination towards industrial growth and the use of innovative business methods and investment through companies, as well as the collection of small investments of capital and liberation from the constraints and financial dependency on the major foreign powers, were all included in a very similar proposal for the establishment of Iran's National Bank.

Those for and against the Economy Movement

This movement, like any other collective movement, had its supporters and opponents. Guilds, clergy, landlords and farmers were among the groups that joined this movement. The Isfahan Guilds' Union declared in a resolution titled 'The Homeland is in Danger' that they would no longer use 'foreign goods' but would be content with Iranian products and would refrain from spending money on 'luxury goods and decorative items' that only 'benefit foreigners'. They believed that the country's backwardness was due to 'continuous neglect and failure to adhere to the principles of so-called progress'.[41] The report from the Qazvin police department also mentioned the participation of guilds and merchants in the gatherings of the Economy Movement.[42] The participation of guilds and merchants was seen in most collective movements during this period. However, the intellectual leadership of these uprisings belonged to the merchants, while guilds followed their lead. The Economy Movement's merchant members believed that the trade obstacles in the northern parts of the country undoubtedly had an effect on the imbalance of supply and demand for goods, which directly affected their prices in the domestic market, and certainly had an impact on the businesses of the guilds.

It seems that, in the past, there had been instances of collaboration between clerics and merchants in order to fulfil the latter's demands, but this time, such collaboration was not widespread. In Isfahan, Haj Sheikh Nurollah Esfahani published a statement titled 'Islam in Danger' under an announcement propagated by the Union of Shop Keepers and Artisans, affirming the ideas of the guild members that criticized the prevalence of foreign goods in the country. He considered the use of Iranian goods to be an absolute necessity.[43] Similar statements were previously issued by other clerics in Isfahan in support of the Islamiyeh Company and Iranian goods.[44] However, at that moment in time, this did not become a widespread general movement.

The Economy Movements throughout the country received support from landowners, as well. Due to the close relationship between Iran's foreign trade and agricultural sectors, the interests of these two groups, merchants and landowners, were intertwined. The landowners in Gilan province expressed their support for the Economy Movement through a statement, considering the closure of the northern trade route to be the cause of commercial decline, poverty and hardship for farmers and landowners. They urged supporters of independence and national security to collaborate with the merchants.[45] In response to the landowners' support, farmers in Gilan also wrote a letter to Reza Shah titled 'Supporters of the Gilan Farmers' League', in which they raised demands, including the removal of restrictions on free trade with the Soviet Union and improvements in the transportation infrastructure, which were essential for selling their agricultural products.[46]

It seems that, as this issue was related to the livelihoods of a wide range of social groups, it had garnered considerable support. However, it appears that among merchants themselves, there were those who did not align with the Economy Movement. This discord was interpreted by the Merchants' Union and the Economy Movement as a personal betrayal and adhering to self-interest, which had been strongly condemned. The Economy Movement published a statement in the newspaper *Habl al-Matin* against merchants who engaged in business with Russian trading houses and acted as their brokers, referring to them as traitors to the country and profit-seekers and emphasizing the necessity of collective solidarity to 'maintain collective order and comply with general regulations'.[47] A report from Mashhad described the opposition of some Caucasian merchants, who had gathered in the trading house of Haj Gholam Reza to express their opposition to the general position of merchants in the trade crisis with the Soviet Union and then tore up the telegraph sent by the Merchants' Union of Khorasan and cursed them. The Merchants' Union then telegraphed the Royal Court and Reza Shah, demanding their punishment.[48] They also declared in a telegraph to the Parliament, the government and the Chamber of Commerce that any utterance of comments, letters or statements published by merchants other than through the Merchants' Union and the Economy Movement is 'falsified and not attributed to the Iranian people'.[49]

These cases indicate that there were still a few merchants who prioritized their personal interests over public interests, but this small number mostly consisted of medium-sized trading houses, merchants and brokers associated with Russian trade houses or active Russian traders in Iran who were not very influential in the overall movement of merchants. The Economy Movement declared that representatives of the Soviet government had tried to 'neutralize the movement',[50] either directly or indirectly through statements and by creating rifts among the merchants. 'They have deceived a merchant named Seyyed Mohammad in Rasht into buying a small amount of textiles,[51] and they have compelled nineteen Khorasani merchants to publish declarations contrary to the declaration of the Merchants' Union and the Economy Movement.'[52] The merchants declared in a published statement that they considered all of these divisive actions useless, which they believed had been perpetrated by the Soviets. Since the declarations and statements of the Economy Movement would lose credibility in the absence of practical actions, they severely suppressed any merchants who did not join, even if it was only one person, and even threatened their lives.[53]

Another point to contemplate is that the weakening of the political and economic power of the Soviet government in Iran, along with the anger expressed by the public towards its commercial organizations, could have provided a suitable platform for British political activities against the Soviet government and further undermined the political position of the Soviet Union in Iran. Therefore, the stance and response of the British government regarding the Economy Movement could have been noteworthy, but the documents examined reflect nothing to that effect.

Results of merchants' demands and the Iranian government's performance

With the expansion of demands made by the Economy Movement and the telegraphs and letters sent by this league and the various social classes that chose to support it, the government dispatched its representatives to Rasht in 1927. It was also decided that the merchants' representatives would be present at the telegraph office to negotiate with the Shah directly, allowing the merchants to voice their demands.[54] The government assured the merchants in a statement that 'the interests of the merchants will be taken into account in all aspects' in the forthcoming Iran-Soviet trade agreement.[55] Therefore, the merchants were anticipating a positive outcome from the negotiations of the Iranian delegates sent to Moscow. They expressed their views on the details and provisions of the trade agreement through the Chamber of Commerce and the Supreme Trade Council. The Chamber of Commerce requested the formation of a commission to incorporate the views of the merchants into the Iran-Soviet trade charter, stating that the charter must be drafted with the consent of the merchants. Accordingly, a draft of the agreement was sent to the Supreme Trade Council for the merchants to declare their proposals to the government.[56] Although the widespread and cohesive demands of the merchants facilitated their interaction with the government, the latter's response was also significant at this time. The Iranian government usually tried to prevent direct contact between the merchants and foreign government representatives,[57] as it did not see such relations in its best interests and general benefit. This was one of the reasons for the positive interaction between the Iranian government and the merchants.

The merchants raised the issue of currency exchange and the dire problems it created with the Soviets. Iranian merchants received chervonets,[58] by exporting goods, such as rice, dried fruits and other products, to the Soviet Union. This money was delivered to Ruspersbank and converted into qirans. During this conversion, however, merchants suffered significant losses.[59] Merchants also proposed some points about the transit issue and the right to exchange 50 million manat's worth of commercial goods for both countries, considering the fluctuations in its value to be unfair.[60]

The demands of the merchants led the Iranian government to make greater efforts to conclude a fairer trade agreement with the Soviet Union, despite the fact that the prevailing ideological constraints determining the terms and conditions of these commercial transactions did not change very much. Nevertheless, the meetings of delegates from the two countries and their agreements provided some stability in these matters. The 1927 Customs Treaty included the principle of balance in trade and customs rights, the presence of trade representatives and permission for the transit of Iranian goods through Soviet territory. The balance of exports and imports between the two countries was to be improved by determining the list of necessary goods. Although not all the demands of the merchants were met, during the following years, in 1932, 1935 and 1940, new trade treaties were concluded between the two countries.[61] It should be mentioned that the approval of Iran's Foreign Trade Monopoly Law in 1931 not only authorized the government to monitor commercial affairs but also led to its control of them. Thus, Iranian merchants put an end to their last collective, cohesive and widespread organization that was formed during these critical years.

Conclusion

The Economy Movement is worth considering from different perspectives. It came into being after the domestic economic crisis, which stemmed from the Russian Revolution, and also the political and social crises in Iran that were the result of instability caused by the First World War. The downfall of the Qajar dynasty and the subsequent coming to power of the Pahlavi state made the sociopolitical arena ready for merchants to enter a coalition in order to combat the economic crisis. This particular coalition, tactically speaking, was a previously unseen form of cooperation on the part of the merchants that covered the entire country. Although the reason behind the establishment of this merchant coalition came from outside the country, very different layers of society responded in solidarity with the merchants. It was basically a coherent protest made by Iranian merchants who were witnessing their businesses in jeopardy. But contrary to the usual way in which the centre of a protest movement would naturally have arisen in the capital, this time, protests started and were centred in the north of the country. Petty shopkeepers, who had proved to be reliable allies of the merchants all through the Qajar era, were indeed allies of the merchants in this protest movement, too. Clerics, landowners and farmers were mainly in agreement with the protest movement, yet, interestingly enough, the medium-sized merchants who acted and did business as brokers of Russian trading houses actually opposed the movement but were silenced by the huge wave of protests made by the League of Merchants' Union all over the country.

The Economy Movement was witness to the vitality of Iranian society and the fact that very influential large merchants could play a prominent role in protesting against the state and foreign powers and also exert pressure on those who chose to oppose the movement. It is worth mentioning that the Iranian state had positive interactions with the merchants, though, at the same time, it tried to prevent the merchants from negotiating directly with the Soviets by trying to be their sole counterpart. Although the political and economic situation in the Soviet Union made any attempts at interacting with this country very difficult, the Iranian government strove to find a solution to the economic crisis and put an ultimate end to trade conflicts with this country through successive rounds of negotiations and the conclusion of consecutive agreements. The cohesive, powerful and nationwide Merchants' Union, which, in the years immediately after the Great War, was once again autonomously organized, showed how powerfully and effectively it could take action and persuade the Iranian government to respond in a suitable way to its demands. This was in spite of the fact that, prior to advent of the Merchants' Union, there happened to be other merchants' organizations, such as Majles-e Vokala-ye Tojjar and Anjoman-e Tojjar (Merchants' Society), which had never been in a position to achieve anything so worthwhile.

The Iranian government, which was under huge internal pressures and facing nationwide protests by merchants and other layers of society, on one hand, negotiated the matter with merchants' representatives in order to find out what their grievances were, and, on the other hand, dispatched delegates to the Soviet Union, which resulted in the conclusion of a series of trade agreements. By the end of 1927, after the signing and ratifying of the new trade agreement between Iran and the Soviet Union, the Economy Movement, which no longer had any raison d'être, gradually ceased its activities, and its members returned to their daily commercial affairs.

Notes

1 Ann Lambton, *Qajar Persia: Eleven Studies* (Austin: University of Texas Press, 1988), 112–15.

2 Ibid., 110–11.

3 Mohammad Taghi Sepehr, *Naskh al-Tavarikh: Salatin-e Qajarieh*, vol. 1 (Tehran: Islamiyeh, 1344/1965), 248.

4 Concerning issues about customs, see Majid Yektayi, *Tarikh-e Darayi-ye Iran* (Tehran: Piruz, 1340/1961), 398–404; Pio Carlo Terenzio, *Reqabatha-ye Rus va Englis dar Iran va Afghanestan*, trans. Abbas Azarin (Tehran: Entesharat-e Elmi va Farhangi, 1364/1985), 42; Fereydun Adamiyat, *Amir Kabir va Iran* (Tehran: Kharazmi, 1348/1969), 396–7.

5 A. Ashraf and H. Hekmat, 'Merchants and Artisans and the Developmental Processes of Nineteenth-Century Iran', in *The Islamic Middle East, 700–1900: Studies in Economic and Social History*, ed. A. L. Udovitch (Princeton: The Darwin Press, Inc., 1981), 734; For a statistical comparison of Iran's trade with Russia and Britain, see Louis Jadot, 'La Russie, l'Angleterre et la Perse', *Bulletin du Comité de l'Asie française*, no. 27 (June 1903): 251–8.

6 Charles Issawi, *Tarikh-e Eqtesadi-ye Iran*, trans. Yaghoob Azhand (Tehran: Gostareh, 1362/1983), 208.

7 Amin al-Zarb Archives. Parvandeh-ye Dadkhastha tavassot-e Amin al-Zarb beh Shah: 'Nameh az Mohammad Hassan Amin al-Zarb beh Nasser al-Din Shah', 1301 AH (1883), quoted in: Fereydun Adamiyat and Homa Nategh, *Afkar-e Ejtemaei va Siyasi va Eqtesadi dar Asar-e Montasher Nashodeh-ye Dowran-e Qajar* (Tehran: Agah, 1356/1977), 308–9.

8 Amin al-Zarb Archives. Asnad-e Ettehadiyyeh-ye Tojjar: 'Asami-ye Ozv-e Tojjar dar Ettehadiyyeh-ye Tojjar', n.d.; 'Ketabcheh-ye Nezamnameh-ye Esasi-ye Heyat-e Ettehadiyyeh-ye Tojjar-e Tehran', 1338 AH (1920): 1–2; 'Davatnameh beh Mohammad Hossein Amin al-Zarb tavassot-e Ettehadiyyeh-ye Tojjar', 1337 AH (1919).

9 *Tableau general du commerce avec les pays etrangers pendant l'annee 21 Mars 1913–20 Mars 1914* (Tehran: Customs General, 1915), see 'Tables' section.

10 National Archives and Library of Iran (NLAI), [293]/18/147/2. 'Gozaresh-e Vaziyyat-e Eqtesadi-ye Mazandaran, Farmandar-e Barfarush', n.d., Vezarat-e Dakheleh.

11 *Tableau general du commerce 21 Mars 1913–20 Mars 1914*, see 'Tables' section.

12 *The General Booklet of Trade with Foreign Countries in 1332–1333 AH/21 March 1914–20 March 1915* (Tehran: Customs General, 1334 AH/1915), 26.

13 *Tableau general du commerce avec les pays etrangers pendant l'annee 21 Mars 1916–20 Mars 1917* (Tehran: Customs General, 1918), see 'Tables' section.

14 *Tableau general du commerce avec les pays etrangers pendant l'annee 21 Mars 1917–20 Mars 1918* (Tehran: Customs General, 1919), xii, 2–3.

15 Soheila Torabi Farsani, *Tojjar, Mashrutiyyat va Dowlat-e Modern* (Tehran: Tarikh-e Iran, 1384/2005), Appendices: Table No. 9.

16 Hossein Makki, *Mokhtasari az Zendegani-ye Siyasi-ye Soltan Ahmad Shah Qajar: beh Zamimeh-ye Chand Pardeh az Zendegani-ye Dakheli va Khususi-ye U* (Tehran: Amir Kabir, 1357/1978), 251–83.

17 'Ahdnameh-ye Iran va Rus', *Habl al-Matin* 35, no. 2–3 (29 Jamadi al-Avval 1345/4 December 1926): 26–9.

18 Abdollah Mostowfi, *Sharh-e Zendegani-ye Man: Tarikh-e Ejtemaei va Edari-ye Dowreh-ye Qajariyeh*, vol. 3 (Tehran: Zavvar, 1370/1991), 551.
19 Torabi Farsani, *Tojjar*, 392.
20 NLAI, [240]/251/48/(58–60). 'Gozaresh az Edareh-ye Gomrok-e Shomal (Mashhadsar)', 1302 (1923), Vezarat-e Darayi. This report mentions three Soviet trade organizations, Rupeto, Tsentrosoyuz and Khlopkom.
21 NLAI, [240]/251/48/146. 'Gozaresh az Edareh-ye Gomrok-e Astara beh Edareh-ye Kol-e Gomrok', 3 Khordad 1301 (25 May 1922), Vezarat-e Darayi.
22 'Ekhtariyyeh (2): Raje beh Tejarat-e Shomal', *Ettelaat*, no. 437 (2 Esfand 1306/22 February 1928): 3.
23 'Sadd Rah-ye Bajgiran', *Habl al-Matin* 32, no. 3 (3 Zelhajjeh 1342/7 July 1924): 10.
24 NLAI, 290/4/611/(2). 'Az Vezarat-e Khareji beh Vezarat-e Dakheleh', 25 Ordibehesht 1307 (15 May 1928).
25 'Maramnameh-ye Majma-ye Eqtesad-e Esfahan'; 'Bayannameh-ye Majma-ye Eqtesadiyun-e Esfahan', *Habl al-Matin* 35, no. 14–15 (24 Ramazan 1345/29 March 1927): 8 and 9–11.
26 'Bayaniyyeh-ye Jamiyyat-e Nahzat-e Eqtesad', *Habl al-Matin* 35, no. 9 (12 Shaban 1345/15 February 1927): 5–7.
27 For more on the Merchants' Union, see Torabi Farsani, *Tojjar*, 376–90.
28 NLAI, [293]/44/39/1. 'Telegraf az Ettehadiyyeh-ye Tojjar-e Hamadan beh Maqamat-e Ali-ye Mamlekati', 6 Bahman 1306 (27 January 1928), Vezarat-e Dakheleh.
29 NLAI, 310/43/2/1. 'Telegraf az Ettehadiyyeh-ye Tojjar-e Hamadan beh Vezarat-e Tejarat va Falahat', 27 Ramazan 1348 (25 February 1930), Daftar-e Nokhost Vazir.
30 NLAI, [293]/44/35/6. 'Gozaresh az Edareh-ye Polis-e Qazvin beh Farmandar', 9 Bahman 1305 (30 January 1927), Vezarat-e Dakheleh; NLAI, [293]/44/35/7. 'Gozaresh az Shahrdari-ye Qazvin beh Vezarat-e Dakheleh', 17 Bahman 1305 (7 February 1927), Vezarat-e Dakheleh.
31 NLAI, [293]/44/35/1, 3–5. 'Gozaresh az Edareh-ye Polis-e Qazvin beh Farmandar', 23 Esfand 1305 (15 March 1927), Vezarat-e Dakheleh; 'Az Markaz-e Farmandehi-ye Edareh-ye Polis beh Vezarat-e Dakheleh', 7 Farvardin 1306 (28 March 1927), Vezarat-e Dakheleh; 'Az Farmandari-ye Qazvin beh Vezarat-e Dakheleh', 10 Bahman 1305 (31 January 1927), 24 Esfand 1305 (16 March 1927), Vezarat-e Dakheleh.
32 NLAI, [293]/44/35/9. 'Bayaniyyeh-ye Jamiyyat-e Nahzat-e Eqtesad-e Qazvin', 14 Bahman 1306 (4 February 1928), Vezarat-e Dakheleh.
33 NLAI, [293]/44/35/1. 'Gozaresh az Edareh-ye Polis-e Qazvin beh Farmandar', 23 Esfand 1305 (15 March 1927), Vezarat-e Dakheleh.
34 Amin al-Zarb Archives. 'Bayaniyyeh-ye Jamiyyat-e Nahzat-e Eqtesad-e Khorasan', 18 Esfand 1305 (10 March 1927).
35 'Nahzat-e Eqtesad-e Tabriz', *Habl al-Matin* 35, no. 14–15 (24 Ramazan 1345/29 March 1927): 28–9.
36 NLAI, [293]/5/104001. 'Telegraf az Shiraz beh Nokhost Vazir', 19 Mehr 1306 (12 October 1927), Vezarat-e Dakheleh.
37 'Maramnameh'; 'Bayannameh', 8 and 9–11.
38 Ibid.
39 'Bayaniyyeh-ye Jamiyyyat-e Nahzat-e Eqtesad-e Markaz', *Habl al-Matin* 35, no. 21–2 (22 Ziqadeh 1345/24 May 1927): 25–6.
40 NLAI, [293]/44/56/1–2. 'Bayaniyyeh-ye Jamiyyat-e Nahzat-e Eqtesad-e Tehran', 1 Esfand 1305 (21 February 1927), Vezarat-e Dakheleh; 'Baz Ham Nahzat-e Eqtesad', *Habl al-Matin* 36, no. 2 (25 Jamadi al-Sani 1346/20 December 1927): 23.
41 NLAI, [310]/1/53/5/1. 'Qatnameh-ye Ettehadiyyeh-ye Asnaf-e Esfahan', 11 Azar 1305 (3 December 1926), Daftar-e Nokhost Vazir.

42 NLAI, [293]/44/35/6. 'Gozaresh az Edareh-ye Polis-e Qazvin beh Farmandar', 9 Bahman 1305 (30 January 1927), Daftar-e Nokhost Vazir.
43 NLAI, [310]/1/53/4. 'Bayaniyyeh-ye Sheikh Nurollah Esfahani', 11 Azar 1305 (3 December 1926), Daftar-e Nokhost Vazir.
44 Musa Najafi, *Andisheh-ye Siyasi va Tarikh-e Nahzat-e Bidargeraneh-ye Haj Aqa Nurollah Esfahani* (Tehran: n.p., 1369/1990), 38–40.
45 'Bayaniyyeh-e Malekan-e Gilan', *Habl al-Matin* 35, no. 16 (9 Shavval 1345/12 April 1927): 13–14.
46 NLAI, [310]/3/19/4. 'Az Heyat-e Hamiyan-e Zare-ye Gilan beh Shah', 19 Tir 1305 (11 July 1926), Daftar-e Nokhost Vazir.
47 'Tajer', *Habl al-Matin* 35, no. 14–15 (24 Ramazan 1345/29 March 1927): 15.
48 Presidential Research and Documents Centre. 'Az Vezarat-e Darbar beh Iyalat-e Khorasan', 6 Bahman 1305 (27 January 1927), Vezarat-e Darbar; 'Telegraf az Ettehadiyyeh-ye Tojjar-e Khorasan beh Vezarat-e Darbar', 5 Bahman 1305 (25 January 1927), Vezarat-e Darbar.
49 NLAI, 1584/104010. 'Telegraf az Tojjar beh Nokhost Vazir va Majles', 14 Bahman 1305 (4 February 1927).
50 'Telegraf az Rasht', *Habl al-Matin* 35, no. 21–2 (22 Ziqadeh 1345/24 May 1927): 26.
51 'Iran va Hokumat-e Showravi', *Habl al-Matin* 35, no. 14–15 (24 Ramazan 1345/29 March 1927): 6–7.
52 Ibid., 6–7.
53 Ibid.
54 Ibid.
55 'Shekayat-e Tojjar', *Habl al-Matin* 35, no. 1 (15 Jamadi al-Sani 1345/21 December 1926): 19.
56 'Nazariyyat-e Tojjar', *Habl al-Matin* 35, no. 4 (6 Rajab 1345/11 January 1927): 21.
57 NLAI, [293]/4/104001. 'Az Vezarat-e Falahat va Tejarat va Favayed-e Ammeh beh Riyasat-e Vozara', 23 Aban 1306 (15 November 1927), Vezarat-e Dakheleh; NLAI, [293]/4/104001. 'Az Vezarat-e Dakheleh beh Riyasat-e Vozara', 11 Azar 1306 (3 December 1927), Vezarat-e Dakheleh; NLAI, [293]/4/104001. 'Az Riyasat-e Vozara beh Vezarat-e Dakheleh', 4 Azar 1306 (26 November 1927).
58 One Soviet chervonets equalled ten manat, the local currency of Azerbaijan.
59 'Az Rasht Minevisand: Ezmehlal-e Tojjar-e Shomal ba Amal-e Hamsayeh', *Habl al-Matin* 34, no. 6 (2 Shaban 1344/16 February 1926): 16–17.
60 'Raje beh Nezamnameh', *Habl al-Matin* 36, no. 9 (14 Shaban 1346/7 February 1928): 24.
61 For more information see: Akbar Valizadeh, *Ettehad-e Jamahir-e Showravi va Reza Shah: Barresi-ye Ravabet-e Iran va Showravi mian-e Do Jang-e Jahan* (Tehran: Markaz-e Asnad-e Enqelab-e Eslami, 1385/2006), 194–6; Mahmoud Taher Ahmadi, *Asnad-e Ravabet-e Iran va Showravi (Dowreh-ye Reza Shah: 1304–1308)* (Tehran: Sazman-e Asnad-e Melli-ye Iran, 1374/1995), 141–8.

Bibliography

Archives and libraries

Amin al-Zarb Archives, Tehran
Customs Education and Research Library of Iran, Tehran
National Library and Archives of Iran, Tehran
Presidential Research and Documents Centre, Tehran

Periodicals

Ettelāʿāt
Habl al-Matin

Secondary sources

Adamiyat, Fereydun. *Amir Kabir va Irān*. Tehran: Kharazmi, 1348 (1969).
Adamiyat, Fereydun and Homa Nategh. *Afkār-e Ejtemāʿi va Siyāsi va Eqtesādi dar Āsār-e Montasher Nashodeh-ye Dowrān-e Qājār*. Tehran: Agah, 1356 (1977).
Ashraf, A. and H. Hekmat. 'Merchants and Artisans and the Developmental Processes of Nineteenth-Century Iran'. In *The Islamic Middle East, 700–1900: Studies in Economic and Social History*, edited by A. L. Udovitch, 725–50. Princeton: The Darwin Press, Inc., 1981.
Issawi, Charles. *Tārikh-e Eqtesādi-ye Irān*. Translated by Yaghoub Azhand. Tehran: Gostareh, 1362 (1983).
Jadot, Louis. 'La Russie, l'Angleterre et la Perse'. *Bulletin du Comité de l'Asie française*, no. 27 (June 1903): 251–8.
Lambton, Ann. *Qajar Persia: Eleven Studies*. Austin: University of Texas Press, 1988.
Makki, Hossein. *Mokhtasari az Zendegāni-ye Siyāsi-ye Soltān Ahmad Shāh Qājār: beh Zamimeh-ye Chand Pardeh az Zendegāni-ye Dākheli va Khususi-ye U*. Tehran: Amir Kabir, 1357 (1978).
Mostowfi, Abdollah. *Sharh-e Zendegāni-ye Man: Tārikh-e Ejtemāʿi va Edāri-ye Dowreh-ye Qājāriyeh*. Vol. 3. Tehran: Zavvar, 1370 (1991).
Najafi, Musa. *Andisheh-ye Siyāsi va Tārikh-e Nahzat-e Bidārgerāneh-ye Hāj Āqā Nurollah Esfahāni*. Tehran: n.p., 1369 (1990).
Sepehr, Mohammad Taghi. *Naskh al-Tavārikh: Salātin-e Qājārieh*. Vol. 1. Tehran: Islamiyeh, 1344 (1965).
Taher Ahmadi, Mahmoud. *Asnād-e Ravābet-e Irān va Showravi (Dowreh-ye Rezā Shāh: 1304–1308)*. Tehran: Sazman-e Asnad-e Melli-ye Iran, 1374 (1995).
Terenzio, Pio Carlo. *Reqābathā-ye Rus va Englis dar Irān va Afghānestān*. Translated by Abbas Azarin. Tehran: Entesharat-e Elmi va Farhangi, 1364 (1985).
Torabi Farsani, Soheila. *Tojjār, Mashrutiyyat va Dowlat-e Modern*. Tehran: Tarikh-e Iran, 1384 (2005).
Valizadeh, Akbar. *Ettehād-e Jamāhir-e Showravi va Rezā Shāh: Barresi-ye Ravābet-e Irān va Showravi miyān-e Do Jang-e Jahān*. Tehran: Markaz-e Asnad-e Enqelab-e Eslami, 1385 (2006).
Yektayi, Majid. *Tārikh-e Dārāyi-ye Irān*. Tehran: Piruz, 1340 (1961).

5

Growth or bread

Craftsmen's reactions to industrialization policies under Reza Shah

Serhan Afacan

> Previously, the matter of Islamic fabrics and textiles, which would be manufactured and woven in Islamic territories and contribute to the prosperity of the homeland, was deliberated in the Council of Commerce. Some advocated for the establishment of a yarn-spinning mill, which would mark the initiation of textile production. Without the presence of such a factory, a significant part of our population would inevitably turn to foreigners to fulfil their textile needs, which would deplete our nation's wealth by trading gold and silver for cotton. This would perpetuate our plight. Others proposed providing resources to weavers, enabling them to accumulate capital and strength to revitalize their businesses. In short, everyone emphasized one of the two approaches to promote and disseminate Islamic textiles. *Whichever is accepted and deemed appropriate.*[1]

Introduction

By the end of Reza Shah's rule in September 1941, extensive industrialization had ushered in significant economic, social and political transformations in Iran. While craft industries persisted throughout this era and beyond, they were perceived as outdated, unappealing and insufficient to satisfy domestic demand or compete with imports. On the other hand, during much of the nineteenth century, Qajar reformists, particularly Mirza Taqi Khan Farahani, otherwise known as Amir Kabir, who served as Nasser al-Din Shah's first premier between 1848 and 1851, had placed considerable emphasis on enhancing and advancing handicrafts as a component of their economic policies while simultaneously introducing the first examples of modern industries into Iran.[2]

Following military setbacks against the Russians in the early 1800s, Iran faced not only political challenges but also economic disadvantages due to the growing influx of

European imports. Throughout the first half of the nineteenth century, interactions with the West prompted many Iranian reformists to recognize the necessity of introducing modern technology and administration to their country. However, 'their efforts in this regard were unsuccessful and, in the minds of ordinary people, modernization and reformism from above soon became associated with failure'.[3]

As a result, from the mid-nineteenth century onwards, a critical and negative narrative gained traction among intellectuals, craftsmen and merchants. This discourse centred on Europe's increasing control over Iran's politics and economy, a concern that was equally shared by the Iranian religious establishment. Furthermore, 'the influx of mass-manufactured products, especially textiles, undermined the traditional handicrafts, and consequently presented for the many bazaars a mutual enemy – the foreigner'.[4] The Constitutional Revolution of 1905–6 can be viewed as a by-product of this collective concern, among other factors. This revolution yielded two significant outcomes: Iran's first constitution and parliamentary-monarchical system. The veneration of the modern state and preoccupation with economic growth among intellectuals and officials were other major consequences that emerged at this time.

In comparison with other cases, such as the neighbouring Ottoman Empire or Muhammad Ali Pasha's Egypt, the modernizing reforms in nineteenth-century Iran were characterized by caution and discontinuity. Iranian reformers and intellectuals hailed the industrial advancements taking place in Europe and, to some extent, in the Ottoman Empire and Egypt, while, at the same time, bemoaning the lack of infrastructure necessary for a comprehensive industrial transformation of Iran. Nevertheless, after the Constitutional Revolution, a strong desire emerged within the National Consultative Assembly (henceforth, the Majles) and among the growing number of domestic newspapers to attain economic growth and prosperity. Hence, 'the revolution against despotism was not fought for purely "idealistic" reasons – that is, merely because the revolutionaries disliked despotism and preferred a "democratic" system; its triumph promised real economic, social and personal gains for the participating classes and individuals'.[5]

Moreover, within the religio-nationalist discourse strategically employed by constitutionalist politicians and writers to resonate with the masses, the attainment of modern economic development was underscored as a crucial prerequisite for the country's independence and progress. While the industrial policies of this era fell short of achieving the projected outcomes, since, by the turn of the century, there barely were any modern factories in Iran, they were nonetheless pivotal in preparing the psychological ground for large-scale industrialization policies under Reza Shah, which will be explored later in this chapter.

Irrespective of large-scale industrialization's degree of success in the 1920s and 1930s, this process displaced, disillusioned and infuriated some artisans who derived their livelihood from handicrafts, particularly in the textile industry. These traditional handicraft workers were intimidated by the increasing number of modern factories, not necessarily because they were technophobic or backward-looking but rather out of a genuine concern for losing their source of bread. Prior to this period, they had endured the influx of European imports but had adapted to them through cost-minimizing strategies. However, the rise of large-scale factories presented them with a more enduring and substantial challenge. Unlike foreign products, it was not easy to compete against, discredit or collectively oppose goods manufactured in Iranian factories.

Ironically, every argument and discursive tool that craftsmen and their supporters had employed against the flow of imports since the mid-nineteenth century could now also be applied in favour of large-scale industrial establishments. These arguments mainly included: reducing reliance on foreign goods, halting the outflow of precious metals from Iran, safeguarding the nation's honour and contributing to the welfare of Iranians. Thus, the discursive weapons of those who advocated for self-sufficiency in order to curtail foreign imports were, in a way, turned against them or at least were perceived as such.

Numerous accounts exist regarding the craftsmen's perceptions of large-scale industrialization during this era and the extent of their feelings of vulnerability. Accordingly, this chapter offers an analysis of these responses as evidenced in their petitions, while also drawing upon other available sources whenever possible. While economic historians primarily deal with analysing changes in the economy and presenting statistics, it is important to note that labour historians predominantly direct their attention towards understanding how these transformations impacted the workplace experiences of labourers and their daily lives. There is a rich collection of scholarship dealing with these aspects of modern Iranian history as far as factory workers and collective labour actions are concerned. Conversely, the experiences and responses of artisans, petty shop owners and small traders remain largely unexplored in the existing body of research on Iranian labour history.

Thus, this chapter aims to contribute towards addressing this gap by examining the reactions of craftsmen to the introduction of cost-saving machinery in factories established during the Reza Shah period. It primarily centres on the petitions of these craftsmen to local and central authorities. Most of the petitions discussed in this chapter originate from Isfahan and primarily pertain to the textile industry, frequently articulating grievances related to the Vatan Factory.

Before delving into this discussion, it is important to establish four key points. The first point pertains to petitions, which are the main source material used in this study. Petitions can be defined as 'demands for a favour or for the redressing of an injustice directed to some established authority'.[6] Furthermore, in order to ensure responses, petitioners may at times exaggerate or alter certain facts to fit their cases. As a result, ascertaining the veracity of these documents is problematic. Thus, one should always read petitions critically. My intention in this chapter has been to show, by examining craftsmen's petitions, how they reacted to industrialization policies of the 1920s–30s, which they thought and/or argued had worked to their disadvantage. The petitions I have analysed in the subsequent sections make almost no mention of any positive outcomes of industrialization in Iran during this period, although factory-made textiles led to the creation of many new crafts and made some of the existing ones more profitable.

The second point is about the terminology employed in this chapter. For the sake of clarity, the term 'craftsmen' will be used with reference to the petitioners. Yet this term was part of a wide spectrum of occupations within the handicraft industry for textiles, which included weavers (men, women and children), employers and traders, who shared similar experiences within their respective occupational spheres. Also, the Persian word for factory (*kārkhāneh*, literally 'work-house') had been used in Iran prior to the existence of modern factories. Thus, in the 1920s, 'factories' (*kārkhānehhā*) could refer to cottage industries (also *kārgāh* or workshop) or those involving large groups of workers and light machinery. Therefore, 'large-scale industrialization' will refer to state policies, particularly in the 1930s, for the factory system's adoption, while 'factory' will be used for the new manufacturing establishments equipped with power-driven machinery.

The third point addresses the predominantly rural character of Iran during this period. Given that most handicraft workers still lived in the countryside, industrialization remained a limited and piecemeal phenomenon in terms of its share in the country's manufacturing sector and geographical reach. Consequently, many of the large-scale industrial establishments faced minimal or no significant resistance from locals. While every individual case may have significance from various angles, one needs to avoid overemphasizing the experiences of urban artisans.

The fourth point concerns the negative perception of industrialization, as elaborated by Braun:

> Industrialisation seems by its very nature to be hostile to community and tradition. We stress 'seems' because we cannot share this attitude. Industrialisation and industrial labour has until now been perceived and judged almost exclusively from the point of view of uprooting, disruption and stereotyping and any discussion generally starts from hidebound assumptions and views: industrialisation and industrial work destroy old crafts, working patterns and associations; they displace ancient folklore, long-lived customs and practices and traditional forms of community; there is a dynamism inherent to the industrial system of production which disregards human and material ties, and so on.[7]

Some contemporaries and historians depict industrial capitalism as having a notably detrimental impact on crafts, a perspective that holds true to a certain extent. However, I contend that craftsmen frequently employed anti-industrialization arguments in their petitions as a discursive strategy and a means to interact with the state, in order to work the system 'to their minimum disadvantage', to borrow Eric Hobsbawm's phraseology.[8] To put it differently, craftsmen's reactions in most instances were directed towards the government's industrialization policies rather than the factories themselves. In the previous sentence, I used 'the government' (*dowlat*) instead of 'the state' (*hukumat*) due to the precise distinction made by the petitioning craftsmen between the two concepts – the latter referring to Reza Shah, whom they frequently praised as 'the just king', 'the father of the nation' and other honorific titles.

The interaction between large-scale industrialization policies and craftsmen will be examined in the subsequent sections of this chapter. Although limited in scope, the data presented still provides valuable insights into a specific facet of Iran's industrialization. In order to provide a broader historical context for the discussion, I will begin by offering a concise overview of large-scale industrialization during Reza Shah's reign with a focus on the primary characteristics of the economic policies of that period. This section will be followed by an exploration of craftsmen's responses to these policies, culminating in my concluding remarks.

Large-scale industrialization under Reza Shah

Industrialization is not merely an economic and political matter since it also has significant social implications. From the late nineteenth century onwards, Iranian political reformists increasingly perceived industrialization as a crucial avenue towards progress and autonomy. To facilitate this, domestic production was encouraged as an initial step to counteract the influx of imported manufactures. Consequently, trade protectionism as an idea and government interventionism as a policy both gained prominence after the Constitutional Revolution, continuing throughout the 1920s–30s.[9] Moreover, the adoption of the factory system had begun to gain greater credibility in Iran than the advancement of craft industries by the end of the 1800s. Likewise, as the twentieth century dawned, various segments of Iranian society had become receptive to the idea of industrialization.

The extensive technological transformations that revolutionized industrial production globally throughout the nineteenth century had a profound impact on Iranian manufacturing. As a result, Iran faced European trade dominance while undergoing a period of modest economic recovery, particularly towards the end of the century. While the flow of imports posed challenges to Iran's manufacturing sector, the utilization of aniline dyes and imported yarns and the expanded use of light machinery enabled Iranian craftsmen to decrease production costs. Moreover, in pursuit of further cost reductions, women and children were widely employed, especially in carpet weaving, and were often subjected to unfavourable working conditions while receiving very low wages.

Hence, during the nineteenth and early twentieth centuries, Iranian economic policies did not overtly favour the adoption of the factory system. Instead, emphasis was placed on promoting domestic industries through any feasible means. In this milieu, rural and urban artisans were not appreciably apprehensive about government policies or the central state's regulatory influence, particularly concerning industry. However, this situation changed dramatically under Reza Shah's rule. More specifically, the official industrialization strategy during this period 'was based on the view that more factories are better than less factories, that state factories are better than private factories, that big plants are better than small plants and that capital-intensive production is preferable to labour-intensive production'.[10]

Ironically, state-led industrialization on a large scale ended up having a more detrimental impact on Iran's craft industries than foreign goods. This impact was most acutely felt during Reza Shah's push for industrialization in the 1930s. In the preceding decades, due to unsuccessful attempts to industrialize, the output of the newly emerging factories remained relatively insignificant in terms of quantity, particularly within the textile industry, compared with the extant craft industries. However, under Reza Shah, an import substitution policy was effectively employed to expedite

Iran's industrialization. By the end of his reign in 1941, numerous factories had been established, producing a range of commodities, including sugar, matches, soap, oil and leather, along with textile goods representing a significant portion of this expansion.[11]

At the same time, the legislative foundation for the state's industrialization drive was established during the initial years of Reza Shah's rule. The unfavourable economic terms imposed on Iran by the Treaties of Golestan (1813) and Turkmenchay (1828), following Iran's defeats in conflicts with Russia, coupled with subsequent trade agreements signed with European powers, significantly curtailed Iran's control over its tariff policies.[12] Consequently, due to the absence of economic independence, several measures were implemented to promote the use of domestically produced goods. One such example was the Law for the Use of National Clothes, which was enacted in February 1923.[13] This law mandated that all state employees, including the military, wear clothing manufactured in Iran from native fabrics.

Between 1925 and 1941, a substantial amount of legislation concerning industrialization and related matters (211 laws and 934 decrees) was passed or issued.[14] For instance, in 1925, a law was enacted to grant a ten-year exemption from import duties for industrial and agricultural machines, as well as their component parts.[15] During the same year, a new commercial code was ratified, recognizing joint-stock companies and embracing other principles of modern Western commerce. Additionally, three significant developments unfolded in subsequent years. In May 1927, the country's first national bank (Bank-e Melli-ye Iran) was established. Secondly, in May 1928, Iran achieved full tariff autonomy by terminating the capitulation regime, which was then replaced by new bilateral treaties.[16] Finally, as a result of these measures, 'the number of registered companies rose from 93 with 143 million rials of capital in 1311 [1932] to 1,735 companies with 1.862 billion rials of capital in 1319 [1940]'.[17]

Then, in December 1928, the Uniform Dress Code Law was approved. Its first article stated: 'All male Iranian subjects who are [not] required to wear special clothing in conformity with service in the government shall wear uniform clothing within the country; and all government employees, whether civil or judicial, shall, when on government duty, wear civil or judicial clothing, as officially prescribed, and at other times, they shall wear the uniform attire.'[18] Thus, this law mandated that Iranian males adopt Western-style attire and abandon their traditional clothing.

Initiatives were also launched to establish the necessary infrastructure for a nationwide market, exemplified by the Trans-Iranian Railway project connecting the Caspian Sea to the Persian Gulf via Tehran. This concerted push for industrialization was bolstered by the establishment of government-managed monopolies, which initially began with sugar and tea and subsequently expanded to encompass various other goods. Additionally, a law passed in February 1931 fully monopolized foreign trade. This legislation granted exclusive control over the import and export of both natural and industrial products to the government, with the authority to grant foreign trade privileges to individuals or entities.[19]

The onset of the Great Depression in 1929 not only compelled but also facilitated the implementation of etatist and protectionist economic and monetary policies under Reza Shah, like in much of the world. It is worth noting that while private sector participation overwhelmingly drove industrial growth, the industrialization programme as a whole remained a state-initiated and controlled endeavour. Consequently, in the early 1930s, the government made the most of its monopolistic authority by displaying a clear preference for the establishment of large-scale industries with support for private entrepreneurs.[20] The most conspicuous manifestation of such industrialization fervour was observed in the textile sector. Pre-existing industries, such as the Vatan Factory, were supported by the state, and new ones were founded, particularly in Isfahan, Shiraz, Tabriz, Kashan and Yazd, among other prominent locations. The modernization of the textile industry was fuelled by the importation of machinery from Britain and Germany.[21] Although Iranian craftsmen retained their relevance in the textile industry well into the twentieth century, the new factory system was the most conspicuous facet of Reza Shah's industrialization.

The government's favouritism towards large-scale factories was also evident in the Factory Act of 1936, which introduced several significant measures to regulate working conditions in factories with ten or more workers.[22] Ironically, the act placed greater liability on the employees than the employers. Furthermore, it prohibited employees from forming or taking part 'in any union or association prejudicial to the factory's interests'.[23] Furthermore, to eliminate any impediments to industrial growth, trade unions and collective labour actions were effectively suppressed during the 1930s.

The strategies employed by Iranian workers in various industries to voice their demands and concerns through collective action or non-confrontational means, as well as how they dealt with Reza Shah's repressive policies, have been relatively well-examined in the existing scholarship.[24] However, the same level of analysis is lacking for those engaged in crafts or cottage industries, who were equally apprehensive about losing their livelihoods in the face of advancing industrialization. The subsequent section will delve into this dimension of Iran's industrialization.

Craftsmen's reactions

Our understanding of artisan ideology, their political inclinations and labour organizations in both urban and rural contexts remains limited. Similarly, there is a dearth of comprehensive studies on their potential cultural, economic or political motivations for resisting industrial capitalism. However, two distinct discourses employed by Iranian craftsmen can be discerned. During the 1920s, when the number of new factories was still negligible, the supplicants' discourse echoed the anti-import arguments that had circulated in the preceding decades. Conversely, with the factory system's emergence in the 1930s, the petitioners shifted their focus to domestic industrial enterprises, attributing their declining businesses and misfortunes to these establishments.

It is important to note that references in the writings from this period and subsequent scholarship often allude to the disintegration of artisanal production in Iran. Yet, as previously mentioned in this chapter, the extent of this disintegration should not be overstated. It is true that numerous craftsmen abandoned their trades throughout the nineteenth century, either seeking employment in nascent industries – often ending up among the ranks of the urban unemployed – or attempting to seek their fortunes in other countries, particularly Tsarist Russia.[25]

This trend emerged due to various factors, including the erosion of the traditional master-journeyman-apprentice craft-based system, natural calamities, like famines, and broader economic shifts, such as Iran's increasing integration into the global economy, especially from the mid-1800s onwards. Over time, the master craftsman's role became less significant, particularly by the 1920s–30s. However, many craftsmen remained relatively unaffected by these changes and managed to weather the challenges posed by European imports. A major contributing factor to this situation was the absence of a unified countrywide market. This lack of integration was largely due to Iran's challenging geography, inadequate transportation routes and infrastructure – especially in inland regions – and ongoing security concerns along the roads. Thus, even as the twentieth century began, 'Iran could in no way be regarded as a single economic unit'.[26]

The impact of imported goods on handicraft workers in the countryside was relatively less severe. As elsewhere in the Middle East, small-scale plants 'which survived could only do so either by dominating or developing some part of the local market which was protected from foreign imports by cost, taste, or fashion; or by learning to make efficient use of some of the cheaper products which the outside world could provide such as cotton thread or simple machines'.[27] On the other hand, the flood of foreign goods impelled craftsmen, petty shop owners and traders in urban centres to petition the government to implement measures to reduce imports and safeguard domestic craft industries.[28] In the early twentieth century, besides foreign companies operating in Iran, native merchants who collaborated with foreign firms were also held accountable for the nation's economic predicament. In March 1923, a petitioner from Iranian Azerbaijan vehemently criticized these merchants for importing manufactured articles 'into our sacred country' instead of selling 'the goods that are domestically produced in quantities sufficient to meet the needs of the people, and whose production rescues craftsmen from destitution'.[29]

Likewise, craftsmen outside the textile sector were frustrated by the limitations of the previously mentioned law on the use of national clothing. Shoemakers, for instance, conveyed their dissatisfaction regarding the content of the law through a petition they submitted to the Majles in March 1923, shortly after its enactment:

> It is undoubtedly true that the very purpose behind the establishment of this national regime and the foundation of the constitutional system is to secure the means of well-being and safety for all, while procuring benefits for Iranians and eliminating detriments. [. . .] You should not forget the principle of equality.
>
> As shoemakers, we have consistently made sacrifices and led the way in the establishment of the sacred Constitution. Concurrently, we have considerably advanced our craft in recent years, rendering our handiwork more exquisite and appealing. Regrettably, in response to our efforts, certain deputies completely disregarded our trade during their deliberations about the use of native fabrics and domestically made products . . . Of course, our remarks pertain to a number of deputies who wear foreign-made shoes, not those who have been accustomed

> to wearing domestically produced shoes from an early age . . . We wish to capture your esteemed attention and earnestly request that you extend your consideration to native footwear, like your attention to native textiles. We kindly ask you to include a provision in the supplemental legislation concerning native footwear and promote the advancement of this craft as well.[30]

As evident in this example and subsequent petitions, the supplicants employed a particularly critical tone when addressing the Majles, an institution they closely followed through newspapers and various political organizations. Furthermore, these petitions consistently established a connection between nationalism and the preservation of domestic craft industries. In another petition sent in January 1926, the Hamadan Merchants' Union expressed its dissatisfaction with foreign investment and the industrialization of Iranian industries in this critical statement:[31]

> Throughout Iran, one can witness the demoralized and disheartened craftsmen, whose number is already dwindling. If you happen to find some time, you could even visit what could be called their crypts [*dakhmeh*] which are the factories of twentieth-century Iran . . . Among the most noteworthy of these factories are those engaged in carpet-weaving, which are under foreign control. Go and observe how young boys and girls toil there for an entire day in exchange for a paltry sum. If foreigners buy Iranian carpets, it is because of these meager wages. In contrast, labourers in industrialized nations around the world earn considerably more money, despite working a six to eight-hour day. So, we work but cannot accrue earnings, and whatever we do manage to earn is invariably spent on foreign textiles and other commodities.

Similarly, in a petition dated 15 September 1927, the brocade weavers of Yazd voiced their grievances about the decline of their business which they attributed to the influx of cheaper imports and the inefficacy of the government's economic policies.[32] In addition to calling for the safeguarding of the textile industry, they requested an instructor to train the offspring of 'factory' owners in the art of using permanent dyes. On 17 November, the Majles forwarded this proposal to the Ministry of Agriculture, Commerce and Public Works. The ministry responded on 26 November, referring to 'the Law for the Use of National Clothes' as 'the best encouragement for factory owners and workers' and added that its limited budget did not allow for the appointment of an instructor.[33] Instead, factory owners and manufacturers were advised to travel to Tehran at their own expense to receive the necessary training.

In certain instances, petitioners adopted an exceptionally critical tone when addressing the government's economic policies. A vivid example of such a petition was composed by a brocade weaver named Mohammad Ali Yazdi, who intriguingly identified himself as 'Dust-e Pahlavi' (Pahlavi's Friend). In this lengthy petition, forwarded to the Majles in January 1929, he openly criticized these policies, particularly the Uniform Dress Code Law, in the following manner:

> You proclaim yourselves to be advocates for labourers [*tarafdārān-e ranjbar*], and I wish that, from time to time, you could turn these words into actual deeds.

> Have you ever taken a moment to contemplate the plight of the wretched people of Yazd? . . . Have you ever pondered the consequences of the Uniform Dress Code Law for the silk fabric makers of Yazd? Their products are no longer in demand among the public . . . Today, due to a lack of consideration, their products are neither sold nor utilized. The responsibility for this lies with your lack of consideration and indifference towards this community. Why is this? It is because both Iranians and the entire world have become imitators, and as you are aware, it is those at the top who set the example. When you wear European socks, trousers, shirts and even walking sticks, the lower classes strive to emulate you, resulting in the disappearance of Iranian industries and handicrafts, much like the people who craft those goods. The populist gentlemen [*aqāyān-e sūrat-e mardom*] prefer foreign fabrics over Iranian ones, and they have no need for the silk producers of Yazd and Kashan . . . This malady [Law for the Use of National Clothes] had begun to spread a few years ago, but did not gain widespread recognition. Also, it would be beneficial if, during the winter, prominent figures donned woollen cloaks [*ʿabā*] produced in Nain to keep themselves warm! But, of course, how funny would the Pahlavi hat [*kolāh-e pahlavi*] appear when paired with an *ʿabā*! It must be complemented by an overcoat, jacket or dressing gown! . . . If you seek to shield yourselves from the cold and stay warm, you could achieve both with the *ʿabā* produced in Nain. But why bother? It is simpler to use the revered fabric of any foreign brand produced by Mr. Foreigner![34]

Yazdi writes that he sent a copy of his petition to a newspaper in Tehran, which suggests that he wanted to draw public attention to these issues. His use of forceful and critical language in the petition, which the relevant official referred to as 'vulgar, hateful and impolite', reflects the depth of his frustration and dissatisfaction with the government's policies. The official also remarked: 'He mentions that he has sent a copy of this petition to a newspaper in Tehran. In this way, he reached the people who swear most.' By sharing his concerns with a wider audience in print, he likely hoped to garner support for his cause and put pressure on the authorities to address the issues faced by his fellow craftsmen and artisans. Although Yazdi's use of strong language was uncommon in petitions of this period, essentially, it resembled others with similar content.

In numerous other petitions, craftsmen from Isfahan complained about the Uniform Dress Code Law, arguing that it was damaging their businesses. On 18 March 1929, Isfahan Municipality issued an announcement addressing these concerns.[35] The announcement encouraged the residents of Isfahan to comply with the law and urged them to consider using domestically produced fabrics when making clothing, rather than purchasing expensive imported fabrics. It specifically highlighted the affordability of locally produced jersey (*keshbāf*) and canvas (*karbās*), suggesting that their use would not only support weavers and textile producers in Isfahan and other parts of the country but would also encourage other workers. It was envisioned that the revival of this craft, which had declined due to neglect, would result in economic benefits. These benefits were expected to be shared by the 'country's servants' (*ʿabid-e mamlekat*), referring to those who were dedicated to the nation's well-being and actively participated in its prosperity and challenges.

Nevertheless, people turned to imported goods or modern factories for trousers, shirts, overcoats and hats. In an undated petition addressed to Reza Shah, most likely from September 1929, craftsmen from Isfahan protested the Uniform Dress Code Law, on the grounds that it damaged their business, which had raised concern both at local and central levels.[36] On 23 September, Prime Minister Mehdi Qoli Hedayat responded to this petition by urging them to produce more attractive goods that could also be used for everyday clothing (*lebās-e ma'mūl*).[37]

In October 1931, yet another petition requested that the Majles encourage the use of domestic fabrics:

> As a humble servant, I am neither a shroud-seller nor a canvas-seller, and I am presenting this [petition] solely to assist the unemployed and the impoverished. How long must we persist in clothing our deceased in foreign fabrics? . . . Instead of sacred prayers, one finds Jewish or foreign words on the shroud; for instance, 'no. 17 from Manchester' . . . While we are alive, we do not wear clothes of the homeland [*lebās-e vatan*] and use foreign shoes. At the very least, let our deceased be buried in Iranian fabrics.[38]

Up to the late 1920s, the government had not yet adopted the factory system. However, driven by a strong desire to transform Iran into a self-reliant country, the Pahlavi elites firmly believed that 'they had to create a social and technological infrastructure from scratch'.[39] Consequently, large-scale industrialization became a cornerstone of state economic policies throughout the 1930s, further exacerbating the concerns of craftsmen, petty shop owners and traders. An early expression of this concern can be identified in a petition sent by cigarette sellers to the Majles in March 1932, protesting 'the news' regarding the construction of a cigarette-rolling factory:

> We, the members of the cigarette-selling guild, who have endured numerous hardships in the past, have come across news in the newspapers regarding the importation of rolling machines by certain traders in our industry, along with other individuals. These machines have a daily production capacity equivalent to that of a hundred workers, and they have not yet reached full operation. As a result, all the workers in our profession are in a state of deprivation, along with their families. We humbly implore your highness to extend your benevolence to the livelihoods of these few thousand workers, ensuring that they do not plunge into misery and destitution along with their families.[40]

While the process of industrialization began to affect various handicraft producers across Iran, within Isfahan's textile industry, the Vatan Factory became a focal point of concern for local craftsmen. The factory was initially established by Mirza Fazlollah Khan (Ata al-Molk) Dehesh, an entrepreneur from Isfahan, around 1921. However, the factory's actual production did not commence until 1925. Due to financial constraints, Dehesh eventually formed a joint venture with Haj Mohammad Hossein Kazeruni, a prominent merchant from Isfahan.[41] However, during the course of their partnership, disputes arose between the two businessmen, leading to a lawsuit filed in court. As a result, Dehesh sold his share of the factory to Kazeruni. Subsequently, the Vatan Factory became so closely associated with the latter that it was often referred to in various sources as the 'Kazeruni Factory'. Shortly thereafter, the factory expanded its presence, opening retail stores in cities such as Tehran, Shiraz, Mashhad and Rasht.

The concept of establishing such a factory can be traced back to efforts in the late nineteenth century that aimed to counter textile imports. In 1899, the Islamiyeh or Islam Company (Sherkat-e Eslamiyyeh) was founded as 'a rare collaborative venture on the part of different Isfahanis to promote the manufacture and use of local textiles, as opposed to foreign imports'.[42] Kazeruni, who was the company's president, played a significant role in this endeavour. Other notable founding members included Massoud Mirza Zell al-Soltan, who served as the governor of Isfahan from 1872 to 1907, and prominent ulema, such as Haj Aqa Nurollah Esfahani.

From the beginning, the Vatan Factory enjoyed the state's support. This support was so pronounced that Reza Khan, then known as 'Sardar-e Sepah' (Commander-in-Chief), personally intervened between Dehesh and Kazeruni in order to mediate and resolve their dispute, and 'to reassure Kazeruni of the future of this factory', he 'placed a substantial order with the factory for army uniforms'.[43] Moreover, in June 1929, *Akhgar*, a local newspaper in Isfahan, reported that Seyyed Yaqub, a Majles deputy, had proposed the promotion of domestic manufacturing, with a specific emphasis on textiles produced by the Vatan Factory.[44] Again, on 30 January 1930, it reported that the factory had been rescued from bankruptcy by government support.[45] In November 1933, the Isfahan Municipality also placed an order for sportswear that further bolstered the Vatan Factory's operations.[46]

Furthermore, the Vatan Factory benefitted significantly from the Uniform Dress Code Law, as people began to purchase the mandatory clothing in compliance with its regulations. In 1935, when the government decreed that schoolchildren and the Ministry of Education's employees had to wear uniforms, the factory secured orders for these garments.[47] These examples, along with similar cases, underscored the state's overt and continuing support for the Vatan Factory. At the same time, this support generated discontent among craftsmen, particularly in Isfahan.

According to *Akhgar*, as early as February 1929, the weavers of Tehran protested against the Vatan Factory.[48] The newspaper also mentioned that the weavers of Yazd had lost their means of livelihood due to the expansion of textile factories. Moreover, on 17 February, it published the following statements of some Majles deputies, which conveyed their discontent:

> A distressing chaos and uproar have arisen among the impoverished workers of Yazd and Kashan. This turmoil stems from the inability of the Kazeruni Factory to compete effectively against foreign factories, forcing it into competition with manufacturers from Yazd, Kerman and other regions . . . Other deputies also have expressed their dissatisfaction, noting that despite receiving three hundred tomans a month, they could not afford Kazeruni's clothing. They instead opt for foreign worsted, which they can use for up to ten years, costing them two tomans per meter. In contrast, Kazeruni's domestic *barak* [a kind of thick fabric made

of camel's hair] and worsted cost 18 tomans and barely last for a single winter season.[49]

In a petition sent to the Majles on 29 March 1930, the *barak* weavers in Isfahan aired their grievances against the Vatan Factory. They contended that the factory was responsible for their dire circumstances and impoverishment and appealed for the following:

> Therefore, it is incumbent upon the government, other authorities and especially the esteemed deputies of the Majles to equally consider the interests of guildsmen and industrialists. Their sole concern should be the welfare of our country and the development of our guilds, without discrimination against any individual, since all members of the society share the same rights. A labourer and a millionaire are the same. We, the *barak* weavers of Sedeh [now Khomeini Shahr, Isfahan province], number over ten thousand people. We secured a contract to produce overcoats for the armed forces in southern Iran and finished these garments with our sweat and toil. Each unit of our finished products costs the state three tomans and has a lifespan of three years. In contrast, the Vatan Factory, which obtained the same contract last year, produced each unit for three tomans and a fraction, with a duration of usability of only two years. As your humble servants, we invite the qualified individuals to confirm the durability of our products, which last for three years, compared to those from the Vatan Factory, lasting only two. Furthermore, since the ultimate objective of the authorities is to promote domestic goods, it is worth considering that we are ten thousand residents of this homeland, while the owner of the Vatan Factory is only one individual... Ultimately, the peaceful resolution lies within your esteemed presence, and may Allah extend your fortunes.[50]

Unlike the craftsmen's previous petitions, which drew attention to the detrimental impact of imports on the country's economic development, those launched against the Vatan Factory could not present such a compelling argument. In another collective petition sent to the governor of Isfahan in February 1934, the cloak makers of Isfahan voiced similar grievances about their craft:

> Following the decline of cloak-weaving, we engaged in fabric-weaving under the command of His Excellency, the Most Powerful Shah of Shahs, and Our Beloved Father, whose sovereignty may Allah perpetuate. However, since foreign fabrics are sold at relatively lower prices, our own fabrics suffered wear and tear, piled up and became unsellable. Consequently, we found ourselves in overwhelming hardship and destitution. Ultimately, we were compelled to sell our products at a loss. When we conveyed our plight to His Most Glorious Excellency, the Source of Light, we were advised to turn to your esteemed office. Thus, we humbly beseech you to consider the establishment of an institution where we can receive guidance from qualified instructors. This would prevent future unemployment and the necessity of selling our products at a loss. Alternatively, you could issue a decree to the

> esteemed offices of the army and the police, urging them to purchase certain portions of their required clothing from us. This would enable us, your devout subjects, to earn our livelihood. At present, they exclusively procure their clothing from the Kazeruni Factory, while we, a group of helpless craftsmen, struggle to find buyers for our products. Moreover, to enhance the quality of our goods, it would be feasible to establish a company that could import machinery to aid in fabric production. We implore you not to withhold your assistance from your praying subjects.[51]

Notably, the words expressing complaints about the privileges granted to the Vatan Factory were deliberately blacked out, likely within the governor's office, making them barely legible. This suggests that the factory enjoyed the protection of local authorities. Similarly, in 1931, the striking workers of the factory submitted a petition addressed to Reza Shah. In it, they complained that local authorities paid little attention to their grievances regarding Mirza Jafar Kazeruni, the son of Haj Mohammad Hossein Kazeruni, who allegedly resorted to bribery to achieve his objectives.[52] In fact, the conflict between these disgruntled craftsmen/labourers and the Vatan Factory's owners was rooted in the tension between promoting the economic growth of large-scale industrialization and maintaining the working classes' source of bread.

Conclusion

This chapter has attempted to understand how the Iranian government's industrial and other economic policies during the 1920s and 1930s affected Iranian craftsmen, as reflected primarily in their petitions. These petitions offer a unique glimpse of these craftsmen's voices. However, it is important to reiterate that Iran's transition to the factory system in the textile industry, as well as other sectors, except for oil, was a gradual and prolonged process and most craft industries managed to survive Reza Shah's reign and beyond.

Reports on the number of factories in the early 1940s vary, but they certainly did not exceed a few hundred.[53] Additionally, a significant percentage of the labour force still worked outside of these factories at that time. Nonetheless, from the 1930s onwards, those specializing in handicrafts increasingly faced the mechanization and division of their labour among less skilled workers. Consequently, those who depended on handicrafts to earn their bread, particularly in urban areas, described themselves as abandoned, devastated and impoverished. The loss of this work also eroded self-esteem and impacted social relationships. As their 'traditional' products were clearly falling out of fashion, craftsmen and artisans resented the fact that state industrialization policies were working against their interests. This turn of events estranged them from the government.

One of my main objectives in this chapter has been to illustrate the striking contrast between the craftsmen's success in countering the influx of imports during the 1920s and their failure to do so in response to modern large-scale factories during the 1930s. Here, the crux of the matter was that the religio-nationalist discourse employed against foreign goods could not be effectively applied to the country's own factories. Moreover, the anti-import campaign was bolstered by a broad alliance of craftsmen, merchants, ulema and intellectuals who regarded the promotion of domestic manufactures as a precondition for Iran's independence and progress. However, the overarching aspiration of this alliance was to propel Iran towards self-sustaining growth and eliminate the dependency on foreign products by any means possible. Hence, advocating for local craft industries and their social milieu found support among many politicians, ulema and intellectuals when the progress of large-scale industrialization was minimal. Conversely, such support became less tenable once the factory system's benefits became achievable on a wider geographic scale. Thus, large-scale industrialization served the underlying purpose of this alliance.

In general, I have not intended to portray Iranian craftsmen as mere victims, nor am I suggesting that we should interpret their petitions literally. On the contrary, a critical approach to these petitions is necessary, for although they are invaluable for comprehending the craftsmen's world and their responses to socio-economic change, they can sometimes be misleading if we take them at face value. Just like other petitioners, craftsmen primarily aimed to seek redress for their grievances rather than providing an objective account of the facts. In order to ensure the desired responses to their cases, they might use dissimulation and even distort some details. Nevertheless, these discourses still offer significant insights into their circumstances and experiences. In addition, the abundancy of this documentation offers a unique source and fertile ground for a more comprehensive understanding of the interaction between craftsmen and others working in the handicraft sector and the process of industrialization during the 1920s–30s. These documents can also answer questions that have not been sufficiently addressed in the extant historiography. Finally, it is my view that a careful analysis in these petitions of the experiences of Iranians engaged in various craft industries and living in diverse regions of the country can enrich our knowledge and understanding of the significant socio-economic transformations that took place throughout the 1920s and 1930s – with political consequences for the decades that followed.

Notes

1 *Ruznameh-e Anjoman-e Moqaddas-e Melli-ye Esfahan* 1, no. 17 (14 Rabi al-Awwal 1325/27 April 1907): n.p. Quoted in: Abdoulmehdi Rajaei, *Esfahan az Enqelab-e Mashruteh ta Jang-e Jahani-ye Avval: Gozideh-ye Ruznamehha* (Isfahan: Daneshgah-ye Esfahan, 1386/2007), 319. The italicized quote is a line from Hafez of Shiraz: 'Tā cheh qabul oftād va cheh dar nazar ayād.'

2 Fereydun Adamiyat, *Amir Kabir va Iran* (Tehran: Kharazmi, 1362/1983), 393.

3 Ali Gheissari, *Iranian Intellectuals in the Twentieth Century* (Texas: University of Texas Press, 1998), 3.

4 Ervand Abrahamian, *Iran Between Two Revolutions* (Princeton: Princeton University Press, 1982), 59.

5 Homa Katouzian, *The Political Economy of Modern Iran: Despotism and Pseudo-Modernism, 1926–1979* (London: Macmillan, 1981), 103.

6 Lex Heerma van Voss, 'Introduction', Supplement 9: Petitions in Social History, *International Review of Social History* 46 (2001): 1.
7 Rudolf Braun, *Industrialization and Everyday Life*, trans. Sarah Hanbury Tenison (Cambridge: Cambridge University Press, 1990), 2.
8 Eric Hobsbawm, 'Peasants and Politics', *The Journal of Peasant Studies* 1, no. 1 (1973): 13.
9 See: Serhan Afacan, 'Foreign Goods, Native Consumption: Popular Reactions to Foreign Economic Domination in Iran (1921–3)', in *Iran in the Middle East: Transnational Encounters and Social History*, eds. Houchang E. Chehabi, Peyman Jafari and Maral Jefroudi (London: I.B. Tauris, 2015), 137–60.
10 Julian Bharier, *Economic Development in Iran, 1900–1970* (London: Oxford University Press, 1971), 87.
11 Massoud Karshenas, *Oil, State and Industrialization in Iran* (Cambridge: Cambridge University Press, 1990), 77.
12 Charles Issawi, ed., *The Economic History of Iran, 1800–1914* (Chicago: University of Chicago Press, 1971), 72–3.
13 Afacan, 'Foreign Goods', 154.
14 Zahra Sadeghi, *Siyasatha-ye Sanati-ye Dowran-e Reza Shah, 1304–1320* (Tehran: Khojasteh, 1388/2009), 60.
15 Library, Museum and Document Centre of the Iranian Parliament (LMDCIP), dore4-k25-j12-p31, 'Moein al-Tojjar', 8 Tir 1301 (30 June 1922). There already were similar proposals for the development of the country's industry. For example, Haj Mohammad Moein al-Tojjar Bushehri, a prominent merchant, constitutionalist and former deputy of the First and the Third Majles, submitted a petition to the Fourth Majles to this effect in mid-1922. After emphasizing the importance of getting rid of foreign goods, he proposed a law for the exemption of machines from import duties. See The National Archives, Public Record Office, Foreign Office Files (FO) 307/10158. Seyyed Hassan Taqizadeh made a similar proposal. When asked about ways to develop domestic industry, he proposed, inter alia, the abolition of import duties on machinery. See also Bharier, *Economic Development*, 176; Willem Floor, *Labor and Industry in Iran, 1850–1941* (Washington, DC: Mage Publishers, 2009), 124. However, the law ultimately passed in 1925 did not apply to many small-scale capital goods, such as sewing and knitting machines, printing and engraving equipment and so on, which, as Floor rightly observes, showed the state's bias in favour of large-scale industries.
16 Michael Zirinsky, 'Riza Shah's Abrogation of Capitulations, 1927–1928', in *The Making of Modern Iran: State and Society under Riza Shah, 1921–1941*, ed. Stephanie Cronin (London: RoutledgeCurzon, 2003), 94.
17 Ebrahim Razaqi, *Eqtesad-e Iran* (Tehran: Ney, 1367/1988), 18–19. Quoted in: Mahmoud Delfani, 'Gozareshi az Vaziyyat-e Sanaye va Moassesat-e Amuzesh-e Fanni-ye Iran dar Sal-e 1315 Shamsi', *Ganjineh-ye Asnad*, no. 7–8 (1371/1992): 65.
18 Houchang E. Chehabi, 'Staging the Emperor's New Clothes: Dress Codes and Nation-Building under Reza Shah', *Iranian Studies* 26, no. 3–4 (1993): 213.
19 Dariush Rahmanian, Gholam Reza Zarifian, Simin Fasihi and Shahram Gholami, 'Qanun-e Enhesar-e Tejarat-e Khareji-ye Iran-e 1309: Zaminehha, Ahdaf va Peyamadha', *Tarikh-e Islam va Iran* 21, no. 11 (1390/2011): 29.
20 Floor, *Labor and Industry*, 124.
21 FO 371/17909, 'Annual Report', 1933; FO 371/20052, 'Annual Report', 1935.
22 For the act's full translation, see: Laurence Paul Elwell-Sutton, 'Appendix III', in *Modern Iran* (London: George Routledge and Sons, Ltd., 1944), 213–24.

23 Elwell-Sutton, *Modern Iran*, 219.
24 For a discussion of this scholarship see Chapter 2 of this volume.
25 Hojjat Fallah Tootkar, 'Faaliyyatha-ye Ejtemaei va Siyasi-ye Asnaf va Sanatgaran az Enqelab-e Mashruteh-ye Iran ta Faraz-e Reza Shah, 1285–1304' (PhD diss., Tarbiat Modares University, 1382/2003), 33.
26 Bharier, *Economic Development*, 7.
27 Roger Owen, 'The Study of Middle Eastern Industrial History: Notes on the Interrelationship between Factories and Small-Scale Manufacturing with Special References to Lebanese Silk and Egyptian Sugar, 1900–1930', *International Journal of Middle East Studies* 16, no. 4 (1984): 476.
28 For a discussion of this period's anti-import campaign, see: Afacan, 'Foreign Goods', 137–60.
29 LMDCIP, d4/k25/j12/-p52, 'Az Taraf-e Mohammad Ali Aynehsaz beh Namayandegan-e Mohtaram-e Majles-e Moqaddas', 27 Esfand 1301 (19 March 1923). The petitions discussed in this chapter were translated by the author and used in his dissertation, if not otherwise stated: Serhan Afacan, 'State, Society, and Labour in Iran, 1906–1941: A Social History of Iranian Industrialization and Labour with Reference to the Textile Industry' (PhD diss., Leiden University, 2015).
30 LMDCIP, d4/k25/j12/p14, 'Az Taraf-e Kaffashiyan', 12 Esfand 1301 (4 March 1923).
31 Raziyeh Yousefi Nia, *Asnad-e Tejari-ye Advar-e Avval ta Panjom Majles-e Showra-ye Melli, 1285–1304* (Tehran: Ketabkhaneh, Muzeh va Markaz-e Asnad-e Majles-e Showra-ye Eslami, 1388/2009), 503.
32 LMDCIP, d6/k59/j27/p69, 'Beh Riyasat-e Majles', 29 Shahrivar 1306 (21 September 1927).
33 LMDCIP, d6/k59/j27/p69, 'Az Taraf-e Vezarat-e Keshavarz va Tejarat va Ammolmanfaeh beh Riyasat-e Majles', 4 Tir 1306 (26 June 1927).
34 LMDCIP, d7/k155/j35.1/13, 'Beh Rayis-e Mohtaram-e Majles-e Showra-ye Melli', 27 Dey 1307 (17 January 1929).
35 NLAI, 290/8508, 'Elan az Taraf-e Baladiyyeh-e Esfahan', 27 Esfand 1307 (18 March 1929).
36 NLAI, 290/8508, 'Beh Arz-e Ali Miresanad', n.d.
37 NLAI, 290/8508, 'Senf-e Ababafan-e Esfahan', 1 Mehr 1308 (23 September 1929).
38 LMDCIP, 8/7/20/3/102-Gilan, 'Mohammad Shafei Nili Darbareh-ye Kafanha', 17 Mehr 1310 (10 October 1931).
39 Floor, *Labor and Industry*, 113.
40 LMDCIP, 8/168/6, 'Az Taraf-e Sigar Forushan', 3 March 1932.
41 Habib Borjian, 'Kazeruni Family', in *Encyclopaedia Iranica Online,* accessed 26 August 2023 (print version: vol. 16, fascicle 2, 217–21), https://www.iranicaonline.org/articles/kazeruni-family.
42 Vanessa Martin, 'Aqa Najafi, Haj Aqa Nurullah, and the Emergence of Islamism in Isfahan 1889–1908', *Iranian Studies* 41, no. 2 (2008): 161.
43 Borjian, 'Kazeruni Family'.
44 *Akhgar* (19 Khordad 1308/9 June 1929). Quoted in Abdoulmehdi Rajaei, *Esfahan az Negah-e Akhgar* (Isfahan: Sazman-e Farhangi va Tafrihi-ye Shahrdari-ye Esfahan, 1393/2014), 49.
45 Rajaei, *Esfahan az Negah*, 89.
46 *Akhgar* (15 Aban 1312/6 November 1933). Quoted in: Rajaei, *Esfahan az Negah*, 125.
47 NLAI, 297/6434, 'Az Taraf-e Vezarat-e Amuzesh va Parvaresh va Mowqufat-e Dini va Honarha-ye Ziba beh Edareh-ye Bazresi', 12 Mehr 1314 (5 October 1935).

48 *Akhgar* (18 Bahman 1307/7 February 1929). Quoted in: Rajaei, *Esfahan az Negah*, 125.
49 Rajaei, *Esfahan az Negah*, 32. See also NLAI, 291/954, 'Az Taraf-e Nahiyyeh-ye Nohom-e Edareh-ye Amar va Savabeq beh Farmandar-e Esfahan', 25 Esfand 1309 (16 March 1931). The Ninth District of the Directory of Statistics and Records concluded that the Vatan Factory unjustly charged higher prices because it was the only supplier of the necessary clothes in the region.
50 LMDCIP, d7/k102/j14.2/p89, 'Beh Majles-e Bashokuh', 9 Farvardin 1309 (29 March 1930).
51 NLAI, 291/2480, 'Beh Farmandar-e Mohtaram-e Esfahan', 6 Esfand 1312 (25 February 1934).
52 Serhan Afacan, 'Revisiting Labor Activism in Iran: Some Notes on the Vatan Factory Strike in 1931', *International Labor and Working-Class History (ILWCH)* 93 (2018): 213.
53 Karshenas, *Oil, State and Industrialization*, 77.

Bibliography

Archives

Library, Museum and Document Center of the Iranian Parliament
National Library and Archives of Iran
The National Archives, London

Periodicals

Akhgar
Ruznāmeh-e Anjoman-e Moqaddas-e Melli-ye Esfahān

Secondary sources

Abrahamian, Ervand. *Iran Between Two Revolutions*. Princeton: Princeton University Press, 1982.

Adamiyat, Fereydun. *Amir Kabir va Irān*. Tehran: Kharazmi, 1362 (1983).

Afacan, Serhan. 'Foreign Goods, Native Consumption: Popular Reactions to Foreign Economic Domination in Iran (1921–3)'. In *Iran in the Middle East: Transnational Encounters and Social History*, edited by Houchang E. Chehabi, Peyman Jafari and Maral Jefroudi, 137–60. London: I.B. Tauris, 2015.

Afacan, Serhan. 'Revisiting Labor Activism in Iran: Some Notes on the Vatan Factory Strike in 1931'. *International Labor and Working-Class History (ILWCH)* 93 (2018): 201–20.

Afacan, Serhan. 'State, Society, and Labour in Iran, 1906–1941: A Social History of Iranian Industrialization and Labour with Reference to the Textile Industry'. PhD diss., Leiden University, 2015.

Bharier, Julian. *Economic Development in Iran, 1900–1970*. London: Oxford University Press, 1971.

Borjian, Habib. 'Kāzeruni Family'. In *Encyclopaedia Iranica Online*. Accessed 26 August 2023 (print version: vol. 16, fascicle 2, 217–21). https://www.iranicaonline.org/articles/kazeruni-family.

Braun, Rudolf. *Industrialization and Everyday Life*. Translated by Sarah Hanbury Tenison. Cambridge: Cambridge University Press, 1990.

Chehabi, Houchang E. 'Staging the Emperor's New Clothes: Dress Codes and Nation-Building under Reza Shah'. *Iranian Studies* 26, no. 3–4 (1993): 209–33.

Delfani, Mahmoud. 'Gozāreshi az Vazʿiyyat-e Sanāyeʿ va Moʿassesāt-e Āmuzesh-e Fanni-ye Irān dar Sāl-e 1315 Shamsi'. *Ganjineh-ye Asnad*, no. 7–8 (1371/1992): 64–94.

Elwell-Sutton, Laurence Paul. *Modern Iran*. London: George Routledge and Sons, Ltd., 1944.

Floor, Willem. *Labor and Industry in Iran, 1850–1941*. Washington, DC: Mage Publishers, 2009.

Gheissari, Ali. *Iranian Intellectuals in the Twentieth Century*. Texas: University of Texas Press, 1998.

Hobsbawm, Eric. 'Peasants and Politics'. *The Journal of Peasant Studies* 1, no. 1 (1973): 3–22.

Issawi, Charles, ed. *The Economic History of Iran, 1800–1914*. Chicago: University of Chicago Press, 1971.

Karshenas, Massoud. *Oil, State and Industrialization in Iran*. Cambridge: Cambridge University Press, 1990.

Katouzian, Homa. *The Political Economy of Modern Iran: Despotism and Pseudo-Modernism, 1926–1979*. London: Macmillan, 1981.

Martin, Vanessa. 'Aqa Najafi, Haj Aqa Nurullah, and the Emergence of Islamism in Isfahan 1889–1908'. *Iranian Studies* 41, no. 2 (2008): 155–72.

Owen, Roger. 'The Study of Middle Eastern Industrial History: Notes on the Interrelationship between Factories and Small-Scale Manufacturing with Special References to Lebanese Silk and Egyptian Sugar, 1900–1930'. *International Journal of Middle East Studies* 16, no. 4 (1984): 475–87.

Rahmanian, Dariush, Gholam Reza Zarifian, Simin Fasihi, and Shahram Gholami. 'Qānun-e Enhesār-e Tejārat-e Khāreji-ye Irān-e 1309: Zaminehhā, Ahdāf va Peyāmadhā'. *Tarikh-e Islam va Iran* 21, no. 11 (1390/2011): 25–55.

Rajaei, Abdoulmehdi. *Esfahān az Enqelāb-e Mashruteh ta Jang-e Jahāni-ye Avval: Gozideh-ye Ruznāmehhā*. Isfahan: Daneshgah-ye Esfahan, 1386 (2007).

Rajaei, Abdoulmehdi. *Esfahan az Negāh-e Akhgar*. Isfahan: Sazman-e Farhangi va Tafrihi-ye Shahrdari-ye Esfahan, 1393 (2014).

Razaqi, Ebrahim. *Eqtesād-e Irān*. Tehran: Ney, 1367 (1988).

Sadeghi, Zahra. *Siyāsathā-ye Sanʿati-ye Dowrān-e Rezā Shāh, 1304–1320*. Tehran: Khojasteh, 1388 (2009).

Tootkar, Hojjat Fallah. 'Faʿāliyyathā-ye Ejtemāʿi va Siyāsi-ye Asnāf va Sanʿatgarān az Enqelāb-e Mashruteh-ye Irān tā Farāz-e Rezā Shāh, 1285–1304'. PhD diss., Tarbiat Modares University, 1382 (2003).

van Voss, Lex Heerma. 'Introduction'. Supplement 9: Petitions in Social History, *International Review of Social History* 46 (2001): 1–10.

Yousefi Nia, Raziyeh. *Asnād-e Tejāri-ye Advār-e Avval tā Panjom Majles-e Showra-ye Melli, 1285–1304*. Tehran: Ketabkhaneh, Muzeh va Markaz-e Asnad-e Majles-e Showra-ye Eslami, 1388 (2009).

Zirinsky, Michael. 'Riza Shah's Abrogation of Capitulations, 1927–1928'. In *The Making of Modern Iran: State and Society under Riza Shah, 1921–1941*, edited by Stephanie Cronin, 81–98. London: RoutledgeCurzon, 2003.

Part III

Economic development and the state

6

Iran's quest for economic autonomy

Foreign trade, banking, companies and industry, 1921–46

Mary Yoshinari

Introduction

This chapter will discuss the emergence and growth of Iran's foreign trade and banking systems, companies and industry. These four fundamental and interrelated sectors formed the basis of the Iranian modern economy. Breaking with the periodization of Reza Shah's reign (1925–41), this chapter discusses Iran's pursuit of economic independence (1921–46), which was activated by the signing of the Treaty of Friendship with Soviet Russia on 26 February 1921.[1] The treaty's annulment of the Capitulations (special legal and economic privileges granted to Imperial Russia in 1828 after Iran's defeat) established a new basis for bilateral commercial relations. Equally if not more important, this treaty empowered the Fourth Majles (National Consultative Assembly or Iranian Parliament) to reject the 1919 Anglo-Persian Agreement in June 1921, which would have relegated Iran to a British protectorate.[2] Thereafter, through diplomatic battles with the British, Iran finally achieved autonomy in its banking operations and continued to pressure the Soviets for an equitable trade balance. This chapter concludes with 1946, when Iran reclaimed its territorial sovereignty from the Soviet Union and thus ended the Allied occupation.

Monopolization of foreign trade

During the 1920s, a newly independent Iran joined a complex system of interwar transnational trade. First and foremost, the Iranian government aimed to correct its unequal trade balance with the Soviet Union and Great Britain; however, both were reluctant to cede their spheres of influence in the northern and southern regions of the country. From 1921 until 1930, Great Britain remained Iran's number one trading partner.[3] The Soviet Union held the number two position from 1924 onwards, finally overtaking the British in 1931. The Soviets maintained this ranking until they were usurped by the Germans in 1938. They had encouraged German trade at the expense of the British until confronted by the rise of Nazi expansionism within Iran.

From the outset, the Iranians sought profitable trade with the Soviets while resisting the latter's commercial monopolization of the country. Thus, Iranian merchants were granted the right to trade at the Nizhny Novgorod and Baku fairs in 1922.[4] At the first fair, they 'concluded five contracts with major Soviet trade organizations'.[5] Besides eighty-four registered merchants, many more sold nearly 110,000 pounds of leather, wool, rice, cotton, dried fruits, nuts and other goods. At the second fair, 138,856 pounds of Iranian goods were exported, and 69,594 pounds of Soviet imports were brought back to Iran.[6] As a result, Iran's trade balance with the Soviet Union was quite favourable in 1923/4. According to 1914 values, Iranian exports amounted to 18,504,000 roubles versus 7,506,000 roubles of Soviet imports crossing their common borders.[7]

On the other hand, negotiations for a new trade treaty were unresolved until 1927. Beyond the economic realpolitik of both countries, the Soviets aspired to increase their political influence in Iran through closer commercial ties with some big Iranian merchants and other social classes. Many Soviet officials adhered to the Marxist belief that the rise of Iran's bourgeoisie would lead to a revolution of the underclasses. Hence, the Soviet mixed companies were created and 'tasked with the mission of eliminating foreign competition in northern Iran and expanding into the central and southern regions of the country'.[8] However, the hegemonic and unfair trading practices of these Soviet organizations ultimately backfired, as the Iranians had 'started to think about the creation of monopolistic agencies' in the interests of 'self-preservation'.[9]

Iran achieved a trade surplus in the export of goods with the Soviet Union in 1934/5, and Germany in 1931/2 and 1933/4, while maintaining mostly positive balances with the United States, Iraq and Turkey from 1926 to 1936.[10] Although trade with the USSR was geographically inevitable, the Iranians strove to diversify their commercial links with other countries, especially during disputes with the Soviets. Iran also favoured 'the adoption of autonomous customs tariffs' in order to protect new domestic industries from foreign competition.[11] As a result, in May 1928, the Sixth Majles approved 'special customs agreements with foreign governments',[12] and the Iranian government cancelled its 'unequal treaties' with the United States, France and Great Britain, among others.[13] Soon, new agreements were signed with these countries, as well as Germany and Italy.[14]

The following year, however, Iran and the Soviet Union signed a new customs convention with minimal tariff rates.[15] Then, in February 1930, the Soviet trade fairs were cancelled.[16] These disappointing developments, as well as the Soviet Union's 'refusal to adhere to the principal of the balance of trade' in the 1927 Trade Treaty,[17] prompted the Iranian government to monopolize all foreign trade on 25 February 1931,[18] thereby securing 'the right to import and export all natural and industrial products' and determine their amounts. On 11 March, a supplementary law was approved by the Eighth Majles, stating that the importation of foreign goods was conditional upon the exportation of Iranian products of equal value.[19]

Despite its imperfections and subsequent amendments,[20] Iran's foreign trade monopoly had a profound effect on the shape of the Iranian national economy. Ten days after ratifying the latest commercial agreement with the Soviet Union, the Eighth Majles approved the declaration of lump sugar and sugar to be 'domestic manufactures' on 10 March 1932.[21] Consequently, the Iranian government monopolized these commodities, as well as matches, and their net revenues became 'public profits of the country'. Iran's foreign trade monopoly also caused the dissolution of the Soviet Union's mixed companies that imported sugar and other goods, namely Perssakhr and Sharq, and even its new large transnational commercial organization, Vostgostorg.

Throughout the interwar period, Iran utilized Soviet territory as a transit corridor for trade with Germany and other Western countries. The Iranian government imported machinery for the new domestic factories, mostly from Germany and Czechoslovakia, as well as contingents of modern consumer goods that did not threaten these nascent industries, for example, motor vehicles, bicycles, cameras, films, fedoras, umbrellas, raincoats and electric appliances. Moreover, Iran switched to imports of Japanese cotton textiles and Belgian lump and powdered sugar during the 1932/3 boycott of Soviet goods. As a result, the Soviet Union's exports of these commodities to Iran fell to 56 per cent of Japan's and about 77 per cent of Belgium's in 1933/4.[22]

The signing of 1935–6 bilateral clearing agreements increased Iran's trade with Germany, thereby enabling the Trans-Iranian Railway's completion on 19 August 1938.[23] By 1941, German imports to Iran had reached 47.87 per cent and 'Iranian exports to Germany stood at 42.09 per cent'.[24] However, after the Allied invasion of August–September 1941, Great Britain and the Soviet Union restricted, regulated and requisitioned Iran's foreign trade. As a consequence, Iran was forced to cut all economic ties with Germany. Finally, on 30 September and 1 October 1944, the Fourteenth Majles passed legislation that reinstated Iran's foreign trade monopoly.[25] In a speech delivered on 30 March 1946, Prime Minister Qavam declared that Iran's foreign trade monopoly was 'the foundation' of state economic policy for the country's revival.[26]

Taxation, budgets and banks

The Iranian government took significant steps to establish autonomy, solvency and stability with regard to the country's finances during the interwar period. The creation of national banking institutions, the conservation of foreign exchange for state reserves and industrialization, the prevention of capital flight and the stabilization of the rial were among the most important objectives to be realized. As stipulated in the Friendship Treaty, the Soviet government transferred the assets of the Discount and Loans Bank of Persia (Banque d'Escompte et Prêts de Perse or Bank-e Esteqrazi), which formerly had belonged to Imperial Russia, to Iran's Ministry of Finance in September 1922. These assets became 'the Bank of Iran', a prototype for the National Bank (Bank-e Melli), and they provided capital for the founding of the Bank of Agriculture and Industry (Bank-e Falahat va Sanat).

Concurrently, the first American mission led by Arthur Chester Millspaugh was tasked with the modernization of Iran's state finances and taxation system during the 1922–6 period.[27] One important outcome was a bill 'embodying a permanent program of road construction and maintenance, and proposing new taxes to carry out the program'.[28] Thus, the Fifth Majles approved the construction and repair of Iran's 'essential roads' in 1925.[29] Then, on 28 September 1926, the Sixth Majles ratified the Iranian government's policy programme for the founding of the country's state and agricultural banks from the revenues of the gradual sale of crown lands.[30] Subsequently, on 5 May 1927, the same Majles deputies authorized the founding of the National Bank of Iran 'for the advancement of commercial, farming, agricultural and industrial affairs'.[31]

By the end of 1929, all of the Iranian government's accounts had been transferred from Britain's Imperial Bank of Persia to Iran's National Bank.[32] In spite of the Great Depression of 1929–33, the Iranians pushed ahead with their plans for currency modernization.[33] Iran's Minister of Court Abdol Hossein Teymurtash agreed to compensate the Imperial Bank with a payment of £200,000 for the 'sole right of note issue', which was ceded to the National Bank on 20 March 1931. Thereafter, the Eighth Majles approved the issuance of 340 million rials of banknotes in 5, 10, 20, 50, 100 and 500 denominations on 21 March 1932.[34] After some deliberation, the Iranian government wisely decided to remain on the silver standard instead of switching to gold.[35]

In addition to the National Bank, a new financial institution was required for further economic development. Consequently, on 11 June 1933, the Ninth Majles authorized the Bank of Agriculture and Industry's establishment with 20 million rials of capital, derived from 'all of the Bank of Iran's movable and immovable property, demands, et cetera and the current assets of the National Bank of Iran's Agricultural Branch'.[36] Subsequently, the Majles approved the Bank of Agriculture and Industry's annual loan of £600,000 from the National Reserve for five years, which was to be held in a special fund for credit to assist entrepreneurs with the 'expansion, completion and transformation' of their factories.[37] In total, the bank was to grant 350 million rials in loans for industrial and agricultural assistance over a ten-year period.[38]

During the spring and summer of 1932, the Iranian government earmarked export-derived foreign exchange for the purchase of imports, industrialization and 'an exchange rate stabilization reserve',[39] as well as setting the official exchange rate to stabilize the rial and attempting to curtail capital flight.[40] Furthermore, in 1935/6, the Iranian government monopolized principal exports and negotiated barter agreements with various countries in order to increase foreign exchange reserves for railway construction, the expansion of industry and ports and military orders – all hampered by the rial's recent fall in value.[41] Supplementary legislation continued to address these issues in 1936–8.[42] Soon afterwards, the Trans-Iranian Railway was completed at a total cost of approximately 2.4 billion rials or 'nearly £30 million'.[43]

Throughout the 1930s, Iran's annual budgets also began to rapidly expand. The Soviets noted that the Iranian government's spending for 'national-economic requirements' rose from 36 per cent/361.8 million rials in 1934/5 to 49 per cent/657.7 million rials in 1935/6 and 48 per cent/707.4 million rials in 1936/7.[44] Although Iran's oil revenues were excluded from these budgets, they were substantially increased – dating back to 1931/2 – by the controversial 1933 Agreement with the Anglo-Iranian Oil Company

(AIOC).[45] Moreover, Iran's government-supported corporations contributed 'nearly 65 per cent of all state revenues' in 'taxes and trade income' in 1938/9.[46] By 1940, Iran also had four domestic financial institutions: the Mortgage Bank, the National Bank, the Bank of Agriculture and Trades and Crafts and Sepah Bank.[47]

The outbreak of the Second World War caused Iranian food prices to rise dramatically in 1939–43.[48] Inflation was exacerbated by the printing of 1.5 billion rials for Allied expenditures and Iran's purchase of grain and other staples for domestic consumption in 1942.[49] Due to a shortfall in revenues, the Iranian government obtained a $12 million advance payment from AIOC and a loan from the National Bank in 1943.[50] Millspaugh's taxation reform did not generate sufficient revenue in 1944/5, either.[51] The National Bank's governor Abol Hassan Ebtehaj concluded that Millspaugh also had not used Iran's import quotas efficiently – which were considered to be the worst in the region.[52] Nonetheless, days after Iran's territorial integrity had been restored with the final exit of Soviet troops, the Bank of Industry and Mining (Bank-e Sanat va Madan) was registered with 2.5 billion rials of fully paid-up capital on 4 June 1946.[53]

Patterns of companies' growth

On 14 February 1925, the regulations for joint-stock (*sahāmi*), limited liability (*zamānati*) and limited partnership (*mokhtalet*) companies, and cooperatives (*ta'āvani*), were ratified in the Law of Commerce.[54] Thereafter, in 1931/2, all Iranian and foreign firms – established and headquartered in Iran – were encouraged to

Table 6.1 Iranian Companies and Their Statistics, 1940/1

Company Type	English Equivalent	Total (March 1941)	Total Capital (Rials)
Sherkat-e sahāmi	Joint-stock company (corporation)	612	1,512,150,000
Sherkat-e nesbi	Proportional liability partnership	556	198,300,000
Sherkat-e tazamoni	General partnership	268	147,290,000
Sherkat bā mas'uliyat-e mahdud	Limited liability company	424	104,790,000
Sherkat-e mokhtālet-e gheyr-e sahāmi	Limited partnership	See below	See below
Sherkat-e mokhtālet-e sahāmi	Limited joint-stock partnership	See below	See below
Sherkat-e ta'āvoni-ye towlid va masraf	Manufacturing and consumer cooperative	13 (includes two above categories)	5,740,000 (includes two above categories)

Source: 'Statistique des sociétés enregistrées en 1319 (1940–1941)', *Bulletin de la Banque Mellié Iran*, no. 61 (September–October 1942), 258–64.

register and pay tariffs corresponding to the amount of capital invested.[55] Then, on 3 May 1932, the Eighth Majles approved an updated version of this law,[56] defining seven types of firms (shown in Table 6.1), which have existed until the present day. By 1936/7, joint-stock companies had become the predominant form of commercial organization, which was partly reflective of the government's role in foreign trade, industry and agriculture. Moreover, general partnerships, relative to their lesser number, amassed a significant amount of capital. There also was a geographical divide: proportional liability partnerships were more numerous in the provinces, whereas limited liability companies proliferated in Tehran.[57]

The commercial laws encouraged a variety of business partnerships, for example, the Qomash Corporation, Shams Azar Proportional Liability Partnership and Rabi va Sherka General Partnership, which were all founded during the 1930s.[58] As shown in Figure 6.1, the total capital invested in Iranian companies had crossed the 1.4 billion rial threshold between April 1936 and March 1937. By March 1941, it had almost reached the 2 billion rial mark, and there were 1,873 companies.[59] Additional data from the same source as Figure 6.1 illustrates that the total capital of Tehran companies nearly doubled between April 1936 and March 1937, then briefly contracted before rebounding between April 1938 and March 1941 to surpass 1 billion rials. Conversely, provincial companies grew more gradually, yet steadily, approaching 1 billion (913.51 million) rials of capital by March 1941.

What explains this dramatic spike and fallback? Figure 6.2 partly answers this question. Between April 1936 and March 1937, the capital of Tehran's joint-stock companies increased by about 75 per cent, reaching 873.95 million rials – 91 per cent of the share for all companies in this city – and almost 59 per cent for all companies in Iran. Furthermore, joint-stock companies continued to proliferate, amounting to nearly a third (32.7 per cent) of the total number by March 1941. Significantly, the

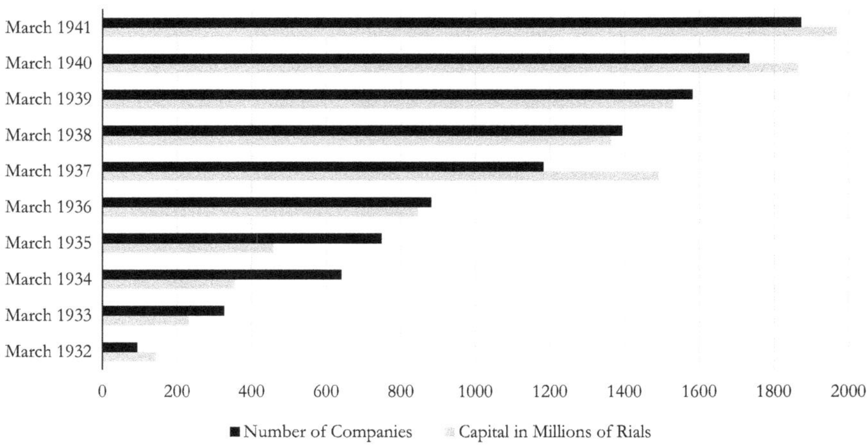

Figure 6.1 All registered companies in Iran, 1932–41. *Source*: 'Statistique des sociétés enregistrées en 1319 (1940–1941)', *Bulletin de la Banque Mellié Iran*, no. 61 (September–October 1942), 256.

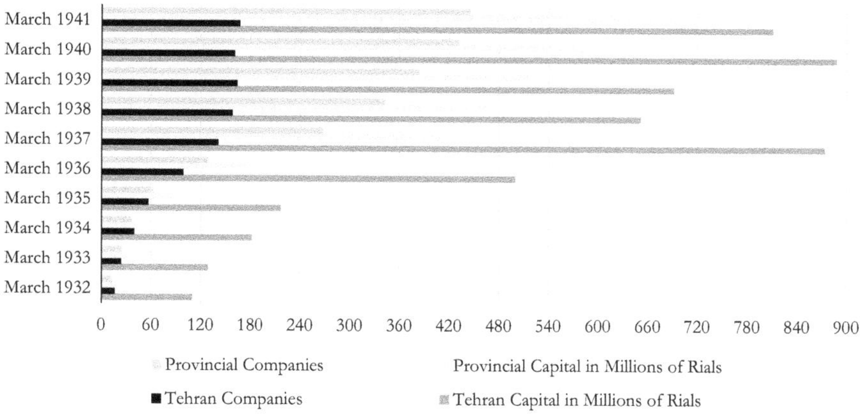

Figure 6.2 Registered joint-stock companies in provinces and Tehran, 1932–41. *Source:* 'Statistique des sociétés enregistrées en 1319 (1940–1941)', *Bulletin de la Banque Mellié Iran*, no. 61 (September–October 1942), 258.

combined capital of these corporations accounted for more than three quarters (76.8 per cent) of the total amount for all Iranian companies. Thus, much of Iran's domestic capital was concentrated in the joint-stock companies, and those in the provinces increasingly claimed a greater share – which was nearly equal to their counterparts in Tehran by March 1941.

Thanks to AIOC and the Imperial Bank, Britain's investment capital in Iran was nearly eight times that of all other countries combined, totalling £19.5 million by March 1936.[60] The British had founded twenty-eight companies, the Germans had nine and the Soviets had six, including Iransovtrans (formerly Persbiuro), Gostrakh and Intourist for shipping, its insurance and tourism, respectively, as well as Iransovneft (formerly Persazneft) for petroleum products.[61] From 1933 onwards, no further Soviet companies were registered, and by autumn 1936, the mixed company for cotton gins, Iransovkhlopok (formerly Perskhlopok), was dissolved, and the capital of shipping firm Iransovtrans (later Soviranturktorg) was increased by 275,000 rials.[62] Conversely, Rusiranbank (formerly Ruspersbank) was classified as an Iranian joint-stock company, having been founded and headquartered in Tehran.[63] Presumably, this was also true of the fisheries company, Iranryba (formerly Persryba), which was jointly run by the Iranians and the Soviets.

On 28 April 1940, the Twelfth Majles approved the transfer of Iran's semi-state monopolies and joint-stock companies to the Ministry of Finance's new 'Economic Section'.[64] Later in the year, the Sakhteman Consortium and the Rahparvar Corporation for construction and public works were registered with a total of 7 million rials of fully paid-up capital.[65] Concurrently, the Iranian government was planning to build an enormous stock exchange complex in Tehran,[66] which was interrupted by the Allied invasion. Afterwards, as Iran's economy returned to regular operations in 1946, general merchants, exporters, importers, building contractors and other entrepreneurs established companies. One of the largest was a joint-stock distributor of local textile factory products, North Textile Distributor (Pakhsheh-ye Mansujat-e Shomal)

Company Limited, which was registered with 40 million rials of fully paid-up capital in Tehran.[67]

State and private industry

In the early 1920s, new laws began to encourage the growth of domestic industry in Iran. For instance, the Khoei Brothers were accorded tax exemptions and other incentives for their match factory in Tabriz.[68] Moreover, in 1925, machinery imports were exempted from customs duties for two years, and Iranian merchants were authorized to establish and operate 'every type of factory'.[69] Textile and yarn-spinning factories in Isfahan and Tehran also were granted loans in the country's annual budgets in the late 1920s.[70] Thanks to state legislation – and the national banks, foreign trade monopoly and corporations – by 1936, 'industrial centers . . . [were] arising in the country, where, 10-15 years ago, there had been no trace', as noted by the Soviets.[71]

Concurrently, a significant number of factories and workshops – mostly private sector enterprises – had been founded or revived in forty Iranian cities by 1931/2.[72] Some of these cities were commodity processing hubs: textiles in Tehran, wool in Tabriz, tea in Lahijan, tobacco in Isfahan and grain in Bushehr, which housed eight mills. Conversely, Rasht was a diversified manufacturing centre, producing soap, hulled rice, ice, socks, silk thread, electric lighting and lemonade. In north-eastern Iran, some municipalities partnered with local entrepreneurs for the electrification of their cities. The Soviet mixed companies, Perssholk and Perskhlopok, in contrast to their exploitative peers that sold sugar and other goods at high prices, supported the expansion of Iranian silkworm farms and cotton-cleaning plants in this region.[73]

Notably, among the entrepreneurs who participated in the April 1936 Exposition of Iranian Products in Tehran, there were two women. Gol Bangiz (see Figure 6.3) had founded the first factory and technical institute for the production of opaque and coloured glass in 1932, supplying offices, institutions, homes and shops.[74] She employed eight workers for the production of mirrors, street lights, globe lights, tube lighting and small bottles, including those for medicine. Likewise, Betul Khanom Mohajer-Qarabaghi's artificial flowers were on display at the 1936 Exposition.[75] After the Department of General Trade had denied her request to import artificial flowers in 1934, including orange blossoms, which were prohibited, she established her own enterprise, equipped with imported machinery for the manufacture of such flowers using domestic fabric. Some of these flowers, for example, imitation Damask roses, orange and cherry blossoms, pansies, nasturtiums and narcissus, were used to decorate women's dresses and hats. It is interesting to note that both of these women were working solo (i.e. there was no mention of family partnerships) and were producing domestic consumer goods whose imported analogues had been banned by law.

The Iranian government's far-reaching plans for domestic industrialization on a larger scale also began to take shape in 1931/2. Firstly, the Ministry of the National Economy's 'economic installations [*tasisāt-e eqtesādi*]' were allocated 9,091,640 rials in the annual budget.[76] Secondly, regulations pertaining to a wide range of industrial and

Figure 6.3 Gol Bangiz, glassware entrepreneur, Tehran, *c.* 1936. *Source*: 'Kala-ye Iran: Ghorfehha-ye Namayeshgah va Tafsil-e Har Yek', *Majalleh-ye Otaq-e Tejarat*, no. 133 (Ordibehesht 1315/April 1936), 19–20.

consumer goods were ratified in the Commercial Trademarks and Inventions Law.[77] Thirdly, legislation for machinery imports that facilitated the improvement of Iranian exports and/or 'the elimination of the need of foreign products and manufactures' was passed.[78] Imports of sugar, cement, textiles and other products would fill the gap in domestic consumption until Iranian factories could produce sufficient quantities. These factories were fuelled by multiple coal mines, which were being exploited in the 1930s.[79]

Thanks to increasing government control over foreign trade, a network of large modern factories arose throughout Iran during the 1930s. The monopolization of staple goods, such as tobacco, sugar and matches, paved the way for their domestic production. For example, the construction of tobacco factories was partly funded by the monopoly revenue from this commodity.[80] Foreign exchange profits from oil and exports also financed the lump sugar factories in Kahrizak, Karaj, Varamin, Shahi, Shahabad, Miandoab, Marvdasht and Abkuh.[81] In 1934, the Ninth Majles authorized the Ministry of Finance to withdraw £250,000 of credit from the National Reserve to purchase equipment for 'a whole series of factories', producing sugar, textiles, silk, tarred railway sleepers and other products, and to borrow 30 million rials from the National Bank.[82]

Iran's unprecedented economic expansion was overseen by the Departments of Industry, Agriculture and Mining, the Ministry of Finance and the Bank of Agriculture and Industry, which were instructed by the Council of Ministers (Cabinet or Heyat-e Vaziran) to hold weekly sessions 'for the proper functioning of state factories and industrial establishments'.[83] Thus, these concerted efforts had led to the establishment of 150 major factories, either partially or entirely state-owned, by 1938.[84] The Soviets observed that Iranian textile technology was advancing 'comparatively quickly', attracting domestic and foreign consumers alike.[85] Similarly, Iran's cement imports began to decrease in 1937 with the recent founding of factories in Rey and Bandar-e Pahlavi.[86] The British reported that the Rey Factory was 'turning out 300 tonnes of cement per day'.[87]

Even after the Allied occupation's severe disruption of Iran's economy, there were at least 213 domestic factories operating in 1946; about half were cotton or wool processors.[88] The Behshahr Chintz Factory was one of the largest, established in 1938, operating at nearly 80 per cent capacity with an output of 9,580,385 metres of fabric. Both operating at about 50 per cent capacity, the Shahi Linen and Chalus Silk Factories produced 1,952,000 metres of linen fabric plus 137,500 bundles of yarn, and 367,483 metres of silk textiles, respectively.[89] The Kazeruni family's Vatan Factory in Isfahan had an output of 489,895 metres of woollen fabric and 31,727 wool blankets.[90] Five mills in Kerman, Tabriz, Kashan and Shiraz also produced 125,782,125 kilograms of cotton batting.[91] Tehran and Rasht were manufacturing hubs for socks and knitwear.

Likewise, the Kahrizak, Karaj, Miandoab and Marvdasht Lump Sugar Factories, and the Khosravi Leather and Pashmineh Wool Factories in Tabriz, had continued to operate throughout 1941–6.[92] The two leaders among fifteen domestic producers, Tehran's Darugar and Mak, churned out 247,530 kilograms of laundry detergent and 1,171,000 bars of soap, respectively.[93] Tehran also boasted thirteen glass manufacturers, whose output totalled 6,800,000 pieces of glassware and 1,800 kilograms of glass. Momtaz-e Iran of Tabriz and Saadat of Zanjan were at the top of the list of twenty-four match factories, manufacturing a total of 103,302,000 boxes.[94] Last but not least, Rasht's gunnysack factories had an output of 36,200 kilograms of twine and 1,823,483 metres of burlap sacks, and Karaj's cardboard manufacturer produced 200,000 kilograms.[95]

Remarkably, the growth of Iranian industry had continued during the Second World War. For instance, six state tea factories and nine rice mills sprang up in northern Iran from 1932 to 1945, processing 790 tonnes of tea and almost 12,600 tonnes of rice in 1946.[96] In the same year, a refractory brick factory, which had opened in 1942, produced 1,332,555 kilograms of bricks,[97] and the Rey factory churned out 36,567 tonnes of cement. Three more productive enterprises had been founded in 1943: the Varamin Oil-Extraction Plant, the Amin Abad Sodium Bicarbonate Factory and the Shahi Cannery. In 1946, the first yielded 127,068 kilograms of cottonseed oil, the second was operating at full capacity and the third was among a group of domestic fish canneries that had turned a total net profit of 10,848,500 rials.[98] Moreover, by this point, there were seven grain silos in Tehran, Tabriz, Isfahan, Ahvaz, Mashhad, Kermanshah and Shiraz.[99]

Conclusions

Why was the Iranian government in such a hurry to implement all of these large-scale economic modernization projects simultaneously? In answer to this question, it should be noted that Iran faced at least four simultaneous impediments: (1) delayed economic development due to its semi-colonial status during the Qajar period, which still posed significant challenges to its newfound independence; (2) an unfavourable global economic climate for such development; (3) a limited window of opportunity for autonomous economic modernization between two world wars; (4) being an oil-producing nation in a strategic location vis-à-vis the power politics of international relations.

Since the 1800s, the Great Powers, Russia and Britain, had prevented the implementation of these projects. The spectre of British protectorate (or even Soviet satellite) status lent a further urgency to Iran's quest for economic sovereignty. Even after the 1921 Friendship Treaty's signing, Iranians faced an uphill battle to maintain their economic independence, given the imperialistic tendencies and geopolitical ambitions of these two powers. This threat was fully confirmed when the Allies began to raise objections to Iran's increasing trade ties with Germany, which prompted their invasion and occupation of Iranian soil and their imposition of authority over the country's inhabitants, resources and infrastructure.[100]

The Iranian government decided to monopolize domestic resources for the national economy's rapid expansion, given the dearth of foreign loans and currency during the interwar period as well as the country's unequal position in foreign trade. By centralizing capital and resources, it was able to plan and expedite multiple projects for the railway, roads, ports, mines and factories simultaneously throughout the country. Moreover, the state monopolization of foreign trade was intended to improve the standard and volume of exports, and protect 'the consumer of foreign products from excessive [price] increases',[101] which were a consequence of the rial's fluctuating value as well as exploitative Soviet trading practices. Also, rather than 'checking the level of private consumption',[102] as Daftary claims, Iranians were encouraged to buy domestic sugar, textiles and other goods.

By integrating foreign trade, industry, mining and agriculture into a centralized system with the support of the new national banks, Iran was able to displace the Soviet Union's commercial organizations and strengthen its financial autonomy in relation to Great Britain, which still controlled the oil industry. Consequently, British and Soviet officials displeased by their waning dominance over Iran's economic affairs, including Victor Mallet and Maksim Litvinov, criticized Iranian assertiveness.[103] Likewise, Reader Bullard and Millspaugh exhibited prejudice while blaming the Iranian government for their own mistakes in the 1940s.[104]

The diversification of economic relations with 'third countries' during the 1920s–30s was another effective way of curbing Soviet and British influence. Apart from Millspaugh and his team of experts, the Americans – and their investment capital – were mostly absent from the Iranian economic landscape during this period. Instead, Iran turned to the continental powerhouse, Germany, as well as rising industrial manufacturers in Eastern Europe. These countries were willing to supply modern machinery at lower prices and/or in exchange for agricultural exports. Thus, Czech and German firms, such as Škoda and Allgemeine Elektricitäts-Gesellschaft AG (AEG), were awarded contracts during the 1930s.[105] Škoda provided much of the equipment for the Rey Cement Factory,[106] as well as the Varamin, Shahi and Miandoab Lump Sugar Factories.[107] Similarly, Iranian semi-state joint-stock corporations were partly inspired by German syndicates and combines.[108]

One of the main drivers of these policies was Reza Shah, whose nationalism, ambition and belief in the necessity of rapid economic modernization – partly motivated by like-minded officials, merchants, guilds, farmers and other groups from the wider society – impelled him to embark on a number of complex and costly projects all at once. Unfortunately, this modernization drive displaced craftspeople and artisans,[109] and led to the demise of the talented Teymurtash and 'hard-working' Mirza Ali Akbar Khan Davar, who as finance minister had overseen 'the gigantic and growing burden of . . . the railway, the factories, the monopoly companies, and the control of trade and exchange' until February 1937.[110] Admittedly, this was mainly urban-centred economic development, yet, as outlined in this chapter, many economic reforms were implemented in stages and/or in tandem with one another, which were evidence of foresight and planning.

Furthermore, this development was advanced by the capital and expertise of merchants and other entrepreneurs, especially the Chambers of Commerce, as well

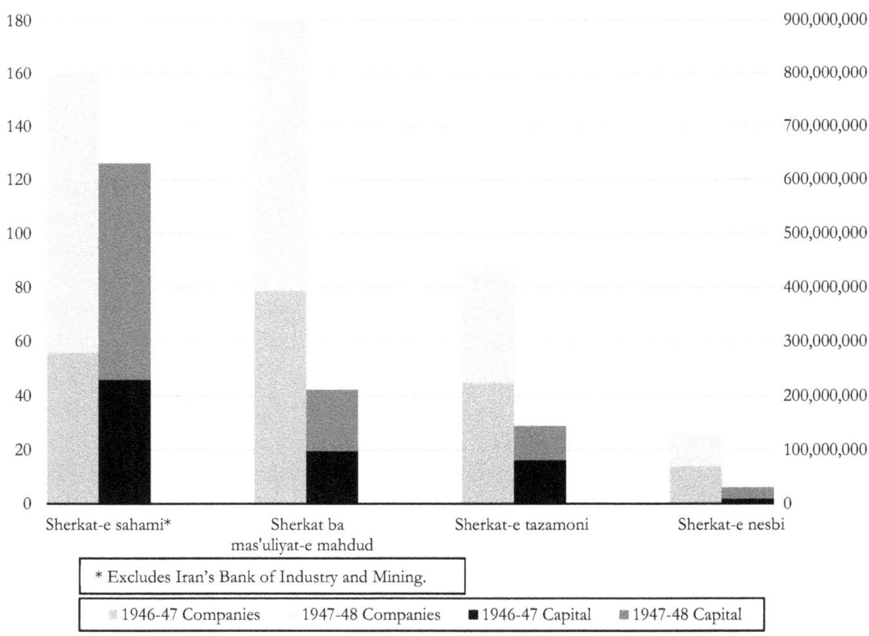

Figure 6.4 New registered companies in Tehran and their capital (millions of rials), 1946–8. *Source*: 'Companies Registered in Iran and the Provinces in 1325–1326 (March 1946–March 1948)', *Supplement to Bank Melli Iran Bulletin No. 99* (April–May 1949), 2–51. My sincere thanks to Dr Sima Rabbani for assisting with this graph's preparation.

as statesmen who defended Iran's economic autonomy, such as Teymurtash, Davar, Qavam, Mohammad Ali Forughi and, collectively, the Majles. For example, Davar and his colleagues oversaw a 66.6 per cent increase in joint-stock companies during the first quarter of 1934.[111] That is, fifty-nine corporations were created with 28,603,602 rials of capital in less than a year since the Bank of Agriculture and Industry's establishment. Then, between January and March 1935, sixteen corporations for exports, imports and industry were founded with 47,651,496 rials. This sudden increase in firms with multiple shareholders led the Soviets to remark that 'the centralization of capital in Iran . . . has accelerated'.

Finally, as discussed earlier, the growth of private sector industries during the 1920s–30s suggests that the state had played a role in encouraging such entrepreneurship. In addition, the Iranian government's plans for a massive stock exchange – said to rival New York's – was a bold response to rising wartime inflation that anticipated the private sector's future expansion.[112] The fact that Iran's first stock market was to be built within the vicinity of the Tehran Bazaar indicated that the state considered the traditional marketplace to be the ideal hub for modern commerce and finance. Although this pioneering initiative for the Iranian financial market's expansion was halted by foreign intervention, by 1946/7, Tehran's companies, especially joint-stock, limited liability and proportional liability partnerships, plus a smaller number of general partnerships, had increased in number and capital (see Figure 6.4).[113] Thus, Iran's economic modernization began anew in the post-war period.

Notes

1 *Ruznameh-ye Rasmi-ye Keshvar: Bakhsh-e Avval, 1300–12* (Tehran: Ruznameh-ye Rasmi-ye Jomhuri-ye Eslami-ye Iran, 1388), 4–7. In December 1921, the Fourth Majles ratified the Treaty and Iran's membership in the League of Nations, which had been accepted on 10 January 1920.

2 Ira M. Lapidus, *A History of Islamic Societies* (New York: Cambridge University Press, 2014), 549. The 1921 Treaty's 'very favorable' terms enabled Iran to reject the '1919 treaty with Britain'. See also Arthur Chester Millspaugh, *The Financial and Economic Situation of Persia, 1926* (New York: the Imperial Persian Government under the auspices of The Persia Society, 1926), 33. Iran's external debt was 'exclusively owing to Great Britain and the Imperial Bank of Persia' after the Soviet government 'waived its claim to repayment of [Imperial Russian] loans'.

3 'Le commerce extérieur de l'Iran pendant l'année 1317/18 (1938/39)', *Bulletin de la Banque Mellié Iran*, no. 42 (December 1939): 612. See Table No. 8 for these statistics.

4 *Dokumenty Vneshnei Politiki SSSR*, vol. 5, 1 January–19 November 1922 (Moscow: Gosudarstvennoe izdatel'stvo politicheskoi literatury, 1961), 416.

5 Ibid., 746 n. 102. The merchants had their own pavilion and a warehouse with a capacity of 150,000 pounds for storing their goods.

6 Ibid., 577–8 and 758 n. 142. See also Étienne Forestier-Peyrat, 'Red Passage to Iran: The Baku Trade Fair and the Unmaking of the Azerbaijani Borderland, 1922–1930', *Ab Imperio* 4 (2013): 88–9, 91. By 1927, Iran's share of trade at the Baku fair had increased to 74 per cent (23,166,000 roubles – versus 524,000 roubles in 1922) with

226 companies, representing 27 per cent of its total volume of trade with the Soviet Union.

7 *Dokumenty Vneshnei Politiki SSSR*, vol. 7, 1 January–31 December 1924 (Moscow: Gosudarstvennoe izdatel'stvo politicheskoi literatury, 1963), 690–2, 697. Iranian exports represented more than 50 per cent of the total for all countries via the USSR's Asian borders. See also 'Amar-e Tejarat-e Khareji-ye Iran dar 1279–1343', Vezarat-e Eqtesad, Edareh-ye Kol-e Amar-e Bazargani, vol. 82, no. 18 (Bahman 1344/January–February 1966): 13; Millspaugh, *Financial and Economic Situation*, 30. Iran's non-oil exports rose by 170 per cent from 1921/2 to 1924/5, and customs revenues grew by almost 92 per cent from 1920/1 to 1924/5.

8 Mary Yoshinari, 'A Unique Event in Iran-Soviet Economic Relations: The 1935 Iranian Trade Delegation to the USSR', *Iranian Studies* 49, no. 5 (2016): 797, 810 nn. 33–8. See also Robert Wesley Davenport, *Soviet Economic Relations with Iran, 1917–1930* (New York: Columbia University, 1953), 83, 109–10, 132. These companies relied on 'the capital and business connections of Iranian merchants'.

9 Rossiiskii gosudarstvennyi arkhiv sotsial'no-politicheskoi istorii (RGASPI), f. 82, op. 2, d. 1217, ll. 1–2. This was the warning of the People's Commissar of Foreign Affairs of the USSR, Georgy Vasil'evich Chicherin, in December 1924.

10 'Le commerce extérieur de l'Iran pendant l'année commerciale 1314–15 (22 Juin 1935–21 Juin 1936)', *Bulletin de la Banque Mellié Iran*, no. 14 (August 1937): 42–7.

11 Miron Rezun, *The Soviet Union and Iran: Soviet Policy in Iran from the Beginnings of the Pahlavi Dynasty until the Soviet Invasion in 1941* (Alphen aan den Rijn: Sijthoff and Noordhoff International Publishers; Geneva: Institut Universitaire de Hautes Etudes Internationales, 1981), 124.

12 *Ruznameh: Bakhsh-e Avval*, 264–83. This law was to be in effect for eight years.

13 *Dokumenty Vneshnei Politiki SSSR*, vol. 11, 1 January–31 December 1928 (Moscow: Gosudarstvennoe izdatel'stvo politicheskoi literatury, 1966), 721–2 n. 96.

14 Ibid., 312–13, 722 nn. 96–7.

15 *Dokumenty Vneshnei Politiki SSSR*, vol. 12, 1 January–31 December 1929 (Moscow: Gosudarstvennoe izdatel'stvo politicheskoi literatury, 1967), 120–4.

16 Forestier-Peyrat, 'Red Passage', 110.

17 R. M. Burrell and R. L. Jarman, eds, *Iran Political Diaries, 1881–1965*, vol. 8 (Cambridge: Archive Editions, 1997), 603.

18 *Ruznameh: Bakhsh-e Avval*, 476. See also R. M. Burrell and R. L. Jarman, *Iran Political Diaries, 1881–1965*, vol. 9 (Cambridge: Archive Editions, 1997), 13.

19 *Ruznameh: Bakhsh-e Avval*, 476–8.

20 'Nouvelles Économiques: Éclosion des Sociétés', *Bulletin de la Banque Méllié Iran*, no. 5 (June 1935): 43; RGAE, f. 413, op. 13, d. 1084, ll. 14–16. As a consequence of the Foreign Trade Monopoly Law, the Qomash (Textile) Corporation was founded on 22 November 1934.

21 *Ruznameh: Bakhsh-e Avval*, 605. These monopolies could borrow a maximum of 3 million tomans from Iran's National Bank or 'another bank' for the 1932/3 economic year.

22 'Le commerce extérieur de l'Iran pendant l'année économique 1312 (22.6.33–21.6.34)', *Bulletin de la Banque Mellié Iran*, no. 5 (June 1935): 16.

23 R. M. Burrell and R. L. Jarman, eds, *Iran Political Diaries, 1881–1965*, vol. 10 (Cambridge: Archive Editions, 1997), 544–6; *Ruznameh: Bakhsh-e Avval*, 201–2. The Railway linked the Caspian Sea (Bandar-e Gaz) to the Persian Gulf (Khorramshahr/Khur-e Musa).

24 Jennifer Jenkins, 'Iran in the Nazi New Order, 1933–1941', *Iranian Studies* 49, no. 5 (2016): 728; idem, 'The Trouble with Third Powers: German-Iranian Relations to 1941', *Iran Nameh* 28, no. 1 (2013): 62–85.
25 *Ruznameh-ye Rasmi-ye Keshvar, 1321–30* (Tehran: Ruznameh-ye Rasmi-ye Jomhuri-ye Eslami-ye Iran, 1388), 251–2. See also Arthur Chester Millspaugh, *Americans in Persia* (Washington, DC: The Brookings Institution, 1946), 232–3. On 28 August 1944, the State Department advised that Iran 'handle its imports through normal commercial channels'.
26 Center for Documents and the History of Diplomacy of the Ministry of Foreign Affairs of Iran, SH1325-02-115.3-5. Domestic 'raw materials' would be used while reviving local industry.
27 Arthur Chester Millspaugh, *The American Task in Persia* (New York: The Century Co., 1925), 21, 38.
28 Ibid., 237–8.
29 *Ruznameh: Bakhsh-e Avval*, 112, 132, 141. In February 1926, a related law was passed for 'the preparation of roads and vehicles' towards 'the northern and western provinces'.
30 Ibid., 192. This policy programme of Prime Minister Mirza Hassan Khan Mostowfi al-Mamalek's Cabinet also called for the creation of an iron smelting factory.
31 *Ruznameh: Bakhsh-e Avval*, 218. The Bank's 15 million tomans of foundational capital was to be raised from the sale of state jewels. See also R. M. Burrell and R. L. Jarman, eds, *Iran Political Diaries 1881–1965*, vol. 7 (Cambridge: Archive Editions, 1997), 194, 387. Despite the Imperial Bank's opposition, Mohammad Ali Foroughi defended the National Bank's founding.
32 Burrell and Jarman, *Iran Political Diaries*, vol. 8, 653–4.
33 Ibid., 656–7.
34 *Ruznameh: Bakhsh-e Avval*, 606–7. A New York company printed these notes.
35 'La Monnaie Persane', *Bulletin de la Banque Mellié Iran*, no. 1 (January 1934): 6. The Iranian government had been aware of Britain's decision to abandon the gold standard in 1931.
36 *Ruznameh: Bakhsh-e Avval*, 836–7.
37 Ibid., 859–61 and 871. This legislation was ratified on 7 January 1934. A March 4 law allowed domestic factory owners to obtain loans from the Bank.
38 These loans were to be issued, as follows: first to third year: 20 million rials; fourth year: 30 million rials; fifth to eighth year: 40 million rials; ninth and tenth years: 50 million rials.
39 *Ruznameh: Bakhsh-e Avval*, 725, 768, 770.
40 Burrell and Jarman, *Iran Political Diaries*, vol. 9, 236, 340–1. See also *Ruznameh: Bakhsh-e Avval*, 773.
41 RGAE, f. 413, op. 13, d. 3504, l. 4. The Soviets explained that 'although all of these payments were foreseen by the Iranians in the balance of payments . . . foreign currency inflow channels are providing less than . . . planned'.
42 *Ruznameh-ye Rasmi-ye Keshvar: Bakhsh-e Dovvom* (Tehran: Ruznameh-ye Rasmi-ye Jomhuri-ye Eslami-ye Iran, 1388), 1117–18, 1207, 1241, 1274–5, 1351–3. The Tenth Majles ratified the Foreign Exchange Transactions Law on 1 March 1936. Related legislation was passed eight months later; subsequently, six foreign exchange directives were issued.
43 Burrell and Jarman, *Iran Political Diaries*, vol. 10, 545.
44 RGAE, f. 413, op. 13, d. 1852, ll. 20–1.

45 Burrell and Jarman, *Iran Political Diaries*, vol. 9, vi. See also Peter J. Beck, 'The Anglo-Persian Oil Dispute 1932–33', *Journal of Contemporary History* 9, no. 4 (1974): 123–51; Mohammad Malek, 'Oil in Iran between the Two World Wars', in *Anglo-Iranian Relations since 1800*, ed. Vanessa Martin (London: Routledge, 2005), 128–36.
46 RGAE, f. 413, op. 13, d. 2553, l. 4. One quarter of this revenue had been generated by the Central Corporation, Qomash and Shekar, which competed with Soviet firms.
47 *Ruznameh: Bakhsh-e Dovvom*, 1354–9, 1393, 1408–12, 1420, 1483–5. The Bank of Agriculture and Trades and Crafts had been previously named the Bank of Agriculture and Industry, and Sepah Bank had been formerly known as Pahlavi Bank. See also R. M. Burrell and R. L. Jarman, eds, *Iran Political Diaries 1881–1965*, vol. 11 (Cambridge: Archive Editions, 1997), 40. The Mortgage Bank was established with 200 million rials of capital in 1939.
48 Stephen L. McFarland, 'Anatomy of an Iranian Political Crowd: The Tehran Bread Riot of December 1942', *International Journal of Middle East Studies* 17, no. 1 (1985): 53. Bread prices rose from six cents to one dollar from January to May 1942. See also Millspaugh, *Americans*, 58. Millspaugh noted that inflation had started before 1937, and by February 1943, the cost of living had risen more than 700 per cent. Moreover, the Allies' shipping demands disrupted domestic production and reduced imports to Iran.
49 Kamran M. Dadkah, 'The Iranian Economy during the Second World War: The Devaluation Controversy', *Middle Eastern Studies* 37, no. 2 (2001): 183. See also Abol Hassan Ebtehaj, *Khatirat-e Abol Hassan Ebtehaj*, vol. 1 (Los Angeles: Ketab Corporation, 2010), 589–91; McFarland, 'Anatomy', 55; *Ruznameh, 1321–30*, 1, 19.
50 Millspaugh, *Americans*, 105, 109.
51 Ibid., 98–9 and 111. Millspaugh was General Director of Iran's Ministry of Finance in 1943–4. See also 'Doktor Milspaw dar Majles', *Ettelaat*, no. 5317 (18 Aban 1322/ November 10, 1943): 1; *Ruznameh, 1321–30,* 95–8; R. M. Burrell and R. L. Jarman, eds, *Iran Political Diaries 1881–1965*, vol. 12 (Cambridge: Archive Editions, 1997), 498. The British reasoned that such tax reforms had to be implemented over 'a number of years'.
52 Frances Bostock and Geoffrey Jones, *Planning and Power in Iran: Ebtehaj and Economic Development Under the Shah* (New York: Routledge, 2013), 57.
53 'Companies Registered in Iran and the Provinces in 1325–1326 (March 1946–March 1948)', *Supplement to Bank Melli Iran Bulletin No. 99* (April–May 1949): 6–7.
54 *Ruznameh: Bakhsh-e Avval*, 89–110.
55 Ibid., 542–3, 651, 661, 817.
56 Ibid., 677–704.
57 'Statistique des sociétés enregistrées en 1319 (1940–1941)', *Bulletin de la Banque Mellié Iran*, no. 61 (September–October 1942): 258–64.
58 'Chegonegi-ye Vaz-e Sherkatha dar Iran', *Majalleh-ye Otaq-e Tejarat*, no. 160 (June–July 1937/Tir 1316): 27–8.
59 Ahmad Minai, *Economic Development of Iran under the Reign of Reza Shah (1926–1941)* (Washington, DC: American University, 1960), 212.
60 'L'éclosion des sociétés en Iran pendant les dernières années – Les sociétés provinciales et les des sociétés étrangères', *Bulletin de la Banque Mellié Iran*, no. 10 (March 1937): 3–4.
61 Ibid., 2–4.
62 'Sociétés enregistrées en Iran pendant l'année 1315 et les changements apportés en 1315 dans les status des sociétés enregistrées en Iran durant les années 1310 à 1314',

Supplément au Bulletins Nos. 15 et 18 (Septembre et Décembre 1937) de la Banque Mellié Iran, 76.

63 'Sherkatha-ye Tejarati', *Majalleh-ye Otaq-e Tejarat*, no. 82–3 (Salnameh dar Aghaz-e 1313/March–April 1934): 31–40; 'L'éclosion des sociétés', 4.

64 *Ruznameh: Bakhsh-e Dovvom*, 1672–3. 'Up to 50 per cent' of this capital was earmarked for state monopolies and corporations by obtaining a loan from domestic banks and institutions.

65 'Sociétés enregistrées à Tehran en 1319', *Supplément au No. 61 de la Banque Mellié Iran* (September–October 1942): 350–1.

66 'Burs-e Tehran', *Majalleh-ye Otaq-e Tejarat*, no. 232–3 (Shahrivar 1319/August–September 1940): 1–6. This complex would include: (1) a stock market for the rial and foreign currencies, securities and currency exchange; (2) a commodity exchange and reserves; and (3) a private stock exchange.

67 'Companies', 14–15.

68 *Ruznameh: Bakhsh-e Avval*, 25, 135, 223.

69 Ibid., 71, 94–5.

70 Ibid., 197–8, 244, 274.

71 RGAE, f. 413, op. 13, d. 1083, l. 45. The Soviets concluded that Iran's rapid economic expansion had been fostered partly by the laws supporting domestic factories of 1925/6.

72 'Karkhanejati Keh Folan dar Iran Dayer Ast', *Salnameh-ye Pars*, vol. 7 (1311/1932–33): 162–7.

73 N. M. Mamedova, 'Russia ii. Iranian-Soviet Relations (1917–1991)', in *Encyclopaedia Iranica Online*, accessed 1 June 2024, https://iranicaonline.org/articles/russia-ii-iranian-soviet-relations-1917-1991.

74 'Kala-ye Iran: Ghorfehha-ye Namayeshgah va Tafsil-e Har Yek', *Majalleh-ye Otaq-e Tejarat*, no. 133 (Ordibehesht 1315/April 1936): 19–20. See also Mary Yoshinari, 'Assessing the Role of Iranian Entrepreneurs in the Interwar Period via *Otaq-e Tejarat*', *Iran Nameh* 30, no. 1 (2015): 59, 62.

75 'Kala-ye Iran: Ghorfehha-ye Namayeshgah va Tafsil-e Har Yek', *Majalleh-ye Otaq-e Tejarat*, no. 134 (Ordibehesht 1315/May 1936): 14–15. See also Yoshinari, 'Iranian Entrepreneurs', 59–60, 67.

76 *Ruznameh: Bakhsh-e Avval*, 480.

77 Ibid., 655–9. See regulations dated 23 June 1931.

78 Ibid., 562. This law was approved on 4 October 1931.

79 RGAE, f. 413, op. 13, d. 1083, l. 44. Shemshak fuelled a new power station and numerous factories in Tehran, including Rey's cement factory. See also *Ruznameh: Bakhsh-e Avval*, 320.

80 *Ruznameh: Bakhsh-e Avval*, 609, 732. Iran's banks were to loan 55 million rials to the state tobacco monopoly for 'profit-generating capital and preliminary expenses'.

81 Ibid., 840. In 1933, £360,000 was to be transferred from the National Reserve to the General Department of Industry and Agriculture's fund for six lump sugar factories. See also Burrell and Jarman, *Iran Political Diaries*, vol. 9, 671.

82 'Nouvelles Économiques: Industrialisation', *Bulletin de la Banque Mellié Iran*, no. 3 (June 1934): 25–6. See also *Ruznameh: Bakhsh-e Dovvom*, 922.

83 'Nouvelles Économiques: Surveillance des Entreprises Gouvernementales', *Bulletin de la Banque Mellié Iran*, no. 3 (June 1934): 28. This project was presented to the Ninth Majles. For a list of the officials involved, see Burrell and Jarman, *Iran Political Diaries*, vol. 9, 501.

84 L. P. Elwell-Sutton, *Modern Iran* (London: George Routledge and Sons, Ltd., 1941), 105.
85 RGAE, f. 413, op. 13, d. 2178, ll. 46–7.
86 'L'industrie iranienne: 3 – L'industrie de ciment', *Bulletin de la Banque Mellié Iran*, no. 21 (March 1938): 3 and 24. See also RGAE, f. 413, op. 13, d. 1083, ll. 40–1.
87 Burrell and Jarman, *Iran Political Diaries*, vol. 10, 353.
88 SH1325-K2-P113.30-15 to 39.37. Twenty-eight cotton mills were founded in 1937–41.
89 SH1325-K2-P113.30-15.
90 SH1325-K2-P113.30-35.
91 SH1325-K2-P113.30-29.
92 SH1325-K2-P113.30-38. Seven factories produced 32,663,151 kilograms of sugar in 1946.
93 SH1325-K2-P113.30-31.
94 SH1325-K2-P113.30-32.
95 SH1325-K2-P113.30-30.
96 SH1325-K2-P113.30-29 and 37. Twelve plants cleaned 23,212,059 kilograms of rice in 1946.
97 SH1325-K2-P113.30-26 and 38.
98 *Ruznameh, 1321–30*, 102.
99 SH1325-K2-P113.30-39.37. The Tehran and Ahvaz silos could hold 64,000 and 30,000 tonnes of grain; the rest had capacities of 16,000 tonnes, but the Shiraz silo lacked machinery.
100 The Soviets and the British reassumed control over their former spheres of influence in northern and southern Iran. See Mehdi Heravi, *Iranian-American Diplomacy* (Brooklyn: Theo. Gaus' Sons, 1969), 78–9. The Soviets banned grain shipments from northern Iran to other regions of the country, causing near-starvation, and even deaths, in 1942. See also George Lenczowski, *Russia and the West in Iran, 1918–1948: A Study in Big-Power Rivalry* (Ithaca: Cornell University Press, 1949), 195–6.
101 'L'éclosion des sociétés', 3–4.
102 Farhad Daftary, 'Development Planning in Iran: A Historical Survey', *Iranian Studies* 6, no. 4 (1973): 178.
103 Burrell and Jarman, *Iran Political Diaries*, vol. 9, 433–4. See also Yoshinari, 'Unique Event', 798. Litvinov, who was the People's Commissar of Foreign Affairs of the USSR during the 1930s, maintained a negative stance towards Iranian demands for a fair balance of trade.
104 McFarland, 'Anatomy', 53. In April 1942, British minister Plenipotentiary Bullard decided that less than 20 per cent of the 160,000 tonnes of wheat requested by the Iranian government would be shipped. He claimed that 'Iran would have to make up any shortfall from supposed vast hoards held by speculators, though American officials denied the existence of such hoards'. See also Millspaugh, *Americans*, 107. Conversely, Millspaugh admitted to mistakes made in the provision of staple goods.
105 RGAE, f. 413, op. 13, d. 3502, l. 89.
106 RGAE, f. 413, op. 13, d. 1083, ll. 40–1. The rotary kiln was imported from Denmark.
107 RGAE, f. 413, op. 13, d. 1841, ll. 15–15ob. See also Burrell and Jarman, *Iran Political Diaries*, vol. 9, 399 and 580.
108 'Khatt-e Mashi-ye Ayandeh-ye Sherkat', *Majalleh-ye Otaq-e Tejarat*, no. 100 (Azar 1313/November–December 1934): 7. 'The creation of big corporations' in Iran was said to be 'one of the growth factors of commercial life of the present epoch' and

was part of a global trend, including the rise of large syndicates and combines in Germany.
109 Serhan Afacan, 'Workers as Petitioners: Discursive Practices of Iranian Textile Workers, 1906–1941', *Cihannüma* 6, no. 2 (2020): 164–70.
110 Burrell and Jarman, *Iran Political Diaries*, vol. 10, 318, 449, 476. The British also supposed that Reza Shah had 'insisted on an ever-increasing supply of funds to finance a programme', whose domestic resources were likely 'insufficient to meet . . . the pace demanded'.
111 RGAE, f. 413, op. 13, d. 1086, l. 4.
112 Millspaugh, *Americans*, 34.
113 'Companies', 2–74. Overall, joint-stock companies were greater in number and capital share. Isfahan, Tabriz and Mashhad had a smaller number of companies.

Bibliography

Archives and libraries

Center for Documents and the History of Diplomacy of the Ministry of Foreign Affairs of Iran, Tehran
Library, Museum and Document Center of the Iranian Parliament, Tehran
Robarts Library, University of Toronto
Russian State Archive of the Economy (RGAE)
Russian State Archive of Socio-Political History (RGASPI)

Primary sources

'Āmār-e Tejārat-e Khāreji-ye Irān dar 1279–1343'. Vezarat-e Eqtesad, Edareh-ye Kol-e Amar-e Bazargani. Vol. 82, no. 18 (Bahman 1344/January–February 1966): 13–15.
Burrell, R. M. and R. L. Jarman, eds. *Iran Political Diaries, 1881–1965*. Vol. 7-12. Cambridge: Archive Editions, 1997.
Dokumenty Vneshnei Politiki SSSR (January 1922–December 1929). Vol. 5, 7, 11, 12. Moscow: Gosudarstvennoe izdatel'stvo politicheskoi literatury, 1961–1967.

Periodicals

Bulletin de la Banque Mellié Iran
Ettelāʿāt
Majalleh-ye Otāq-e Tejārat
Ruznāmeh-ye Rasmi-ye Keshvar
Salnāmeh-ye Pars

Secondary sources

Afacan, Serhan. 'Workers as Petitioners: Discursive Practices of Iranians Textile Workers, 1906–1941'. *Cihannüma* 6, no. 2 (2020): 157–77.

Beck, Peter J. 'The Anglo-Persian Oil Dispute 1932–33'. *Journal of Contemporary History* 9, no. 4 (1974): 123–51.
Bharier, Julian. *Economic Development in Iran, 1900–1970*. London: Oxford University Press, 1971.
Bostock, Frances and Geoffrey Jones. *Planning and Power in Iran: Ebtehaj and Economic Development Under the Shah*. New York: Routledge, 2013.
Dadkah, Kamran M. 'The Iranian Economy during the Second World War: The Devaluation Controversy'. *Middle Eastern Studies* 37, no. 2 (2001): 181–98.
Daftary, Farhad. 'Development Planning in Iran: A Historical Survey'. *Iranian Studies* 6, no. 4 (1973): 176–228.
Davenport, Robert Wesley. *Soviet Economic Relations with Iran, 1917–1930*. New York: Columbia University, 1953.
Ebtehaj, Abol Hassan. *Khātirāt-e Abol Hassan Ebtehāj*. Vol. 1. Edited by Alireza Aruzi. Los Angeles: Ketab Corporation, 2010.
Elwell-Sutton, Lawrence Paul. *Modern Iran*. London: George Routledge and Sons, 1941.
Floor, Willem M. *Industrialization in Iran, 1900–1941*. Occasional Paper Series, no. 23. Edited by John Dewdney and Heather Bleaney. Durham: University of Durham Centre for Middle Eastern and Islamic Studies, 1984.
Floor, Willem M. *Labor and Industry in Iran, 1850–1941*. Washington, DC: Mage Publishers, 2009.
Forestier-Peyrat, Étienne. 'Red Passage to Iran: The Baku Trade Fair and the Unmaking of the Azerbaijani Borderland, 1922–1930'. *Ab Imperio* 4 (2013): 79–112.
Heravi, Mehdi. *Iranian-American Diplomacy*. Brooklyn: Theo. Gaus' Sons, 1969.
Issawi, Charles. 'De-Industrialization and Re-Industrialization in the Middle East since 1800'. *International Journal of Middle East Studies* 12, no. 4 (1980): 469–79.
Issawi, Charles, ed. *The Economic History of Iran, 1800–1914*. Chicago: University of Chicago Press, 1971.
Issawi, Charles. 'The Iranian Economy 1925–1975: Fifty Years of Economic Development'. In *Iran under the Pahlavis*, edited by George Lenczowski, 129–35. Stanford: Hoover Institution Press, 1978.
Jenkins, Jennifer. 'Iran in the Nazi New Order, 1933–1941'. *Iranian Studies* 49, no. 5 (2016): 727–51.
Jenkins, Jennifer. 'The Trouble with Third Powers: German-Iranian Relations to 1941'. *Iran Nameh* 28, no. 1 (2013): 62–85.
Karshenas, Massoud. *Oil, State and Industrialization*. Cambridge: Cambridge University Press, 1990.
Lapidus, Ira M. *A History of Islamic Societies*. New York: Cambridge University Press, 2014.
Lenczowski, George. *Russia and the West in Iran, 1918–1948: A Study in Big-Power Rivalry*. Ithaca: Cornell University Press, 1949.
Malek, Mohammad. 'Oil in Iran between the Two World Wars'. In *Anglo-Iranian Relations since 1800*, edited by Vanessa Martin, 128–36. London: Routledge, 2005.
Mamedova, N. M. 'Russia ii. Iranian-Soviet Relations (1917–1991)'. In *Encyclopaedia Iranica Online*. Accessed 1 June 2024. https://iranicaonline.org/articles/russia-ii-iranian-soviet-relations-1917-1991.
McFarland, Stephen L. 'Anatomy of an Iranian Political Crowd: The Tehran Bread Riot of December 1942'. *International Journal of Middle East Studies* 17, no. 1 (1985): 51–65.
Millspaugh, Arthur Chester. *Americans in Persia*. Washington, DC: The Brookings Institution, 1946.

Millspaugh, Arthur Chester. *The American Task in Persia*. New York: The Century Co., 1925.

Millspaugh, Arthur Chester. *The Financial and Economic Situation of Persia, 1926*. New York: the Imperial Persian Government under the auspices of The Persia Society, 1926.

Minai, Ahmad. *Economic Development of Iran under the Reign of Reza Shah (1926–1941)*. Washington, DC: American University, 1960.

Mojaver, Farshid. 'A Cost-Benefit Analysis of the Trans-Iranian Railway: Was It a Reasonable Investment?' Presentation at the International Iranian Economic Association's Fourth International Conference on the Iranian Economy, University of Marburg, Germany, 17–18 June 2016.

Rezun, Miron. *The Soviet Union and Iran: Soviet Policy in Iran from the Beginnings of the Pahlavi Dynasty until the Soviet Invasion in 1941*. Alphen aan den Rijn: Sijthoff and Noordhoff International Publishers; Geneva: Institut Universitaire de Hautes Etudes Internationales, 1981.

Rostow, W. W. 'The Take-Off Into Self-Sustained Growth', *The Economic Journal* 66, no. 261 (1956): 25–48.

Rostow, W. W. *The World Economy: History and Prospect*. Austin: University of Texas Press, 1978.

Yoshinari, Mary. 'Assessing the Role of Iranian Entrepreneurs in the Interwar Period via *Otaq-e Tejarat*'. *Iran Nameh* 30, no. 1 (2015): 48–69.

Yoshinari, Mary. 'A Unique Event in Iran-Soviet Economic Relations: The 1935 Iranian Trade Delegation to the USSR'. *Iranian Studies* 49, no. 5 (2016): 791–815.

7

The political economy of social policy developments in Iran, 1920s–70s

Reza Omidi

Introduction

This chapter discusses the organizational and institutional changes in the formation and development of welfare policies in Iran from 1925 to 1978, demonstrating that various political, economic and social factors influenced the three historical periods under review. During the first period, the government prioritized the formation of the state and the nation. However, in the second period, social and worker demands gained more attention. In the third period, the government assumed a greater role in the development of welfare policies due to its control of the labour and leftist movements through various mechanisms, as well as the acceleration of industrialization from the early 1960s. Furthermore, the government aimed to improve the well-being for various social groups, by expanding its organizations and state-affiliated charities, as well as implementing various welfare and social assistance programmes. This was done while also exercising multiple forms of social control and supervision.

Social policy developments during the Reza Shah period (1925–41)

This included the implementation of various economic and social welfare plans, such as the construction of railways and telephone lines, the establishment of the first Iranian banks and airline flights, the development of small and medium-sized factories and the transformation of industries through technical and vocational schools. Between 1921 and 1941, following the First World War and the establishment of the Pahlavi government, Iran underwent a period of modernization. The first Pahlavi government was built 'on two main pillars: the military and the bureaucracy'.[1] The expansion of the army and administrative system was made possible by revenues from oil royalties, collected back taxes, increased customs duties and taxes imposed on consumer goods. At the beginning of Reza Shah's rule, the central government was 'a haphazard collection of semi-independent mostowfis, monshis, and titled grandees. But by 1941, it had eleven full ministries employing in excess of 90,000 salaried civil servants.'[2] The expansion of the armed forces continued, particularly after the Conscription Law's approval in 1925. Establishing a standing army during this period also had significant social implications, according to Messkoub: 'The defense budget increased by fivefold from 1926 to 1942. The introduction of conscription, establishment of a military academy, and a career structure for a professional corps quadrupled . . . the armed forces.'[3] Moreover, 'despite harsh conditions', military service had 'a lasting modernizing influence' on Iranian soldiers, as these young people 'learned about each other as well as the rules of a hierarchical structure'. These rules were based 'more on merit than nepotism or divine rule'. Later, literacy classes were held in the army, as well as training in basic skills, such as driving and car mechanics, which 'proved useful to the enlisted after their discharge'.

On 14 December 1922, the National Employment Law was approved by the Majles (Parliament).[4] Articles 43 and 44 of this law dealt with the retirement of state employees, including the right to receive pensions from the government and the amount of pensions. In addition, the 'Pension Fund and Duties of the Heirs of Employees' was founded to administer pension affairs. The Ministry of Finance also established the 'Pension Office' under the General Department of Personnel.[5] In 1927, this section was renamed the 'National Pension Department', becoming an independent office in the Ministry of Finance, and, in 1937, its name was changed to the 'Civil Servants' Pension Department'. The Army Pension Fund was also established in 1935.

Concurrently, with the nationwide implementation of the railway project, the Council of Ministers (Cabinet) established the Road and Railway Workers' Provident Fund in 1931. This was the first generation of Iranian social insurance. Health care and treatment of persons who are injured or sick during work, financial compensation for physical impairment while working, permanent disability and survivors of job-related death were among the services provided, according to the Fund's regulations. In August 1936, the Cabinet approved regulations for factories and industrial institutions due to the expansion of factories, mining activities and other productive economic institutions. These regulations were based on the proposal of the General Department of Industry and Mines. In accordance with these regulations, workers in other industrial and mining workplaces were gradually covered by the Workers' Provident Fund.[6] In fact, the gradual expansion of the wage-earning and salaried classes (i.e. workers and government employees) led to the establishment and expansion of social insurance in Iran.

In addition to the provident and pension funds, charitable institutions affiliated with the Imperial Court were created during this period, the most important being the Agency for the Support of Mothers and Infants, which was founded in 1940. Funded by benefactors, the purpose of this charity 'was to support mothers, babies and the poor'.[7] Since it was chaired by Princess Fawzia (wife of the Crown Prince), this charity 'benefitted from the services of state institutions and officials' and received some financing from the public budget. Cabinet ministers and Parliament members also contributed to this charitable organization. Thus, 'considering that this public institution relied on state resources in practice and its administration was under the authority of the court and government officials, it was included among the public institutions under the umbrella of the government's support'.

Akbari has shown that out of all the social security laws and regulations approved during the 1915–41 period 43.7 per cent were related to insurance matters and 55.5 per cent were related to support matters.[8] Furthermore, the Cabinet paid more attention to insurance matters and parliamentarians paid more attention to support matters. From the establishment of Parliament until 1921, all enacted laws and regulations exclusively pertained to assistance and protection affairs. It is noteworthy that the initial insurance law was officially sanctioned in 1922. Also, more than 88 per cent of the laws and regulations enacted were related to financial resource allocation. Most of the decisions of this period were aimed at expanding coverage of insurance and support services.

Social security initiatives and legislation of the 1925–41 period indicate that workers' welfare and labour conditions were fundamental considerations in the creation of institutions and the formulation and approval of rules and regulations. The majority of the government's decisions were focused on supporting workers and employees. Provident and pension funds were established to provide organized government support to the workforce and government employees against work-related hazards, and employee cooperative funds were founded to support vulnerable employees. The experience of industrialized countries and global and external requirements also played a role in the creation and continuation of these developments. For example, the Iranian government started cooperating with the International Labour Organization (ILO) in 1932 and implemented some of its conventions in the same year.[9] Such partnerships and collaborations resulted in the consideration of some workforce-related values in government policymaking.

The idea of public education was put on the political agenda during the Constitutional period and helped to establish the public education system in Iran. But the development of public education at the national level was related to the Reza Shah period:

> The educational reforms were the most impressive of the civilian reforms. Between 1925 and 1941, the annual allocations for education increased in real terms by as much as twelvefold. In 1925, there had been no more than 55,960 children enrolled in 648 modern primary schools administered by state officials, private boards, religious communities, or foreign missionaries. By 1941, there were more than 287,245 children in 2,336 modern primary schools, almost all administered by the Ministry of Education.[10]

Meanwhile, the number of registrants in traditional schools did not increase much. During this period, in order to unify the country's education system, missionary schools and educational institutions of religious minorities were declared national, and traditional schools were also integrated into public high schools. According to Messkoub, 'on the eve of the Second World War, Iran had . . . clear objectives and was progressing modestly' with regard to education.[11]

The government also implemented limited measures for sanitation and public health, by constructing sewage and piped water systems and establishing medical facilities. However, no significant success was achieved and the high mortality rate of children due to tuberculosis, diarrhoea, measles, typhus and malaria continued. Iran's Red Lion and Sun Society was also established in 1922 as a humanitarian relief organization. Providing health care in cases of natural disasters, combating public diseases, assisting the poor and helpless, especially during famines, maintaining and educating orphaned and destitute children, establishing free public clinics and fixed and mobile hospitals were among the duties of this relief organization.[12]

At the end of the Reza Shah period, efforts were also made to prepare economic and development plans. In April 1937, with the Cabinet's approval, the Economic Council was formed in order to prepare an economic plan and establish coordination between the economic measures of the ministries and economic institutions, and it started working under the chairmanship of Abol Hassan Ebtehaj. Increasing employment, providing the minimum cost of living, extending health services to the general public and improving the general situation were among the other tasks assigned to this institution. However, as Ebtehaj mentions in his memoirs, planning was not possible during this period and the Economic Council was effectively discontinued.[13]

From the fall of Reza Shah until the coup (1941–53)

With the onset of the Second World War (1941–5) and the entry of the Allied forces into Iran, the central government's authority disintegrated. Following the exile of Reza Shah, there was an opportunity for leftist groups and intellectual tendencies to engage in political activities in the country. According to Abrahamian, the political structure's collapse in September 1941 revealed the existence of class conflicts, especially in the cities. During this period, the economic pressure on the general public, on one hand, and the increasing wealth of merchants and landowners, on the other hand, threatened the social structure, and the lower classes were extremely dissatisfied with the severe lack of food, clothing, medicine, health care and education. In such a situation, the Tudeh Party officially announced its existence, and by 1945, 'It had six parliamentary seats in addition to that of Isfahan. It had three cabinet ministries: education, health, and trade. Its main newspaper, *Rahbar* (Leader), boasted a record-breaking circulation of more than 100,000 – triple that of the semi-official *Ettela'at*.'[14]

When Ahmad Qavam took office in 1946, extensive social programmes were put on the agenda. Qavam's coalition government, which cooperated with centre-left parties and politicians, promised that its social programmes would include the 'distribution of state lands, women's suffrage, provincial assemblies, full employment' and the 'construction of rural clinics, schools and irrigation projects'.[15] He also commissioned the Supreme Economic Council to design plans for the country's development, based on the two principles of raising the standard of living by increasing production and consumption and adjusting the distribution of productive wealth. Moreover, Qavam 'initiated a far ranging labor reform program that included recognition of the trade unions allied to one of his coalition parties (the Tudeh Party) and appointment of a Supreme Labor Council to introduce unemployment insurance, wage scales, and committees for managing industrial relations'.[16]

In May 1946, the Cabinet approved the Labour Law proposed by the Supreme Labour Council. This law 'considered certain rights for workers in terms of working conditions, minimum wages, health, the work environment's safety, the formation of an unemployment fund, labour unions, as well as the formation of a health fund and a cooperative fund'.[17] The Qavam government's establishment of the Rural Cooperative Fund in June 1946 was yet another measure in line with its social goals. These funds were tasked with taking care of the disabled, including those injured due to accidents, as well as needy and homeless elderly people, orphans and poor patients, providing social insurance, establishing kindergartens, elementary schools, hospitals and pharmacies and employing mobile doctors. They were financed with landowner profits (*bahreh-ye mālekāneh*) and a percentage of income from owners of cattle farms, mills and orchards.[18] The Social Welfare Agency's charter also was approved in May 1947, in order to centralize and supervise the workplace funds' affairs under the Labour Law.[19]

Another turning point occurred at the end of the 1940s, when 'the intellectuals and workers who had been mobilized by the Tudeh Party since 1941, and . . . the National Front with a broad coalition of the new middle class, traditional moderate bazaaris and the lower middle classes under Mohammad Mossadegh's leadership, challenged the influential classes'.[20] In July 1949, the Formation of Municipalities and Association of Cities and Towns Law was approved. According to Article 39 of this law, taking care of the health and welfare of city residents, establishing soup kitchens, founding nurseries and orphanages for poor and orphaned children, preventing begging and obliging beggars to do industrial work were the duties of municipalities.[21] In addition, the Workers' Cooperative and Insurance Fund was established in 1949, which 'by extending the provision of compulsory insurance to all workers and their family members, expanded insurance obligations to non-work related accidents and illnesses, and therefore, for the first time, the workers' social insurance model was implemented in the country'.[22]

When Mossadegh came to power in April 1951, social policies continued to develop. Apart from the political tensions caused by oil nationalization, the labour unions that had been suppressed in 1946–51 were reactivated during the Mossadegh era. Meanwhile, accompanied by the National Movement, workers organized massive marches in protest against low wages and living and working conditions. Furthermore, after the incident of 21 July 1951 (30 Tir 1331), Mossadegh 'cut the military budget by 15 percent . . . cut the palace budget . . . [and] placed royal charities under government supervision'.[23]

In the autumn of 1952, a series of social development and insurance policies were designed and implemented. The government approved the establishment of the Village, Rural District and Regional Development and Cooperation Fund in support of villages in October 1952. According to this law, landowners were required to donate 20 per cent of their profits: 10 per cent to farmer producers and the other half to the Construction and Cooperative Fund, to be spent on village construction and social affairs in consultation with local councils.[24] These funds were intended to help build low-cost houses, provide health and care for orphans, help to care for debilitated elderly people and patients without families, help to hire mobile doctors and prevent local diseases.

Concurrently, the Formation of Municipalities Law was amended in October 1952 and then approved by the government as the Municipal Law. According to this updated law, in addition to their previous duties, municipalities were tasked with taking the necessary measures to provide low-cost housing for poor people living in urban areas.[25] Subsequently, in November 1952, the Cabinet approved the establishment of the Commission to Help the Poor and Create Employment for Them, whose financial resources were provided by taxes on gasoline sales. The provision of heated housing, food and clothes for the unemployed poor, as well as work tools to persuade them to work, and the construction of public buildings were among the duties of this commission.[26]

Based on the extraordinary powers he received from the Parliament, Mossadegh passed the Workers' Social Insurance Law in January 1953. In accordance with this law, the Workers' Social Insurance Organization was established in April 1953. As a result, all factories and companies subject to the Labour Law, which had been updated in 1949, were obliged to insure their workers under this organization. In addition to expanding the coverage of compulsory insurance in the country, the Workers' Social Insurance Law increased the comprehensiveness of insurance services. Moreover, this law helped to centralize and standardize the implementation of social insurance affairs, while 'creating a legal guarantee for the provision of income . . . [Thus,] many of today's achievements in social insurance may be attributed to this transformation'.[27]

During this period, the country's First Development Plan (1948–55) was approved. This plan allocated 28.5 per cent of its financial resources to social and urban reforms, such as building low-cost housing, supplying piped water to cities, improving the level of public health and training of technical employees, finding work for the unemployed and increasing craftsmen and farmers' technical knowledge.[28] However, as a result of the oil industry's nationalization, 'oil revenues, which were the main source of funding for the Development Plan, were cut off between 1951 and 1954. This caused only one-third of the projected revenues to be realized during the plan.'[29] Despite the government's inevitable need to adopt austerity policies, Mossadegh increased the salaries and benefits of teachers, doctors and nurses and expenditures on education and health.

In March 1947, the Social Services Association was established as a public institution in order to improve the country's health situation and treat poor patients and was later renamed the Imperial Social Services Organization. This organization operated under the Shah's supervision and the deputyship of his sister, Ashraf Pahlavi, and its board members included 'a number of ministers and heads of banks, and . . . twelve people were chosen by the president of the association'.[30] In 1953, the National Association for the Protection of Children also was established to cooperate with the United Nations International Children's Fund (UNICEF) by the order of Ashraf Pahlavi.[31]

Between the coup and the Revolution (1953–1979)

During this period, extensive measures were taken to reduce social freedoms, while limiting the activities of political parties and labour organizations. Moreover, following the implementation of the Land Reform Law in 1963, there were changes in the social and economic structure of the villages. The reduction of the power and influence of big landowners and the expansion of the government's influence in villages, the formation of a class of small-scale farmers and the intensification of the migration of villagers to cities were among these changes.[32]

After the 1953 coup, Mohammad Reza Shah consolidated his power. A new contract with a Western oil consortium increased Iran's oil revenues from about 34 million dollars in 1954 to more than 344 million dollars in 1958. This allowed him to expand the army, bureaucracy and support system of the Imperial Court as much as possible. As a result, 'between 1954 and 1977, the military budget grew twelvefold and its share of the annual budget went from 24 to 35 percent – from $60 million . . . to $7.3 billion'.[33]

During the post-coup period, the activities of independent trade unions were prohibited. Ashraf and Banuazizi show that with the government's permission to form labour unions under the Ministry of Labour's supervision in 1963, their number increased from 16 unions in 1964 to more than 519 in 1972.[34] The economic policies of the 1960s also led to an increase in factories and the growth of a new industrial working class. In order to supervise these unions, the government formed the Workers' Organization of Iran in 1967. Moreover, after the suppression of the June 1963 Uprising, a security section under SAVAK's (secret police and intelligence service) supervision was established in each factory. In addition, the government was able to control industrial workers with beneficial policies to a large extent: 'the regime . . . obliged the employers, who had a lot of economic power due to the government's unreserved support, to pay relative attention to the workers' well-being. The expansion of social insurance, special benefits and workers' participation in the shares of factories led to the emergence of relatively prosperous working classes.'[35]

In line with increasing the Ministry of Labour's social welfare duties, it was renamed the Ministry of Labour and Social Services in 1962 and then the Ministry of Labour and Social Affairs in 1964. Its new tasks included: expanding social insurance, establishing vocational training centres for workers, providing for workers' welfare and improving their living standards and centralizing and coordinating all social service activities throughout the country. Due to these changes, a series of associations and organizations were established under the ministry. In January 1968, a rehabilitation association affiliated with the Ministry of Labour and Social Affairs was established in order to provide vocational and job training for disabled people.[36] The Fund for the Education of Workers' Children was also established in November 1972.[37]

Concurrently, in May 1969, the Villagers' Social Insurance Law was approved, and based on this legislation, the Villagers' Social Insurance Organization was founded. This organization was obliged to cover villagers and their families in case of work-related accidents, diseases, disability, death and other losses.[38] At the time of this law's ratification, the parliamentary representative of Abhar, Manuchehr Saeidvaziri, commented on its significance:

> It is one of the most important steps taken for the completion of the land reforms' goals and the provision of a better life for free peasants . . . By creating such an organization, the government will be able to penetrate the hearts of the villages in

> the true sense of the word . . . and if it is really intended to penetrate and influence the villager's heart and make the villager more interested in the country, as he really should be, and make him attached [*delbasteh*] to the village, he should definitely be provided with a doctor and a clinic.[39]

The Villagers' Social Insurance Organization was created in line with the goals of land reforms, and the aspect of patronage and social and political control was evident in its creation.

There were a number of other state insurance institutions established during this period, including the Public Administration and Recruitment Organization in June 1966, the Medical Services Organization for First-Class Families of Officers, Soldiers and Army, Gendarmerie and Police Employees in March 1973, the Retirement and Pension Fund for Employees of State Companies in May 1973 (affiliated with the Administrative and Employment Affairs Organization), the Medical Services Organization for Government Employees in 1973 and the Retirement and Pension Fund for Permanent Municipal Employees in July 1974.

Furthermore, the Pahlavi Foundation, which was established for the expansion of the Imperial Court's support system as a tax-exempt charitable institution in 1958, began:

> holding in trust for the nation the previous shah's landed estates. It then incorporated most of the fixed assets of the current shah as well as those of his sixty-four family members . . . At its height, the Pahlavi Foundation had assets worth in excess of $3 billion, with shares in 207 companies active in such diverse fields as mining, construction, automobile manufacturing, metal works, agrobusinesses, food processing, banking, insurance, and tourism (casinos, cabarets, and grand hotels). It also had shares in international corporations such as Krupp and General Electric . . . *The New York Times* reported in 1979 that: 'Behind the façade of charitable activities the foundation is apparently used in three ways: as a source of funds for the royal family, as a means of exerting control over the economy, and as a conduit for rewards to supporters of the regime.'[40]

During this period, welfare policies also had been growing within Iran's development plans. Between 1955 and 1973, four such plans were approved and implemented. In the Second Development Plan (1955–62), 14.9 per cent of funding was allocated to public health and education. Although the plan was revised in 1957 with a 28 per cent increase in funding, the amount and share for social affairs decreased drastically. The reduction of social welfare funding occurred in the Second Plan's early years while the country was facing massive protests by workers and employees due to inflationary stagnation.[41]

On the other hand, 'in the early 1960s, the American government, which was worried about the situation in Iran, especially due to the Iraqi coup in 1958,[42] and the increase in propaganda by the Soviet Union against the Iranian regime, put pressure on the regime to carry out social and economic reforms'.[43] In such a situation, as the prime minister, Ali Amini was responsible for the formation of the government in

1962. He entrusted the Ministries of Justice,[44] Education and Agriculture to three of the Shah's critics.[45] From the very beginning, Hassan Arsanjani initiated the land reform programme in the Ministry of Agriculture.[46] In January 1963, the Shah put the six-point plan known as the White Revolution to a referendum. These six points were: the division of agricultural land, nationalization of forests, sale of state factories to private investors, sale of factory shares to workers, giving women the right to vote and creating the Knowledge Corps.

Within this context, the Third Development Plan (1962–8) was formulated as Iran's first comprehensive development programme in cooperation with Harvard University. According to the Harvard Advisory Group's research, budgetary indiscipline and interference in the tasks of decision-making institutions were the most important reasons for the disruption of the formulation and implementation of development policies. Regarding the latter problem, this group explained:

> There are a large number of Committees, High Councils and Higher Councils as well as other governmental institutions with formal responsibility for enunciating and enforcing major economic policies. Thus, at any one moment in time, there are a number of agencies with legal or constitutional authority for making economic policy, and in recent years, the relative importance of these institutions has shifted rapidly, almost from month to month. It has been relatively easy to block a policy decision by playing one institution against another or to prevent implementation of one agency's decision by referring the matter to another organization or 'Council' with parallel powers. It is an obvious corollary that no Council or organization can be held responsible for the success or failure of policies and programs when every decision is subject to conflicting interpretations and jurisdictional uncertainty. The system has produced few basic policy decisions and almost no consistent or purposeful enforcement of decisions taken.[47]

The Third Plan's main goal was to increase the annual national income by at least 6 per cent, and a more equitable distribution of income was a secondary goal. In a meeting held to explain the plan, the Shah emphasized 'the need to increase the income and purchasing power of the people in order to curtail the doubts being created by subversive elements [communists]'.[48] According to the Planning Organization, due to the limited possibility of investment in the agricultural sector, investment should be focused on industry.[49] The argument of the planners was that, with the growth of the industry, agricultural workers would be transferred to the industrial and service sectors, and cities would expand, and as a result, investment in education, health and other aspects of social welfare would increase. According to Abrahamian, while the land reforms of the 1960s 'transformed the countryside, five-year plans . . . brought about a minor industrial revolution'.[50] Improvement of port facilities, expansion of the cross-country railway to Mashhad, Tabriz and Isfahan, asphalting of main roads and the construction of a dam, petrochemical plants and oil refineries and Ahvaz and Isfahan's steel factories were among the important infrastructural facilities built during this decade. By adopting tariff and monetary support policies, the government also encouraged some old landowning families to become industrial entrepreneurs.

The Fourth Plan (1968–73) also considered the acceleration of economic growth and the multiplication of national income by increasing the power of production with more reliance on industrial development and raising capital efficiency. While the share of education and health funding from monetary sources in the Third Plan was about 13.4 per cent, it decreased to 10.2 per cent in the Fourth Plan. On the other hand, a separate section was dedicated to social welfare in the Fourth Plan for the first time, which emphasized:

> Social welfare's general goal is that all welfare activities are gradually… [transferred] from the current limited and charitable phase… [to] the government's supervision in a public organized role, and at the same time, are coordinated with the welfare services of various public, social and private organizations to make it possible for everyone to use minimum services and benefit from social rights.[51]

In this regard, the Supreme Council of Social Welfare was formed in order to coordinate planning work and prevent the overlap of duties, duplication of work and waste of resources.

In March 1973, the Fifth Development Plan (1973–8) was approved. Pesaran and Vafaei consider the most important issues of this period to be: increasing income inequality in urban and rural areas due to the unbalanced economic growth of the Third and Fourth Plans, shortcomings in education, health, social welfare and housing, the expansion of marginalization, environmental pollution and unhealthy urban development.[52] In this regard, the Fifth Plan prioritized welfare goals, such as improving education and health levels, fairer distribution of income, paying attention to the rapid increase in the cost of living and welfare of low-income groups, creating regional equality and preserving the environment. The share of social affairs funding from the Plan's financial resources reached about 30 per cent, 18.1 per cent of which was allocated to education and health. The Social Insurance Section was renamed Social Security and its scope was also expanded. In the sphere of welfare and social security, a regional-demographic targeting approach was formed and the prioritization of service delivery was based on three principles:

1. Low-income level (prioritizing groups from underdeveloped urban and rural areas and simple workers).
2. Social importance (prioritizing children due to their role in the future society and teachers due to their sensitive role in raising and educating future generations of society).
3. Disability and vulnerability (prioritizing the improvement of the physically, mentally and socially disabled in terms of human dimensions and social support).[53]

The fourfold increase in the price of oil in 1973 led to extensive changes in economic and social policies. In March 1974, the First National Seminar on the Country's Social Welfare was held. At the opening of the seminar, the Shah's wife, Farah Pahlavi, spoke about the need to focus on welfare and social security: 'One of the goals of this seminar, without compromising the institutional and legal form of these . . . welfare service organizations, such as the Red Lion and Sun Society and Imperial Social Services Organization, is to create close coordination and cooperation between these organizations by creating an opportunity to exchange opinions and discuss the society's future requirements.'[54] The lack of social security experts and specialists was considered to be one of the main obstacles. This weakness in the expertise of personnel could lead to delays in preparing and approving the plans, changes in content during their drafting, difficulties in their implementation and conflicts arising between the departments implementing them. In the seminar, it was emphasized that 'there is no authority . . . officially responsible for interpreting the laws and finding a logical solution for such cases . . . the Supreme Council of Social Welfare . . . also with the present composition has neither the power nor the authority to implement such work.'[55]

A primary goal emphasized in the seminar's final resolution was coordination between the activities of non-governmental welfare institutions and the government's welfare programmes, while performing these activities with the optimal speed and system. Moreover, given that the Social Security, Welfare and Youth Section's various programmes and divisions (within the Fifth Development Plan) were not directly supervised by any specific state organization, it was announced that a responsible central organization should be identified to undertake tasks, such as planning and determining rules and standards, preparing and organizing the required bills and regulations, coordinating between the active welfare units, supervising the correct implementation of the regulations, approved laws and standards and evaluating the units' activities. The final resolution also mentioned the strengthening of the Ministry of Interior's Social Affairs Branch in order to develop social welfare services with social organizations and institutions, especially by attracting the cooperation and participation of municipalities and affiliated organizations.[56]

In 1974, the Fifth Plan was revised and its financial resources were more than doubled. As a result, government spending on education, health and social welfare increased significantly in its subsequent years. Before the Fifth Plan's revised text was presented to the Parliament, there were changes in the government. In April 1974, Prime Minister Amir Abbas Hoveyda explained the reason for these changes in the Parliament:

> our industrial and agricultural progress and the country's economic progress in general reached such [a level] of growth that a new look at the Fifth Plan and changes in the volume of investments and examination of priorities compelled the government to prepare an amended program, and I hope we will present it to the legislature this summer . . . In any case, this issue caused us to progress with a 40 per cent growth [rate] . . . Our state of progress required us to make changes in our administrative system . . . Based on this principle, some changes were made in our organizations . . . Another change that . . . is very important is the subject of social welfare . . . in the Fifth Plan . . . we gave great importance to social welfare . . . The Shah decreed that this plan will be the welfare program of the country of Iran. So, in order to coordinate these works, the Ministry of Social Welfare has decided that the relevant minister will try to adapt his programs without trying to centralize all

these organizations in one place to maintain coordination. Two billion tomans are being spent by charity groups and aid in the government budget for progress.[57]

Following these changes, on 23 July 1974, the Law of Establishing the Ministry of Social Welfare was approved.[58] According to Article 1 of this law, the duties of this ministry included: the provision of universal medical insurance, social security (such as social insurance and social support), welfare services for age groups and families and rehabilitation services, as well as the supervision of non-governmental welfare organizations, treatment of drug addicts, membership in international organizations and implementation of welfare programmes approved by the Supreme Council of Social Welfare. According to Article 2 of the law, some government organizations and institutions were to be placed under the Ministry of Social Welfare's authority, as follows:

1. Social Insurance Organization and related units (formerly under the Ministry of Labour and Social Affairs)
2. Workers' Welfare Bank (formerly under the Ministry of Labour and Social Affairs)
3. Villagers' Social Insurance Organization (formerly under the Ministry of Cooperatives and Rural Affairs)
4. Medical Services Organization (formerly under the Ministry of Health)
5. Rehabilitation Association (formerly under the Ministry of Labour and Social Affairs)
6. Implementation of the Law for the Protection of Employees from the Effects of Old Age, Disability and Death (formerly under the Ministry of Labour and Social Affairs)
7. Affairs concerning drug addicts' treatment and rehabilitation and related treatment units (formerly under the Ministry of Health)
8. Affairs concerning mental patients' treatment and rehabilitation and related treatment units (formerly under the Ministry of Health)

According to Article 3 of this law, coordination of the activities of non-governmental welfare organizations was the Supreme Council of Social Welfare's responsibility. The members of this council were: the Minister of Social Welfare, the Minister of Health, the Minister of Education, the Minister of the Interior, the Minister of Cooperatives and Rural Affairs, the Minister of Labour and Social Affairs, the Minister of the Advisor and the Head of the Planning and Budget Organization, the Minister of Science and Higher Education, the CEO of the Red Lion and Sun Society of Iran and the CEO of the Imperial Social Services Organization.

The parliamentary opposition to the new ministry's establishment had criticized its possible control of public benefit institutions and foundations, insufficient services and support within its legal framework and inadequate organizational structure. Nonetheless, the Ministry of Social Welfare's establishment can be considered the most important government measure towards the centralization and organization of welfare and social security services in Iran. In February 1975, the Minister of Social

Welfare, Shojaeddin Sheikholeslamzadeh, proposed the establishment of two new institutions: the Welfare Services Organization and the Social Security Organization. Sheikholeslamzadeh, who considered the ministry's formation to be an achievement of the First Welfare Seminar and a step towards creating coordination, management and greater centralization in welfare affairs,[59] spoke about the Welfare Services Organization's formation in the Parliament:

> both in terms of political stability and internal and external security, and . . . economic prosperity, the country has been provided with the means and facilities that will enable the government to plan and implement extensive and comprehensive programs to ensure the welfare of all . . . it necessary to remind the honourable representatives that the government's general welfare policy . . . is that it strives to cover all the residents of the country through the expansion of . . . medical, retirement, disability, unemployment and accident insurance . . . in such a way that no natural or accidental event disturbs their well-being . . . [while] providing the minimum livelihood and material and spiritual needs of the Iranian family. However, until [these] types of insurance have covered all of the country's residents, the Ministry of Social Welfare has the duty to provide the necessary organizations, institutions and manpower . . . with the implementation of programs that are researched and formulated with the help of experts and specialists.[60]

It is evident that the increase in Iran's oil revenues of the early 1970s was the most important factor in the development of welfare services, especially the Ministry of Social Welfare and its affiliated organizations. Firstly, the Welfare Services Organization was founded in order to organize social support affairs. Secondly, the Social Security Organization was established in July 1975 in order to promote and expand social insurance coverage, by merging the Social Insurance Organization and the Villagers' Social Insurance Organization. According to Article 4 of the Establishment of Organizations Law, those eligible were: people who work in any capacity in exchange for wages or salaries, holders of professions and occupations and recipients of retirement, disability and death benefits. Article 28 also noted that, for the first time, the government had funded insurance and undertook to pay 3 per cent of the insurance premium.[61]

However, the weakness of the economic, political and social conditions and structures at this time in Iran caused the development and expansion of social services to face fundamental challenges, and as a result, the Ministry of Social Welfare was merged with the Ministry of Health. The bill proposing to merge these two ministries in order to form the Ministry of Health and Welfare was approved in July 1976.[62] On the day of Sheikholeslamzadeh's introduction as the Minister of Health and Welfare to the Parliament, Hoveyda explained the reasons for the merger of the two ministries, as follows:

> It is important to inform you that the new ministry will not be centralized, in the sense that there will be a small core in Tehran for planning, while all executive work will be carried out at provincial, county and district levels, and we hope . . .

> those who deal with health and medical treatment issues at regional levels will help us in preparing this law to insure its successful implementation.[63]

Moreover, given that the Ministry of Social Welfare had been established to centralize the management and provision of the country's welfare and social security services, its subsequent integration with the Ministry of Health indicated the necessity of decentralizing its activities.

Coinciding with the debate over the merger of the Ministries of Social Welfare and Health, the Second National Seminar on Social Welfare was held in May 1976. At this seminar, it was emphasized: 'Regarding the complex dimensions that the country's rapid economic growth has presented to us, the Second National Seminar on Social Welfare, rather than paying attention to various groups, deals with the fundamental issues and topics that are inclusive of all groups and social strata in every field and in every case.'[64] The Minister of Health and Welfare, Sheikholeslamzadeh, said the following about the main challenges of the Ministry of Social Welfare in the seminar's opening speech:

> From the very first months of the [Ministry of Social Welfare's] work, two facts gradually became clear. First, welfare, medical and health services are very closely related to each other, and supplying these services separately, both from the point of view of the provider and the consumer is not logical and cost-effective. The second fact is related to the decision-making and management approach. With the ever-increasing expansion of welfare programs and the rapid increase of social security coverage, it gradually became clear to our implementing officials and experts that the existing centralized system, along with the ethos of its Tehran bureaucracy, was one of the significant obstacles to the progress of [our] work.[65]

Concerning the above-mentioned challenges, the first indicated the necessity of a comprehensive approach to welfare and social security services, and therefore, in the Second Seminar, emphasis was 'placed on the formulation of a comprehensive plan and system and expandable service capability as a part of the country's development plan.'[66] This issue was taken into consideration for the Sixth Development Plan (1978–82) so that half of the committees (i.e. eighteen out of a total of thirty-six) for its formulation were dedicated to the social and welfare dimensions of development, including macro and trans-sectoral committees (e.g. quality of life, social welfare and development) and committees for specific social sectors (e.g. housing, education, health and medical treatment). Regarding the Sixth Plan's outline, it was stated: 'in determining the development priorities, increasing the national gross product has been replaced by providing more welfare for the people, especially those with the lowest levels of income and social security.'[67]

Conclusion

During the Reza Shah period, nation-building, which was one of the institutional factors in the formation of social policies, had a significant impact, especially in the areas of public education and housing (including the settlement of the nomadic population). Concurrently, state programmes were implemented to train a technical workforce, increase the skill level of workers and create workers' provident funds, which were all influenced by the economic efficiency factor. This period can be considered the starting point of social policies in its modern sense. It is also important to consider the influence of social democratic ideas during the Constitutional era and the rise of a developmental approach among constitutional elites. Another factor that had an impact, especially with regard to the expansion of social insurance, was the government's cooperation with global organizations, including the International Labour Organization. Such interactions, which began in the early 1930s, created obligations for the Iranian government, which led to the adoption of the policies and mechanisms of these international institutions. In fact, from this point of view, a kind of theoretical and policy synchronization with global models was created, but from a practical standpoint, it seems that the political, social and economic structure of Iran was not ready for the comprehensive implementation of such policies, and serious resistance coalesced against them.

After September 1941, a different type of relationship between the government and society appeared and class divisions became evident. The extensive activities of the Tudeh Party also highlighted this issue. Therefore, especially when the Qavam government came to power, various social programmes were implemented for education, health, employment and income distribution, which included the formulation of the first labour law and the establishment of the Villagers' Cooperative Fund. Moreover, in line with social welfare goals, various types of insurance and support organizations were established in the country from the mid-1940s onwards, covering different demographic groups. This process of development continued with Mossadegh's government. The approval of the Workers' Social Insurance Law and the establishment of the Workers' Social Insurance Organization were among the most important measures taken by his government to improve the situation of workers. In general, during the second period (1941–53), class interests as well as the Iranian social movements, elites and left-wing parties were the main factors in the evolution of social and welfare policies.

Another major factor was the tenfold increase in oil revenues of the late 1950s, which provided the conditions for the formulation and implementation of industrial development programmes. This economic growth coincided with international developments, especially, the Soviet-backed coup in Iraq, which raised American concerns about the political situation in Iran, thus strengthening attention to social welfare reforms. This issue was particularly evident in the Third Development Plan, which was prepared by the Harvard Advisory Group. As noted by Abrahamian, with the implementation of the Land Reform Program and the Third and Fourth Development Plans, a small industrial revolution was effected in Iran from the early 1960s to the mid-1970s. Also, from the mid-1960s, social and welfare policies were gradually included in the development plans.

During the Fourth Plan's implementation in 1968–73, many governmental and non-governmental organizations and institutions were established in the welfare and social security sector with state financial support. Throughout this decade, more than forty associations, communities and welfare organizations were established, which were often funded by the government and connected to the Imperial Court while operating outside of state supervision. These institutions often began their operations as charities and gradually became dependent on the government's annual budget. This situation increased the inclusiveness and comprehensiveness of social services but led to bureaucratic issues, for example, inconsistency, parallel work and interference.

The Supreme Council of Social Welfare was established in order to resolve these inconsistencies. The government's efforts to establish organizational coherence and order in social insurance and welfare matters intensified from the early 1970s and resulted in the Ministry of Social Welfare's formation. With its establishment, some non-governmental organizations became governmental or were placed under state supervision. During this period, efforts were made to expand services through existing organizations instead of creating new ones; however, incoherence and inefficiency still posed a serious challenge.

As shown in the documents of the Second National Social Welfare Seminar and the committees related to the Sixth Plan's formulation, it seems that achieving a comprehensive welfare strategy posed a problem for development policymakers and more serious attention was paid to the existing social security structures and systems, distribution of services, target groups, service providers, the government's role and the non-governmental sector's position in the mid-1970s. From the mid-1960s, and as a result of the growth of bureaucratic rationality, the internal consistency of policies increased, but the instability and continuous changes in structures, especially after the sudden increase in oil revenues, disrupted the efficiency of policymaking. At the same time, it seems that the acceleration of 1960s industrialization, despite its economic achievements, had extensive social consequences, which, in turn, influenced the government's increasing activities in social and welfare affairs.

Based on the findings of the historical documentation and theoretical approaches of this chapter, the author has concluded that a mixed methods approach should be used to explain social policy developments, rather than only focusing on a single factor, which potentially excludes or distorts important aspects of historical developments.[68] This also explains why welfare policies have been typically interpreted in piecemeal fashion, and this issue is especially evident in countries such as Iran that historically have not had a stable and enduring structure of political economy nor a developed relationship between the government and the nation.

Notes

1 Ervand Abrahamian, *A History of Modern Iran* (Cambridge: Cambridge University Press, 2008), 66.

2 Ibid., 67.

3 Mahmood Messkoub, 'Social Policy in Iran in the Twentieth Century', *Iranian Studies* 39, no. 2 (2006): 229.

4 'Qanun-e Estekhdam-e Keshvar', approved 22 Azar 1301 (14 December 1922), accessed 17 December 2023, https://rc.majlis.ir/fa/law/show/90706.

5 Mohammad Ali Akbari, *Barresi-ye Barnamehrizi-ye Dowlati dar Howzeh-ye Tamin-e Ejtemaei-ye Iran* (1285–1320), vol. 1 (Tehran: Moasseseh-ye Ali-ye Pazhuhesh-e Tamin-e Ejtemaei. 1382/2003), 44–53.
6 Valim Peyrovian and Abdolhossein Jivar, *Qavanin va Moqarrarat-e Tamin-e Ejtemaei: Majmueh-ye Kamel* (Tehran: Moasseseh-ye Ali-ye Pazhuhesh-e Tamin-e Ejtemaei, 1381/2002), 3–8.
7 Akbari, *Barresi*, vol. 1, 69.
8 Ibid., 77–9.
9 Ibid., 169.
10 Ervand Abrahamian, *Iran Between Two Revolutions* (Princeton: Princeton University Press, 1983), 144–5.
11 Messkoub, 'Social Policy', 229.
12 Akbari, *Barresi*, vol. 1, 61.
13 Abol Hassan Ebtehaj, *Khaterat-e Abol Hassan Ebtehaj*, ed. Alireza Aruzi (Tehran: Elmi, 1371/1992), 303.
14 Abrahamian, *Modern Iran*, 108.
15 Messkoub, 'Social Policy', 230.
16 Ibid.
17 Mozaffar Karimi, 'Zaminehha-ye Tarikhi-ye Peydayesh-e Nezam-e Jame-ye Refah va Tamin-e Ejtemaei dar Iran', *Faslnameh-ye Hoquq-e Tamin-e Ejtemaei* 1, no. 1 (1384/2005): 38.
18 Mohammad Ali Akbari, *Barresi-ye Barnamehrizi-ye Dowlati dar Howzeh-ye Tamin-e Ejtemaei-ye Iran* (1320–1357), vol. 2 (Tehran: Moasseseh-ye Ali-ye Pazhuhesh-e Tamin-e Ejtemaei, 1383/2004), 50–2.
19 Ibid., 54.
20 Ahmad Ashraf and Ali Banuazizi, *Tabaqat-e Ejtemaei, Dowlat va Enqelab dar Iran*, trans. Soheila Torabi Farsani (Tehran: Nilufar, 1388/2009), 83.
21 Akbari, *Barresi*, vol. 2, 58–9.
22 Bahram Panahi, *Karkardha-ye Tamin-e Ejtemaei dar Iran: Zaruratha-ye Barpayi-ye Nezam-e Jame-ye Refah va Tamin-e Ejtemaei* (Tehran: Moasseseh-ye Ali-ye Pazhuhesh-e Tamin-e Ejtemaei, 1385/2006), 22.
23 Abrahamian, *Modern Iran*, 118.
24 Karimi, 'Zaminehha', 40.
25 Akbari, *Barresi*, vol. 2, 59.
26 Ibid., 60–1.
27 Peyrovian and Jivar, *Qavanin*, 77.
28 Gholamreza Ghaffari and Reza Omidi, *Keyfiyyat-e Zendegi: Shakhes-e Towseeh-ye Ejtemaei* (Tehran: Shirazeh, 1388/2009), 130–1.
29 Julian Bharier, *Economic Development in Iran, 1900–1970* (London: Oxford University Press, 1971), 90.
30 Akbari, *Barresi*, vol. 2, 121.
31 Ibid., 125.
32 Hossein Bashiriyeh, *Mavane-ye Towseeh-ye Siyasi dar Iran* (Tehran: Gam-e Now, 1382/2003), 87–95.
33 Abrahamian, *Modern Iran*, 124.
34 Ashraf and Banuazizi, *Tabaqat-e Ejtemaei*, 102.
35 Ahmad Ashraf, 'Kalbodshekafi-ye Enqelab: Naqsh-e Kargeran-e Sanati dar Enqelab-e Iran', *Goftogu*, no. 55 (1389/2010): 58.
36 Akbari, *Barresi*, vol. 2, 91.

37 Ibid., 98.
38 Ibid., 94.
39 *Mashruh-e Mozakerat-e Majles-e Showra-ye Melli va Eslami* (Tehran: Majles-e Showra-ye Eslami, 1390/2011), dowreh-ye 22, jalaseh-ye 128.
40 Abrahamian, *Modern Iran*, 127–8.
41 Ghaffari and Omidi, *Keyfiyyat-e Zendegi*, 137.
42 The coup was led by Abdul Karim Qasim and supported by the Iraqi Communist parties, and the Soviet Union played a prominent role.
43 Massoud Karshenas, *Naft, Dowlat va Sanati Shodan dar Iran*, trans. Ali Asghar Saeidi and Yusef Haji Abdolvahab (Tehran: Gam-e Now, 1382/2003), 137.
44 Abrahamian, *Iran Between Two Revolutions*, 423. Nuraldin Alamuti, one of the Tudeh Party's former leaders who had joined Qavam in 1947, became Minister of Justice.
45 Ibid. Mohammad Derakhshesh, who, as the teachers' spokesperson, had both the Tudeh Party and the National Front's support, became Minister of Education.
46 Ibid. Hassan Arsanjani, one of Qavam's colleagues and a supporter of land reforms since the early 1940s, became Minister of Agriculture.
47 Thos. H. McLeod, *National Planning in Iran: A Report Based on the Experiences of the Harvard Advisory Group in Iran* (Regina, n.p., 1964), 241.
48 *Jalaseh-ye Tarikhi-ye Barresi-ye Barnameh-ye Sevvom* (Tehran: Sazman-e Barnameh, 1341/1962), 19.
49 *Moqaddameh-ye Barnameh-ye Omrani-ye Sevvom-e Iran* (Tehran: Sazman-e Barnameh, 1340/1961), 20–2.
50 Abrahamian, *Modern Iran*, 133.
51 *Osul va Hadafha-ye Barnameh-ye Omrani-ye Chaharom* (Tehran: Sazman-e Barnameh va Budjeh, 1347/1968), 99.
52 Mohammad Hashem Pesaran, 'Refah-e Ejtemaei ve Barnamehrizi', in *Majmueh-ye Maqalehha-ye Dovvomin Seminar-e Melli-ye Refah-e Ejtemaei, 18–22 Khordad Mah 2535 [1355]*, vol. 1, Komite-ye Towseeh va Refah-e Ejtemaei (Tehran: Sazman-e Barnameh va Budjeh, 1355/1976), 4–70; Changiz Vafayi, 'Eqtesad-e Refahi va Toseeh-ye Ejtemaei', in *Majmueh-ye Maqalehha-ye Dovvomin Seminar-e Melli-ye Refah-e Ejtemaei, 18–22 Khordad Mah 2535 [1355]*, vol. 1, Komite-ye Towseeh va Refah-e Ejtemaei (Tehran: Sazman-e Barnameh va Budjeh, 1355/1976), 273–340.
53 *Barnameh-ye Panjom-e Omrani-ye Keshvar, 1352–1356* (Tehran: Sazman-e Barnameh va Budjeh, 1351/1972), 796.
54 *Seminar-e Melli-ye Refah-e Ejtemaei 18–22 Esfand Mah 1352: Qatnameh-ye Seminar* (Tehran: Sazman-e Barnameh va Budjeh, 1352/1973), 5.
55 *Barnameh-ye Panjom*, 12–14.
56 *Seminar-e Melli: Qatnameh*, 20–21.
57 *Mashruh-e Mozakerat-e Majles*, dowreh-ye 23, jalaseh-ye 164.
58 Qanun-e Tashkil-e Vezarat-e Refah-e Ejtemaei, approved 1 Mordad 1353 (23 July 1974), accessed 17 December 2023, https://rc.majlis.ir/fa/law/show/97121.
59 'Sokhanrani-ye Shojaeddin Sheikholeslamzadeh, Vazir-e Behdari va Behzisti dar Eftetah-ye Seminar', *Dovvomin Seminar-e Melli-ye Refah-e Ejtemaei*, vol. 2 (Tehran: Sazman-e Barnameh va Budjeh, 1355/1976), 7.
60 *Mashruh-e Mozakerat-e Majles*, dowreh-ye 23, jalaseh-ye 208.
61 Akbari, *Barresi*, vol. 2, 115–17.
62 Some consider the reason for the Ministry of Social Welfare's merger to have been its inability to deal with charitable institutions affiliated with the Imperial Court. This issue can be considered one of the primary reasons because the Minister of the

Economy Alinaghi Alikhani also resigned from his position in 1969 due to challenges with the Special Office of Farah Pahlavi. See also Mohammad Yeganeh, *Khaterat-e Mohammad Yeganeh*, eds. Habib Ladjevardi and Zia Sedqi (Tehran: Sales, 1385/2006), 117–18.

63 *Mashruh-e Mozakerat-e Majles*, dowreh-ye 24, jalaseh-ye 22.

64 'Sokhanrani-ye Abdol Majid Majidi, Vazir-e Moshaver va Rayis-e Sazman-e Barnameh va Budjeh dar Eftetah-ye Seminar', *Dovvomin Seminar-e Melli-ye Refah-e Ejtemaei*, vol. 2 (Tehran: Sazman-e Barnameh va Budjeh, 1355/1976), 4.

65 Ibid., 7.

66 Ibid., 27.

67 *Khotut-e Kolli, Hadafha, Siyasatha va Khatt-e Mashiha-ye Barnameh-ye Omrani-ye Sheshom* (Tehran: Sazman-e Barnameh va Budjeh, 1356/1977), 238.

68 For further discussion, see Reza Omidi, 'Tahavvolat-e Siyasatgozari-ye Ejtemaei dar Asr-e Pahlavi: Faraz va Forud-e Ravabet-e Dowlat va Mellat', *Barnamehrizi-ye Refah va Towseeh-ye Ejtemaei* 7, no. 28 (1395/2016): 151–60, https://doi.org/10.22054/qjsd.2017.7144.

Bibliography

Archives

Library and Document Center of the Planning and Budget Organization of Iran
Library, Museum and Document Center of the Iranian Parliament
National Library and Archives of Iran

Primary sources

Barnāmeh-ye Panjom-e ʿOmrāni-ye Keshvar, 1352–1356. Tehran: Sazman-e Barnameh va Budjeh, 1351 (1972).

Dovvomin Seminār-e Melli-ye Refāh-e Ejtemāʿi. Tehran: Sazman-e Barnameh va Budjeh, 1355 (1976).

Gozāresh-e Omumi-ye Dovvomin Seminār-e Melli-ye Refāh-e Ejtemāʿi va Gozāreshhā-ye Komitehhā-ye Panjgāneh-ye Seminār. Tehran: Sazman-e Barnameh va Budjeh, 1355 (1976).

Jalaseh-ye Tārikhi-ye Barresi-ye Barnāmeh-ye Sevvom. Tehran: Sazman-e Barnameh, 1341 (1962).

Khotut-e Kolli, Hadafhā, Siyāsathā va Khatt-e Mashihā-ye Barnāmeh-ye ʿOmrani-ye Sheshom. Tehran: Sazman-e Barnameh va Budjeh, 1356 (1977).

Majmuʿeh-ye Maqālehhā-ye Dovvomin Seminār-e Melli-ye Refāh-e Ejtemāʿi, 18–22 Khordād Māh 2535 [1955]. Tehran: Sazman-e Barnameh va Budjeh, 1355 (1976).

Mashruh-e Mozākerāt-e Majles-e Showrā-ye Melli va Eslāmi. [DVD]. Tehran: Majles-e Showra-ye Eslami, 1390 (2011).

Moqaddameh-ye Barnāmeh-ye 'Omrāni-ye Sevvom-e Irān. Tehran: Sazman-e Barnameh, 1340 (1961).

Osul va Hadafhā-ye Barnāmeh-ye Omrāni-ye Chahārom. Tehran: Sazman-e Barnameh va Budjeh, 1347 (1968).

Seminār-e Melli-ye Refāh-e Ejtemā'i 18–22 Esfand Māh 1352: Komiteh-ye Ta'min-e Ejtemā'i, Majmu'eh-ye Maqālehhā. Tehran: Sazman-e Barnameh va Budjeh, 1352 (1973).
Seminār-e Melli-ye Refāh-e Ejtemā'i 18–22 Esfand Māh 1352: Qat'nāmeh-ye Seminār. Tehran: Sazman-e Barnameh va Budjeh, 1352 (1973).

Secondary sources

Abrahamian, Ervand. *A History of Modern Iran*. Cambridge: Cambridge University Press, 2008.
Abrahamian, Ervand. *Iran Between Two Revolutions*. Princeton: Princeton University Press, 1982.
Akbari, Mohammad Ali. *Barresi-ye Barnāmehrizi-ye Dowlati dar Howzeh-ye Ta'min-e Ejtemā'i-ye Irān (1285–1320)*. Vol. 1. Tehran: Moasseseh-ye Ali-ye Pazhuhesh-e Tamin-e Ejtemaei, 1382 (2003).
Akbari, Mohammad Ali. *Barresi-ye Barnāmehrizi-ye Dowlati dar Howzeh-ye Ta'min-e Ejtemā'i-ye Irān (1320–1357)*. Vol. 2. Tehran: Moasseseh-ye Ali-ye Pazhuhesh-e Tamin-e Ejtemaei, 1383 (2004).
Ashraf, Ahmad. 'Kālbodshekāfi-ye Enqelāb: Naqsh-e Kārgerān-e San'ati dar Enqelāb-e Irān'. *Goftogu*, no. 55 (1389/2010): 55–124.
Ashraf, Ahmad and Ali Banuazizi. *Tabaqāt-e Ejtemā'i, Dowlat va Enqelāb dar Irān*. Translated by Soheila Torabi Farsani. Tehran: Nilufar, 1388 (2009).
Bashiriyeh, Hossein. *Mavāne'-ye Towse'eh-ye Siyāsi dar Irān*. Tehran: Gam-e Now, 1382 (2003).
Bharier, Julian. *Economic Development in Iran, 1900–1970*. London: Oxford University Press, 1971.
Ebtehaj, Abol Hassan. *Khāterāt-e Abol Hassan Ebtehāj*. Edited by Alireza Aruzi. Tehran: Elmi, 1371 (1992).
Ghaffari, Gholamreza and Reza Omidi. *Keyfiyyat-e Zendegi: Shākhes-e Towse'eh-ye Ejtemā'i*. Tehran: Shirazeh, 1388 (2009).
Karimi, Mozaffar. 'Zaminehhā-ye Tārikhi-ye Peydāyesh-e Nezām-e Jāme'-ye Refāh va Ta'min-e Ejtemā'i dar Irān'. *Faslnameh-ye Hoquq-e Tamin-e Ejtemaei* 1, no. 1 (1384/2005): 27–53.
Karshenas, Massoud. *Naft, Dowlat va San'ati Shodan dar Irān*. Translated by Ali Asghar Saeidi and Yusef Haji Abdolvahab. Tehran: Gam-e Now, 1382 (2003).
McLeod, Thos. H. *National Planning in Iran: A Report Based on the Experiences of the Harvard Advisory Group in Iran*. Regina: n.p., 1964.
Messkoub, Mahmood. 'Social Policy in Iran in the Twentieth Century'. *Iranian Studies* 39, no. 2 (2006): 227–52.
Moridi, Siavash. *Farhang-e Bimehhā-ye Ejtemā'i*. Edited by Ali Kayal. Tehran: Moasseseh-ye Ali-ye Pazhuhesh-e Tamin-e Ejtemaei, 1378 (1999).
Omidi, Reza. 'Tahavvolāt-e Siyāsatgozāri-ye Ejtemā'i dar 'Asr-e Pahlavi: Farāz va Forud-e Rāvabet-e Dowlat va Mellat'. *Barnamehrizi-ye Refah va Towseeh-ye Ejtemaei* 7, no. 28 (1395/2016): 151–92 .
Panahi, Bahram. *Kārkardhā-ye Ta'min-e Ejtemā'i dar Irān: Zarurathā-ye Barpāyi-ye Nezām-e Jāme'-ye Refāh va Ta'min-e Ejtemā'i*. Tehran: Moasseseh-ye Ali-ye Pazhuhesh-e Tamin-e Ejtemaei, 1385 (2006).

Pesaran, Mohammad Hashem. 'Refāh-e Ejtemā'i va Barnāmehrizi'. In *Majmu'eh-ye Maqālehhā-ye Dovvomin Seminār-e Melli-ye Refāh-e Ejtemā'i, 18–22 Khordād Māh 2535 [1355]*, 1–47. Vol. 1, Komite-ye Towse'eh va Refāh-e Ejtemā'i. Tehran: Sazman-e Barnameh va Budjeh, 1355 (1976).
Peyrovian, Valim and Abdolhossein Jivar. *Qavānin va Moqarrarāt-e Tamin-e Ejtemā'i: Majmu'eh-ye Kāmel.* Tehran: Moasseseh-ye Ali-ye Pazhuhesh-e Tamin-e Ejtemaei, 1381 (2002).
Vafayi, Changiz. 'Eqtesād-e Refāhi va Towse'eh-ye Ejtemā'i'. In *Majmu'eh-ye Maqālehhā-ye Dovvomin Seminār-e Melli-ye Refāh-e Ejtemā'i, 18–22 Khordād Māh 2535 [1355]*, 273–340. Vol. 1, Komite-ye Towse'eh va Refāh-e Ejtemā'i. Tehran: Sazman-e Barnameh va Budjeh, 1355 (1976).
Yeganeh, Mohammad. *Khāterāt-e Mohammad Yegāneh.* Edited by Habib Ladjevardi and Zia Sedqi. Tehran: Sales, 1385 (2006).

8

The Commercial Bank of Iran

The first private bank, from establishment to merger

Ali Tatari[1]

Introduction

Although the negative economic consequences of the Second World War of 1939–45 (1318–24 SH) were evident to the whole world at that time, it was catastrophic for Iran, which had a weak but growing economy during those years. Iran, after the occupation by the Allied forces, suffered from imposed sociopolitical and economic ruptures, the consequences of which were evident for years. The monetary situation of the country was transformed, and all the standards and regulations that were necessary to maintain an economic system were gradually lost. Although the Second World War ended in 1945, the resulting political and economic consequences of wartime conditions continued in the Middle East, where there had not been peace before the war, and unrest, disorder and disorganization had replaced the relative stability of the past.

As a country that officially declared neutrality in the Second World War, Iran was not damaged any less than the countries involved in the war. In addition to various economic and political hardships that this international conflict brought to Iran, the influence of foreign countries was a serious obstacle that prevented any constructive activities. Of course, other factors contributing to the calamitous conditions in Iran of those days should not be overlooked, such as the influence of the security apparatuses of the occupying countries among the members of the people's classes and their effectiveness, the general public's poverty and misery, the existence of weak and reckless governments and the lack of internal security.

Economic situation of Iran in the 1940s

Cost of living index

One of the measures of the economic situation in any country is the extraction and refinement of the quality of life index, affected by economic, social and political factors. Based on this, the cost of living index was 100 in 1936 (1315), and this number increased to 946 in 1949 (1328).[2] Hence, the cost of living in Iran increased ninefold in thirteen years.

Annual budget deficit

Another serious problem of those years was the annual budget deficit. That is, during the period from 1941 (1320) to 1954 (1333), successive governments faced problems with resources and expenditures for the provision of the annual budget. Due to the experience of the modern bureaucracy of the middle and final years of Reza Shah's reign, the country's budget bill was balanced, and according to a regular routine, usually in early March of each year, the annual financial plan of the following year was approved by the National Assembly (Parliament or Majles). But after the occupation of Iran and the increase in the cost of living, and the unbridled inflation that was the result of the war, the amount of state expenses increased dramatically in such a way that the government was forced to approve the annual budget in one or two-twelfths within a period of six or twelve months to pay the salaries of employees.[3]

Development plans

With the subsiding of some political and social crises, the Government of Iran considered the implementation of a series of plans for the country's economic development from 1948 (1327), when the First Development Plan of the Country was formulated and approved, and then implemented during a seven-year period.[4] With the approval of this development plan, the government felt the need to establish financial and credit institutions to advance its goals; hence, it took the initiative by establishing several state and semi-state banks and did not create any obstacles for the establishment of private banks. This was an opportunity for the Commercial Bank (Bank-e Bazargani) to start working in January 1949 (Bahman 1328),[5] benefiting from the Law of Commerce by means of shares.[6]

Establishment of first banks in Iran

Although Iranians had a long familiarity with money changing and financial institutions, the first bank in Iran was officially established by the British in 1888. The British New East Bank was created due to England's industrialization and increasing colonial possessions, and to sell its industrial products in different countries, especially colonies, and to buy raw materials needed by British industries in different countries and colonies. Its central office was in London, and branches were opened all over the world, including Tehran.[7]

Years later, in April 1925, the first Iranian state-owned bank, the Pahlavi Army (Qashun) Bank, was opened in some shops located on Sepah Street in Tehran. This bank, whose initial capital was 3,883,950 rials (the balance of the army officers' pension fund),[8] expanded its activity from the end of 1933 as Sepah Bank.[9] Meanwhile, a bill for the establishment of Iran's National Bank was presented to the Parliament during the early days of Reza Shah's reign and Mostowfi al-Mamalek's government, and it was approved on 27 April 1927 (6 Ordibehesht 1306), and the government was allowed to hire experts from Germany or Switzerland. With the Parliament's permission, a delegation of German experts was hired under the chairmanship of Kurt Lindenblatt, and the National Bank started working in August 1928 (Shahrivar 1307).[10] The establishment of the National Bank, which was a long-standing aspiration of Iranians, was accomplished with the aim of eliminating foreign banks from the economic arena of Iran. Therefore, it was directly supported by Reza Shah Pahlavi and the governments of that time. Although several other state banks, such as agricultural, mortgage, industrial and mining banks, were established in subsequent years, it seems that the conditions for the establishment of a private bank were not available until the late 1940s.

Antecedents of private banks

The history of private banks in Europe dates back to the nineteenth century. Germany and England were pioneers in this sector. Even in nineteenth-century Germany, banking operations in nearly all dimensions were carried out by private banks.[11] In Germany, these banks were also called 'all-round banks' because they conducted all kinds of credit transactions.[12] Private banks in England were known for their accuracy and stringency in work, and of course, simplicity in regulations, and these banks granted more short-term loans and credit, both in England and in Germany.[13]

In Iran, the idea of establishing a non-governmental bank was by no means an easy task. At first glance, it was impossible to gain public trust in those years, and on the other hand, the influence of foreigners could be considered a serious obstacle in the administrative structure and public opinion. In addition, as mentioned in the introduction, Iran's economy was experiencing one of its most adverse periods. Apart from this, there was still no administrative and legal infrastructure for private banks to operate within, and this was a primary reason why applicants faced unforeseen problems in administrative mazes. On the other hand, gaining public trust was a difficult task in those years. Besides the fact that there was no track record of private financial institutions in the country, the livelihood and economic situation of the people was such that they could not entrust their capital to the private sector's new institutions. Moreover, private investors feared foreign banks and their potential encirclement of the country's monetary economy.[14]

The problems and obstacles to establishing a private bank did not end here, as the state banks were also serious competitors. In those years, some believed that only the National Bank should be strengthened, and the people and the government should focus on its activity and agency. This was the view of the National Bank's director, Abol Hassan Ebtehaj. In fact, these state banking officials were pursuing an important goal, which was to repel the two Soviet and British banks, and on the other hand, they did not have confidence in the private sector's capability to establish financial institutions. Although Ebtehaj initially resisted the establishment of private banks, years later, in 1960 (Bahman 1338), he founded the Iranian Bank.

Opening of the Commercial Bank

The Commercial Bank of Iran officially opened for business on 26 February 1950 (6 Esfand 1328) on Bouzarjomehri Street (now 15 Khordad Street), across from Soltani Mosque, in the vicinity of Dar al-Shafa school in Tehran.[15] The day of the bank's establishment was chosen to coincide with the day of Bahmangan, on 2 Bahman, which was considered one of the most important holidays of Iranians in ancient times, and various festivals and ceremonies were held on that day.[16] Mostafa Tajaddod (see Figure 8.1), the founder and CEO of the bank, who was born in 1908 (1278 SH) in Sari, had worked previously in the Ministry of Justice and the National Bank. In early 1934 (end of 1312), he resigned from the National Bank and left for Europe to complete his studies in law and economics. After twelve years of studying and working in financial institutions in Germany and France, he returned to the country at the beginning of 1946 (end of 1324). At first, he was employed in the Bank of Industry and Mining.[17]

Later, during the eighteenth and nineteenth terms of the Majles, he was elected as the senator representing the people of Sari from the fourth to seventh terms of the Senate. He also held the position of Secretary General of the Supreme Economic Council in the Ministry of Commerce in the later years of his life.[18] At the same time, he was successful in the Tehran Chamber of Commerce's elections and was an active member of this private sector organization. He also mastered three languages: German, English and French.

In addition to the aforementioned jobs and responsibilities, Tajaddod was the CEO and chairman of the Bank of Commerce's board of directors from January 1950

Figure 8.1 Mostafa Tajaddod, *c.* 1968. *Source*: Ettelaat Newspaper and Photo Archive.

(1328) to 1979 (1358),[19] when the bank was merged with Tejarat (Trade) Bank. The Bank of Commerce's first board of directors included: board members Mohammad Ali Saffari and Vajehollah Fazel Sarjooyi, alternate members Yeganeh Haeri and Jafar Kafaei and auditors Mohammad Ali Moffarah and Javad Sadr.[20] On the opening day, the Commercial Bank had nineteen employees and attendants, most of whom were experienced personnel from the Industrial and Mining Bank.[21] On Wednesday 22 February 1950 (3 Esfand 1328), *Ettelaat* newspaper wrote:

> The Commercial Bank of Iran has recently been established to carry out banking and commercial affairs with 100 million rials of capital, of which 40 million rials has been paid up. This bank is a joint-stock company and is the first institution that was established with people's capital through the sale of shares. The Commercial Bank will start working next week in the former location of the Shahi Bazaar Bank.[22]

News of the bank's establishment was published in other newspapers, including *Keyhan*.[23]

The Commercial Bank's Articles of Association, which were formulated in thirty articles,[24] determined its duties as follows:

1. Paying promissory notes and bills of exchange
2. Granting credit
3. Granting loans against goods, shipping documents and other commercial collateral
4. Accepting demand and term deposits
5. Transferring funds from one city to another
6. Carrying out any type of foreign exchange transactions (with the permission of the Foreign Exchange Commission)
7. Issuance of credit bonds
8. Opening a current account with banks
9. Accepting representation and providing any type of banking facilities for customers
10. Any manner of banking and exchange operations and transactions

The first challenge

After completing the initial formalities of opening and setting up the new private bank, based on the laws of that day, it was necessary for private and state banks to open an account in the National Bank, and this issue itself caused the first serious challenge to the Commercial Bank's establishment. On 22 February 1950, the Commercial Bank officially requested (in paragraphs 20 and 21 of a letter) that the National Bank open two accounts on its behalf in the latter's Central and National Bazaar branches.[25]

However, in correspondence number 437/10, dated 6 March 1950 (15 Esfand 1328),[26] the National Bank replied:

1. Article 5 of that bank's statute states that 40 per cent of its capital is paid in cash, and in Article 6 of the same statute, it is explicitly stated that all of its shares are anonymous. On the other hand, the last section of Article 29 of the Law of Commerce, approved on 13 Ordibehesht 1311 [3 May 1932] stipulates that until 50 per cent of the nominal price of the shares has been paid, anonymous shares cannot be issued with temporary anonymous confirmation.

Also, the National Bank stated another reason:

2. Article 52 of the Law of Commerce stipulates that the director of this joint-stock company must deposit shares in the company's fund with a name to guarantee their administrative actions, and [these shares] cannot be transferred. On the other hand, all the shares of that bank are anonymous, according to Article 6 of your own statute. Therefore, the shares provided for in Article 14 of that bank's statute must also be anonymous, and this arrangement will be against the express text of Article 525 of the Law of Commerce.

The National Bank made the opening of the accounts subject to the elimination of defects and, in view of the above legal defects, refused to open these accounts for the Commercial Bank. This conflict between the National Bank and the Commercial Bank lasted about six months. The Commercial Bank considered the National Bank's director, Abol Hassan Ebtehaj, to be the cause of this crisis and tension between the two banks and in a special issue commemorating its tenth anniversary substantiated this claim, writing:

> Despite all these objections and obstructions, the bank's board of directors did not stop pursuing the matter for the advancement of the work and the achievement of the goal, and with their reasoned explanations before the competent authorities and frequent visits and correspondence, they overcame such problems and were able to reach their objective to end this conflict between the National Bank and this bank that had lasted for six months. On the 2 Shahrivar 1329 [24 August 1950], the Commercial Bank of Iran managed to open a current account in its own name with the number 52160 in the National Bank of Iran.[27]

Ironically, on the same day that Ebtehaj resigned from the management of the National Bank and was appointed as Iran's ambassador to France, the news of the opening of the Commercial Bank's account and Ebtehaj's departure to France was simultaneously published on page eight of *Keyhan* newspaper. With the abatement of this crisis, it seems that the process of development and progress in the Commercial Bank intensified. The second branch of the bank was opened in November 1950 (Aban 1329) in Rasht by Mohammad Majid, the governor of Gilan province.[28]

With the increase in government revenues and, especially, the encouragement to invest in the banking sector, at some points in the 1940s and 1950s, government officials supported the establishment of a private bank, but there was a pessimistic view, on the contrary, which said:

> [Private banks] . . . were formed by a small group of big and allied capitalists, who, at the same time, controlled the ownership of large production groups, and their main motive was to establish a direct financial link between these banks and the aforementioned groups, in order to increase their monopoly power while exerting influence on the banking system by using the banking network's extensive credit and facilities.[29]

Another concern was the lack of organizational and individual experience in this sector, which, of course, could not be proven in the case of the Commercial Bank and Mostafa Tajaddod, since he had chosen the core of the bank's employees from personnel with experience in the banking sector.

However, during the initial years of the Commercial Bank's activity, especially between 1949 (1328) to 1953 (1332), an array of political and economic crises overshadowed Iran, and the economy struggled with a kind of bankruptcy, and business was not prosperous. Nor were positive statistics recorded in sectors such as industry and agriculture, and on the other hand, the influx of nomadic and agricultural communities into cities had reached its peak in these years. Hoarding and the black market trade in goods were an institutionalized legacy of the Second World War, as well.

Nonetheless, several important and decisive factors should not be overlooked. Firstly, there was a small number of active banks in the country, all of which were state-owned, and there was no significant competition between them, and secondly, the National Bank, with some initiatives and support from the government and the people, was able to weaken the British and Soviet banks, and these factors had prepared the sector for the Commercial Bank's activity, to a certain extent.

Buying a new building

In the late 1940s, with the intensification of Iran's economic recession, foreign banks turned to contractionary policies and wanted to reduce their expenses and current costs. At the same time, strict laws were imposed by the Iranian government to limit the activities of foreign banks.[30] Hence, in 1951 (1330), the British Bank of Iran and the Middle East, which did not find it profitable to continue working due to currency restrictions and other considerations, decided to close its branches in Iran.[31] Taking advantage of this opportunity, the Commercial Bank's management first bought the buildings of the British bank's Isfahan and Khorramshahr branches, and then, in September 1952 (Shahrivar 1331), they purchased its central branch on the eastern side of Sepah (Tupkhaneh) Square in Tehran, which had been the location of the former Imperial (Shahanshahi) Bank in previous decades.[32] The central building of the Imperial Bank was purchased for the amount of 29.6 million rials (£331,096). The British estimated the value of this building to be 60 million rials.[33] The Commercial

Bank's central branch was officially opened in this building (see Figure 8.2) in November 1952 (Aban 1331), and Prime Minister Mohammad Mossadegh was invited for the opening day.

This turn of events pleased the Iranian people and statesmen and brought a great deal of prestige to the Commercial Bank, while also coinciding with the political currents that led to the nationalization of the country's oil industry and a spectrum of political movements actively campaigning against British colonialism in the region. The British considered the building's significance and the Imperial Bank's influence to be the second symbol and sign of their power in Iran, after the importance and glory of their embassy, and they referred to the bank's closure as 'a sad end to the sweet story

Figure 8.2 Commercial Bank of Iran, *c.* 1968. *Source*: Ettelaat Newspaper and Photo Archive.

of British efforts'.[34] Moreover, Tajaddod mentioned the purchase of the British bank's central building to Mohammad Reza Shah Pahlavi during the opening ceremony of the Construction Bank on 15 September 1952 (24 Shahrivar 1331).[35] Apparently, the National Bank also had been negotiating with the British to buy this building since 21 March 1952 (1 Farvardin 1331).[36]

In addition to gaining favour with the Royal Court and Prime Minister Mossadegh's government, Tajaddod and the Commercial Bank acquired a positive reputation in public opinion and further credibility within the society by purchasing the British bank's buildings. This event also was publicized in the Commercial Bank's charters, advertising and correspondence. For example, a letter addressed to Mossadegh, which was published by the bank, called him 'the beloved leader' while explaining that after ending the tenure of colonial officials, the Commercial Bank of Iran succeeded in purchasing the British bank's real estate in Khorramshahr, Isfahan (and Tehran), and with this act, it prevented further damage to the country's economic affairs.[37]

The annual balance sheets of the bank between the years 1950 (1329) and 1976 (1355) indicate the increasing growth of the Commercial Bank's net profits. Although the annual and periodical reports may have been arranged in such a way to present the most hopeful outlook for the banking system and to reassure the shareholders, the ever-expanding development of the bank's units, activities and employees paints a positive picture on the whole (see Figure 8.3).

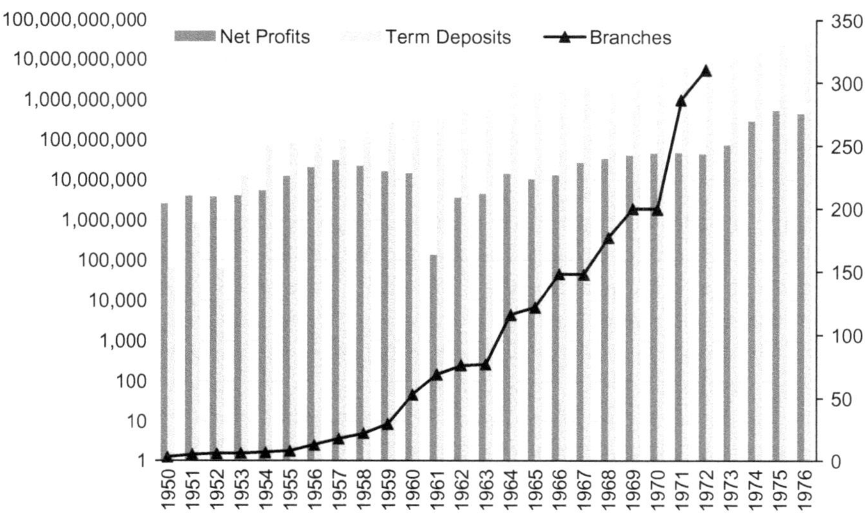

Figure 8.3 Commercial Bank's net profits, term deposits and branches/kiosks, 1950–76.
Source: Central Bank of Iran Archives, *Taraznamehha-ye Salha-ye 1329–1355, Bank-e Bazargani.*

Cultural activities

In addition to economic affairs, the Commercial Bank was active in various cultural fields during its thirty-year existence, including the publication of its monthly magazine. From 1966 (1345) until 1971 (1350), sixty-seven issues were published, and subsequently, the four-page magazine was expanded to twenty-five to fifty-five pages, and the content was improved. Each chapter of the magazine covered a variety of subjects, including the bank's internal news and historical and scientific topics for the improvement of employees' technical knowledge. The last known issue was published in the spring of 1977 (1356).[38] The bank also published its performance report on various occasions, including two ten-year and fifteen-year reports. In these reports, the date of the bank's establishment and its role in Iran's economy with accompanying statistics and figures are of particular interest. The bank's balance sheet (*tarāznāmeh*) was also published in Persian and English every year.

The Commercial Bank's printing house was located next to its central building in Sepah Square,[39] and was probably established around the same time as the bank, since its name is engraved on the first charters, including the balance sheet of 1950 (1329). The printing house published many books, such as: *Divan-e Abol Qasem Hassan bin Ahmad Ansari*;[40] Haj Mirza Mohammad Hassan Vaqayenegar's *Pokernameh*; *Kolliyyat-e Mosavvar-e Mirzadeh Eshghi* by Ali Akbar Moshir Salimi; Noosh Azar Asadi's *Garmsar*; Reza Lotfi's *Romuz-e Estentaq*; Mohammad Rashad's *Manteq*; *Modiriyyat-e Shahrdari* by Ali Niami;[41] *Salnameh-ye Amuzeshgah-ye Andisheh-ye Don Bosko Tehran, 1342–1343*; *Joghrafiya-ye Eqtesadi* by various authors; *Baghestan-e Eshgh* by Habibollah Chaichian (Hesan); Foruzan Kermani's *Yusef-e Iran*; Persian translations of Plato's *Crito* and *A Christmas Carol* by Charles Dickens;[42] *Ravesh-e ʿAmali-ye Sherkatha-ye Taʿavoni* by Ali Akbar Nurad; Mehdi Soheili's *Do Qatreh-ye Ashk*; and Yadollah Maftun Amini's *Deryacheh*.

Use of new technologies

One of the benefits of the presence of private banks in Iran's banking network was the use of the latest techniques and technology to provide better services and, of course, earn more money. Mostafa Tajaddod's experience as a commercial bank manager in the banking and foreign currency exchange sector laid the groundwork for many initiatives and innovations that had to be quickly defined and implemented. Especially after Iran's banking network expanded significantly in the early 1960s, it became necessary to use advanced tools and facilities to manage and monitor this system.

Tajaddod, with a background of studying and working in West Germany, had a detailed knowledge of its advanced banking system. The importance and role of private commercial banks in the West German economy is well demonstrated by their share of the country's credit transactions in 1960: 60 per cent of all demand and term deposits of individuals and commercial and manufacturing institutions, 80 per cent of domestic transactions with foreign countries and 95 per cent of foreign bank deposits were concentrated in these banks.[43] He travelled to West Germany in 1953 (1332), and while visiting several banking and business study centres, he met with Dr Hjalmar Schacht, the director of Schacht Bank and a famous professor of economics, and after initial negotiations, he invited him to Tehran for a three-week period. During his stay in Iran, in addition to meeting with Mohammad Reza Shah Pahlavi and other heads of government, Schacht held training courses in the Commercial Bank and prepared a comprehensive report on the situation of that day and the future of the bank.[44] Schacht's presence was widely reflected in the Iranian media of that day. Moreover, from 1968 (1347) onwards, the bank started using electronic calculators in financial and accounting systems, and from 1969 (1348), preparations were made to use a number of computers in several large branches of the bank. Gradually, the bank's structure and work methods were adapted to the new conditions.[45] Also, in order to learn about the latest technical developments and increase the expertise of its personnel, the bank implemented an annual programme in 1954 (1333) for its trainees and employees to study modern banking methods in Germany, England, France and the United States.[46]

Bank's international activities

Twelve years of living in European countries, where, besides studying, Tajaddod had held responsible positions in Germany and France's financial and economic sectors, had made him familiar with the economic environment of Europe and the world. Also, his mastery of German, English and French allowed him to communicate directly with international organizations. Therefore, he actively participated in most of the important financial conferences and meetings in the world. Having acquired this valuable international experience, Tajaddod later opened two European branches of the Commercial Bank in London and Hamburg, which were to have a presence in world markets. Reporting on his trip abroad in 1956 (1335), he wrote in the introduction of the balance sheet:

> On my way back from my trip to America, I stopped in London for a few days, and while looking into the situation of [our new UK] branch, I met and became acquainted with the British bank's VIPs. It is fully hoped that introducing us abroad with the opening of this branch will yield good results. I travelled to America at the invitation of several international monetary funds and banks to participate in the eleventh conference held in Washington, and I was fortunate enough to attend these meetings to get a valuable opportunity to personally contact the executives of various banks and make arrangements to cooperate with them.[47]

Taking into account his international business in the banking sector and all the conditions and aspects of an effective presence in economic circles abroad, Tajaddod chose two locations, England and Germany, to establish the new global branches. In addition to the fact that Iranians had a more effective presence in these two countries, which dated back to the 1940s, the banking systems of these countries were very

Table 8.1 Commercial Bank's Foreign Exchange Transactions, 1956–9

Total	Year
$23,330,409	1956
$55,634,444	1957
$85,763,036	1958
$92,146,456	1959

Source: Astan Qods Razavi Libraries and Archives, *Panzdah Salegi-ye Bank-e Bazargani* (Tehran: Bank-e Bazargani-ye Iran, n.d.), 12–13.

extensive and advanced. Thus, the Commercial Bank's new branches were officially opened on 23 July 1956 (1 Mordad 1335) in London, and later, in Hamburg, on 15 April 1959 (25 Farvardin 1338).[48] Furthermore, the bank regularly published advertisements in the *Financial Times*, *The Times*, the *Guardian* and the *Handelsblatt* to attract foreign capital.[49]

In 1956 (1335), the Commercial Bank entered a new stage of economic activity by conducting foreign exchange transactions and, within a short distance from its foreign exchange unit, communicating with the banking network abroad. Thus, as an administrative organization, it was able to establish a good relationship with foreign brokerage. The increasing volume of foreign exchange transactions between 1956 (1335) and 1959 (1338) was significant (see Table 8.1).

Social responsibility

With a series of initiatives, the Commercial Bank rendered assistance in many domestic crises by giving donations to semi-governmental institutions, charities and social organizations, attracting the public's attention more than ever before. Social responsibility, which is referred to as a set of duties and obligations that are carried out by institutions and companies to help society, became purposeful in Iran when the first serious private sector institution, the Tehran Chamber of Commerce, was formed around 1926 (1305). Since then, some companies and non-governmental and economic institutions have taken measures in this direction, according to their conditions and financial capacity. But it seems that the Commercial Bank had a respectable track record in the field of social responsibility, compared to other private and public banks. From the very first months of its establishment, that is, in 1950 (1329), this bank allocated 2 per cent of its monthly profits to the current accounts of charitable institutions associated with the Red Lion and Sun Society (Jamiyyat-e Shir va Khorshid-e Sorkh) of Iran.[50] This action was unprecedented for any Iranian Bank up to this point.

Moreover, in a series of measures planned to support the urban middle class, the bank granted low-interest loans to educators and government employees. The report of the Commercial Bank's CEO to the General Assembly in 1966 (1345) stated:

> In order to ensure the material well-being of educators and other government employees, the Commercial Bank of Iran, which always enjoys the unwavering

> support of the country's intellectuals, has paid a total of 328,193,035 rials to government employees in 1345/1966. Also, currently, loans are continuing to be given to educators at a regular price for the welfare of teaching staff during the summer vacation season.[51]

For some natural disasters and accidents, the Commercial Bank provided assistance in kind and in cash. During the flood of November 1963 (Aban 1342), which covered areas of the cities of Amol, Babol and Nur in Mazandaran province, in addition to donating necessities for the earthquake victims, Mostafa Tajaddod sent 50,000 rials in cash.[52] Also, in order to fight illiteracy and provide education fees for underprivileged children, a new account named 'Hope of Youth' was established in December 1966 (Azar 1345) in all of the Commercial Bank's branches to grant donations as well as the bank's own financial assistance.[53] In addition, the bank decided to open a free hospital for the health and treatment of domestic and non-domestic animals, and for this endeavour, it allocated 10 million rials to the construction of a well-equipped veterinary hospital in 1963 (1342).[54]

New banking services

During its thirty-year existence, the Commercial Bank competed with some of the most powerful foreign, state and private banks in Iran, thanks to its initiative and creation of new banking services. According to former managers of this bank, most of the innovations in commercial banking services were invented by Mostafa Tajaddod.[55] Besides increases in the bank's resources and the amount of credit granted to commercial and economic affairs in Iran, based on its balance sheet's statistics during this period, a large network of branches had spread throughout the country, even in some small villages and towns. In this regard, the bank was trying to take the initiative and cover all sections of the society with its programmes and services, which was unprecedented for the country's banking system.

One of the Commercial Bank's new initiatives was the 'mobile account', which had a great impact on attracting people's funds in the 1950s and 1960s. Beginning in 1952 (1331),[56] account holders could make withdrawals and deposits by presenting their account book in any branch of the Commercial Bank.[57] Customers of the mobile account also could transfer up to 100,000 rials without any banking fee,[58] and since 1959 (1338), prizes had been awarded to the owners of this account by lottery.[59]

Another innovative idea was to provide monetary services to Iranian pilgrims attending the Hajj in 1964 (1343), which had never been done before. At the Commercial Bank's suggestion and with the government's approval, a delegation from the bank was stationed in the cities of Jeddah, Medina and Mecca to provide the necessary funds to the pilgrims,[60] who could even get the money they needed as a cash advance with a receipt during the Hajj from the bank's representatives in Saudi

Arabia, later repaying this amount to the Commercial Bank after returning to Iran.[61] This unprecedented financial service, which gained spiritual credibility among Iran's religious classes, probably encouraged the flow of much of their monetary capital to the bank. Coincidently, when the Arab-Israeli War of Attrition intensified in May 1970 (Ordibehest 1349), three famous Iranian clerics announced three bank account numbers in their speeches and propaganda brochures in order to attract people's financial aid in support of the Palestinian people. These accounts belonged to the Commercial Bank.[62]

Yet another novel initiative of the Commercial Bank was its account lottery. This prestigious ceremony was held in Tehran and other Iranian cities twice a year, often in the presence of senior local officials and members of the public with special ceremonies. For example, the lottery ceremony for Yazd Commercial Bank's customers, which was formalized with the attendance of the governor and city officials on 6 February 1964 (17 Bahman 1342), appeared in *Ettelaat* newspaper,[63] as well as an advertisement for the lottery ceremony in Tehran on its first page.[64] The bank's seasonal lottery was held in Mordad every year, and its local lottery was held on the second day of Bahman annually.[65]

A further initiative of the Commercial Bank was to open an account for babies in such a way that parents had the possibility to deposit any amount of money, and the bank also gave about 10 per cent of this amount back as a bonus, but the parents did not have the right to withdraw funds until the child turned eighteen.[66]

Other commercial activities

Like other private enterprises throughout the world, the Commercial Bank needed a variety of commercial activities to expand and strengthen its economic foundations. Until the 1960s, it was not very common for banks to invest directly in other sectors, such as construction, industries and tourism. Based on documentary evidence, the Commercial Bank started extensive activity in the construction sector and the buying and selling of land from the initial years of its existence. Two major companies were founded in this sector,[67] one was Omran Ameri Company, which bought many properties in the Khuzestan region and was active in construction, and the second was Pargar Construction Company, which was established on 26 April 1967 (6 Ordibehesht 1346), with registration number 11433.[68]

Tajaddod was also interested in the tourism and hotel management sector. He entered the tourism industry by launching Ahavan Company in 1969 (1348) with the aim of promoting tourism and hotel management.[69] He also worked in Khorasan province by setting up a lump sugar factory and several compote and tomato paste factories.[70] In the leasing industry, the Commercial Bank was the first Iranian banking institution to operate in the home appliances sector.[71]

Thus, the aforementioned activities of the Commercial Bank were divided into two categories:

1. Buying land, which was maintained for a certain period, then sold; establishing several construction companies that were operating in the housing construction sector.
2. Establishing affiliated companies under different names, which were engaged in various economic activities to increase the bank's capital.

Bank's welfare measures for employees

Compared to other banks before the Revolution, the Commercial Bank had acceptable amenities. In addition to the fact that this issue was raised in an interview with two former senior employees of this bank,[72] it is also evident from the documents that remain from the bank's archives and charters. In total, the employee welfare measures of the bank can be analysed in the following four sections:

1. Monthly salary and other benefits
   The Commercial Bank, which started its operations in January 1950 (Bahman 1328) with about nineteen employees, had managed to increase its personnel to 3,981 in 1977 (1356).[73] As a result, it was necessary to pay sufficient salaries and benefits to these personnel during its nearly thirty years in business. According to the bank's financial documents, the salaries and benefits of its employees were increased and paid at a specific annual rate. The bank's board of directors also tried to improve the salaries of the personnel and give them a noticeable increase on various occasions. In 1956 (1335), changes were made in the bank's statutes and the amount of its legal reserve from net profits increased from 10 to 15 per cent and the bonus of bank employees increased from 5 to 10 per cent.[74]

   Also, in January 1975 (Bahman 1353), on the occasion of the twenty-fifth anniversary of the establishment of Mostafa Tajaddod's bank, in a ceremony held in the hall of the bank's central office, he announced that, in addition to increasing the annual salary of the employees, another amount would be added to their salaries, and at the same time, privileges would be given to the retired employees of the bank.[75] In another measure, the bank paid annual travel expenses to employees.[76]
2. Health and medical treatment
   Concerning the health and safety of its employees, the Commercial Bank provided the appropriate conditions from the very beginning of its establishment, along with the creation of a health department within the administrative structure. A clinic was established in the bank's central branch, and for the welfare of the bank employees, a portion of shares in Tous Hospital was purchased.[77] Also, the personnel could go to any of the hospitals, clinics and laboratories of the bank's contracting party by getting a letter of

introduction from the central branch and only pay 20 per cent of the visiting fee.[78]

3. Consumer cooperative company, bank store and hairdressers
Every six months, the bank allocated free food items and groceries to the employees, the amount of which varied in different years, so that it fluctuated from 35 kilos of rice and 15 kilos of vegetable oil to 60 kilos of rice and 25 kilos of vegetable oil. Of course, it should be noted that free food had been distributed regularly since 1966 (1345).[79] In addition, a hairdressing salon was opened in the central branch by order of the bank's directorship, which provided free hairstyling services to the staff.[80]
4. Celebrations and ceremonies honouring employees
In the last days of every year, the Commercial Bank honoured its selected employees by holding a ceremony. This ceremony was held for the first time in 1962 (1341) and continued until the end of the bank's life.[81]

Bank merger

Mostafa Tajaddod was an influential and active figure in the Iranian political scene of the second Pahlavi period, who attended multiple periods of the Parliament and the Senate and chaired their specialized commissions. At the same time, he established an effective image of entrepreneurship in the contemporary history of Iran with five decades of participation in banking, construction, industry, tourism and philanthropy, employing about 4,000 personnel. Overcoming many difficulties that were encountered along the path to establishing the first private bank in Iran, Tajaddod focused on the growth, expansion and modernization of the Commercial Bank, which paved the way for subsequent private banks in the country. On the other hand, his performance has been criticized by some researchers.[82] Nonetheless, overall, his was a defensible performance: by the end of 1977 (1356), the Commercial Bank had 102 branches in Tehran, 104 branches in other Iranian cities, towns and villages, as well as two branches abroad, with the total number of bank employees reaching 3,081.[83]

According to its financial reports, until the end of 1977 (1356), the Commercial Bank enjoyed significant growth in all areas and was in good condition. However, during the events of 1978–9 (1357) that led to the victory of the Islamic Revolution, the bank gradually had to face the economic and political realities of Iran at that time. During the demonstrations of the Pahlavi regime's final months, a number of the Commercial Bank's branches were damaged in Tehran and other cities,[84] yet the bank continued to operate after a short break and until a few months after the Islamic Revolution.

In a radio message on 7 June 1979 (17 Khordad 1358), Mehdi Bazargan, the prime minister of the Provisional Government, announced the nationalization of all the country's banks. This law was formulated in two articles, as follows:

> Article 1. In order to safeguard the law and national capital, and to put the country's wheels of production to work, and to guarantee people's deposits and savings in banks while accepting the principle of conditional legitimate ownership, and concerning: 1. the manner of acquiring, the revenue of banks and the illegal transfer of assets abroad; 2. the fundamental role of banks in the country's economy and the natural connection between the country's economy and banking institutions; 3. banks' indebtedness to the government and their need for state supervision; 4. the need to coordinate the activities of banks with other organizations of the country; 5. the need to channel banks' activity towards Islamic operations and profit. From the date of this law's approval, all national banks will be announced and the government is obliged to appoint bank directors.
>
> Article 2. As of this date, only the signatures of the directors appointed by the government for the banks have legal validity.[85]

This decision would seem to have been taken without the knowledge of the owners of capital and entrepreneurs and faced serious problems in practice. Although the government guaranteed the career future of bank employees and counted all of them as state employees, in order to solve and alleviate the problems in the implementation of Article 17 of the Banking Affairs Law, ratified on 25 September 1979 (3 Mehr 1358) by the Revolutionary Council, a merger plan for banks was also approved by the General Assembly of Banks. According to this plan, the country's banks were divided and then merged into three categories: commercial, specialized and provincial.[86] After its implementation, the Irano British Bank, the Credit Bank of Iran, the Bank of Iran and the Middle East, the Mercantile Bank of Iran and Holland, the Commercial Bank of Iran, Iranshahr Bank, the Bank of Iranian Industries, Shahriyar Bank, Iranians' Bank, the Labour Bank and the International Bank of Iran and Japan were all merged into the newly formed Trade Bank (Bank-e Tejarat) and continued to operate.[87]

Conclusion

The founding of the Commercial Bank in 1949 (1328) encountered serious opposition from the public opinion of Iranian society at that time. At first, due to the political and economic conditions that Iran was facing in the years after the Second World War, people could not fully trust a private banking institution, so they preferred to deposit all of their money and wealth in state or foreign banks that had the necessary support. On the other hand, the financial laws and regulations regarding the operation and activity of private banks were unclear at that time in Iran.

In fact, contrary to the past perception that the main reason for the delay in the establishment of Iranian private banks was the existence of strict and convoluted regulations, it must be acknowledged that it was mostly the fear of powerful foreign banks and their encroachment on the monetary economy of the country that made investors hesitate to establish a private bank. However, the legal obstacles that had been created in the financial structure of Iran since the late 1940s made it difficult for foreign banks to survive, which prepared the ground for the establishment of domestic private banks. With the arrival of private banks, especially the emergence of the Commercial Bank of Iran, new pages appeared in the history of Iran's modern banking system, and gradually other bank investors began to participate in this growing sector, and during the golden era of Iran's economy in the 1960s, the role of private banks became irreplaceable. In addition to being the first private bank in the country, the Commercial Bank was able to create lasting innovations in the history of banking. By using the weaknesses of its banking competitors and implementing a series of fruitful initiatives, it consolidated its position in the economic arena of Iran during three decades of effective activity.

Creating self-confidence among Iranian capitalists to establish their own private banks was one of the most important results of the Commercial Bank's presence, in such a way that, as the bank passed its ten-year mark in the late 1950s by founding hundreds of bank branches inside and outside the country, many entrepreneurs and owners of capital were convinced that with careful planning and diligent efforts, it was possible to set up a private bank in Iran.

Furthermore, prior to the Commercial Bank's formation, state and foreign banks dominated the country's financial and monetary activity, and, as a result, they were less inclined to solve defects in their systems and work. Likewise, the concentration of government revenues and people's money in state banks had largely deprived the directors of those banks of the necessary ingenuity and initiative. However, the entry of private banks, which aimed to gain customers' satisfaction as much as possible in order to acquire capital, led to changes in the state banks, as well. In fact, private banks tried to attract more funds by capitalizing on the weak points of their state competitors. The creation of a mobile account, which was one of the Commercial Bank's initiatives, was one of these measures.

Attention to social responsibility, which was a characteristic of financial institutions of modern societies of the world at that time, was also evident in the Commercial Bank's activities. In addition to giving spiritual credibility to the bank, this principle attracted material capital during its lifetime. Moreover, the managerial role of Mostafa Tajaddod should be considered instrumental in the Commercial Bank's success. Besides the fact that he had considerable political influence in the upper echelons of the government, he had the necessary knowledge and literacy in banking management. His international interactions and familiarity with the latest scientific and technical achievements in the banking sector led to many of the measures necessary for the bank's success and dynamism that arose from his creative mind. Of course, the establishment of some companies that were active in the construction and real estate sectors, including agricultural land, may have been somewhat far from the bank's mission, and this remains a criticism of his performance. Nevertheless, in total, his entrepreneurship employed about 4,000 people, while donating revenue to the current accounts of charitable institutions, creating mobile savings accounts and profits for savings account holders as well as holding biannual lotteries for the bank's customers and so forth, all of which provided an important basis for the Commercial Bank's accreditation. Finally, the bank's management supported the educated urban middle classes, including cultured people, teachers and intellectuals, as well as showing a great interest in the general development and improvement of the society. Such a bank also displayed nationalistic views in the public sphere.

Notes

1 Tatari.info@gmail.com.
2 National Library and Archives of Iran (NLAI), *Majalleh-ye Bank-e Bazargani: Beh Monasebat-e Bist o Panj Saleh-ye Tasis-e Bank-e Bazargani*, no. 87 (Winter 1353/1974), 41.
3 Central Bank of Iran Archives (CBIA), *Dah Sal dar Khedmat-e Eqtesad-e Keshvar: Beh Monasebat-e Payan-e Dahomin Sal-e Tasis-e Bank-e Bazargani-ye Iran* (Tehran: Edareh-ye Entesharat va Amar va Barresiha-ye Eqtesadi, n.d.), 26–7.
4 'Tarikhcheh-ye Tanzim-e Barnameh-ye Haft Saleh-ye Omran va Abadi-ye Iran', *Zamimeh-ye Majalleh-ye Shomareh-ye 98 Bank-e Melli-ye Iran* (Bahman-Esfand 1327/ February 1949), 4.
5 Sadeq Barzegar, *Bankdari* (Tehran: Madreseh-ye Ali-ye Bazargani, 1350/1971), 26.
6 Before 1955 (1334), there was no special law for banks and banking, and banks were often registered as joint-stock companies and conducted banking operations according to their articles of association. For more information, see the Commercial Bank's balance sheets in 1953 (1332) and 1955 (1334).
7 Ahmad Rafiei, *Bank va Bankdari* (Tehran: n.p., 1351/1972), 47.
8 *Gozaresh-e Amaliyyat-e Si Saleh-ye Bank-e Sepah* (Tehran: Entesharat-e Bank-e Sepah, n.d.), 2.
9 *Majalleh-ye Bank-e Sepah*, no. 1 (Khordad 1341/June 1962): 54.
10 *Habl al-Matin* 36, no. 20 (3 Ziqadeh 1346/24 April 1928): 23–4.
11 Rafiei, *Bank va Bankdari*, 47.
12 Ziaoddin Hemmat, 'Sistem-e Banki-ye Jomhuri-ye Federal-e Alman-e Gharbi', *Majalleh-ye Kanun-e Bankha* 1, no. 1 (Shahrivar 1343/August–September 1964): 21.
13 Ibid., 37 and 47.
14 Hamid Deyhim, 'Naqsh-e Bankha dar Towseeh-ye Eqtesadi-ye Iran' (Bachelor's thesis, University of Tehran, 1345–46/1966–67), 112.
15 *Dah Sal*, 96.
16 *Majalleh-ye Bank-e Bazargani*, no. 87, 12.
17 *Tehran Ekonomist*, no. 520 (5 Bahman 1342/25 January 1964), 14.
18 Baqer Aqeli, *Sharhehal-e Rajal-e Siyasi va Nezami-ye Moaser-e Iran*, vol. 1 (Tehran: Goftar; Elm, 1380/2001), 492–3.
19 Tajaddod died in 1358 at the age of 71. Aqeli, *Sharhehal*, vol. 1, 492–3.
20 CBIA, *Taraznameh-ye Sal-e 1329, Bank-e Bazargani*, 17.
21 *Dah Sal*, 17.
22 *Ettelaat*, no. 7161 (3 Esfand 1328/22 February 1950), 8.
23 *Keyhan*, no. 2061 (13 Esfand 1328/4 March 1950), 8.

24 Ayatollah Boroujerdi Library, *Asasnameh-ye Bank-e Bazargani-ye Iran*, registration no. 854, 1–2.
25 *Dah Sal*, 23–4.
26 National Bank of Iran Archives (NBIA), 122945_20220501.
27 *Dah Sal*, 24. See also *Keyhan*, no. 2208 (2 Shahrivar 1329/24 August 1950), 8. The Commercial Bank also opened a current account (number 37405) at the National Bank's Bazaar branch.
28 *Majalleh-ye Bank-e Bazargani*, no. 87, 19.
29 CBIA, *Gozaresh-e Tahavvolat-e Bankdari dar Iran* (Tehran: Edareh-ye Barresiha-ye Eqtesadi-ye Bank-e Markazi-ye Iran, 29 Mehr 1369/21 October 1990), 2.
30 Deyhim, 'Naqsh-e Bankha', 113.
31 *Majalleh-ye Bank-e Bazargani*, no. 87, 16.
32 Ibid., 17.
33 Geoffrey Jones, *Tarikhcheh-ye Bank-e Shahi dar Iran [Banking and Empire in Iran]*, trans. Nasser Moafaqian (Tehran: Moasseseh-ye Tahqiqat va Towseeh-ye Olum-e Ensani, 1393/2014), 406.
34 Ibid., 381.
35 Ibid., 17.
36 NBIA, 56-20220501–122412.
37 NLAI, 0230-017362–0006.
38 Mansour Hosseinzadeh, 'Ravabet-e Omumi dar Sherkat-e Sahami-ye Bank-e Bazargani-ye Iran' (Bachelor's thesis, Allameh Tabatabaei University, 1354/1975), 53–4.
39 Seyyed Reza Ebrahimi, interview by Ali Tatari, 27 April 2022 (7 Ordibehesht 1401), Tejarat Bank Archives (TBA), Tehran, Iran; CBIA, *Taraznameh-ye Sal-e 1329, Bank-e Bazargani*, 17.
40 University of Tehran Library and Document Centre.
41 Specialized Library on the History of Islam and Iran.
42 Grand Ayatollah Boroujerdi Library.
43 Hemmat, 'Sistem-e Banki', 21.
44 CBIA, *Taraznameh-ye Sal-e 1332, Bank-e Bazargani*, 5.
45 *Majalleh-ye Bank-e Bazargani*, no. 87, 27.
46 *Dah Sal*, 46; *Majalleh-ye Sepid o Siyah*, no. 401 (22 Ordibehesht 1340/12 May 1961): 5.
47 CBIA, *Taraznameh-ye Sal-e 1335, Bank-e Bazargani*, 2.
48 *Dah Sal*, 47–8.
49 NLAI, 023681-2-27, 'Agahi-ye Bazargani' (31 Khordad 1355/21 June 1976).
50 *Ettelaat*, no. 7189 (10 Farvardin 1329/30 March 1950): 5.
51 CBIA, *Gozaresh-e Modir-e Amel beh Majma-ye Omumi va Taraznameh-ye Sal-e 1345, Bank-e Bazargani*, 5.
52 *Eteraf*, no. 376 (4 Aban 1342/26 October 1963): 1.
53 CBIA, *Gozaresh-e Modir-e Amel beh Majma-ye Omumi va Taraznameh-ye Sal-e 1354, Bank-e Bazargani*, 6.
54 *Majalleh-ye Asiya-ye Javan*, no. 657 (12 Bahman 1342/1 February 1964): 3.
55 Seyyed Reza Ebrahimi, interview.
56 CBIA, *Taraznameh-ye Sal-e 1333, Bank-e Bazargani*, 7.
57 CBIA, *Taraznameh-ye Sal-e 1335*, 4–5.
58 CBIA, *Taraznameh-ye Sal-e 1336, Bank-e Bazargani*, 4.
59 CBIA, *Taraznameh-ye Sal-e 1338, Bank-e Bazargani*, 12.
60 *Donya*, no. 835 (1 Esfand 1343/20 February 1965): 1.

61 *Majalleh-ye Bank-e Bazargani*, no. 87, 121.
62 This data was obtained from the Ministry of Information and Tejarat Bank's Digital Archives.
63 Seyyed Reza Ebrahimi, interview.
64 *Ettelaat*, no. 1023 (24 Bahman 1342/13 February 1964): 11.
65 *Majalleh-ye Sepid o Siyah*, no. 401, 50.
66 Seyyed Reza Ebrahimi, interview.
67 Ibid.
68 'Sherkat-e Sakhtemani-ye Pargar', Rasmio, accessed 3 December 2023, https://rasm.io/company/10100451744/شرکت ساختمانی پرگار/.
69 Seyyed Reza Ebrahimi, interview.
70 Planning and Budget Organization of Iran Library, *Chehreh-ye Khorasan* (n.p.: Otaq-e Bazargani va Sanaye va Maaden-ye Iran va Mashhad, 1349/1970), 79.
71 Seyyed Reza Ebrahimi, interview.
72 Ibid.; Reza Keshavarz, interviews by Maryam Zarei and Fatemeh Eskandari, April 2022 (Ordibehesht 1401), Tehran, Iran.
73 *Majalleh-ye Bank va Eqtesad*, no. 11 (Shahrivar 1379/August–September 2000): 60.
74 CBIA, *Taraznameh-ye Sal-e 1335*, 1.
75 *Majalleh-ye Bank-e Bazargani*, no. 87, 120.
76 Ibid.
77 Seyyed Reza Ebrahimi, interview.
78 Hosseinzadeh, 'Ravabet-e Omumi', 44.
79 Ibid.
80 Seyyed Reza Ebrahimi, interview.
81 Hosseinzadeh, 'Ravabet-e Omumi', 46.
82 Ibid.
83 *Majalleh-ye Bank va Eqtesad*, no. 11, 60.
84 This data was obtained from the Islamic Propaganda Organization's Art Archive.
85 *Ayandegan*, no. 3370 (19 Khordad 1358/9 June 1979), 1.
86 CBIA, *Gozaresh-e Tahavvolat*, 6–7.
87 CBIA, *Niru-ye Ensani va Amuzesh dar Bankha-ye Keshvar* (Tehran: Edareh-ye Amuzesh va Motaleat-e Niru-ye Ensani, Tir 1360/June–July 1981), 5.

Bibliography

Archives

Digital Document Center of Tehran Chamber of Commerce, Industries, Mines and Agriculture
Ettelaat Newspaper and Photo Archive
Grand Ayatollah Boroujerdi Library
Institute for Iranian Contemporary Historical Studies
Islamic Propaganda Organization Art Archive
Keyhan Newspaper and Photo Archive
Library and Documentation Center of the Monetary and Banking Research Institute, Central Bank of Iran
Library and Document Center of the Planning and Budget Organization of Iran

Library, Museum and Document Center of the Iranian Parliament
Ministry of Foreign Affairs, Center for Documents and History of Diplomacy
Ministry of Information, Center for the Study of Historical Documents
Mofid University Library
National Bank of Iran Document Center and Museum
National Library and Archives of Iran
Organization of Libraries, Museums and Document Center of Astan Qods Razavi
Specialized Library on the History of Islam and Iran
Tehran University Library and Documentation Center
Tejarat Bank Archives and Digital Archives

Periodicals

Āyandegān
Donyā
E'terāf
Ettelā'āt
Habl al-Matin
Keyhān
Māhnāmeh-ye Bānk va Eqtesād
Majalleh-ye Āsiyā-ye Javān
Majalleh-ye Bānk-e Bāzargāni
Majalleh-ye Bānk-e Melli-ye Irān
Majalleh-ye Bānk-e Sepah
Majalleh-ye Kānun-e Bānkhā
Majalleh-ye Otāq-e Bāzargāni
Majalleh-ye Sepid o Siyāh
Tehrān Ekonomist

Secondary sources

Aqeli, Baqer. *Sharhehāl-e Rajāl-e Siyāsi va Nezāmi-ye Mo'āser-e Irān*. Vol. 1. Tehran: Goftar; Elm, 1380 (2001).
Ardalan, Abbas Gholi. *Osul-e Bānkdāri*. Tehran: Sazman-e Barnameh, 1339 (1960).
Bani Kamali, Massoud. 'Ravābet-e Omumi dar Sherkat-e Sahami-ye Bānk-e Bāzargāni'. Bachelor's thesis, Allameh Tabatabaei University, 1354/5 (1976).
Barzegar, Sadeq. *Bānkdāri*. Tehran: Madreseh-ye Ali-ye Bazargani, 1350 (1971).
Chehreh-ye Khorāsān. n.p.: Otaq-e Bazargani va Sanaye va Maaden-ye Iran va Mashhad, 1349 (1970).
Dah Sāl dar Khedmat-e Eqtesād-e Keshvar: Beh Monāsebat-e Pāyān-e Dahomin Sāl-e Tāsis-e Bānk-e Bāzargāni-ye Irān. Tehran: Edareh-ye Entesharat va Amar va Barresiha-ye Eqtesadi, n.d.
Deyhim, Hamid. 'Naqsh-e Bānkhā dar Towse'eh-ye Eqtesādi-ye Irān'. Bachelor's thesis, University of Tehran, 1345/6 (1967).
Ebtehaj, Abol Hassan. *Khātirāt-e Abol Hassan Ebtehāj*. Vol. 1 and 2. Edited by Alireza Aruzi. Tehran: Elmi, 1371 (1992).

Ganjbakhsh, Shirindokht. 'Pazhuhesh dar Bānk-e Bāzargāni-ye Irān va Chegunegi-ye Kār-e Ravābet-e Omumi dar Ān'. Bachelor's thesis, Allameh Tabatabaei University, 1353/4 (1975).
Gozāresh-e Amaliyyāt-e Si Sāleh-ye Bānk-e Sepah. Tehran: Entesharat-e Bank-e Sepah, n.d.
Hosseinzadeh, Mansour. 'Ravābet-e Omumi dar Sherkat-e Sahami-ye Bānk-e Bāzargāni-ye Irān'. Bachelor's thesis, Allameh Tabatabaei University, 1354 (1975).
Jones, Geoffrey. *Tārikhcheh-ye Bānk-e Shāhi dar Irān [Banking and Empire in Iran]*. Translated by Nasser Moafaqian. Tehran: Moasseseh-ye Tahqiqat va Towseeh-ye Olum-e Ensani, 1393 (2014).
Pānzdah Sālegi-ye Bānk-e Bāzargāni. Tehran: Bank-e Bazargani-ye Iran, n.d.
Rafiei, Ahmad. *Bānk va Bānkdāri*. Tehran: n.p., 1351 (1972).

9

The role of workers and the state in Iranian mining, 1920s–50s

Abdolreza Alamdar

Introduction

This chapter presents a chronological narrative of mining expansion in Iran during four critical decades (1920s–50s) of the twentieth century. It examines both the industrial dimension as well as the social dimension of mining development, focusing on the dynamics of the two main agents: workers and the state. It documents the role of governmental planning and state institutions within the social and political context of mining development and their impact on workers' conditions. It also underscores the political agency of the mineworkers and the role they played in formulating and promoting their status, which has rarely been identified in the historiography of modern Iran. The dearth of enquiry into the condition of miners in Iran's contemporary past does not stem merely from structural causes, for instance, underdeveloped mining with a small workforce or mines being located in remote areas; it also echoes the discourses dominant at the time, which generated a specific order of knowledge regarding Iran's contemporary past. In order to restore the standing of mineworkers and revitalize their history, this chapter will examine archival documents and oral narratives as well as literary works.

Modern mining's early development, 1925–41

In the late nineteenth century, Iran's modern economy was embryonic with little interaction with the outside world. Pre-industrial relationships dominated, with agriculture being the main source of income for most inhabitants. It is estimated that, in 1900, Iran's population was 9.86 million, with urbanization at 21 per cent; a fifth of the population lived in 100 towns and cities.[1] According to another estimate, 90 per cent of those who worked outside the home were in the agricultural and nomadic sectors, while the remaining 10 per cent worked in trade, service and handicrafts.[2]

There are no precise figures for the number of mineworkers, and indeed, in general, scholars researching the history of mining in Iran face a critical shortage of any documentation concerning miners' lives, working conditions or numbers in the nineteenth and twentieth centuries. Without adequate information, there sometimes emerges an inaccurate picture of mining, which occasionally misleads researchers. For instance, Abdullaev, in his report on the number of Iranian workers in various economic sectors in the early twentieth century, has claimed that there were 200 mineworkers. This same figure (for 1882 and circa 1910) appears in two important works on Iran's economy and labour, *The Economic History of Iran* by Charles Issawi,[3] and *Industrialization in Iran* by Willem Floor.[4] Although we have no precise data on the total number of mineworkers, we do have some documents which reveal that 200 is much lower than localized figures. For instance, a report by A. Kassis, the representative of Bank-e Esteqrazi (Russian Discount and Loans Bank of Persia), mentions that in 1910, 250 to 300 workers laboured at a single site, the Kuh-e (Dehqan-e) Siyah copper mine, adjacent to the mountains near Sabzevar, in north-eastern Iran.[5] Clearly then, the figure of 200 workers in the mining sector of the late nineteenth and early twentieth centuries is far from the actual one. This report's observations leave us with the impression that working conditions for miners at Kuh-e Siyah were not too demanding. The mine owner provided small houses for the workers, and because the mine was isolated, there was a small grocery shop to provide for the workers' immediate needs. The same report revealed that in 1900, fifty workers were involved in mining activity in the Kuh-e Gomai copper mine in Khorasan province, where almost 300 kilograms of copper ore was extracted every day, which would yield about 36 kilograms of pure copper. The mine was being leased to Mohammad Esmaeil Arbab at 500 tomans (5,000 qirans) per month.[6] While the average wage of a turquoise miner or a stone cutter in the 1880s was 5 or 2 qirans, respectively,[7] in the years just before the First World War, miners earned 3 qirans on average.[8] It seems that mineworkers' wages in the early 1910s were similar to those of other sectors, such as textiles and fisheries.

During the interwar period, Reza Shah (1925–41) launched a project of economic modernization, initially through focusing on restructuring the existing state institutions. He began by overhauling the bureaucratic system, based on a modern structure, thereby considerably improving the state's administration. In addition to reforming the existing ministries, new ones were established to cover agriculture, commerce, transport and industry. Reza Shah's state-centric industrial reform programme was outstandingly successful, with the Ministry of Industry building around 300 industrial plants for the production of copper, cement, electricity, rice, sugar and cigarettes, compared with fewer than twenty industrial units in 1925 of which only five had more than fifty employees.[9]

At the same time, the industrial expansion of this period increased the number of workers, most of them in the new industries.[10] While agriculture had accounted for 90 per cent of the labour force in 1906, that amount gradually decreased to 85 per cent in 1926 and 75 per cent in 1946.[11] Other statistics also show a dramatic rise in the number of workers: by the end of Reza Shah's rule, there were more than 260,000 workers in different sectors, such as mining, construction, industry and transport.[12] It is estimated that 50,000 to 60,000 workers were employed in 200 factories by 1941.[13]

At that time, oil had no substantial input into the Iranian economy, with an appreciable amount of oil income being allocated for the purchase of military equipment and a certain percentage expended on foreign components for investment projects.[14] Most of the government's revenue was derived from the collection of delayed taxes, raising customs duties and imposing a new tax on consumer goods, which led to the overall growth of state income.[15] That in turn created a proper environment for the state to launch its economic programme by encouraging the local bourgeoisie to invest in mining and industries. The state then introduced a high tariff to support domestic production and granted loans to the private sector at low rates of interest for its involvement in manufacturing.[16] According to Arthur Millspaugh, the head of the Iranian government's financial administration in 1926, Iran had numerous and rich mineral resources that mostly had not been extracted.[17] The Ministry of Agriculture, Commerce and Public Works proclaimed that the state warmly invited Iranian entrepreneurs, as well as foreigners, to invest in Iran's mining and other industrial sectors.[18] The rapid industrial growth of the 1930s increased coal consumption as the main fuel of industrial plants at the time. The state then developed coal mining, in order to feed the domestic demand with internal resources, rather than importing from abroad. It presented an incentive policy with the intention of attracting local entrepreneurs to exploit the coal mines. For instance, by passing a concession law that assigned the exclusive right to exploit the coal mine in Mashhad and twelve surrounding *farsakh* (about 75 kilometres) to Mohammad Vali Khan Asadi, his company was tax exempt for five years, thereafter paying 5 per cent of its net profits to the state.[19] The Iranian Parliament assigned another concession to Masoud Khan Adl to exploit the coal mines in the city of Tabriz and its surroundings in 1932.[20]

However, the state's incentive policies fell short of expectations, as the local mercantile bourgeoisie had scant interest because of two factors: limited capital and negligible knowledge of moving from commerce to the mining sector. As a result, in the absence of a robust private sector, the state became the chief stakeholder and investor in medium- and large-scale mining projects.[21] The state then established the Zirab Coal Mine at one of the largest coal deposits in northern Iran, located in the Central Alborz range. The Zirab coal reserve was estimated to hold a definite quantity of 16 million tonnes and a possible deposit of 65 million tonnes. The state's projection was to extract 60,000 *kharvār* (18,000 metric tonnes) of coal by 1935.[22] The Zirab and Galanderoud coal reserves mostly supplied fuel to the Parchehbafi-ye Shahi, Chitsazi-ye Behshahr and Gunibafi-ye Shahi enterprises, which produced fabric, chintz and gunnysacks.[23]

The state also invested in a number of extant coal mines in the South Alborz range, such as those in Shemshak, Gajereh and Lalun. The Shemshak Coal Mine was a medium-sized mining project, in which the state invested 900,000 to 1 million tomans,[24] and was projected to have an annual extraction of 65,000 *kharvār* (19,500 metric tonnes) of coal by 1935.[25] The Iranian Parliament allocated the budget annually and distributed funds acquired from various sources.[26] For instance, they passed a bill in 1928 for the allocation of 200,000 tomans from the expenditures of the Mining Department,[27] which was under the Ministry for Public Works, to develop the Shemshak coal mining project and construct the Shemshak Road. The sum was obtained from income generated by the state monopoly on sugar and lump sugar.[28]

The state's participation led to a significant increase in domestic coal mining: the 5,000 tonnes of coal annually extracted by state companies in 1938 jumped to 64,000 tonnes in 1939 and was estimated to increase up to 100,000 tonnes in 1940.[29] The state also expanded exploration for iron ore in the area around Mesgarabad, Tehran province and Bafq country in Yazd province. It also commenced the exploitation of copper ore deposits in the Anarak district of Isfahan province, the extracted copper ore being transported to Ghaniabad Smelting Plant in Shahr-e Rey, just south of Tehran.[30]

Following governmental restructuring, aimed at increasing institutional efficiency, the Ministry of the National Economy (Eqtesad-e Melli) was disbanded and replaced by the three separate administrative offices of Industry and Mining (Sanat va Madan), Agriculture (Falahat) and Commerce (Tejarat) in 1936. The management of mining affairs was transferred to a dedicated Department of Mines, headed by Engineer (Mohandes) Ali Zahedi. It was approved that the Department's budget should be derived from the income of three state coal mines: Shemshak, Gajereh and Lalun.[31] Later in the same year, the Department of Mines was subsumed into the Ministry of Labour (Kar) and Trades and Crafts (Pisheh va Honar), remaining under the control of that ministry until 1947, when it became part of the Institute of Industrial Affairs.

Along with mining development, Iran's first Law of Mines was enacted by the Iranian Parliament on 11 February 1939.[32] The government was prompt in considering the necessity of mining regulation, and slightly less than six months later, on 5 June 1939, the Mine Exploration Law was issued by the Ministry of Labour and Trades and Crafts.[33] Thereafter, the prime minister approved the proposed Mining Code Legislation on 16 November 1939.[34] After the passing of the first mining law, an outline plan was drafted for a coal-fuelled steelworks to be built in the city of Karaj. Copper refining also commenced at the Ghaniabad plant.[35] The plant in Shahr-e Rey had been designed for the daily production of 3.5 tonnes of refined copper for military use, supplied with raw ore from various mining sites, but predominantly, the Anarak mine in central Iran.[36] According to a report of the Headquarters of Mines in 1939, 260 tonnes of copper were produced in 1938, 500 tonnes in 1939 and a projected 1,200 tonnes in 1940.[37]

The first approved technical regulation of mines in December 1939 was based on two main points. Firstly, it stipulated regulations for workers' health and safety, and secondly, it specified the principles for exploration and extraction. Rather progressively, in a move that supported workers' rights against the power of their employers, the new regulations made employers responsible for working conditions and the safety of the workplace. Various matters were covered, such as adequate lighting and ventilation in mines, the precise forms and designs of tunnels, which should facilitate movement inside mine shafts and galleries, and communication with the surface in hazardous circumstances or case of accident. Attention was given to health and medical requirements, as well. The permanent presence of a doctor and surgeon was required for any mine with more than 1,000 workers; a doctor alone was required for mines with between 300 and 1,000 workers; while for fewer than 300 workers, there had to be a proper medical room with first aid staff and a nurse permanently present. Article 44 of the regulations considered the living conditions of the miners. It obliged employers to provide temporary houses for miners in areas lacking accommodation. Finally, working underground was prohibited for children under fourteen years old as well as for women.[38]

Five years of Allied occupation

Iran's declaration of neutrality in the Second World War did not shield it from that war's adversities. The Great Powers had been planning to depose Reza Shah for quite some time, and the outbreak of the war, together with Iran's geopolitical position, therefore, provided a pretext to occupy the country. Accordingly, on 25 August 1941, the Soviet Union invaded Iran from the north while British forces entered from the south. This incursion of the two imperial powers overtook the Iranian army, and the country came under the control of the Allies, which immediately forced a power shift within the political system: Reza Shah was coerced into resigning in favour of his son and heir, Mohammad Reza.

The destructive consequences of the Second World War devastated the lives of ordinary Iranians, including mineworkers, during the five years of occupation, from 1941 to 1946. The common people and lower classes toiled under the pressure of poverty. A wide gap of inequality in wealth distribution and class distinction was on the rise, which the British Consul in Kermanshah described as being like 'Britain before 1832 when there were two main classes in society, one was living in power and wealth, the other was completely powerless and survived in absolute poverty'.[39] There also were countless civilian fatalities and casualties. At the same time, the country plummeted into social and economic crises, as state income dropped and the government confronted a huge deficit and high inflation. Moreover, the majority of the country's resources were allocated to service of the Allies, leaving people in some regions faced with famine.[40] Limited cereal resources, as well as the rapid growth in bread consumption with the influx of foreign troops, incited bread riots in some cities, although it may be said that the hoarding of wheat and other cereals was the root cause of the shortages. To survive the famine, the state rationed bread in most cities, including Tehran, with workers being allocated 800 grams daily; the rest of the adult population and children received 400 grams and 200 grams, respectively.[41]

In addition, the war severely threatened public health across the country. The Minister of Health Ali Asghar Hekmat wrote to the prime minister in April 1942 that typhus was spreading, and that it was highly probable that there would be epidemics of other contagious diseases, given the large number of foreigners entering the country.[42] Furthermore, the paucity of food and the consequent malnutrition were expected to weaken the society's immune system and resistance to all diseases. There also was a scarcity of medicine, with the Allies having taken possession of Iranian hospitals in order to press them into their war service. That too played a significant role in the spread of debilitating diseases throughout the country.[43]

Contrary to the economic and social instability of these years, the structural conditions in Iran paved the way for a more liberated political atmosphere. Authority was not entirely in the Shah's hands from 1941 to 1953, with other power centres, such as the Royal Court, the Cabinet, the Parliament and even street politics, influencing domestic political relations to a considerable extent.[44] The 1940s and early 1950s, up until the coup d'état of 1953, were a progressive time for workers' social and political activities. The political atmosphere of the wartime and immediate post-war period created fertile ground for re-emerging socialist movements, mainly organized by the Tudeh Party (Communist Party of Iran), which provided an opportunity to unify workers. The same workers played a crucial role in improving their work conditions by pursuing their demands through different forms of grievance, complaint, strike, protest and, in rare cases, open revolt. Strike action, as a civil collective action, has historically been one of the main instruments workers can utilize to put their employers, or the government, under pressure. For instance, less than five months after the abdication of Reza Shah, 1,500 construction workers held the first prominent strike on 8 February 1942 in Tehran,[45] and that action ultimately came to a successful conclusion as the workers achieved their trade union demands.

The miners, like most workers in other sectors of the Iranian economy, were affected by harsh wartime conditions. They also were inspired by more liberating political settings, as more mineworkers' demands can be traced within the documents. The fragile economy sometimes prevented the government from providing them with even the basic essentials. For instance, the Anarak mines could supply food for only two days to 2,500 miners and their families.[46] The government was responsible for supplying their monthly inventory of food supplies, including 30,000 kilograms of wheat, 3,000 kilograms of rice, 6,000 kilograms of grain and 1,000 kilograms of cooking oil, which usually came from Isfahan, the largest city in the province.[47] Even though the state was required to allocate a monthly budget for these supplies beforehand, the government correspondence has shown that the Anarak mineworkers did not receive their food on time.

Some mines were unable to withstand the pressure of a lack of buyers, falling prices and rising costs, which made the mineworkers' jobs vulnerable and insecure. Mine closures or job losses among mineworkers occurred frequently during this period, for instance, at the Farmand Chromite Mine at Sanjabad,[48] the copper and lead mine in Khalkhal,[49] the Baycheh-Bagh Copper Mine in Zanjan,[50] and the Sungun Copper Mine in the Arasbaran region of East Azerbaijan province.[51] All of these mines were closed and their workers were dismissed. However, outright closure was not always the ultimate consequence for every mine. Some shifted the pressure to their labour force by firing workers or delaying payment of wages until there was an improvement in the company's financial situation, or perhaps state support. For example, the Anarak mines deferred payment of workers' wages for six months in 1945/6. In a petition to the Iranian Parliament, the Anarak mineworkers detailed their families' plight: they were hungry and people's lives were at risk.[52] This petition exhorted the government to issue an order for payment; however, it was not implemented for a further four months. The governor of Yazd meanwhile declared that the disbursement of 500,000 rials was spent on food for the workers, which left no remuneration for their wages.[53] In another case, the Abbasabad copper mines' delayed payment of wages caused unrest among the workers. Since the price of copper had increased, and the Iranian army, as the main purchaser and consumer for this mine's output (and the one in Anarak), was in deficit, no customers effectively existed. A few months later, both mines could no longer sustain the economic pressure and thus reduced their labour forces.[54]

It must be emphasized that militancy was not common practice among the miners, who rarely even crossed the government's red lines or infused their protests with political demands, mostly making petitions through their trade union, wishing to care for their families and shield them from ever-worsening deprivation. The rhetoric of grievances was usually peaceable with no intimidating language from the workers' side. Even under radical conditions, their correspondence usually conveyed a 'bottom-up' view. For instance, a petition from the workers of the Anarak mine to the Iranian Parliament read as follows: 'Following a telegram dated 1324/08/20 [11.11.1945], no money has been received by the Anarak mineworkers for the four months of delayed wages. Hunger has spread throughout Anarak. The lives of thousands of workers and their families are in danger. We would ask the authorities to kindly consider our harsh conditions in this severe winter.'[55] Another telegram, from the Abbasabad Choghondar Sar mineworkers in eastern Semnan Province to the Ministry of Labour and Trades and Crafts, states:

> We, the Abbasabad Choghondar Sar mineworkers, who live in a desert far from the cities, have not received our wages for five months and our indignance has heightened. We have been able to survive this living death by selling our possessions, but now our only chance is to bring our indignance to the attention of the authorities. We therefore ask you kindly to preserve the innocent women and children from a lingering death. Now that the head of the mine has come to Tehran for that purpose, please take action to remit our delayed salaries.[56]

That said, the miners' methods of making demands were not always determined by petitioning. Sometimes they applied more radical approaches, including protest and strike, as occurred at the Shemshak Coal Mine on 18 November 1945, when miners protested over the four months' delayed wage payment. This campaign escalated into a bloody clash, which culminated with one dead and twenty injured.[57] Sometimes the miners also became embroiled in political action and even armed confrontation against the government. In a telegram to the prime minister on 22 November 1945, in addition to support for the Zirab and Galanderoud miners, who had not been paid for four months, the Shemshak workers demanded that 'all banned newspapers of Jebheh-ye Azadi [Liberty Front] and all banned clubs of freedom-loving parties must be allowed to resume their activity. Moreover, all detained people and workers must be released'.[58] This telegram was sent not only from the miners but also from 'all the workers in Mazandaran province' and was signed by forty-two of these workers. The last lines of the telegram were imbued with threat, articulating that if their demands were not considered, there would be a forceful reaction by the nation. The miners' resistance inspired intellectuals and writers, as reflected in literary form, including a short story, a novel and a poem. For instance, in his collection of seven short stories, entitled 'Az Ranji Keh Mibarim' (Of Our Suffering), Jalal Al-e Ahmad dedicated the first two, 'Dareh-ye Khazanzadeh' (Valley of the Afflicted Autumn) and 'Zirabiha' (People of Zirab), to the miners' struggle against the state.[59] A critical realism framed the writer's imagination, using incidents from the outside world to create a story. The author praised the miners' resistance, which was contrary to the narrative of the state apparatus.

After the Allied occupation, 1946–53

The stories of Jalal Al-e Ahmad echoed another real incident that occurred the following year: a bloody, armed confrontation at Zirab Coal Mine in Mazandaran province on 3 December 1946 (12 Azar 1325). State-orientated news published in *Keyhan* newspaper expounded that some miners were killed in an unsuccessful attempt to unarm the mine's guards.[60] In reality, the state arrested the rebels, which led to the execution of some offenders and imprisonment of many others. State forces also abducted around forty people, along with their families.[61] In an interview, the Minister of Labour claimed: 'The people who were executed, imprisoned or abducted were not mineworkers, but a group who had plotted an armed riot against national security. We discovered numerous guns, pistols and explosives. They intended to plot a coup by blowing up the train station and the bridges.'[62]

Clearly, the 1940s and early 1950s, up until the coup of 1953, were a radical time in workers' social and political activism. The Central Council of Labour Unions (Showra-ye Markazi-ye Ettehadiyeha-ye Kargari) represented 60,000 oil workers, 45,000 construction workers, 40,000 textile workers, 20,000 carpet and rug weavers, 11,000 dockworkers and 8,000 mineworkers. The oil workers, who were the labour force of Iran's most strategically significant industry, organized a strike on 1 May 1946. These workers marched at the Abadan refinery, but there were no major clashes. However, on 14 July 1946, a general strike was instigated at the refinery, which saw three days of bloody fighting, ending with 50 fatalities and 165 casualties.[63] This labour action remains the largest and bloodiest strike in the history of the Middle East.[64] The number of major industrial actions during the same year totalled 183; however, this number fell to just eight in 1947. Then, economic pressure provoked a gradual increase in strikes, from four to five in 1948–50, soaring to forty-two in 1951, fifty-five in 1952 and seventy-one in the first eight months of 1953.[65]

After the coup in August 1953, the Shah and the government applied various measures in an attempt to dominate those social groups who might have been effective in the political arena. These measures included the dissolution of the unions and prohibition of all labour activism. The repression continued with minor action by the unions being under the control of the state and the Ministry of Labour.[66] At the same time, intelligence activity was expanded and major industrial centres were more closely controlled. The secret police and intelligence services, SAVAK (Sazman-e Ettelaat va Amniyat-e Keshvar), colluded with the Ministry of Labour in order to monitor trade unions, and, as a result, the seventy-nine labour strikes that had occurred in the industrial sector in 1953 dropped to seven in 1954 and a mere three in 1955–7.[67] However, the ban on trade unions did not prevent the workers from making non-provocative demands.[68]

Despite the fluctuation in the frequency of labour activities throughout the 1940s and 1950s, the workers' achievements had been significant during this period. The ratification of the first comprehensive labour legislation in 1946, for instance, was an outstanding attainment. According to the 1946 Labour Law, the maximum working hours had to be decreased to forty-eight hours per week as well as having one day off for every six working days. Also, child employment was restricted with the legal working age becoming twelve, although this could be reduced to ten for apprenticeships. Moreover, the Labour Law of 1946 addressed the issue of maternity leave, which was an important statement to secure the employment of women workers.[69]

Following the Allied occupation, in 1946, the Supreme Economic Council was established and the First Development Plan was drafted. According to George Benedict Baldwin, the head of the First Harvard Advisory Group in Iran: 'The first seven-year development plan that focused on the years 1948–55 called for a public investment expenditure of 21 billion rials ($656 million), which later increased to 26.3 billion rials.'[70] The plan was comprised of two sections, covering economic and social development. The economic section contained programmes for construction, water resource and agricultural development, the modification and establishment of new industries and the development of communications and infrastructure. The latter programme included the development of more efficient and modernized postal services, telephone and telegraph communications, roads, railways, ports and airports. A budget of 3 billion rials was allocated for mining and industrial development, with the major share allotted to industry.[71]

However, the first plan did not meet its goals, which meant that the actual expenditure was only 16 per cent of the planned investment for the whole seven-year period.[72] This was due mainly to the crisis with Britain caused by Iran's oil nationalization, as well as the political turbulence created by the United States and Britain, which orchestrated a coup in 1953 against Prime Minister Mohammad Mossadegh (in office: 1951–3). Mossadegh was an anti-imperialist and nationalist politician who followed the 'Negative Equilibrium' doctrine in international relations, which advocated the rejection of an alliance with either the United States or the Soviet Union, in the dichotomy of global power after the Second World War. While it was a time which inevitably drew developing countries to ally with one side or the other, Mossadegh averred that any such alliance would prepare the ground for more foreign intrusion in Iran domestic affairs.[73]

Mossadegh also insisted on nationalizing Iran's oil industry, which was under the dominance of the British. This predicament coincided with Britain's faltering supremacy in the world; therefore, the nationalization of Iranian oil could trigger a decline in Britain's global authority if it lost control over an extensive source of the most strategic commodity of the twentieth century. In order to thwart Mossadegh, Britain promptly imposed hefty sanctions against the sale of Iran's oil and threatened to make an official complaint to international organizations against countries that continued to deal with Iran. British threats proved to be effective, and the embargo, in effect, turned into a heavy international sanction against Iran.

The oil embargo prompted the Iranian government to expand its sources of income, therefore, mining once again became the focus of the state's attention. The state established the Mines Council in early 1952, whose members included the Minister of the National Economy (or deputy), the head of the Planning and Budget Organization (or deputy), a representative of the Ministry of Finance, the managing director of the Qeshm and Hormozgan Mines Corporation and the managing director of the Discovery and Extraction of Mines Agency. The incentive policy of the Mines Council played an instrumental role in the expansion of mining within the private sector so that there was a dramatic growth in the number of applications for exploration licences in the years 1953–6 (see Table 9.1). The forty-four mining companies that were active in 1950 increased to 105 in 1953, and their capital rose from 506 million to 664 million rials.[74]

During this period, the state passed a bill to protect the rights and interests of both the owner and the exploiter of mines under three categories: non-metallic mineral mines, metal ore mines and oil and radioactive mines. There was no restriction on the exploitation of non-metallic mineral mines and there was no need to apply for an exploitation licence, but the owner had to release 5 per cent of the extracted minerals to the state or pay the equivalent market price. The exploitation of metal ore mines by either a state or a private company was permitted, depending on who was being granted a licence. However, the exploiter had to assign 4 per cent of the extracted minerals, or pay its equivalent market price, to the state. Oil and radioactive mines were public property, and the state was the only legitimate party permitted to exploit such mineral resources. Exploitation licence holders of the first and second categories were obliged to pay 10 rials per square kilometre of the mine to the Ministry of Finance. Also, the first category of licence holders had to pay a stipend of 2 per cent of the extracted minerals as a royalty disbursement to the landowner. This same percentage was paid to the state by the second category of licence holders as ground rent. Moreover, to protect the discoverer's rights, the exploiter was required to give 0.5 per cent of the extracted

Table 9.1 Number of Requests for Issuance of Discovery Licence for Group Two Mines, 1940–65

Year	Number of Submitted Applications for Discovery Licences	Number of Issued Discovery Licences
1940–6	67	27
1947–51	640	312
1952	1,217	465
1953	1,618	1,186
1954	1,315	1,197
1955	1,592	870
1956	3,320	1,143
1957	1,084	837
1958	1,341	824
1959	512	507
1960	486	406
1961	416	324
1962	461	332
1963	342	264
1964	464	328
1965	948	508

Source: Farshad Momeni and Bahram Naghsh Tabrizi, *Eqtesad-e Iran dar Dowran-e Dowlat-e Melli* (Tehran: Nahadgara, 1394/2015), 105.

minerals, or their equivalent market price, to the discoverer. The exploitation licence was issued for a maximum of thirty years. According to the law, 25 per cent of the state income from non-oil mineral resources was allocated to mining development for such purposes as the equipping of exploring machines and mapping instruments.

The aforementioned turn in economic policy that led to a new focus on industry and mining also resulted in the formation of a new large state enterprise. In mining, two state companies – Sherkat-e Maaden-e Zoghal-e Sang (the Coal Mines Company) and Sherkat-e Maaden-e Felezi va Ekteshafat (the Company of Metallic Ore Mines and Exploration) – were combined, and a new company was established, called Sherkat-e Maaden va Zob-e Felezat (the Mines and Metal Smelting Corporation). As it was the Iranian government's intention to establish a steel industry in the near future, for which both iron ore and coal were required, the amalgamation of the two state companies was considered to be more efficient and would encourage better cooperation.[75] A total amount of 680 million rials was allocated for industrial and mining plans, out of which 240 million rials were allotted to mining development.[76]

During the tenure of Mossadegh's government, in 1952, the first Workers' Social Insurance Law was passed, which coincided with the establishment of the Organization of Workers' Social Insurance. According to this legislation, all enterprises and agencies mentioned in the 1946 Labour Law had to insure workers for the following contingencies: accident, disease, disability and periods off work (e.g. family allowance, retirement, funeral expense payment, support for the family members of deceased workers and unemployment insurance).[77] Although the labour law improved employment conditions in some aspects, such as raising wages and stemming child labour in state enterprises, it had less impact on enhancing safety in industrial workplaces, especially in the mining industry. There are no regular reports on workplace incidents and causalities; however, sporadic news articles show that working conditions were inadequate. For instance, some miners were killed in a major explosion at Galanderoud Coal Mine in Mazandaran province in February 1953. A subsequent investigation revealed that the ventilation system had broken down so that flammable gas was discharged inside the tunnel. The glass of the only mining light had also been broken, which led to the explosion of compressed gas.[78] Similarly, in another accident, a few months later, eleven miners were killed when a tunnel collapsed at the Gajereh Coal Mine in northern Iran.[79]

Conclusion

Contrary to other economic sectors, including oil and manufacturing, mining has been profoundly ignored in the historiography of modern Iran. This is particularly true when it comes to the labour conditions of mineworkers and their resistance. In order to fill the gap and provide fresh ground for further studies, this chapter has overviewed mining expansion during the first half of the twentieth century in Iran, while focusing on the two key agents of worker and state within economic and political contexts. It has deconstructed the involvement of so-called influential forces, including the state, which has laid the ground to examine the role of other agents, especially workers, and highlight their involvement within a particular political and economic structure.

This study has looked back on the mid-1920s and 1930s in order to document the mining development and industrial expansion that commenced with the Reza Shah period. It has demonstrated how the interwar modernization project, along with the local economic structure and political elements, gradually led to the dominance of state interventionism in Iran's economy, particularly in the mining industry. The economic structure, including the weakness of local entrepreneurs and the capital-intensive development of mining, led to the state incentive policy that had less success in attracting entrepreneurs to the mining industry. This outcome paved the way for the establishment of a state-centric mining industry, and the Iranian government then became the leading actor in mining development. The state ran educational programmes to train mining experts and mining industry strategists as well as establishing relevant institutes to articulate law and regulations. These measures also shaped the workers' living and working conditions and placed the majority of miners in a direct relationship with the state as their employer. This economic development increased the population of mineworkers, who become a force of resistance for the improvement of their living and working conditions.

These developments did not occur in isolation but were shaped by social and political conditions. The momentum of mining reforms during the Reza Shah period was interrupted by five years of the Allies' occupation of Iran (1941–6) during the Second World War and their intervention in Iranian political and economic affairs. The war also created a period of impoverishment for workers, including the miners. Following the departure of the Allies in 1946, and Mohammad Reza Shah's gradual establishment of a structure of political power and governance, the mining industry began to return to normal. The structural specifications of mining curbed the miners' previous social activism for the betterment of the working class; however, they continued to gain concessions for the improvement of their living and working conditions, mostly through petitioning and protesting, as well as armed resistance. Yet, that did not last long, as the country faced further international crises, generated by Britain's embargo on Iranian oil. The sanctions instigated by the nationalization of the Iranian oil industry, which was a measure to end Britain's domination of domestic oil reserves, signalled a backlash from Britain, which banned the sale of Iranian oil on the international market. However, the economic pressure on the oil industry led the state to encourage the private sector development of other industries, including mining. The nationalization of the oil industry, consequently, also unified external powers with domestic forces to overthrow the prime minister, Mohammad Mossadegh, through a coup in 1953, backed by the United States and Britain. During Mossadegh's tenure, the first Workers' Social Insurance Law was approved, which coincided with the founding of the Organization of Workers' Social Insurance.

Notes

1 Julian Bharier, *Economic Development in Iran, 1900–1970* (London: Oxford University Press, 1971), 25–8. 'Urban' is defined as settlements with a population of over 5,000 people.

2 Fred Halliday, *Iran: Dictatorship and Development* (London: Penguin Books, 1978), 14.
3 Charles Issawi, ed., *The Economic History of Iran, 1800–1914* (Chicago: University of Chicago Press, 1971), 282–3. Here, it only refers to the turquoise mines of Nishapur.
4 Willem M. Floor, *Industrialization in Iran, 1900–1941*, Occasional Paper Series, no. 23, ed. John Dewdney and Heather Bleaney (Durham: University of Durham Centre for Middle Eastern and Islamic Studies, 1984), 5.
5 Tsentral'nyi gosudarstvennyi istoricheskii arkhiv v Leningrade (TsGIAL), f. 600, op. 10, d. 321, ll. 15–16. This data comes from Issawi, *Economic History*, 299.
6 One toman equalled 10 qirans, and a qiran was equal to 1 rial. The average currency rate at this time was 1 dollar to 11 qirans in Majid Pourshafei, *Eqtesad-e Kucheh: Gozaresh-e Pul-e Melli-ye Iran, Hazinehha-ye Zendegi va Dastmozdha dar Do Sadeh-ye Gozashteh 1157–1357* (Tehran: Gam-e No, 1385/2006), 191. See also Iraj Kia, *Moruri bar Tarikhcheh-ye Mokhtasar-e Maaden-e Iran* (Tehran: Negin, 1374/1995), 67–8.
7 Issawi, *Economic History*, 283.
8 Zakir Zul'fugarovich Abdullaev, *Promyshlennost' i zarozhdenie rabochego klassa Irana v kontse XIX–nachale XX vv* (Baku: Akademii Nauk Azerbaidzhanskoi SSR, 1963), 224–30, extracts reproduced in Issawi, *Economic History*, 41.
9 Ervand Abrahamian, *Iran Between Two Revolutions* (Princeton: Princeton University Press, 1983), 146.
10 Farhad Kazemi, *Poverty and Revolution in Iran: The Migrant Poor, Urban Marginality and Politics* (New York: New York University Press, 1980), 105.
11 Bharier, *Economic Development*, 34.
12 Zakir Zulfugarovich Abdullaev, cited in Ahmad Ashraf and Ali Banuazizi, *Tabaqat-e Ejtemaei, Dowlat va Enqelab dar Iran* (Tehran: Nilufar, 1388/2009), 98.
13 Parvin Alizadeh, 'The Process of Import Substitution Industrialization in Iran (1960–1978) with Particular Reference to the Case of the Motor Vehicle Industry' (PhD diss., Sussex University, 1984), 99.
14 Farhad Daftary, 'Development Planning in Iran: A Historical Survey', *Iranian Studies* 6, no. 4 (Autumn 1973): 178.
15 Ervand Abrahamian, *A History of Modern Iran* (Cambridge: Cambridge University Press, 2014), 67.
16 Abrahamian, *Iran Between Two Revolutions*, 148.
17 Arthur Chester Millspaugh, 'The Financial and Economic Situation of Persia, 1926', in *Vaziyyat-e Mali va Eqtesadi-ye Iran dar Dowreh-ye Reza Shah (Majmueh-ye Gozareshat)*, ed. and trans. Shahram Gholami (Tehran: Tarikh-e Iran, 1395/2016), 30.
18 'Elan az Taraf-e Vezarat-e Falahat, Tejarat va Favayed-e Ammeh', *Ettelaat*, no. 101, 21 Azar 1305 (13 December 1926): 6.
19 The concession holder had to start exploiting the mine within six months of being granted the concession and was obliged to provide the coal needed for Mashhad and its surrounding areas from year three onwards. The company also had to be able to meet the rise in demand by expanding its activities and had no right to more than a 20 per cent profit margin. If the discovered mines were on state-owned lands, their exploitation was free, but if they were on private land, the company had to obtain the landowner's permission by renting or buying the land or allocating a share of business to the landowner. See 'Qanun-e Emtiyaz-e Enhesari-ye Estekhraj-e Maaden-e Zoghal-e Sang-e Atraf-e Mashhad beh Aqa-ye Mohammad Vali Khan Asadi', 27 Mehr 1309 (19 October 1930), The Islamic Parliament Research Centre, accessed 17 September 2023, https://rc.majlis.ir/fa/law/show/91950.

20 The same terms and conditions applied unless the margin dropped from 20 to 10 per cent for the state's coal demand. See 'Qanun-e Eta-ye Emtiyaz-e Estekhraj-e Zoghal-e Sang-e Atraf-e Shahr-e Tabriz beh Aqa-ye Masoud Khan Adl', 24 Khordad 1311 (14 June 1932), The Islamic Parliament Research Centre, accessed 17 September 2023, https://rc.majlis.ir/fa/law/show/92393.
21 It must be noted that the state also imprinted its presence on the economy by founding new institutions. The intervention proceeded apace, with legislation designed to bring foreign trade wholly under state control. The new law assigned exclusive rights to the government to import and export all industrial products and raw commodities as well as determining the status of an import or export. See 'Qanun-e Vagozari-ye Enhesar-e Tejarat-e Khareji-ye Mamlekat beh Dowlat', Mosavvab-e 6 Esfand 1309 (25 February 1931), The Islamic Parliament Research Centre, accessed 29 August 2023, https://rc.majlis.ir/fa/law/show/92304.
22 An old unit of weight measurement in Iran, 1 kharvar is the equivalent of 300 kilograms.
23 See Mohammad Taghi Razavian, *Manabe-ye Enerzhi-ye Iran* (Tehran: Daneshgah-e Azad-e Eslami, Vahed-e Tehran-e Jonub, 1373/2004), 50; Fathollah Saadat and Amir Houshang Amini, *Joghrafiya-ye Eqtesadi-ye Iran* (Tehran: Daneshkadeh-ye Olum-e Ertebatat-e Ejtemaei, 1350/1971), 104; National Library and Archives of Iran (NLAI), N104017-2035, 'Edareh-ye Maden, Mahsul-e Pishbini Shodeh-ye Zoghal az Maden-e Zirab baraye Sal-e 1314 [1935], 1313 [1934]', in Mahshid Latifi Niya, *Asnad-e Maaden-e Iran, 1300–1332* (Tehran: Sazman-e Asnad-e Melli-ye Iran, Pazhuheshkadeh-ye Asnad, 1376/1997), 124.
24 One toman equalled 10 rials. From May 1933 until September 1941, the official rate was 1 dollar to 16.35 rials. See Mohsen Bahmani-Oskooee, 'History of the Rial and Foreign Exchange Policy in Iran', *Iranian Economic Review* 10, no. 14 (Fall 2005): 4.
25 NLAI, N104017-2035, 'Edareh-ye Maden, Mahsul-e Pishbini Shodeh-ye Zoghal az Maden-e Shemshak, 1314 [1935], 1313 [1934]', in Latifi Niya, *Asnad-e Maaden*, 124–5.
26 'Rayis-e Kol-e Sanat va Falahat (Aqa-ye [Mirza Mostafi Qoli] Bayat)', *Mashruh-e Mozakerat-e Majles-e Showra-ye Melli*, dowreh-ye 9, jalaseh-ye 69, 13 Esfand 1312/4 March 1934 (Tehran: Matbaeh-ye Majles, 1314/1935), pp. 1012–13.
27 One dollar was equal to 11.20 rials in May 1933. See Bahmani-Oskooee, 'History of the Rial', 4.
28 See 'Qanun-e Etebar-e Devist Hezar Toman baraye Estekhraj-e Maaden-e Zoghal-e Sang, Mosavvab-e 20 Mordad 1307 [11 August 1928]', The Islamic Parliament Research Centre, accessed 1 September 2023, https://rc.majlis.ir/fa/law/show/91682.
29 NLAI, N104017-2143-8, 'Edareh-ye Kol-e Maaden, Estekhraj va Ekteshafat-e Maaden az Nazar-e Tamin-e Ehtiyajat-e Dakheli, 1318 [1939]'.
30 'Maaden-e Iran', *Ettelaat*, 22 Shahrivar 1316 (13 September 1937): 2.
31 Seyyed Mehdi Farrokh, *Khaterat-e Siyasi-ye Mehdi Farrokh (Motasem al-Saltaneh)* (Tehran: Amirkabir, 1347/1968), 298.
32 NLAI, N113005-5445, 'Majles-e Showra-ye Melli, Qanun-e Maaden', 22 Bahman 1317 (11 February 1939), Shomareh-ye 4691.
33 Ibid.
34 NLAI, N113005-5445, 'Nokhost Vazir, Ayinnameh-ye Fani-ye Maaden', 24 Aban 1318 (16 November 1939), Shomareh-ye 9785/1654.

35 Mohammad Ali Kazemzadeh, *Tarikh-e Mes-e Sarcheshmeh-ye Kerman* (Tehran: Sherkat-e Melli-ye Sanaye-e Mes-e Iran, 1360/1981), 5.
36 NLAI, N104017.2143-1, 'Gozaresh-ye Raheh beh Barnameh-ye Bahrehbardari-ye Maaden-e Iran, 1319 [1940]'.
37 Ibid.
38 NLAI, N113005-5445, 'Nokhost Vazir, Ayinnameh-ye Fani-ye Maaden', 24 Aban 1318 (16 November 1939), Shomareh-ye 9785/1654.
39 The National Archives, Public Record Office, Foreign Office Files (FO) 371/Persia 1942/34–31402, 'British Consul in Kermanshah, Monthly Diary (October)'. Although this comment had not been prompted by any especially close observation of local conditions, and in fact ignored the diversity and dynamics of Iranian society, it certainly made an undeniable point about the high economic inequality of this period.
40 For instance, see 'Qahti dar Fars', *Keyhan*, no. 24, 2 Tir 1321 (23 June 1942): 4; 'Fars Misuzad', *Keyhan*, no. 27, 6 Tir 1321 (27 June 1942): 1.
41 *Ettelaat*, no. 5071, 11 Azar 1321 (2 December 1942) 1.
42 Presidential Research and Documents Centre, 111003-278, 'Nameh-ye Ali Asghar Hekmat beh Nokhost Vazir', 21 Farvardin 1321 (10 April 1942).
43 'Dar Baharestan', *Keyhan*, no. 24, 2 Tir 1321 (23 June 1942): 2–4; Behrouz Tayarani, 'Tasir-e Jang-e Jahani-ye Dovvom bar Vaziyyat-e Behdashti-ye Mardom', *Ganjineh-ye Asnad*, no. 33–4 (Bahar va Tabestan 1378/Spring and Summer 1999): 96–7.
44 Abrahamian, *Modern Iran*, 99.
45 Habib Ladjevardi, *Labor Unions and Autocracy in Iran* (Syracuse: Syracuse University Press, 1985), 37.
46 NLAI, K201001708, 'Telegraf az Sadri beh Vezarat-e Darayi', 7 Tir 1321 (28 June 1942).
47 NLAI, K2910011708, 'Nameh-ye Edareh-ye Pisheh va Honar-e Ostan-e Dahom beh Ostandari-ye Isfahan', 27 Ordibehesht 1321 (17 May 1942), Shomareh-ye 851.
48 NLAI, N104017-2060, 'Edareh-ye Kol-e Maaden, Nameh-ye Vezarat-e Tejarat, Kar va Pisheh va Honar beh Nokhost Vazir', 19 Bahman 1322 (9 February 1944), Shomareh-ye 12368.
49 NLAI, K293005887, 'Nameh-ye Ostandari-ye Kaghazkonan beh Ostandari-ye Khalkhal', 27 Mordad 1329 (18 August 1950), Nomreh-ye 297.
50 Rabi Badiei, *Joghrafyia-ye Sanati-ye Iran* (Tehran: Omur-e Towseeh-ye Niru-ye Ensani, 1338/1959), 260.
51 Ibid., 260.
52 NLAI, N104017-2126, 'Telegraf az Kargaran-e Madan-e Anarak beh Majles-e Showra-ye Melli', Tarikh-e Daryaft 30 Aban 1324 (21 November 1945).
53 NLAI, N104017-2126, 'Telegraf az Ostandari-ye Yazd beh Nokhost Vazir', 20 Esfand 1324 (11 March 1946), Shomareh-ye 5966.
54 NLAI, N104017-2127, 'Nameh-ye Edareh-ye Kol-e Maaden beh Nokhost Vazir', 9 Khordad 1325 (30 May 1946), Shomareh-ye 2756/4842.
55 NLAI, N104017-2126, 'Telegraf az Kargaran', 30 Aban 1324 (21 November 1945).
56 NLAI, N104017-2126, 'Telegraf az Farmandari-ye Yazd beh Nokhost Vaziri', 20 Esfand 1324 (11 March 1946).
57 NLAI, N104017-2126, 'Nameh-ye Rayis-e Edareh-ye Zoghal-e Sang beh Edareh-ye Kol-e Maaden', 1324 (1945).
58 NLAI, N104017-2126, 'Telegraf az Kargaran-e Mazandaran beh Nokhost Vazir', Tarikh-e Daryaft 1 Azar 1324 (22 November 1945).

59 Jalal Al-e Ahmad, *Az Ranji Keh Mibarim* (Tehran: Amirkabir, 1357/1978). The first edition was published in 1947. Publication of the book was banned at the fifth meeting of the Showra-ye Vaziran (Council of Ministers or Cabinet), held on 26 Shahrivar 1357 (17 September 1978). However, along with rising revolutionary protests at that time, which led to the undermining of political stability, the book was permitted to be published later. See Ebrahim Safaei, *Chehel Khatereh az Chehel Sal* (Tehran: Elmi, 1374/1995), 175. Jalal Al-e Ahmad (1923–1969) was a prominent Iranian author and social critic, whose ideas, along with Ali Shariati, another Iranian intellectual, shaped a hegemonic discourse called 'Bazgasht beh Khishtan' (Return to The Self) in the Iranian intellectual milieu. He was primarily a leftist and a member of the Tudeh Party of Iran. He was a spokesman for the party and editor of its publications, such as *Rahbar* and *Mardom*. Al-e Ahmad left the Tudeh Party of Iran in 1947. He published more than twenty volumes of work, including essays, reviews, translations, travel journals and fiction.

60 'Hadeseh-ye Zirab', *Keyhan*, no. 1118, 16 Azar 1325 (7 December 1946): 4.

61 'Mosabbebin-e Ghaeleh-ye Zirab Tabid Mishavand', *Keyhan*, no. 1122, 19 Azar 1325 (10 December 1946): 4.

62 'Mosahebeh-ye Khabargozari-ye Faranseh ba Vazir-e Pisheh va Honar', *Keyhan*, no. 1135, 5 Dey 1325 (26 December 1946): 4.

63 Ibid., 129.

64 Touraj Atabaki, 'Chronicles of a Calamitous Strike Foretold: Abadan, July 1946', in *On the Road to Global Labour History: A Festschrift for Marcel van der Linden*, ed. Karl Heinz Roth (Leiden: Brill, 2017), 93; John Foran, *Fragile Resistance: Social Transformation in Iran from 1500 to the Revolution* (Boulder: Westview Press Inc, 1993), 279–80.

65 Abrahamian, *Iran Between Two Revolutions*, 367.

66 Ladjevardi, *Labor Unions*, 201.

67 Abrahamian, *Iran Between Two Revolutions*, 420.

68 Maral Jefroudi, 'Revisiting "the Long Night" of Iranian Workers: Labor Activism in the Iranian Oil Industry in the 1960s', *International Labor and Working-Class History* 84 (Fall 2013): 176–94.

69 Fatemeh Hormozi, Fatemeh Hajiha and Forugh Haririan, *Seyr-e Tatavvor-e Moqarrarat va Sazman-e Ejrayi-ye Kar dar Iran* (Tehran: Moasseseh-ye Kar va Tamin-e Ejtemaei, 1387/2008), 22.

70 Ahmad Al-e Yasin, *Tarikhcheh-ye Barnamehrizi-ye Towseeh dar Iran* (Tehran: Samar, 1392/2013), 71; Daftary, 'Development Planning', 179.

71 *Mahnameh-ye Burs*, no. 57, Ordibehesht 1347 (April–May 1968): 83.

72 Daftary, 'Development Planning', 179.

73 Stephen C. Poulson, *Social Movements in Twentieth-Century Iran: Culture, Ideology, and Mobilizing Frameworks* (Lanham: Lexington Books, 2006), 168.

74 Farshad Momeni and Bahram Naghsh Tabrizi, *Eqtesad-e Iran dar Dowran-e Dowlat-e Melli* (Tehran: Nahadgara, 1394/2015), 105.

75 Keramatollah Alipour, *Tarikh-e Zaminshenasi va Madan dar Iran* (Tehran: Sazman-e Zaminshenasi va Ekteshafat-e Madani-ye Keshvar, 1380/2001), 343.

76 *Mahnameh-ye Burs*, 83.

77 Momeni and Naghsh Tabrizi, *Eqtesad-e Iran*, 180.

78 'Cheguneh Aram va Biseda Dasteh Jami Jan Separdand, Ama Cheh Hadeseh-ye Bozorgi Bud Agar beh Gusheh-ye Servat-e Bipayan-e Yeki az Hezar Famil Chap Negah Mishod', *Mardom-e Iran*, 4 Esfand 1331 (23 February 1953): 2.

79 *Mardom-e Iran*, 18 Khordad 1332 (8 June 1953): 2.

Bibliography

Archives and libraries

Library, Museum and Document Center of the Iranian Parliament, Tehran
National Library and Archives of Iran, Tehran
Presidential Research and Documents Centre, Tehran
The National Archives, London

Periodicals

Ettelā ʿāt
Keyhān
Māhnāmeh-ye Burs
Mardom-e Irān

Secondary sources

Abdollahzadeh, Hossein. *Seyri dar Qavānin va Āyinnāmehhā-ye Ejrāyi-ye Ma ʿāden-e Irān dar Yek Qarn-e Gozashteh, 1278–1377*. Tehran: Rahpuyan-e Kherad, 1378 (1995).
Abrahamian, Ervand. A *History of Modern Iran*. Cambridge: Cambridge University Press, 2014.
Abrahamian, Ervand. *Iran Between Two Revolutions*. Princeton: Princeton University Press, 1983.
Al-e Ahmad, Jalal. *Az Ranji Keh Mibarim*. Tehran: Amirkabir, 1357 (1978).
Al-e Yasin, Ahmad. *Tārikhcheh-ye Barnāmehrizi-ye Towse ʿeh dar Irān*. Tehran: Samar, 1392 (2013).
Alipour, Keramatollah. *Tārikh-e Zaminshenāsi va Ma ʿdan dar Irān*. Tehran: Sazman-e Zaminshenasi va Ekteshafat-e Madani-ye Keshvar, 1380 (2001).
Alizadeh, Parvin. 'The Process of Import Substitution Industrialisation in Iran (1960–1978) with Particular Reference to the Case of the Motor Vehicle Industry'. PhD diss., Sussex University, 1984.
Ashraf, Ahmad and Ali Banuazizi. *Tabaqāt-e Ejtemā ʿi, Dowlat va Enqelāb dar Irān*. Tehran: Nilufar, 1388 (2009).
Atabaki, Touraj. 'Chronicles of a Calamitous Strike Foretold: Abadan, July 1946'. In *On the Road to Global Labour History: A Festschrift for Marcel van der Linden*, edited by Karl Heinz Roth, 93–128. Leiden: Brill, 2017.
Badiei, Rabi. *Joghrāfiyā-ye San ʿati-ye Irān*. Tehran: Omur-e Towseeh-ye Niru-ye Ensani, 1338 (1959).
Bahmani-Oskooee, Mohsen. 'History of the Rial and Foreign Exchange Policy in Iran'. *Iranian Economic Review* 10, no. 14 (Fall 2005): 1–20.
Bharier, Julian. *Economic Development in Iran, 1900–1970*. London: Oxford University Press, 1971.
Daftary, Farhad. 'Development Planning in Iran: A Historical Survey'. *Iranian Studies* 6, no. 4 (Autumn 1973): 176–228.
Farrokh, Seyyed Mehdi. *Khāterāt-e Siyāsi-ye Mehdi Farrokh (Mo ʿtasem al-Saltaneh)*. Tehran: Amirkabir, 1347 (1968).

Floor, Willem M. *Industrialization in Iran, 1900–1941*. Edited by John Dewdney and Heather Bleaney. Occasional Papers Series, no. 23. Durham: University of Durham Centre for Middle Eastern and Islamic Studies, 1984.

Floor, Willem M. 'Labour Unions, Law, and Conditions in Iran (1900–1941)'. Occasional Papers Series, no. 26. Durham: University of Durham Centre for Middle Eastern and Islamic Studies, 1985.

Foran, John. *Fragile Resistance: Social Transformation in Iran from 1500 to the Revolution*. Boulder: Westview Press, 1993.

Hormozi, Fatemeh, Fatemeh Hajiha and Forugh Haririan. *Seyr-e Tatavvor-e Moqarrarāt va Sāzmān-e Ejrāyi-ye Kār dar Irān*. Tehran: Moasseseh-ye Kar va Tamin-e Ejtemaei, 1387 (2008).

Issawi, Charles. *The Economic History of Iran, 1800–1914*. Chicago: University of Chicago Press, 1971.

Jefroudi, Maral. 'Revisiting "the Long Night" of Iranian Workers: Labor Activism in the Iranian Oil Industry in the 1960s'. *International Labor and Working-Class History* 84 (Fall 2013): 176–94.

Kazemi, Farhad. *Poverty and Revolution in Iran: The Migrant Poor, Urban Marginality and Politics*. New York: New York University Press, 1980.

Kazemzadeh, Mohammad Ali. *Tārikh-e Mes-e Sarcheshmeh-ye Kermān*. Tehran: Sherkat-e Melli-ye Sanaye-e Mes-e Iran, 1360 (1981).

Kia, Iraj. *Moruri bar Tārikhcheh-ye Mokhtasar-e Maʿāden-e Irān*. Tehran: Negin, 1374 (1995).

Ladjevardi, Habib. *Labor Unions and Autocracy in Iran*. Syracuse: Syracuse University Press, 1985.

Latifi Niya, Mahshid. *Asnād-e Maʿāden-e Irān, 1300–1332*. Tehran: Sazman-e Asnad-e Melli-ye Iran, Pazhuheshkadeh-ye Asnad, 1376 (1997).

Millspaugh, Arthur Chester. 'The Financial and Economic Situation of Persia, 1926'. In *Vazʿiyyat-e Māli va Eqtesādi-ye Irān dar Dowreh-ye Rezā Shāh (Majmuʿeh-ye Gozāreshāt)*, edited and translated by Shahram Gholami, 19–66. Tehran: Tarikh-e Iran, 1395 (2016).

Momeni, Farshad and Bahram Naghsh Tabrizi. *Eqtesād-e Irān dar Dowrān-e Dowlat-e Melli*. Tehran: Nahadgara, 1394 (2015).

Pourshafei, Majid. *Eqtesād-e Kucheh: Gozāresh-e Pul-e Melli-ye Irān, Hazinehhā-ye Zendegi va Dastmozdhā dar Do Sadeh-ye Gozashteh 1157–1357*. Tehran: Gam-e No, 1385 (2006).

Razavian, Mohammad Taghi. *Manābe-ye Enerzhi-ye Irān*. Tehran: Daneshgah-e Azad-e Eslami, Vahed-e Tehran-e Jonub, 1373 (2004).

Saadat, Fathollah and Amir Houshang Amini. *Joghrāfiyā-ye Eqtesādi-ye Irān*. Tehran: Daneshkadeh-ye Olum-e Ertebatat-e Ejtemaei, 1350 (1971).

Safaei, Ebrahim. *Chehel Khātereh az Chehel Sāl*. Tehran: Elmi, 1374 (1995).

Tabrizi, Mirza Mohammad Saleh. *Maʿdan Nāmeh: Fehresti az Maʿāden-e Iran beyn-e Sālhā-ye 1240 tā 1270 Shamsi*. n.p.: n.p., n.d.

Tayarani, Behrouz. 'Tāʿsir-e Jang-e Jahāni-ye Dovvom bar Vazʿiyyat-e Behdāshti-ye Mardom'. *Ganjineh-ye Asnad*, no. 33–4 (Bahar va Tabestan 1378/Spring and Summer 1999): 92–107.

Part IV

Statistics versus family memoirs of labour and industry

10

Workforce, working conditions and labour relations in urban Iran: 1950s–60s

Willem Floor

Industrialization and the formation of the urban workforce took place while Iran was developing from a pre-capitalist, decentralized and agricultural subsistence economy to one that was highly centralized, autocratic and industrializing, while the ranks of the incipient urban industrial labour force were filled by rural migrants. This type of socio-economic transition was not much different from what had happened in the industrialized countries. Much like in Europe one century earlier, the Iranian state and its elite, whether secular or religious, also aimed to keep workers in their place by emphasizing the virtue of submission to its hierarchical order. The centralization of the state under Reza Shah (r. 1925–41), which continued under the reign of his son, Mohammad Reza Shah (r. 1941–78), maintained class privileges and the pre-industrial features of the economy. Although this centralization process took away much of the traditional elite's power by transferring it to the central government, they were induced to support this change, not only by the threat of the use of force by the state but also by the granting of subsidies, credit and other forms of economic protection, especially to merchants and industrialists, including government intervention in wages and working conditions. This not only strengthened the power of government but also gave it a central role in the economy. This state-centrism had consequences for the development of the working class, because given the reluctance, if not aversion, of employers to engage with the labour force in a positive way, workers had to lodge their grievances with the government.

Iran's population grew from 9.86 million in 1900 to 30.35 million in 1970.[1] Improved health conditions after 1900 (presumably, more so during the interwar period) led to an increase in population growth, from under 1 per cent to 1.5 per cent.[2] This rate rose to 2.5 per cent, when, just after the Second World War, infrastructural expansion enabled by the accrual of Allied funds created more job opportunities, and thus, higher income, which also led to access to better health care and information. This rise was followed by vaccination and anti-malaria campaigns, as well as better health and nutrition, which led to a growth rate of 2.9 per cent by the mid-1950s. This growth resulted in an increase in the size of the total population, in particular, in the urban areas due to increased rural migration.

Table 10.1 Workforce in Iran, 1921–76 (Thousands)

Description	1921	1941	1956	1966	1970	1972	1976
Total population	9,707	12,833	18,955	25,789	30,020	30,820	33,375
Population over ten years of age	6,992	9,244	12,784	17,045	19,877	20,435	22,613
Inactive population	3,664	4,899	6,717	9,199	11,200	11,583	13,235
Active population	3,328	4,345	6,067	7,846	8,677	8,852	9,378
Employed	-	-	5,908	7,546	8,471	8,656	-
Unemployed	-	-	159	300	206	196	-
Active population in % of total	34.3	33.9	32.0	30.4	28.9	28.7	28.1
Active population over ten years in %	47.6	47.0	47.5	46.0	43.7	43.3	41.5
Employed/active in %	-	-	97.4	96.2	97.6	97.8	-
Employed/total population in %	-	-	31.2	29.3	28.2	28.1	-

Source: *Iran Almanac and Book of Facts* (Tehran: Echo of Iran, 1978), 421.

After 1935, the urban population began to grow faster than the total population, which was due to internal migration. A considerable part of the rural population, which still represented about 57 per cent of the total population by 1970,[3] existed at the subsistence level. Although most migrants came from rural areas, as indicated by the lower than total growth rate, some of the migration was interurban. This trend is evident, based on the depopulation of some cities in the 1950–60s as well as data on the origins of migrants.[4]

The workforce

The economically active male population over ten years of age in Iran was estimated to be 4.394 million in 1926, with 3.735 million inhabitants engaged in agriculture. This means that the active workforce in urban areas at that time amounted to about 659,000.[5] This figure was undoubtedly higher, and may be estimated at 709,000, owing to the fact that boys under ten were employed in handicrafts, services, commerce and manufacturing. Moreover, quite a substantial number of women and girls were engaged in various urban economic activities, especially weaving carpets and other textiles.

In 1972, about 58 per cent of the population still lived in rural areas.[6] However, the share of agricultural labour in the workforce had declined from 56 per cent in 1956 to 46 per cent in 1966. Nevertheless, the agriculture sector was the most important employer for rural labour.[7] In 1966, the latter were mostly self-employed (55 per cent), wage earners (25 per cent) and unpaid family workers (15 per cent).[8]

Although the total number of workers rose more steadily in Iran from 1956 to 1972 (see Table 10.1), employment in the manufacturing industry grew from 379,000 in 1962 to 936,000 in 1972, at an average rate of 9.5 per cent per year.[9] Employment grew fastest in the textile industry (29 per cent of new jobs), with manufacturers of processed food, wearing apparel and metal products as runners up (together 43 per cent of new jobs). Manufacturing was concentrated in Markazi province (which included Tehran and parts of Isfahan, Zanjan and Semnan provinces until 1977), which was estimated to produce nearly 60 per cent of total value added, while only employing 40 per cent of the workforce, as well as having 35 per cent of the enterprises and 20 per cent of the population. Therefore, the government initiated a policy of regional diversification, by banning new industrial plants within a 120-kilometre radius of Tehran. As a result, the Qazvin area grew significantly. This meant that there was (and still is) a wide disparity between various provinces and regions. Large establishments, which were mainly located in Markazi province, were more productive, and their workforces were better paid. In fact, all other provinces were below the national average in terms of size of establishments and labour productivity.

Urban workforce

Data on overall urban employment before the 1950s is incomplete. However, by the mid-twentieth century, 55 per cent of the population was dependent on agriculture as its main source of income. In 1955, the government of Iran reported that more than 1 million people were gainfully employed in the non-agricultural sector. It further submitted that 25 per cent of this group constituted the main breadwinners. This group of more than 1 million people was composed as follows:

Table 10.2 makes it clear that the Iranian government was the main employer (29.1 per cent), although traditional crafts (25.2 per cent) and the commercial sector (21.5 per cent) together employed more than 46 per cent of the total urban workforce. Conversely, modern industry, both private and state-owned, only employed 24.2 per cent of the urban workforce. However, not all of the workers enjoyed permanent employment. The casual workforce in summer was estimated to be 50,000 men in 1955, which increased to 150,000 in the wintertime.[10] In 1960, the brickmaking industry employed 21,000 people, thus suggesting the potential unemployment of 29,000 workers, assuming that the casual workforce was mostly represented by brickmakers. In the same year, there was a decrease of 72,500 jobs in the construction industry, so total unemployment in the building sector amounted to 101,500. At that time, total underemployment was estimated at 40 per cent of the urban workforce.[11] One other major issue was that of a surplus of employees. In the oil industry and the textile industry, which were major employers, there was an excess of labour that, due to pressure by the government, employers were unable to lay off.[12]

Table 10.2 Non-Agricultural Workforce, 1955

Armed forces, gendarmerie, police	185,000	17.4%
Civil service	125,000	11.7%
Petroleum industry	62,000	5.8%
Government-controlled industries	46,000	4.3%
Private manufacturing industries	150,000	14.1%
Professional, merchant, white collar	229,000	21.5%
Crafts, other private firms, miscellaneous	268,000	25.2%
Total	1,065,000	100%

Source: Philip Clock, 'Basic Survey of Labor Affairs in Iran, 1955', in *The Condition of the Working Class in Iran: A Documentary History, 1911–1979*, ed. Cosroe Chaqueri, vol. 4 (Tehran: Antidote Publications, 1991), 87.

Rural migration made matters worse for casual urban workers. Part of the year, in wintertime, peasants were idle and many migrated to towns to look for work, in order to increase their low incomes. There, they had to compete with one another for the few jobs available to unskilled labourers. This situation had a negative impact on the level of wages, safety and sanitation, as well as the employment ratio. Moreover, this influx of transient rural labour during the winter period sometimes coincided with a reduction of work in the construction industry, in particular, brickmaking, which employed a large number of unskilled and semi-skilled labourers. As a result, most workers earned just enough to get by, and, as a consequence, their diet, health and housing were poor.[13]

Characteristics of the rural workforce

Because much of the urban workforce was of rural origin, it is not only of interest but also essential to have a closer look at working conditions in the agricultural sector; since, although the peasant had left his village, the village had not left the peasant.[14] In fact, most workers were still living and working with the mindset of an agricultural worker. At the same time, many employers of the urban workforce also were of the same rural mindset. Therefore, a brief characterization of the mode of production in Iranian villages prior to the 1962 Land Reform (which was part of the White Revolution) will be offered here.

Until recent times, Iran was a pre-capitalist society with a rather weak central government. In such a society, there were no incentives to pursue long-term economic development as the modern capitalist mode of production. This meant that production factors (i.e. land, labour, capital and entrepreneurship) were not used efficiently. For instance, there was plenty of arable land, but because of a lack of labour, water and energy, it could not be effectively utilized. Also, irrigation systems were inefficient and badly maintained, and there was no product quality control. Labour was underemployed because of low productivity, due to primitive and inefficient equipment and methods, and poor health and living conditions. A change in labour was difficult, however, because peasants were often bound to the soil by indebtedness and the use of force.

Agricultural production was determined by soil, seed, draft animals, human labour and water in the case of non-rain-fed agriculture, which required irrigation. The owners of these five inputs each received roughly 20 per cent of the total output. These production factors were owned by different people, and they could even be subdivided (examples of labour included: ploughing, tilling, harvesting and threshing). Due to the Islamic inheritance law, land might be owned by different people, who would only be remunerated for their share in the worked land. This meant that the idea of a landlord-owned and integrated farm that could be run as an economic enterprise did not exist; rather, it had evolved into the landlords' right to a rent.

Often big landlords owned the soil, seed and water, while peasants usually only contributed labour and often draft animals. In the case of land that was owned by more people, each one of them would only be remunerated for their share of the land. Thus, landlords owned an entire village, or part of it, or even an 'imaginary share' of the land. For land could be, and almost invariably was, owned by more than one person. Therefore, a piece of land might be further divided into a large number of smaller shares. For example, a village or a land unit could be divided as follows:

A village or part of it = 24 peas (*habbeh*)
One pea = 24 barley grains (*jow*)
One barley grain = 24 sesame seeds (*konjed*)

This means that a village or a part of it might be divided into 24 x 24 x 24 shares or 13,824 property titles.

In the case of absentee landowners and the owners of imaginary shares, this meant that there was no tangible relationship between the owners and the village, including its population and land. As a result, the owners were only interested in receiving their part of the output proportionate to the share(s) they owned. Consequently, any incentive for economic management was absent and exploitation of the land and labour was the norm.

Peasants who received the right to till a piece of land in the village (on an annual rotation basis, determined by lottery) formed working units called *boneh* or *sahra*. It was with the *boneh*, not the individual peasant, that the landowner or his manager (*mobāsher*) contracted the annual sharecropping arrangement. Those not part of a *boneh* either worked, or tried to work, as a day labourer in non-agricultural jobs, or had to leave the village. In short, most landlords were unable to know which piece of land they owned, and sharecroppers received a different piece of land each year, although it was more or less the same size, depending on its soil quality.

Apart from being able to determine the percentage of a peasant's share of the crop unilaterally, another reason to invest only the bare minimum in landed property was that labour was a fixed cost. In other words, it could not be freely substituted for capital. Landlords wanted to spend as little as possible on production costs, and instead, they preferred to use money for the purchase of luxury goods. The total amount of goods produced, that is, agricultural products, and the proportion that could be exchanged for other goods determined the landlord's standard of living and to a great extent influenced his place in society. His personal consumption was not as important as his sociopolitical obligations, in particular, to the Shah and powerful magnates. The landlord could reduce his personal consumption but not the purchases for these external obligations, which might force him to raise his share in the output to the detriment of the peasants.

This meant that neither the landlord nor the sharecropper had an interest in improving the land and level of production beyond the minimum, because doing more would only benefit others. Moreover, this dilemma tied the peasant to the landlord (or moneylender), thus further contributing to the consolidation and inflexibility of the system of agricultural production and payments. Furthermore, the peasants' almost total dependence on the landlord or other outsiders created a quasi-feudal relationship between them. The fact that landlords or their representative also made use of thugs (*luti*), if need be, to impose their 'rule' over 'their' peasants also contributed to this quasi-feudalism. This also explains the almost total absence of rural uprisings, for peasants either reacted with passivity or moved to another village that hopefully offered better terms.

The selling of farm products (and carpets) was not done by the producers but either by the owners of the production factors, other than labour, or by middlemen (*dallālān*). In the case of carpets, the owners and/or middlemen often organized the entire production process, taking the lion's share of the profits. Likewise, the weavers often went into debt with the financier/middleman, resulting in a relationship of total dependency. The weaver, like the peasant, only received a small percentage of the proceeds of the sale. This constant skimming of the proceeds without a corresponding financial return for the workers impeded socio-economic progress. This system was called 'rent capitalism', a term coined by the Austrian geographer Hans Bobek, in order to distinguish it from modern capitalism, because rather than being linked to production, it was a parasitical system of trying to increase the rent of one's share in production.

Characteristics of the urban workforce

Although data on the characteristics of the urban workforce in Iran is scant and otherwise varied in nature and detail, while being limited to a few towns, sub-sectors and/or years, it is sufficient in scope and detail to draw a coherent picture. Most data concerns the workforce of Tehran, the largest city with the greatest concentration of both modern and traditional industry. Furthermore, data available from other cities in Iran confirms the results found in Tehran.

A study carried out in 1963 by the University of Tehran among about 290 industrial workers in Tehran concluded that the origins of the industrial labour class of that city were different from those of the total population of Tehran. Most of these industrial workers were in the age groups of twenty-five to thirty-four years (43.3 per cent) and thirty-five to forty-four years (27.9 per cent).[15] Members of the industrial labour class mostly hailed from the provinces, which suggested that the older settled urban population preferred other employment to jobs in industry. In fact, two-thirds of the industrial workforce surveyed had rural origins, nine-tenths had provincial roots and only 10 per cent were Tehranis.[16] Apart from being predominantly rural and provincial, members of the workforce were mostly Turkic speakers, which constituted a barrier to finding employment where knowledge of Persian was a requirement, that is, mainly administrative jobs. As a result, the industrial workforce constituted a sociocultural group that was distinct from the general population of Tehran.

A similar situation existed among the informal sector workers of Tehran, of which the brick kiln workers (see Figure 10.1) constituted the largest share. In the 1960s and 1970s, most of these workers in the Khatunabad district of Pakdasht county, which had the largest concentration of kilns around the province of Tehran, originated from villages in Khorasan province, in particular, from the Turkic-speaking area of Quchan and the Persian-speaking areas of Torbat-e Heydarieh and Torbat-e Jam.[17] The latter were said to represent 45 per cent of the workforce in 1970. The rest were Turkic

Figure 10.1 Khatunabad brickworkers, 1956. *Source*: Library, Museum and Document Center of the Iranian Parliament, 'Kurehha: Sad Hezar Nafar dar Inja Jan Mikonand ta Jan Dashteh Bashand', *Keyhan*, no. 3881 (7 Khordad 1335/28 May 1956), 6.

speakers from Quchan and villages around Hamadan province and Persian speakers from Zabol, in Sistan and Baluchestan province. At this time, the average age of the Khatunabad brick kiln workers was twenty-seven, and the maximum was fifty years old.

In Ahvaz, while we do not have a breakdown of the composition of its workforce, the general population consisted of migrants from many parts of Iran, and so the workforce must have been similarly constituted. The population was divided into two groups: Arabs and what they called 'the ʿAjami' (Persian speakers). Undoubtedly, the Arabs were not all members of the dominant tribe in Khuzestan, the Banu Kaʿb, but also came from other Arab groups, such as the Sabaeans, and from cities, such as Hoveyzeh, and even Iraq. Likewise, the Persian speakers were an ethnically diverse group, ranging from Bakhtiyaris, Shushtaris, Dezfulis and Isfahanis. Those from Isfahan province came mainly from the city of Isfahan, Sedeh Lenjan, Najafabad and so on.[18] A similar situation existed in Abadan, the headquarters of the Anglo-Persian Oil Company (APOC). APOC hired poor Bakhtiyari tribesmen as unskilled labour but employed Europeans for managerial and technical positions and Indian staff for all clerical jobs and skilled and semi-skilled manual tasks.

The literacy rate of the total population of Iran rose from less than 5 per cent in 1900 to under 10 per cent in 1948, 15 per cent in 1956 and about 30 per cent for those over the age of ten in 1966.[19] The literacy rate among the industrial workforce was about 20 per cent in 1948. The Tehran survey shows that 82 per cent of workers of urban origin had received an education, and about 65 per cent of them were literate. Among the rural migrants, 45 per cent had received an education in religious schools (*maktabhā*) and 25 per cent were literate. Moreover, the sons of agricultural labourers had the lowest level of education.[20] About 90 per cent of the brick kiln workers of Khatunabad were illiterate, and only very few were able to read and write fluently.[21] By 1986, 40 per cent of the total employed population in Iran was still illiterate.[22]

Individual industrial workers in Tehran depended on traditional kinship ties (*tāyefeh*) for networking. In the majority of their villages of origin (73.4 per cent), there were three or more *tāyefehhā*, and some had two (10.1 per cent) or only one (7.5 per cent), while only a few had no distinctive *tāyefeh* (0.5 per cent). It is characteristic for members of a *tāyefeh* to be concentrated geographically within the village and the urban quarters. Marriage was endogamic, that is, within the same clan or lineage. This did not mean that there was no rivalry and competition within the group; in fact, this was the rule, for the *tāyefeh* existed mainly as a form of protection against outsiders. This meant that adherence and loyalty to the group also had to have some tangible benefit, such as mutual support in personal and social affairs. In the rural areas, there were often violent conflicts between villages or *tāyefehhā* over water and other resource rights. Although *luti* gangs represented the violent aspect of village life, as exercised by the landlord, to some extent in urban quarters, it was less pervasive and individuals had greater freedom.[23]

In Ahvaz, there was a similar social formation, which translated itself into the monopolization of certain occupations by distinct urban migrant and ethnic groups. Merchants, especially grocers, in spices and fabrics, as well as managers of cafes and hotels, and also certain traditional crafts (e.g. smiths, carpenters and furniture makers) were mostly Isfahanis. Watchmakers, bathhouse managers, tire sellers and repairers, masons, ironworkers, tilemakers and unskilled labourers as well as office staff of the local administration came from Shushtar and Dezful. Bakers were from Shahr-e Kord, the Sabaeans worked as silversmiths and Jews were employed in pharmacies. Endogamy was almost universal among these various groups and imperative among the Bakhtiyaris, Arabs and Jews. Bakhtiyaris and Arabs still maintained their traditional *tāyefeh* organization. These ethnic, cultural and linguistic (Arabic, Lor, Isfahani Persian, etc.) determinants guided people's behaviour and interaction with members of other groups, and sometimes the divisions between them ran deep.[24] Employers tried to exploit these ethnic tensions to their own advantage. A certain industrial entrepreneur in Ahvaz employed Arabs and Persians, but each group had separate workplaces and was paid unequal wages for the same work: '"The Arab is lazy," he tells the better paid Persian, "the Ajami is a liar," he tells the Arab who demands equal pay.'[25]

In the earlier cases, the individual worker had less standing or judicial status independent of the group. Therefore, individuals owed the varying strength of their position to group membership and, more specifically, to their standing within that group in interactions with the landlord, other *tāyefehhā* and so on. Also, the level of influence of a *tāyefeh* did not necessarily depend on its size or agricultural output but rather on its social standing, the strength of its social relations and its use of influence, contacts, information and so on. Thus, the accumulation of wealth was not only achieved through work in the strictly capitalistic sense but also by means of influential social relations.[26]

The protection and safety of belonging to a group, in particular, an influential one, was also important for gaining employment. Casual labour was often hired on a day-to-day basis and part of a worker's pay had to be given to the foreman (*sarkārgar*) or another intermediary responsible for the hiring of this individual.[27] In the oil industry, this system was used, and the *sarkārgar* not only recruited workers, but also supervised them and induced them to stay on the job. In 1912, APOC established a labour office that took the place of the *sarkārgar*.[28] It is noteworthy that initially both Indians and Iranians were hired through a third party. Indian workers were either directly transferred from Burma or were hired through a firm in India (Bombay, Karachi). This system continued until 1926, when APOC cut out the middleman and recruited Indian staff via its office in Bombay.

The *sarkārgar* system also existed in other sectors,[29] in particular, in that of carpet weaving. To avoid the 1959 Labour Law and social insurance coverage for workers, employers usually hired a small number of 'weavers' (i.e. nine or less, because ten or more was classified a factory), who in turn hired others to work for them on a contract basis. These contract workers usually were woman and young children, who worked eight-hour days under appalling conditions for low wages.[30] Because of the presence of intermediaries in the *sarkārgar* system, workers had no direct contact with their employers.

Wages

Not much is known about the level and nature of wages and the regularity of their payment. Also, data is scant, incomplete and unreliable, in particular, when published by the government. It also made a difference whether you worked in a modern factory (and even among those, there were differences) or in a traditional establishment. For instance, the tobacco industry only employed paid workers, while only half of the workers in workshops for the manufacture of furniture and other wood products were paid, usually because they were family members. In other small urban businesses, conditions were not much better, either. Often payment of wages lagged months behind. Workers then were forced to either buy daily necessities on credit, which was costly, or borrow money in the bazaar at high interest rates, where they sometimes competed for the same money with their employers, who received a lower rate.[31] Also, because of intense competition for jobs, workers were willing to work overtime at the standard rate to make ends meet.

The 1959 Labour Law defined the minimum wage for an unskilled worker as being adequate to cover the living expenses of one man, his wife and two children. This wage was to be reviewed every two years. Also, the forty-eight-hour working week was divided into eight hours a day, six days per week.[32] However, in this respect, the law was not adequately applied, either. For example, wages did not keep up with inflation, but always lagged behind, so that real wages were estimated to be 25 per cent lower. Moreover, in 1955, the traditional Nowruz bonus had not been raised since 1945. In that same year, textile workers in Isfahan and many unskilled workers earned 32 rials per day, while expenditures for essential daily food requirements for a family of four were estimated at 50 to 75 rials.[33] In 1958, the Bank-e Melli also conducted a survey of twelve urban centres, including the ten largest cities in Iran. The survey concluded that 76.6 per cent of urban families had a monthly income of less than 5,000 rials. However, it was calculated that an Iranian family of five needed to have an income of 5,200 rials per month for adequate nutrition.[34] In the oil industry, the minimum daily wage was 82 rials in 1956, which was not enough to meet daily needs and old-age saving requirements. In June and July 1956, workers in Abadan and Masjed Soleyman went on strike for short periods.[35] As a result, the minimum wage was raised to 99 rials, although 14 rials were deducted for groceries (*khārobār*).[36] The national newspaper *Ettelaat* hailed this deal as the first collective agreement concluded in the history of Iran.[37] In the same year, about 6,000 workers in Tehran's bakeries earned 3 to 5 tomans (others could get a higher wage), some working as much as eighteen hours per day, from five o'clock in the morning until eleven o'clock at night.[38]

More wage information is available concerning the brick kiln workers (*kurehpaz*), despite the fact that they were not included in the official labour statistics. In 1955, around 100,000 people, of whom about 20 per cent were children below age twelve, lived at the brick kilns of southern Tehran.[39] The workers worked from five o'clock in the morning until seven o'clock in the evening, or a fourteen-hour working day. The men earned 3 tomans and the children were paid 15 rials per day. The wives of the Persian-speaking Khorasani workers (and/or their children) carried the raw bricks and stacked them near the kilns (*khesht-e jam* ʿ *kon*) for firing.[40] In 1954/5 (1333), after a strike, the brick kiln workers received a pay rise of 15 per cent. When, a year later, this pay rise was felt to be insufficient, they went on strike again. The 25,000 workers of the brick kilns, except for the *khākbardārān* (shovellers), received another increase of 25 per cent in early January 1956.[41] They continued to strike in the ensuing years (see Figure 10.2). Workers were not only exploited by their employers but also by the shopkeepers in their area, who sold their products at inflated prices.

In 1964, the weekly *Sepid o Siyah* calculated that an average family needed 2,300 calories per day, which meant that each member of the family had to earn at least 170 rials a day. This figure did not include the cost of housing, clothes and other necessities.[42] In May 1964, the government fixed the minimum wage at 31–40 rials per day, depending on the region,[43] which clearly fell far short of what *Sepid o Siyah* had calculated. In October 1967, Ataollah Khosrovani, the Minister of Labour and Social Services, stated that the minimum wage had been left free to market forces, that is, 'supply and demand'. At that time, he said that the minimum daily wage was 70–80 rials.[44] In 1969, the minimum daily wage of an unskilled labourer in Iran was said to be 80–150 rials a day.[45] While a family of five was estimated to have an annual per capita income of 20,000 rials, given the high cost of living in urban areas, there was usually more than one breadwinner. In March 1969, it was decided to raise the minimum wage for three employment categories to 50, 55 and 60 rials per day, which only benefitted workers earning 'less than these rates'.[46] The government claimed that workers' income was being increased by the 1963 profit-sharing scheme, which set aside 20 per cent of employer profits for workers as part of

Figure 10.2 Khatunabad brickworkers on strike, 1957. *Source*: Library, Museum and Document Center of the Iranian Parliament, 'Kargaran-e Kurehpazkhanehha-ye Tehran Etesab Kerdand', *Keyhan*, no. 4208 (9 Tir 1336/30 June 1957), 1.

collective agreements.[47] However, apart from problems with the actual functioning of this scheme, much of the workforce had no collective agreement and/or their sector was excluded from the scheme (e.g. oil, railway, tobacco and certain other state industries).

Industrial employers' attitude

Factory owners mostly came from bazaar or elite families. This meant that they were part and parcel of the rural-urban exchange system that was accustomed to extracting rents from the agricultural and cottage industry sectors. Therefore, the same 'rent-capitalistic' mindset of the *arbāb* (landowner) was also found among the early factory owners.[48] This modus operandi was quite obvious in the carpet-weaving industry. Whether in rural or market-town cottage industries, the single economic activity of weaving a carpet was subdivided into multiple production factors, the rent of which was often owned by different people. For example, carpet weaving was subdivided into who supplied the labour, loom, wool, wool cleaning, yarns, dyes, pattern and quality control, since each of these factors was commercialized. These factors were organized in various ways, depending on the region and/or city as well as the type of carpet. Also, the fact that many rural workers were casual labour strengthened the hand of the employer.[49]

Landlords or their representatives often had quasi-feudal control over their peasants (*ray'at*) in the countryside. This same state of mind also played a role when rural workers moved to the city, where most neighbourhoods were stratified and vertically structured rather than horizontally organized by one class or social category. Moreover, contrary to the quarters of established urban dwellers, those occupied by rural immigrants were static and unchanging, much like their villages.[50] Consequently, the master-servant attitude generally prevailed in public and private enterprise.[51] The US Labour Relations Advisor wrote in 1960: 'The average Iranian worker looks upon his employer as some sort of superior being. [. . .] Workers often accept the most flagrant violations of their rights with hardly a murmur of protest.'[52]

The same attitude also existed towards the government. For centuries, the only recourse available to peasants to protest against oppression by landlords and/or their agents was to appeal to higher authority, that is, the Shah or his representatives. Moreover, strikes or work stoppages were seldom settled by an agreement between the workers and the employer but more often through informal and rapid government intervention. The provincial Ministry of Labour representative was called, and usually after a few hours, he made his decision known, which was not always in accordance with the requirements of the 1959 Labour Law, and the workers returned to work. If government intervention failed to resolve the matter for whatever reason, including the lack of formal workers' representatives, and the labour dispute dragged on, this would have consequences for the government officials concerned, who would lose their jobs – possibly, even including the provincial governor-general.[53] The US Labour Relations Advisor wrote in 1955:

> The same type of paternalism characterizes labor's relations with Government in Iran, although the Government is, if anything, even more hidebound in outmoded social attitudes than is management. There is a tendency for workers in this country to look to Government for solutions to their problems with management rather than to attempt to deal directly with the source of any particular dispute.[54]

Indeed, most workers did not form labour unions, and even if they did, it was invariably with the encouragement and support of external political actors. In fact, the only individuals who had fought for workers' rights were mostly members of the Tudeh Party, which was outlawed in 1953. Thereafter, any labour 'leader' was vetted for his political reliability, and thus, the labour movement was hijacked by the Iranian government and became merely a façade and an instrument to control the labour force. As a result, labour leaders rather than representing workers' interests only pursued their own. Often, there was more infighting with other so-called labour leaders than taking the fight of workers to employers.[55]

Moreover, many managers were untrained and/or lacked the skills to properly manage their businesses, not even having any idea about, or exhibiting a lack of interest in, their manpower needs and the required recruitment and training activities.[56] The US Labour Advisor reported in 1960:

> There are many modern mills and much machinery, but the same master-servant atmosphere prevails as has prevailed for centuries in the bazaar shops. There is little control over the means of production on the part of management. The mill owners always ask for technical help but when help is forthcoming it is virtually ignored. The mill owners' prime interest in technical assistance appears to be the hope for financial assistance that usually follows. In spite of modern automatic German or Japanese looms that are designed to permit one worker to operate 16 to 22 at a time, Iranian mill owners are content to have one worker operate 4 looms at a time.[57]

This attitude was also evident in the structural lack of skilled workers, which could have been resolved with proper training and more educational facilities.[58] In 1957, there were 4,849 vocational and technical students in Iran, of whom 794 were girls.[59] More than a decade later, in 1969, these figures had risen to 19,059 and 3,701, respectively, including vocational classes (*kelāshā-ye herfeh*) for secretarial and medical assistant jobs. Given that previous efforts had fallen short of labour force needs, it was reported in 1973 that the Ministry of Labour and Social Affairs was offering free four- to six-month training courses in thirty fields at four vocational training centres, located in Tehran, Karaj, Isfahan and Mashhad. Training was offered in welding, casting, modelling, plumbing, lathe operating, metalwork, repairs of household appliances and cars, electrical work, moulding, machinery maintenance, design, cartography and other subjects.[60]

Also, the way in which factory owners marketed their finished products was traditional, outmoded and inefficient, mainly using their bazaar networks and complicated sales contracts.[61] Although the rate of return on the low level of equity capital had to be high enough to attract investors (since debt was usually more than 60 per cent), it was 'not always attributable to an industrial operation by itself' and could be increased if 'integrated firms' sold their products directly 'to the final consumer and thereby [would] appropriate for themselves the traditionally high middleman's profit'.[62]

Moreover, much like in the agricultural and cottage industry sectors, industrial managers did not set labour standards, either, and consequently, working conditions were inadequate, unhealthy and dangerous, which had a negative impact on worker's health as well as on their productivity.[63] This abominable situation was exacerbated by the fierce competition among the vast supply of unemployed casual labourers, as well as a lack of government control, if not disinterest, in the enforcement of labour laws before 1970.[64]

At the same time, the brick kiln workers did not know about the existence of the 1959 Labour Law and their rights under this law.[65] Despite regular demonstrations by various workers' groups in the late 1950s and early 1960s, demanding the implementation of the 1959 Labour Law and the rules of the Social Security Organisation (Sazman-e

Tamin-e Ejtemaei), established in 1950, this did not happen.[66] Employers found it cheaper to bribe government officials than to comply with the Labour Law of 1959.[67] Even after warnings about dangerous situations, the Ministry of Labour only acted after the fact. In addition to this, employers were quite aware of the lack and/or weakness of the Ministry of Labour's enforcement capacity, and the inadequacy of legal penalties, and hence, they had neither fear nor respect for the representatives of the Ministry of Labour.[68]

Therefore, management often sought the easy way out, that is, maintaining the age-old socio-economic gap between worker (*kārgar*) and employer (*arbāb* or its modern iteration, *kārfarmā*). As a result, such entrepreneurs were 'content to spend the great bulk of earnings on present consumption, without regard to implications on future profits', and these industrialists could not 'be induced to expand their own investment without massive injections of new credit'.[69] For instance, government loans that had been provided for investment in the upgrade of their factories were either substituted for their own venture capital or were channelled abroad, while the government's lack of follow-up for their scheduled repayment only encouraged this rent-capitalist behaviour.[70] Also, the fact that government insisted on their employing of redundant labour reinforced this (see earlier in the chapter).

On the other hand, there were employers who wanted to improve conditions for their workers.[71] However, when a worker-friendly employer with a social conscience observed that his actions would negatively impact the interests of his family or friends, he would lose interest in such reforms.[72] In the mid-1960s, younger, more progressive managers started to make changes by rewarding workers for gains in productivity, in line with one of the objectives of the profit-sharing scheme. However, many managers in established industries, such as textiles and food, opposed such an approach.[73] Improvements in productivity were also opposed by many workers, out of fear of job losses.

Despite the post-war wave of industrialization and the economic boom of the 1970s, neither the nature of the urban labour force nor that of the worker's relationship with the employer or government changed much. Iranian workers, especially from the lower classes, may have felt that they belonged to an oppressed and downtrodden part of society, under the control of unjust political leaders and employers, but they developed neither a class conscience nor that of a proletariat, one that might have transformed them into a powerful economic and political force, as the events of the 1978–9 Revolution were about to show in Iran.

Notes

1 Julian Bharier, *Economic Development in Iran, 1900–1970* (London: Oxford University Press, 1971), 26–7.
2 Ibid., 24–5.
3 Ibid., 27.
4 Ibid., 28–30.
5 Ibid., 34.

6 International Bank for Reconstruction and Development (IBRD), *The Economic Development of Iran (Report No. 378a-IRN)*, vol. 2 (Washington, DC, 1974), 1.
7 Bharier, *Economic Development*, 34.
8 Ibid., 140.
9 IBRD, *Economic Development*, 57, 61–2.
10 'Employment and Unemployment', in *The Condition of the Working Class in Iran: A Documentary History, 1911–1979*, ed. Cosroe Chaqueri, vol. 4 (Tehran: Antidote Publications, 1991), 82; Philip Clock, 'Basic Survey of Labor Affairs in Iran, 1955', in *Condition of the Working Class*, 88.
11 'Annual Labor Report, 1961', in *Condition of the Working Class*, 172.
12 Clock, 'Basic Survey', 88.
13 Ibid., 87–8; 'Labor and Social Affairs, 1956', in *Condition of the Working Class*, 101; Bharier, *Economic Development*, 139–41.
14 This section is based on Hans Bobek, 'Rentenkapitalismus und Entwicklung in Iran', in *Interdisziplinare Iran-Forschung: Beitrage aus Kulturgeographie, Ethnologie, Soziologie und Neuerer Geschichte*, ed. Gunther Schweizer (Wiesbaden: Harrassowitz, 1979), 113–24, passim; Eckart Ehlers, 'Rent-capitalism and Unequal Development in the Middle East: The Case of Iran', in *Work, Income and Inequality: Payment Systems in the Third World*, ed. Frances Stewart (London: Palgrave Macmillan, 1983), 32–61, passim; Khosrow Khosravi, *Jameehshenasi-ye Rusta-ye Iran* (Tehran: Payam, 1358), passim.
15 Groupe d'Etudes Sociologiques, *Origine des Ouvriers de Tehran* (Institut d'Etudes et de Recherches Sociales, Universite de Tehran, 1965), 11.
16 Ibid., 9.
17 Willem Floor, 'The Brickworkers of Khatunabad: A Striking Record (1953–1979)', *International Review of Social History* 48, no. 3 (2003): 430.
18 Paul Vieille, *La feodalite et l'Etat en Iran* (Paris: Editions Anthropos, 1975), 222.
19 Bharier, *Economic Development*, 37.
20 Groupe d'Etudes Sociologiques, *Origine*, 102–4.
21 Floor, 'Brickworkers', 430.
22 Hooshang Amirahmadi, *Revolution and Economic Transition: The Iranian Experience* (Albany: State University of New York Press, 1990), 189.
23 Groupe d'Etudes Sociologiques, *Origine*, 20.
24 Vieille, *La feodalite*, 222–5.
25 Ibid., 225. The same 'divide and conquer' stratagem was used by the Tehran kiln owners against their workers, but without success. See also Floor, 'Brickworkers', 430.
26 Groupe d'Etudes Sociologiques, *Origine*, 50–1; Vieille, *La feodalite*, 224.
27 Clock, 'Basic Survey', 88.
28 R. W. Ferrier, *The History of the British Petroleum Company: Volume 1, The Developing Years, 1901–1932* (Cambridge: Cambridge University Press, 1982), 128, 151.
29 Floor, 'Brickworkers', 430–1.
30 Clock, 'Basic Survey', 91.
31 'Wages in Iran, 1955', in *Condition of the Working Class*, 81; 'Annual Labor Report, 1960, 1961, 1963', in *Condition of the Working Class*, 164, 173, 199.
32 *Iran Almanac and Book of Facts* (Tehran: Echo of Iran, 1968), 538.
33 'Wages in Iran', 81; Clock, 'Basic Survey', 90. Most workers in Isfahan received bread free of charge from their employers.
34 'The Campaign Against High Prices', *Echo of Iran*, no. 485 (19 June 1965): 2–3. This undernourishment was borne out by a United Nations survey of the Middle East.

35 In August 1955, there was a strike with the demand for higher wages at the oil fields. In June–July 1957, there was another strike by oil workers, which started at Aghajari and later spread to other localities. Some 5,000 workers were involved, who resumed work after the Iranian Oil Consortium promised to deal with their demands. In September 1957, oil workers at Masjed Soleyman then went on strike, accusing the Consortium of not having kept its promise to increase wages. A wage increase was promised in October, which indeed took place. See 'Recent Labour Strikes', *Echo Reports*, no. 21 (208) (25 June 1959): 2.
36 'Hadde Aqall-e Dastmozd-e Kargaran-e Naft dar 99 Rial Afzayesh Yaft', *Keyhan*, no. 4269 (25 Shahrivar 1336/16 September 1957): 1 and 10; 'Etesab-e Kargaran-e Naft dar Aghajari Payan Yaft', *Ettelaat*, no. 9355 (9 Tir 1336/30 June 1957): 1 and 16; 'Etesab-e Kargaran-e Naft', *Ettelaat*, no. 9413 (20 Shahrivar 1336/11 September 1957): 1 and 13.
37 'Emruz Etesab-e Kargaran-e Naft Payan Miyabad', *Ettelaat*, no. 9417 (26 Shahrivar 1336/17 September 1957): 1.
38 'Akhar va Aqebat-e Ma Shagerd-e Nunvaha Hamineh', *Keyhan*, no. 3884 (10 Khordad 1335/31 May 1956): 6.
39 'Kurehha: Sad Hezar Nafar dar Inja Jan Mikonand ta Jan Dashteh Bashand', *Keyhan*, no. 3881 (7 Khordad 1335/28 May 1956): 6.
40 Floor, 'Brickworkers', 431 and 436–7. The brick moulders' wives were often hired for this difficult job, on top of their daily household chores (e.g. childcare, baking bread and washing clothes).
41 'Kargaran-e Kurehpazkhanehha-ye Tehran Etesab Kerdand', *Keyhan*, no. 4208 (9 Tir 1336/30 June 1957): 1 and 2. In June 1957, there was a strike by Tehran kiln workers, who demanded a 30 per cent increase in their wages. After the kiln owners promised to accede to this demand, the strike was over. However, the kiln workers went on strike again in January 1958 because the kiln owners had not increased their wages. Faced with a forty-eight-hour ultimatum to do so, the kiln owners gave in and raised wages by 25 per cent before the deadline. In June 1959, Tehran kiln workers were striking again, this time demanding a raise of 35 per cent in wages. The kiln owners offered a 20 per cent raise, which was refused, but workers were then forced to resume work. See 'Recent Labour Strikes', 2–3. This weekly stated, 'The increase in wages owing to the constant increase in the cost of living does not help them much. Labour regulations and insurance facilities are not carried out properly due to the inadequate and inefficient departments.'
42 *Iran Almanac*, 1968, 270.
43 *Iran Almanac and Book of Facts* (Tehran: Echo of Iran, 1969), 528.
44 *Iran Almanac*, 1968, 543–4.
45 *Iran Almanac*, 1969, 258–9.
46 Ibid., 528.
47 *Iran Almanac and Book of Facts* (Tehran: Echo of Iran, 1965), 532.
48 Vieille, *La feodalite*, 229.
49 Ehlers, 'Rent-capitalism', 46–55.
50 Groupe d'Etudes Sociologiques, *Origine*, 35–7; Vieille, *La feodalite*, 224–5.
51 'Annual Labor Report, 1961', 179.
52 Clock, 'Basic Survey', 94. This hierarchical attitude was a general feature of Iranian society, even within the family, where an authoritarian father's word was law. See Richard W. Gable, 'Culture and Administration in Iran', *Middle East Journal* 13, no. 4 (Autumn 1959): 407–21, passim.

53 Clock, 'Basic Survey', 93; 'Labor Affairs, Iran, 1969-70', in *Condition of the Working Class*, 224.
54 Philip Clock, 'Labor Affairs in Iran, 1955–57', in *Condition of the Working Class*, 110.
55 Clock, 'Basic Survey', 94; idem, 'Labor Affairs', 113–14; 'Trade Unionism in Iran, 1957', in *Condition of the Working Class*, 119–20; 'Labor Scene in Isphahan and Yazd, 1958', in *Condition of the Working Class*, 141.
56 Richard Elliot Benedick, *Industrial Finance in Iran* (Cambridge, MA: Harvard University Press, 1964), 30; Vieille, *La feodalite*, 229.
57 'Annual Labor Report, 1960', 164.
58 'Annual Labor Report, 1963', 194.
59 *Iran Almanac and Book of Facts* (Tehran: Echo of Iran, 1971), 542. See also David Menashri, *Education and the Making of Modern Iran* (Ithaca: Cornell University Press, 1992), 199–201.
60 'Free Training in 30 Crafts for Workers', *Keyhan International*, vol. 16, no. 4819 (15 Mordad 1352/6 August 1973): 2.
61 'Annual Labor Report, 1963', 199.
62 Benedick, *Industrial Finance*, 49.
63 'Employment and Unemployment', 81; 'Annual Labor Report, 1960, 1961, 1963', 164, 173, 199.
64 'Karfarmayan Sahlengari Mikonand', *Keyhan*, no. 56475 (18 Ordibehesht 1341/8 May 1962): 10. The Ministry of Labour reported that its staff had made inspection visits to 1,158 workshops in 1961/2 (1340) and had found infractions in 237 cases that it subsequently corrected.
65 'Kurehha', 6.
66 'Akhar va Aqebat-e Ma', *Keyhan*, no. 5367 (7 Khordad 1340/28 May 1961): 6; 'Kargaran-e Khabbaz Dowlat Ra Tahdid beh Etesab Kerdand', same issue, 1, 13; 'Ekhtiyarat-e Vezarat-e Kar beh Sandikaha-ye Kargari Montaqel Mishavad', *Keyhan*, no. 6114 (16 Azar 1342/7 December 1963): 1, 11. New unions also were being formed during this period. See 'Sandika-ye Kargaran va Karkonan-e Mosaferbari Tashkil Shod', *Ettelaat*, no. 10934 (6 Aban 1341/28 October 1962): 5, 13.
67 'Annual Labor Report, 1963', 199.
68 'Employment and Unemployment', 81; 'Annual Labor Report, 1960', 165.
69 Benedick, *Industrial Finance*, 50.
70 'Annual Labor Report, 1963', 199.
71 Clock, 'Labor Affairs', 108, 111. One exceptional case was that of Jabbar Saleh-Nia, owner of the Casing Export Company. On family influence on lending and business policy, see Benedick, *Industrial Finance*, 29, 36, 39, 70, 219, 231, 233.
72 Clock, 'Labor Affairs', 108, 111.
73 'Annual Labor Report, 1965', in *Condition of the Working Class*, 211.

Bibliography

Archives

Echo of Iran Archives
Library, Museum and Document Center of the Iranian Parliament
National Library and Archives of Iran

Primary sources

International Bank for Reconstruction and Development (IBRD). *The Economic Development of Iran (Report No. 378a-IRN)*. Vol. 2. Washington, DC: 1974.

Periodicals

Echo Reports
Ettelā'āt
Iran Almanac and Book of Facts
Keyhān
Keyhan International
Post-e Tehrān

Secondary sources

'Annual Labor Report, 1960–1965'. In *The Condition of the Working Class in Iran: A Documentary History, 1911–1979*, edited by Cosroe Chaqueri, 161–214. Vol. 4. Tehran: Antidote Publications, 1991.

Benedick, Richard Elliot. *Industrial Finance in Iran*. Cambridge, MA: Harvard University Press, 1964.

Bharier, Julian. *Economic Development in Iran, 1900–1970*. London: Oxford University Press, 1971.

Bobek, Hans. 'Rentenkapitalismus und Entwicklung in Iran'. In *Interdisziplinäre Iran-Forschung: Beiträge aus Kulturgeographie, Ethnologie, Soziologie und Neuerer Geschichte*, edited by Günther Schweizer, 113–24. Wiesbaden: Harrassowitz, 1979.

Clock, Philip. 'Basic Survey of Labor Affairs in Iran, 1955'. In *The Condition of the Working Class in Iran: A Documentary History, 1911–1979*, edited by Cosroe Chaqueri, 86–100. Vol. 4. Tehran: Antidote Publications, 1991.

Clock, Philip. 'Labor Affairs in Iran, 1955–57'. In *The Condition of the Working Class in Iran: A Documentary History, 1911–1979*, edited by Cosroe Chaqueri, 108–18. Vol. 4. Tehran: Antidote Publications, 1991.

Ehlers, Eckart. 'Rent-capitalism and Unequal Development in the Middle East: the Case of Iran'. In *Work, Income and Inequality: Payment Systems in the Third World*, edited by Frances Stewart, 32–61. London: Palgrave Macmillan, 1983.

'Employment and Unemployment'. In *The Condition of the Working Class in Iran: A Documentary History, 1911–1979*, edited by Cosroe Chaqueri, 81–5. Vol. 4. Tehran: Antidote Publications, 1991.

Ferrier, R. W. *The History of the British Petroleum Company: Volume 1, The Developing Years, 1901–1932*. Cambridge: Cambridge University Press, 1982.

Floor, Willem. 'The Brickworkers of Khatunabad: A Striking Record (1953–1979)'. *International Review of Social History* 48, no. 3 (2003): 427–55.

Gable, Richard W. 'Culture and Administration in Iran'. *Middle East Journal* 13, no. 4 (Autumn 1959): 407–21.

Groupe d'Etudes Sociologiques. *Origine des Ouvriers de Tehran*. Institut d'Etudes et de Recherches Sociales, Université de Tehran, 1965.

Khosravi, Khosrow. *Jāme'ehshenāsi-ye Rustā-ye Irān*. Tehran: Payam, 1358.

Khosravi, Khosrow. *Jāme'eh-ye Dehqāni dar Irān*. Tehran: Payam, 1358.

'Labor Affairs, Iran, 1969–70'. In *The Condition of the Working Class in Iran: A Documentary History, 1911–1979*, edited by Cosroe Chaqueri, 219–28. Vol. 4. Tehran: Antidote Publications, 1991.
'Labor and Social Affairs, 1956'. In *The Condition of the Working Class in Iran: A Documentary History, 1911–1979*, edited by Cosroe Chaqueri, 101–4. Vol. 4. Tehran: Antidote Publications, 1991.
'Labor Scene in Isphahan and Yazd, 1958'. In *The Condition of the Working Class in Iran: A Documentary History, 1911–1979*, edited by Cosroe Chaqueri, 141–4. Vol. 4. Tehran: Antidote Publications, 1991.
Menashri, David. *Education and the Making of Modern Iran*. Ithaca: Cornell University Press, 1992.
'Trade Unionism in Iran', 1957. In *The Condition of the Working Class in Iran: A Documentary History, 1911–1979*, edited by Cosroe Chaqueri, 119–21. Vol. 4. Tehran: Antidote Publications, 1991.
Vieille, Paul. *La féodalité et l'Etat en Iran*. Paris: Editions Anthropos, 1975.
'Wages in Iran, 1955'. In *The Condition of the Working Class in Iran: A Documentary History, 1911–1979*, edited by Cosroe Chaqueri, 81. Vol. 4. Tehran: Antidote Publications, 1991.

11

Recollections of the Risbaf (Carding) Complex in Qom

Ali Gheissari

The Qom Carding and Weaving Corporation (hereafter 'Risbaf', a joint-stock company) was registered initially in Bahman 1314 (January–February 1936) with an investment of 3 million rials, and then in Azar 1316 (November–December 1937) 2 million more rials were added to its capital, and it was opened one year later, in Azar 1317 (November–December 1938).[1] The site of the factory was actually on land in the approximate area of 73,000 square metres in the south-west direction of the city of Qom, which was about 3 kilometres away from the city at the time of its construction.[2] At that time, the Carding and Weaving Corporation's board of directors included Haj Mirza Ali Gheissarieh, Abdol Hossein Nikpour, Mohammad Ali Nosratian, Haj Mohammad Hossein Yazdi, Ali Asghar Zarkesh, Ahmad Akhavan and Haj Abol Qasem Semsarzadeh.[3]

The spinning machinery of the factory was entirely imported from Germany, and in the beginning, with 250 workers and ten hours of work per day, it consumed about 300 tons of cotton annually, producing around 350 to 400 bundles of thread in various grades every twenty-four hours.[4] The powering of the machinery and the electricity needs of the factory were supplied by two generators, which were purchased from the Siemens Corporation. Also, from its initial founding, the spinning factory supplied a major part of Qom's electricity needs for many years.

This brief account, which contains as much of some general recollections from the late 1330s (1950s) to the mid-1340s (1960s) as possible, was the result of the author, accompanied by his family, having the occasional good fortune of travelling to Qom and staying in the Risbaf Complex. Haj Mirza Ali Gheissarieh (c. 1266–1326/1887–1947), the founder of Risbaf and grandfather of the present author, had passed away approximately six years before the author's birth.[5] The visits of the author to Qom during those years often took place in the company of his father, the late Morteza Gheissari (1290–1355/1911–1976).

Figure 11.1 Members of the Tehran Chamber of Commerce, 1935. Front row, left to right: Haj Mohammad Reza Qomi, Haj Kazem Vahabzadeh, Haj Mirza Ali Gheissarieh, Chairman Mirza Abdol Hossein Nikpour, Aqa Reza Bushehri, Hassan Aqa Chaichian, Karam Aqa Khosravani, Malek Mohammad Ramazani. Back row, right to left: (Mirza Gholam Hossein) Kashef, Haj Mirza Ali Asghar Chaichi, (Mirza Abdol Razzaq) Qazizadeh, Mirza Ali Khan Vakili, Aqa Reza Tehranchi, Ahmad Aqa Akhavan, Haj Mohammad Hossein Bolurforushan. *Salnameh-ye Pars* (1935), n.p. (inset).

On the founding of Risbaf

Concerning Risbaf's establishment, the author long ago heard a story from his paternal uncle, the late Ahmad Gheissari (1304–1390/1925–2011), which, even if it differs slightly in some details from documentation and other evidence, probably in general terms can be considered to be close to facts. As the story goes, during the early Pahlavi period when Haj Mirza Ali Gheissarieh and his partners decided to establish and run a carding and weaving factory, they approached Haj Mohammad Hossein Yazdi, who was one of the reputable merchants of Qom, to secure part of the budget that was needed to initiate this work. It is said that Yazdi was managing considerable funds from ulema (religious scholars) and 'was working' with them – that is, like a private bank, by investing this capital or giving out term loans to private individuals. According to the author's paternal uncle (Ahmad Gheissari, mentioned earlier), Haj Mohammad Hossein conveyed the merchants' request to Ayatollah Abdol Karim Haeri Yazdi (1238–1315/1859–1936), the founder of the Qom Seminary, whose considerable portion of funds he had in his possession and was managing. Apparently, Ayatollah Haeri (also known as Haj Sheikh) indicated that there was no objection and asked where the gentlemen wanted to set up the factory. Haj Mohammad Hossein replied that the gentlemen's opinion was, of course, to set it up in Isfahan. According to Ahmad Aqa, then Haj Sheikh apparently further inquired, 'Why Isfahan? Since Isfahan has many factories, why do the gentlemen not come and do this work in Qom, [in order to] raise it from this backward state?' He added, 'You should tell the gentlemen that we will consider allocating a good piece of land to them at a suitable price, and we will not take the Imam's Share [i.e. a portion of *khums*] and other sharia dues from them for a while.' He also mentioned that one of the other advantages was Qom's proximity to Tehran and probably cheaper labourers' wages than Isfahan. Finally, the merchants accepted these suggestions, or, rather, conditions, and began the work.

As it turned out, around the same period, Haj Sheikh further inquired that the gentlemen presumably would be needing electricity for the power required by the factory machines. The reply came that, 'Yes, for the electricity supply, it has been planned to install two generators, one of which will work continuously, and the other one will be in reserve, so that if one of them needs servicing, the work of producing and supplying electricity will not be interrupted.' Haj Sheikh then suggested that the gentlemen bring one or two additional generators and supply electricity to the city and 'turn on the lights of Qom'. This too was done. Thus, in addition to providing its own power, the Risbaf Factory supplied a major part of Qom's electricity for many years. The author remembers very well that at the centre of Qom and near the Holy Shrine, there was a place, or rather an office, which was called 'the Collection Branch' (Shobeh-ye Vosul), where electricity subscribers paid their bills.

In addition to the above account and by way of complementing it, it can further be pointed out that several years prior to the founding of Risbaf, Haj Mirza Ali Gheissarieh used to visit Qom frequently and was well acquainted with Haj Mohammad Hossein Yazdi, and it is also very likely that he emulated – as his *Marja*ʿ – Ayatollah Haeri on religious questions. Thus, as it is also mentioned in other sources, it is possible that he was personally present during those conversations.[6] Likewise, as he had also mentioned among family, inwardly, he believed in the necessity of creating jobs and improving the overall economic situation in Qom.[7] Therefore, regarding the establishment of Risbaf, it cannot be said with certainty that Isfahan was necessarily a priority for the partners at that time. Rather, the founding of Risbaf can be considered a project that was specifically defined for Qom from the very beginning. Furthermore, if the future factory's proximity to Tehran was the only issue of concern, the founding board had other options of a more or less similar (or perhaps even better) quality, in a location closer to the capital.[8] Thus, in view of these points, it can be concluded that at least for the first generation of the founders of Risbaf, building a factory and creating jobs in Qom was a strong motivation.[9]

Factory premises and buildings

The site of the Risbaf Factory was located on a large parcel of land near the city of Qom, to the south. At the beginning of the road that stretched from the city to the factory, there was a relatively high bridge that spanned the railway line. From the centre of the city, the asphalt only extended to some point near the bridge, and the rest was a gravel and dirt road (*chaussée*); each time, be it the factory truck or any car passing along that road, a cloud of dust would go up in the air behind it. Of course, in later years, that road was asphalted and gradually that bridge and all of its surroundings disappeared in new settings. When we were coming from Qom towards the factory, in the middle of the plain, the large campus with its pine trees looked like an oasis in the desert that would always capture our attention. Also, its walls, which enclosed the

Figure 11.2 Haj Mirza Ali Gheissarieh, Farvardin 1315 (March–April 1936). Private collection.

entire complex, as well as the buildings within, including the spinning halls and the engine room, and especially the two ventilation towers, which had beautiful identical structures, were all built with bricks. The design of the upper parts of these towers was inspired by traditional motifs of Iranian architecture. Both from afar and near, those two tall towers gave the atmosphere of the factory a special industrial look and were actually a recognizable sign and symbol of Risbaf. Most likely, and considering the other buildings within the compound, maybe a similar model or template was used in the design and construction of those two towers, because they fitted in well with the rest of the buildings and were completely in harmony with the overall design of the complex.[10]

In the days when we used to go to the factory, the reason for the existence of these two towers with all their awe and charm was always a bit vague for the present author, who did not have enough technical knowledge at that age – because there was no activity inside them, and no work was being done. In other words, the two towers were completely empty, and their inner chamber was large and silent, and even though the distance between them was not more than a few steps, the sound of the engine room could hardly be heard. Perhaps their high walls prevented any sound from entering. The interior of the walls was whitewashed with plaster or thin grout or a similar material. At the upper end of the towers, there were small windows that let the light in. Inside the towers and near the walls, if I am not mistaken, there were always several bales of yarn visible, as well as a large amount of cotton wool, and even raw cotton residues or something like that, which were also often in bales.[11]

Later, I found out that these towers were used for aeration and drying, and a kind of ventilation and purification of yarn fibres, and probably for ventilation of cotton waste, and from this point of view, I had in my mind that they were purification towers or ventilators. Whatever it was, they certainly must have had an important industrial

Figure 11.3 Risbaf Factory Complex in Qom, 1938. *Daftar-e Astaneh-ye Qom, Rahnama-ye Qom, ba 64 Gravur va Yek Naqsheh* (Tehran: Chapkhaneh-ye Majles, n.d.), Figure 59.

use and were interesting to look at from the outside, and they gave the entire factory complex a distinct identity.[12]

The buildings of the Risbaf Complex were a typical example of industrial architecture in the early Pahlavi era. It is worth noting that some of the main buildings of Risbaf in Qom, such as the spinning hall and the engine house, were to some extent the same as the Vatan Factory of Isfahan (which was established in 1304/1925), and probably both used similar designs. Considering that the German national Max Otto Schünemann was directly involved in the preparation of the plans for the construction of the Vatan Factory in Isfahan, it is possible that Haj Mirza Ali Gheissarieh and his partners entrusted the design and supervision of the construction of some or most of the Risbaf buildings in Qom to Schünemann.

Of course, the late Gheissarieh knew Schünemann very well, especially through acquaintances and close mutual relationships that they had with the late Mohammad Hossein Kazeruni (d. 1311/1932) and the late Fazlollah Dehesh (Ata al-Molk) (d. 1338/1959), the founders of Isfahan's Vatan Factory.[13] During the same period, Schünemann had also established a familial relationship with Ata al-Molk Dehesh.

One of the main parts of the factory was its large spinning hall, which had a noticeable industrial feel and a large number of workers worked there at the same time. The main hall had a large area under its roof, where several rows of spinning machines were installed in an orderly manner, and from each of them, many strands of yarn were simultaneously issued and wrapped around the spindles that were installed on the middle part of the machine. The writer does not clearly remember their mechanism now, but their industrial order and continuous work is well remembered. The industrial pace of the work inside the halls was such that no one could stand idly and just watch the machines and stare at the workers.

Transportation service for the workers

The author remembers that a relatively large truck was allocated for the workers to go back and forth between the factory and the city, whose main body and passenger wagon were red and slightly worn on the outside. I had never been inside that truck, but I remember very well that young and middle-aged workers used to get in the big passenger cabin behind it and go to the city. This truck was actually the service vehicle for the workers, which in different shifts brought them from the city to the factory and took them from the factory back to the city. When the truck entered the factory premises, the workers would jump out of this big back cabin. The large size of that truck with its red metal body and its big front wheels is clearly remembered by the author, as well as its wear and tear, which was probably the result of non-stop commuting on the dirt road between the factory and the city several times night and day to pick up and drop off the workers. The face remembered in connection with this truck was that of one of the foremen, or rather the supervisor of the workers boarding the truck, who would give orders when the younger workers got on and off. His hair, which had thinned out, was dyed with henna, and during those years that I remember he always wore a well-worn coat, which was also henna-coloured.

Figure 11.4 Front from right to left: Prime Minister Ali Amini, while visiting Qom Risbaf Factory, and Morteza Gheissari, member of the board of directors, 1 Dey 1340 (22 December 1961).

He always looked like an ill-tempered creature to me, and I think he also had a stick or a disciplinary cane with which he would beat the young workers if they were late or did something that was wrong in his opinion. Not that I ever liked him, for sure, I even resented him.

Water

A point that has always remained in my mind from Qom during those years is the special taste of Qom's (drinking) water, which was noticeably salty, so much so that you could not drink it at all! Maybe that is why we mostly drank buttermilk (*dugh*) or tea there. The author does not remember exactly how far the piped water network of Qom was expanded in the mid-1330s (1950s), and whether it included Risbaf or not, but the taste of the water that was kept either in the kitchen or in the refrigerator was completely salty. Outside the factory area, but from Qom to the surrounding area, it was completely a desert, and the salinity of Qom's water was probably caused by its climatic conditions.

Trees

Another point that the writer remembers is the general campus of the factory and its streets within. The main area and the factory campus were nicely wooded and the author remembers well the poplar (*Tabrizi*) and pine trees of the campus that seemed old (although in fact they were the same age as the factory itself). The factory compound, that is, the area adjacent to the halls, had been planted with trees and paved with streets, and two or three circular or oval ponds were located by design among those relatively narrow and paved walkways. The trees were planted on both sides of these paved passages and also in the middle areas, known as an allotment (*kart*), in this sense, and in contrast to the hot and dry climate of Qom, most of the factory's campus was pleasantly shaded with trees. Therefore, it was not unlikely that one of the tasks of Arbab Hassan (more on him later in the chapter) was watering and taking care of the trees in the area. Of course, the general atmosphere of the area was often dry, but it was definitely irrigated at certain times, which made the trees look a lush green and always lively. I am not sure where the exact source of water for the factory and its trees and summer crops' cultivation areas, garden and so on was supplied from.[14] Maybe it had an underground aqueduct (*qanāt*), and I also do not know if the factory itself used water for industrial purposes or not. Of course, as will be mentioned later, in the 'water reservoir' section, there is a strong possibility that drinking water, at least for the workers, was supplied through the water reservoir. Another thing is that in the main reception quarters and the management hall of the factory, there was indoor plumbing and tap water in the kitchen and bathrooms, but I am not sure if it was supplied from the same place or in any other way. Regarding the general campus, it should be said that although it was green and pleasant, due to the special climate of Qom, I remember that it was always hot and dry.

Habib Aqa, the head steward of the guest house

Whenever we visited the factory, a very pleasant and efficient person named Habibollah was in charge of all receptions at the management residence. He resided in the factory but also had another residence in Qom.[15] He was always smiling and had good manners, and his outfits were impeccably clean, and when he was busy tending the guest house, he always used to wear a pair of high-quality white espadrilles (*giveh*) that were made in Qom, which never rested their heels (such slippers were among the special souvenirs of Qom, which the author also probably emulated and was accustomed to wearing indoors during those years). As a youngster, I used to spend time with some of his children, who were almost the same age. Habibollah's living quarters were also near the main residence and the reception area and were adjacent to the west side of the factory campus. Next to this area was a corridor, the northern end of which contained a few rooms, which I think served as the warehouse for the necessities of this service area, and it led to the yard and a pond on the northern side, above the factory. This whole section had no labour or industrial activity at all, and its southern end was a short distance from a small foyer and a corridor that led to the large reception room of the main guest house. The kitchen and the office pantry (*ābdārkhāneh*, where they used to prepare tea and other beverages) of the management and reception area of Risbaf were also in this section. This entire section was located on the west side of the factory campus and above the main entrance area and was adjacent to the road from Qom to Kashan.

Cycling in the factory area

Another detail that is remembered from our periodic visits to the Qom factory was the use of bicycles, which the author was busy with almost the entire time that we stayed there, and in this sense, Qom was a cycling paradise for him as a youngster, perhaps because during the same period, such freedom of action was very limited for him in Tehran – or was even completely non-existent. Most probably, the author used to pick and use the bicycles belonging to Habib Aqa or his children, and of course, cycling only within the same factory area, which was large enough, as well as being varied and interesting. These bicycles were usually carefully wrapped with coloured tape, and sometimes also had a saddlebag (*khorjin*) on the back wheel, and the writer, either alone or mostly along with one or two fellow riders of the same age from Habib Aqa's children, would constantly ride these bicycles in the streets between the trees in the area and visit every place.

Background music

Another point that is well remembered by the writer was the uninterrupted sound of the electric generators of the factory's 'engine room' (*motorkhāneh*) that worked twenty-four hours a day, which provided enough electricity for both the factory and also for the city of Qom. The engine room had its own separate building, which was built with the same architectural style and similar masonry materials, including brick and tiling in parts of the entrance door and above some of its windows. This building was almost square in shape with a very tall and high ceiling – both from the outside and especially from the inside, the building was quite massive and conveyed the same feeling to the viewer. In fact, this engine room had a kind of industrial beauty of its own and was an environment completely different from that of the outside, and was even different from the main halls of the factory. In the large area inside, I think there were four enormous generators – as far as I know, if I am not mistaken, two of which were working continuously and producing electricity, one of them for the power plant and the other for the city of Qom. Of course, inside the engine room, the sound of the spinning turbines and engine cylinders was quite loud, and outside that building and around the entire factory campus, its echo could always be heard. However, it was not annoying; rather, it had a kind of industrial rhythm and melody. Especially at night, when the campus and the surrounding environment were quieter, the sound of the engine room was like a kind of background music flowing through the atmosphere of that entirely silent environment, which was, of course, very interesting.

Technical management residence

On the west side of the factory and facing south, on the main part of the campus, there was a long building with rooms of different sizes, each of which had its own function. Close to the factory's main entrance gate to the south, there were some rooms for office work, and right next to it, there was a part that was probably reserved for the use and residence of the technical management. During those years, these few rooms were usually closed or seemed to be closed, and the author does not remember ever entering them.

Turnery (machine shop)

On the west side of the factory's main campus overlooking the Qom–Kashan Road, and on the east side overlooking the garden area, next to the rooms and workshops that were built in a row side by side, there were one or two relatively large rooms with high ceilings. These rooms were the workshops for turning, welding and repairing parts of the factory machines, containing about four or five lathes and other tools and equipment. There were always several technicians working there, and it was quite evident that their work was technical and required precision and skill. Of course, having such a workshop was necessary for the factory, because the technical and mechanical operations of the factory machines needed quick and accurate repairs, and it is very likely that Qom did not have such a technical capacity at that time. It was clear that this part was planned and designed along with its details in the original plan of the factory.

Factory store

The factory had a shop, which was situated on the campus overlooking the same wall on its western side, and it was probably next door (or close to) the turning workshop. The workers used to buy goods from this shop, which mostly consisted of lump sugar (*qand*) and tea, and small white sweets (probably *shekar panir*) that mostly the young workers bought and ate. These sweets were most likely made with powdered sugar. Also, frequently as a habit, the young workers bought and ate regular sugar lumps. The author also obtained and chewed the same sugar lumps several times out of curiosity. I think that the shop also had other sweets, such as hard candies (*ābnabāt-qeychi*). The shopkeeper used to sit on a platform, which was in fact a large window, functioning as the shop counter, and the workers below would buy goods from him. I do not remember now whether these transactions were in cash or with credit, which, at any rate, I would not have even noticed then.

Water reservoir

A short distance from the workshop and this store, and of course on the same west side of the factory's inner campus, and a few steps to the south, there was a water reservoir or cistern (*ābanbār*), where we had to go underground, after descending many steps, in order to collect water. It was always dark and damp, and this atmosphere added to its sense of depth; yet, it also had its own peculiar charm. The writer, who went there several times on his own or along with his playmates, always found it a bit strange and at the same time felt that the building had a historical importance and value. It was a brick building, and if I am not mistaken, its entrance had some tilework, and it completely matched the architectural style of the older buildings on the campus. I do not know which architects designed the reservoir's entrance; later, I attributed it to Nikolai Markov because it was in the same style as his other works, although probably this design could have been the work of the same architect or architects who had designed the rest of the buildings, or even more likely, it was the work of Iranian and local architects and experts in the construction of water reservoirs. I do not even think that I had ever taken water out of there myself, but the many downward steps and the depth at the end of the reservoir, and its darkness and dampness, have remained vivid in my memory. In later years, when the factory had closed down, I heard and then saw that all the buildings on the western side of the factory campus, including this old reservoir, had been demolished, in order to widen the road from Qom to Kashan. I was very saddened because it was an interesting and important building in every way. Also, I am not sure if that reservoir had another entrance with a separate stairway on the other side, outside the factory campus, but the main stairway inside the campus was quite interesting and important in itself. There is no trace of these buildings any longer.[16]

Industrial space

Within the entire campus of the factory, including its main and secondary buildings, as far as the author remembers, there was no sign of a mosque, prayer hall or any other place that had a religious connotation. Even though Qom's traditional religious status and atmosphere were quite evident in the city centre, there was no sign of religious expression or any association with it in the working, administrative and reception environment of the factory; yet there was no contrast either.

Arbab Hassan

On the southern grounds of the whole complex of factory lands, there was a relatively large area, most of which was a garden, where vegetables and sometimes fruits were grown. In those years that the author remembers, the manager of that area was a person named Arbab Hassan, who was of an average and somewhat tall stature, and his face was always open and smiling. Arbab Hassan did limited agricultural and mostly horticultural and summer crop work in that area of the factory campus and garden, which was completely separate from the industrial buildings and had a noticeably visible distance from them. In the same area, there was a separate building (like a villa) with white interior walls, and as far as the author remembers, it was abandoned in those years, but evidently it had once been very beautiful and in good repair. I remember that sometimes with my fellow playmates in the rooms on the lower floor there (maybe it was a two-story building or at least part of it was on two floors, although I do not remember exactly), we used to play between the rooms for a while; and on their white walls, people had written and inscribed graffiti. Arbab Hassan himself sometimes came to the management section, and I think he gave reports and did his accounts and calculations in the same main hall or on the outside porch. Maybe the land and the grounds of that area were leased out to him during the time of my late father; I am not sure, but I remember very well that the grounds and garden of that area were very green and must have had a well or an aqueduct (*qanāt*) because that area was full of fruit trees (such as pomegranate) and alfalfa, which consumed plenty of water. In the same area, there was a large pond – which looked like a (rectangular) swimming pool. I think they used it to store water; the author does not remember if that pond was ever full; rather, it often had some water residue or was completely dry, and there were plants and grass growing inside of it. In any case, the overall mood and atmosphere of that part of the factory campus was completely different from the industrial areas, and if I am not mistaken, its south side also had a way out, because the comings and goings of that part did not pass through other factory areas or the main entrance; further to this, I think its exit opened near an area that I later learnt was called 'Salariyeh'.

Mr Habibollah Qaderi

He was a secretary (*munshi*), or more precisely, an accountant and bookkeeper, and a resident of Tehran. I remember him well. His office or working space was allocated in a room in the semi-basement of our city house (in Tehran), and therefore, it was called 'the Qaderi basement'. This 'basement' was adjacent to the main semi-basement section of the house (and both were only a few steps down the general grounds of the yard). Mr Qaderi would normally sit behind two large desks and check various Risbaf accounting books (e.g. correspondence, daybook, balance sheet and general ledger), some of which were quite large in size, and he would copy or extract some items from one and write them into another. In his office, he also had a large abacus with which he regularly added and subtracted figures, and he moved the beads of the abacus with his fingers (especially the index finger and the middle finger of the right hand) back and forth with speed and skill. I remember, with each act of calculation, the abacus beads that collided together would make a sound, and in fact, the background music in the Qaderi basement was the rhythmic sound of the abacus. Later, he also tended to other accounting and bookkeeping tasks of my late father. Mr Qaderi was a polite, dignified and kind person. He was tall, with thick sandy hair, and a round open face, and he always wore a dark suit and a white shirt with a turned-down starched collar but without a necktie. The sandy hair on his head was always combed backwards, like

Figure 11.5 Eid al-Fitr prayer, near the Risbaf Factory in Qom, 4 September 1978. Source: Public Domain 4.

my late father's. Perhaps his initial association with our family dated back to the time of the late Haj Mirza Ali. If I am not mistaken, he may have learned bookkeeping and accounting at a young age after Haj Mirza Ali had brought his father into his establishment. Whenever he came to our city house, he would exchange his usual greetings and converse for a little while in the front yard near the tiled pond and then go straight to his basement, where he tended the accounts and ledgers in his own way.

Concluding note

The subjects that were presented briefly earlier stayed mostly in the past tense (indeed in the perfect participle) and did not include the later periods. If the direct unmediated style of the text were to be altered to reflect the change in perspective and the age of the narrator, then its whole structure should also have been changed and expanded, which in itself would have required a separate occasion and more space. Research in this regard would also require various additional considerations, including delving into variables of the political, and not-so-political, economy, such as the gradual aging of the machinery, the challenge of competing with imports during the 1960s and the multifaceted entanglements with the bureaucracy in the same decade, as well as societal factors, such as the generational turn at the level of management and shareholders, and its often inevitable consequences for the continuity of the operational process, the closure of the factory and then the revolution, followed by all sorts of plans that the revolutionaries had, none of which were realized due to the conditions at that time, and then the (Iran-Iraq) War, followed by the (temporary) resettlement of the war-stricken and other events that could not even be listed in this brief account. Although there are information and scattered references in some reference books and periodicals on the Qom Risbaf Factory and Complex, there is room for a monograph and more independent research about it. Such research will certainly be helpful for a better understanding of the social and economic history of Qom during the past century.

Notes

1 For the original version, see Ali Gheissari, 'Yadi az Majmueh-ye Risbaf-e Qom', in *Sad-Salegi-ye Howzeh-ye Qom*, ed. Rasul Jafarian (Qom: Nashr-e Movarrekh, 1400/2021), 575–622. I am grateful to Rasul Jafarian for his initial invitation and to Mary Yoshinari for translating and editing the chapter, and to Serhan Afacan for its inclusion in the present volume. I would also like to thank Majid Dadashnejad for collecting newspaper information about the Risbaf factory and Mehdi Haj Baqerian for transcribing the report on its opening. For this report, see Appendix 1, and for excerpts from *Ostovar*, see Appendix 2. Concerning *Ostovar*, see Alireza Abazari, '*Ostovar*: Avvalin Gam dar Arseh-ye Ruznamehnegari-ye Qom', *Payam-e Baharestan* (Series 2) 1, no. 4 (Summer 1388/2009): 35–56.

2 See Abdol Hossein Nikpour's report on the opening ceremony of the factory, which took place on 3 Azar 1317 (24 November 1938), in 'Ayin-e Goshayesh-e Karkhaneh-e Risandegi-ye Qom', *Ettelaat*, no. 3671, 4 Azar 1317 (25 November 1938): n.p. (Appendix 1).

This distance was erroneously noted to be 'one kilometre' around the beginning of Risbaf's construction; see 'Karkhaneh-ye Risman-e Risi dar Qom: Sarmayeh-e Sir Takamol-e Bashar Ehtiyaj Ast', *Ostovar*, 22 Esfand 1314 (13 March 1936): 1. Conversely, it was referred to as 'two and a half kilometres' at the time of the factory's inauguration; see: 'Tarikh-e Ejtemaei-ye Qom', *Nashriyyeh-ye Interneti-ye Asr-e Eslam*, accessed 13 Mehr 1399 (4 October 2022), http://www.asrislam.com/fa/news/20026/تاریخ-اجتماعی-قم; with reference to Ali Banaei, ed., *Shenakhtnameh-ye Qom*, vol. 5, part 2 (Qom: Nur-e Mataf, 1390/2011), 56. Concerning the area of the factory premises, 'seventy thousand *zar* [est. 72,800 sq. m.]' was mentioned in 'Karkhaneh-ye Risman-e Risi dar Qom', *Ostovar*, 22 Esfand 1314 (13 March 1936): 1, whereas the report in *Ettelaat* referred to its area as '67,950 square metres'. Elsewhere, this area was said to be 'about seven hectares' (equivalent to 70,000 sq. m.); see: Daftar-e Astaneh-ye Qom, *Rahnama-ye Qom, ba 64 Gravur va Yek Naqsheh, Yadegar-e Goshayesh-e Sakhteman-e Dabirestan-e Hekmat; az Entesharat-e Daftar-e Astaneh-ye Qom (18 Mehr 1317 Motabeq ba 15 Shaban al-Maazm 1357 Qamari [10 October 1938])* (Tehran: Chapkhaneh-ye Majles, n.d.), 138, and another publication mentions 'eight hectares' (i.e. 80,000 sq. m.); see: Mehdi Abbasi, *Tarikhche-ye Kharakdari, Garidari va Doroshkeh Savari dar Qom, beh Enzemam-e Asnad-e Tarikhi* (Qom: Afarineh, 1398/2019), 72 n. 1. The latter publication also contains useful information about the origins of Risbaf's establishment, including the support of Ayatollah Abdol Karim Haeri Yazdi, the founder of the Qom Seminary, and the effective cooperation of Haj Mohammad Hossein Yazdi; see ibid., 72–3 n. 1.

3 'Karkhaneh-ye Risman-e Risi dar Qom', *Ostovar*, 22 Esfand 1314 (13 March 1936): 1; Hossein Mahboubi Ardakani, *Tarikh-e Moassesat-e Tamaddoni-ye Jadid dar Iran*, vol. 3 (Tehran: Moasseseh-ye Entesharat va Chap-e Daneshgah-ye Tehran, 1368/1989), 128–9. In the meantime, Haj Mirza Ali Gheissarieh, Mirza Abdol Hossein Nikpour and Ahmad Akhavan had a history of working together in the Tehran Chamber of Commerce (see Figure 11.1). For more on the Risbaf factory's opening, see: 'Ayin-e Goshayesh-e Karkhaneh-ye Risandegi-ye Qom', *Ettelaat*, n.p. For more on the Tehran Chamber of Commerce, see: Ali Tatari, *Otaq-e Tejarat-e Tehran: Negahi Gozara beh Yeksad o Si o Seh Sal Tarikhcheh-ye Otaq-e Bazargani, Sanaye, Maaden va Keshavarzi-ye Tehran* (Tehran: Edareh-ye Chap va Nashr-e Otaq-e Bazargani, Sanaye, Maaden va Keshavarzi-ye Tehran, 1395/2016).

4 In the terminology of spinning, 'Each bundle of thread has twenty skeins [spun thread] weighing between four and four and a half kilos'. See Fazlollah Heshmati Razavi, 'Boqcheh [Boghcheh]', in *Daneshnameh-ye Jahan-e Eslam*, vol. 3 (Tehran: Encyclopaedia Islamica Foundation, 1393/2014), https://rch.ac.ir/article/Details/6576.

5 He is buried at Imamzadeh Hamzah, within the Abd al-Azim sanctuary, south of Tehran, and the following poem by Gholam Reza Rashid-Yasemi (1275–1330/1896–1951) is engraved on the original gravestone:

Put your trust in the Living One who does not die.
Quran, 25:58
We mourn the loss of Gheissari, a free soul,
Righteous in words and deeds, a seeker after truth.
To serve the public was his lodestar in all he did,
Guided by divine command in every transaction.
Threescore years he lived, and spent it all in righteousness,
The balance of his scale never faltered from fairness.
Forever striving for the public good, but spurning rewards,
Offering his services to the land, without much ado.

He always sought the benefit of his fellow human beings with no expectations,
He offered his services to the land with no pretensions.
In the Solar year three hundred and twenty-six after a thousand,
On the first of Shahrivar he left this house of sorrow.
Thus lamented Rashid Yasemi on this mournful day,
Gheissari has left this world with his worthy fame.
1366 AH (1947)

6 See: Abbasi, *Tarikhcheh*, 72 n. 1.

7 This information was obtained from the author's conversation with the late Forough al-Zaman Gheissari (Samsarzadeh) (1294–1390/1915–2011), daughter of Haj Mirza Ali Gheissarieh, on 3 Mordad 1379 (24 July 2000), Tehran.

8 For example, the Risbaf Factory could have been built in Dowlatabad Gheissarieh in Rey (south of Tehran) or in Aliabad Gheissarieh in Qarchak, Varamin County (also south of Tehran), since Haj Mirza Ali had ownership of both estates.

9 If the above assumption about emulation is correct, it is possible that after the passing of Mr Haeri (in 1315/1936), Haj Mirza Ali Gheissarieh continued to follow him (especially in matters that had a financial commitment) or, less likely, he emulated Haj Mirza Yahya, Emam Jomeh Khoei (1239–1324/1860–1945); although he conducted some of his other business (such as arranging his will) in Tehran in the notary office of Seyyed Mohammad Behbahani (1253–1342/1874–1963). Here, it may be useful to mention that the marriage of his eldest son, Morteza Gheissari, was officiated by both of these gentlemen in Khordad 1321 (June 1942) (Mr Khoei was representing the requesting party [*taraf-e eijab*], and Mr Behbahani was representing the accepting party [*taraf-e qabul*]). It is also worth noting that prior to this period, Haj Mirza Ali Gheissarieh and Seyyed Mohammad Behbahani were both members of the First Constituent Assembly (Majles-e Moassesan) in Azar 1304/December 1925; see: Mozaffar Shahidi, 'Fehrest-e Asami-ye Nemayandegan-e Majles-e Moassesan-e Avval (Azar 1304)', subject code: 323, 'Series 92, Haji Mirza Ali Gheissarieh; Constituency: Savojbolāgh', 'Series 76, Haji Sheikh Mohammad Javad Behbahani, Constituency: Bani Torof', website of the Institute for Iranian Contemporary Historical Studies (IICHS), last modified 19 Shahrivar 1393 (10 September 2014), https://www.iichs.ir/fa/news/323/فهرست-اسامی-نمایندگان-مجلس-مؤسسان-اول-آذر-1304. See also: Fatemeh Masoudi, *Ashnayi ba Tarikh-e Majales-e Qanungozari dar Iran: Avvalin Majles-e Moassesan (15 Azar 1304–22 Azar 1304)* (Tehran: Majles Research Center, 1385/2006). Seyyed Mohammad Behbahani was the son of Seyyed Abdollah Behbahani (c. 1256–1328/c. 1877–1949), one of the leaders of Iran's Constitutional Movement. For more about Emam Jomeh Khoei, see: Hassan Morsalvand, *Zendeginameh-ye Rejal va Mashahir-e Iran (1299–1320 SH)*, vol. 1 (Tehran: Entesharat-e Elham, 1376/1997), 256, and Abbas Aghai Jirahandeh, 'Khoei, Mirza Yahya', in *Daneshnameh-ye Jahan-e Eslam*, vol. 16 (Tehran: Encyclopaedia Islamica Foundation, 1393/2014), https://rch.ac.ir/article/Details/8921; and for more about Seyyed Mohammad Behbahani, see: Mohammad Kazem Asayesh-Talab Tusi, 'Behbahani, Seyyed Mohammad', in *Daneshnameh Jahan-e Eslam*, vol. 4 (Tehran: Encyclopaedia Islamica Foundation, 1393/2014), https://rch.ac.ir/article/Details?id=12,105&&searchText. In addition, regarding the issue of *marjaiyyat* (source of emulation), it can be noted that after the period of Haeri, and with the exception of Seyyed Mohammad Hadi Milani, who was based in Mashhad, the source of emulation (*marja-e taqlid*) was rarely outside of Qom, even in Isfahan or Tehran. Of course, local authorities existed, but it was unlikely that those ulema who had a political disposition, such as Mirza Yahya Emam Jomeh Khoei or Seyyed Mohammad Behbahani, would avail themselves of *marjaiyyat*. I am grateful to Rasul Jafarian for making this point.

10 It is very likely that Max Otto Schünemann (1882–1961) prepared the general plan and, actually, the construction model of Qom's Risbaf Complex, as he had done for Isfahan's Vatan Factory. There is also a small possibility that Nikolai Markov (1883–1957) was invited (e.g. regarding the plans for the electrical engine room building). Moreover, during the same period, the late Gheissarieh assigned the construction of the newer part of his residential house in Tehran, which was connected to its older Qajar section, to Markov, who completed and delivered that project in 1313 (1934). Therefore, perhaps the design of some parts of the Qom complex was entrusted to Markov, but since Schünemann had already provided the plans for the main parts of the spinning sections with a specific industrial pattern, it is unlikely that the engine room's design and construction would have been assigned to another architect. However, in this regard, it can be noted that during the same period, Markov, in addition to a number of prominent administrative and educational buildings, such as the Central Post Office building (1313/1934) and the American College of Tehran (1314/1935) (later known as Alborz High School), handled the design and completion of industrial complexes, such as the Karaj Sugar Refinery (1311/1932) and Varamin Sugar Refinery (1313/1934). For more about Markov and his influence on Iranian interwar architecture, see: Victor Daniel, Bijan Shafei and Sohrab Soroushiani, *Nikolai Markov Architecture* (Tehran: Entesharat-e Did, 1382/2004); see also: Lana Ravandi-Fadai, 'Reconstructions of a Native in Exile: Cossack Brigade Fighter and Architect of Tehran – Nikolai L'vovich Markov (1882–1957)', in *Russians in Iran: Diplomacy and Power in the Qajar Era and Beyond*, eds. Rudy Matthee and Elena Andreeva (London: I.B. Tauris, 2018), 217–39; note in particular, 224–6. For the Persian translation, see: Lana Ravandi-Fadai, 'Baztarif-e Yek Bumi dar Ghorbat: Afsar-e Qazzaq va Memar-e Tehran, Nikolai Lavovich Markof', trans. Fariba Amini and Mehdi Mousavi, *Bukhara* 25, no. 140 (Azar–Day 1399/November–December 2020): 560–89.

11 Here, 'bale' also means a compressed and packed load (be it yarn, cotton or waste); 'cotton wool' also means raw or pure and unprocessed cotton.

12 For more detailed explanations, see Appendix 1.

13 For studies on the beginnings of industrial architecture in Iran and its examples in Isfahan, as well as Schünemann's role, see, for example: Nasrin Faqih, *Aghaz-e Memari-ye Sanati-ye Iran* (Tehran: Muzeh-ye Honarha-ye Moaser-e Tehran, 1357/1978); Morteza Mirzahosseini, Hossein Soltanzadeh and Fariba Alborzi, 'Naqsh-e Mohandesan-e Almani dar Memari-ye Moaser-e Iran (ba Takid bar Dowreh-ye Pahlavi-ye Avval beyn-e Salha-ye 1304 ta 1320)', *Bagh-e Nazar* 16, no. 75 (1398/2019): 53–70; Kamran Afshar Naderi, 'Memari-ye Sanati-ye Iran beyn-e Do Jang-e Jahani', *Majalleh-ye Memar* 25 (1383/2004): 133–44; Mohammad Reza Nilforoushan, 'Memari-ye Sanati-ye Iran dar Dowreh-ye Pahlavi-ye Avval, Motaleeh-ye Mowredi: Naqsh-e Shuneman dar Sanati Shodan-e Esfahan', Haftomin Konferans-e Beynolmelali-ye Towseeh-ye Paidar va Omran-e Shahri, Isfahan, Iran, 1396 (2017), https://civilica.com/doc/701590/; Leila Pahlavanzadeh, 'Maks Shuneman Memar-e Karkhanehha-ye Esfahan', *Nashriyyeh-ye Interneti-ye Memarnet*, accessed 3 September 2014, http://memarnet.com/en/node/2470; idem, *Miras-e Memari-ye Sanati-ye Iran, Bakhsh-e Nakhost: Ostan-e Esfahan* (Isfahan: Entesharat-e Daneshgah-ye Azad-e Eslami, Vahed-e Khorasgan, 1392/2013); idem, 'Sanat va Memari-ye Sanati dar Esfahan', *Faslnameh-ye Abadi* 16, no. 52 (1385/2006): 74–9; and also: Habib Borjian, 'Kazeruni Family', in *Encyclopaedia Iranica Online*, accessed 28 May 2023 (print version: vol. 16, fascicle 2, 217–21), https://www.iranicaonline.org/articles/kazeruni-family. For one of the first reports written about the newly

established factories in Isfahan, see: Hossein Noursadeghi, *Esfahan, Moshtamel bar Chahar Fasl: Tarikh, Joghrafiya, Abniyeh va Asar, Shoara va Bozorgan, ba 41 Gravur* (Tehran: Sherkat-e Matbuat, 1316/1937). It is worth noting that Noursadeghi completed his dissertation under the supervision of Gholam Reza Rashid-Yasemi and the compilation of this work was also probably encouraged by him, see: Abdoulmehdi Rajaei, *Yeksad-o-Yek Nokteh dar Gardeshgari-ye Esfahan* (Isfahan: Sazman-e Refahi va Tafrihi-ye Shahrdari-ye Esfahan, 1400), 244.

14 For information in this regard, see Appendix 1 and Appendix 2.

15 The title of his traditional house in Qom belonged to the late Gheissarieh and was outside the company's property.

16 For information in this regard, see Appendix 1 and Appendix 2.

Bibliography

Periodicals

Ettelāʿāt
Ostovār
Sālnāmeh-ye Pārs

Secondary sources

Abazari, Alireza. '*Ostovār*; Avvalin Gām dar ʿArseh-ye Ruznāmehnegāri-ye Qom'. *Payām-e Bahārestān* 2, year 1, no. 4 (Summer 1388/2009): 35–56.

Abbasi, Mehdi. *Tārikhcheh-ye Kharakdāri, Gāridāri va Doroshkeh Savāri dar Qom, beh Enzemām-e Asnād-e Tārikhi*. Qom: Afarineh, 1398 (2019).

Afshar Naderi, Kamran. 'Meʿmāri-ye Sanʿati-ye Irān beyn-e Do Jang-e Jahāni'. *Majalleh-ye Meʿmār* 25 (1383/2004): 133–44.

Aqaei Jirhandeh, Abbas. 'Khoʾi, Mirza Yahyā'. Vol. 16 of *Dāneshnāmeh-ye Jahān-e Eslām*. Tehran: Encyclopaedia Islamica Foundation, 1393 (2014). https://rch.ac.ir/article/Details/8921.

Asayesh-Talab Toosi, Mohammad Kazem. 'Behbahāni, Seyyed Mohammad'. Vol. 4 of *Dāneshnāmeh-ye Jahān-e Eslām*. Tehran: Encyclopaedia Islamica Foundation, 1393 (2014). https://rch.ac.ir/article/Details?id=12105&&searchText.

Banaei, Ali, ed. *Shenākhtnāmeh-ye Qom*. Vol. 5, Part 2. Qom: Nur-e Mataf, 1390 (2011).

Borjian, Habib. 'Kāzeruni Family'. In *Encyclopaedia Iranica Online*. Accessed 28 May 2023 (print version: vol. 16, fascicle 2, 217–21). https://www.iranicaonline.org/articles/kazeruni-family.

Daftar-e Astaneh-ye Qom. *Rāhnamā-ye Qom, bā 64 Grâvur va Yek Naqsheh, Yâdegār-e Goshāyesh-e Sākhtemān-e Dabirestān-e Hekmat; az Enteshârāt-e Daftar-e Āstāneh-ye Qom (18 Mehr 1317 Motābeq bā 15 Shaʿbān al-Maʿazm 1357 Qamari [10 October 1938])*. Tehran: Chapkhaneh-ye Majles, n.d.

Daniel, Victor, Bijan Shafei and Sohrab Soroushiani. *Nikolai Markov Architecture*. Tehran: Entesharat-e Did, 1382 (2004).

Faqih, Nasrin. *Āghāz-e Meʿmāri-ye Sanʿati-ye Irān*. Tehran: Muzeh-ye Honarha-ye Moaser-e Tehran, 1357 (1978).

Gheissari, Ali. 'Yādi az Majmuʿeh-ye Risbāf-e Qom'. In *Sad-Salegi-ye Howzeh-ye Qom*, edited by Rasul Jafarian, 575–622. Qom: Nashr-e Movarrekh, 1400 (2021).

Heshmati Razavi, Fazlollah. 'Boqcheh [Boghcheh]'. Vol. 3 of *Dāneshnāmeh-ye Jahān-e Eslām*. Tehran: Encyclopaedia Islamica Foundation, 1393 (2014). https://rch.ac.ir/article/Details/6576.

Mahboubi Ardakani, Hossein. *Tārikh-e Moʿassesāt-e Tamaddoni-ye Jadid dar Irān*. Vol. 3. Tehran: Moasseseh-ye Entesharat va Chap-e Daneshgah-ye Tehran, 1368 (1989).

Masoudi, Fatemeh. *Āshnāyi bā Tārikh-e Majāles-e Qānungozāri dar Irān: Avvalin Majles-e Moʿassesān (15 Āzar 1304–22 Āzar 1304)*. Tehran: Majles Research Center, 1385 (2006).

Mirzahosseini, Morteza, Hossein Soltanzadeh and Fariba Alborzi. 'Naqsh-e Mohandesān-e Ālmāni dar Meʿmāri-ye Moʿāser-e Irān (ba Taʿkid bar Dowreh-ye Pahlavi-ye Avval beyn-e Sāl-hā-ye 1304 tā 1320)'. *Bāgh-e Nazar* 16, no. 75 (1398/2019): 53–70.

Mohseni, Seyyed Mohsen. 'Hāj Mirzā ʿAli Gheissarieh va Karkhāneh-ye Risbāf-e Qom'. Report by Mehyar Mousavi. Telegram channel of Qom Research Foundation, 9 Azar 1398 (November 30, 2019).

Morsalvand, Hassan. *Zendeginrāmeh-ye Rejāl va Mashāhir-e Irān (1299–1320 SH)*. Vol. 1. Tehran: Entesharat-e Elham, 1376 (1997).

Nilforoushan, Mohammad Reza. 'Meʿmāri-ye Sanʿati-ye Irān dar Dowreh-ye Pahlavi-ye Avval, Motāleʿeh-ye Mowredi: Naqsh-e Shunemān dar Sanʿati Shodan-e Esfahān'. Haftomin Konferāns-e Beynolmelali-ye Towseʿeh-ye Pāidār va Omrān-e Shahri, Isfahan, Iran, 1396 (2017). https://civilica.com/doc/701590/.

Noursadeghi, Hossein. *Esfahān, Moshtamel bar Chahār Fasl: Tārikh, Joghrāfiyā, Abniyeh va Āsār, Shoʿarā va Bozorgān, bā 41 Grāvur*. Tehran: Sherkat-e Matbuat, 1316 (1937).

Pahlavanzadeh, Leila. 'Māks Shunemān Meʿmār-e Kārkhāneh-hā-ye Esfahān'. *Nashriyyeh-ye Interneti-ye Meʿmārnet*. Accessed 3 September 2014. http://memarnet.com/en/node/2470.

Pahlavanzadeh, Leila. *Mirās-e Meʿmāri-ye Sanʿati-ye Irān, Bakhsh-e Nakhost: Ostān-e Esfahān*. Isfahan: Entesharat-e Daneshgah-ye Azad-e Eslami, Vahed-e Khorasgan, 1392 (2013).

Pahlavanzadeh, Leila. 'Sanʿat va Meʿmāri-ye Sanʿati dar Esfahān'. *Faslnāmeh-ye Ābādi* 16, no. 52 (1385/2006): 74–9.

Rajaei, Abdoulmehdi. *Yeksad-o-Yek Nokteh dar Gardeshgari-ye Esfahān*. Isfahan: Sazman-e Refahi va Tafrihi-ye Shahrdari-ye Esfahan, 1400.

Ravandi-Fadai, Lana. 'Bāztaʿrif-e Yek Bumi dar Ghorbat: Afsar-e Qazzāq va Meʿmār-e Tehrān, Nikolāi Lavovich Mārkof'. Translated by Fariba Amini and Mehdi Mousavi. *Bukhara* 25, no. 140 (Azar–Day 1399/November–December 2020): 560–89.

Ravandi-Fadai, Lana. 'Reconstructions of a Native in Exile: Cossack Brigade Fighter and Architect of Tehran – Nikolai L'vovich Markov (1882–1957)'. In *Russians in Iran: Diplomacy and Power in the Qajar Era and Beyond*, edited by Rudy Matthee and Elena Andreeva, 217–39. London: I.B. Tauris, 2018.

Shahidi, Mozaffar. 'Fehrest-e Asāmi-ye Nemāyandegān-e Majles-e Moʿassesān-e Avval (Āzar 1304)'. Website of the Institute for Iranian Contemporary Historical Studies (IICHS). Accessed 19 Shahrivar 1393 (10 September 2014). https://www.iichs.ir/fa/news/323/1304-فهرست-اسامی-نمایندگان-مجلس-مؤسسان-اول-آذر.

'Tārikh-e Ejtemāʿi-ye Qom'. *Nashriyyeh-ye Interneti-ye ʿAsr-e Eslām*. Accessed 13 Mehr 1399 (4 October 2020). http://www.asrislam.com/fa/news/20026/تاریخ-اجتماعی-قم.

Tatari, Ali. *Otāq-e Tejarāt-e Tehrān: Negāhi Gozarā beh Yeksad-o-Si-o-Seh Sāl-e Tārikhcheh-ye Otāq-e Bāzargāni, Sanāyeʿ, Maʿāden va Keshāvarzi-ye Tehrān*. Tehran: Edareh-ye Chap va Nashr-e Otaq-e Bazargani, Sanaye, Maaden va Keshavarzi-ye Tehran, 1395 (2016).

Appendix 1

(Selections)

'Inauguration Ceremony of the Risbaf (Carding) Factory in Qom', *Ettelaat*, no. 3671, 4 Azar 1317 (25 November 1938).

A report on the factory

At three o'clock yesterday afternoon, the opening ceremony of the carding factory in Qom was held in the presence of many dignitaries, who were invited from Tehran and Qom.

The city of Qom, with these useful facilities as well as many communication links and traffic, due to the construction of a nationwide railway and its connection to all regions of the country, has a bright future. The future deserves more attention from the public, and we will leave our discussion on this issue and Qom's important position for later.

So far, many factories have been opened in the country and ceremonies have been held for each one of them, but the ceremonies that took place at the opening of the Qom Carding Factory yesterday were unprecedented among those of national factories.

A special train prepared by the factory's board of directors departed from Tehran station at 8:00 a.m. The Speaker of the Parliament, the Minister of Trades and Crafts, Acting Minister of Commerce, the Presiding Board of the National Consultative Assembly, the deputy ministers, the heads of the financial and economic departments, the heads of national companies and corporations, members of the Chamber of Commerce, and the board of directors of the Municipal Association along with the management of newspapers and many merchants travelled on this train.

According to schedule, the train arrived at Qom station at 12:30 p.m., and at one o'clock in the afternoon, lunch was served, and at three o'clock in the afternoon, the opening ceremony of the factory took place, detailed proceedings of which can be seen herewith on this page by our dear readers, and at four o'clock in the afternoon, this special train returned to the capital.

The report on the factory was presented by Mr Nikpour, the chairman of the board of directors, and then Mr Mansour, the Minister of Trades and Crafts, gave a speech, and then, Mr Esfandiari, the Speaker of the National Consultative Assembly, made statements, and immediately afterwards the machinery started working, while different parts of the factory were being visited. The board of directors welcomed their esteemed guests with warmth and cordiality all day long, and this remarkable ceremony ended on a happy note. Here is the text of the speeches for our valued readers:

Mr Nikpour's speech
Chairman of the Board

After expressing thanks to the honourable gentlemen for your visit, and especially for the trouble you endured during this trip to inaugurate the factory, this report is herewith presented. Since the economic progress and industrial development of the country is given special attention by His Imperial Majesty the Shah, it is incumbent on all people of the country, especially the merchant class, to act in their turn to implement the royal wishes.

Considering that one of the major items needed by the people of the country is cotton thread and fabrics, and the cotton harvest is obtained in sufficient quantity in the country of Iran, and the increase of its production is also possible with the attention of the guardians of the imperial government, this can be done by establishing factories to produce yarn and cloth within the country. Also, considering that Qom is one of the cotton-producing areas and has been deprived of the benefits of such industries, basically, the implementation of such industrial affairs will be better done by establishing joint-stock companies.

Therefore, in order to establish a carding factory in this city, the joint-stock Risbaf Qom Company was formed with three million rials of capital and registered in the domestic companies registry on 19 Bahman 1314 (9 February 1936) under number (511), and the purchase of land for the construction of the necessary buildings as well as the purchase and installation of factory machinery has been started immediately.

Since, during the course of this work, it was recognized that the initial capital was not enough to cover the expenses of the necessary buildings and to pay for all the machines and their installation expenses, as a matter of necessity, on 9 Azar 1316 (30 November 1937), the equivalent of a further two million rials was added to the initial capital of the partners. Therefore, the total current capital that has been fully paid is five million rials, as described below.

Mr Ali Gheissarieh: 1,900,000 rials
Mr Abdol Hossein Nikpour: 850,000 rials
Mr Ahmad Akhavan: 850,000 rials
Mr Mohammad Ali Nosratian: 815,000 rials
Mr Haj Mohammad Hossein Yazdi: 415,000 rials
Mr Ali Asghar Zarkesh: 85,000 rials
Mr Abol Qasem Semsarzadeh: 85,000 rials
[Total] 5,000,000 rials

Buildings

The building that has been completed thus far consists of a 30-metre long and 18-metre wide engine room. On the northeast side of this building, a tower with a length of 8 metres, width of 7 metres and height of 18 metres has been built. In this tower, a purification device and a water source have been provided.

On the left side of the aforementioned building, a large pool 12 metres long, 10 metres wide and 5 metres deep was built to provide cold water for the engine. From a technical viewpoint, the fuel supply for the engine has been situated in close proximity to both the engine and the water source, so that, in case of fire, the flames could be contained.

Another important building of this factory contains two ginning and spinning salons, the first of which is 30 metres long and 28 metres wide. In order to prevent cotton dust, a tower 8 metres long, 7 metres wide and 24 metres high has been built in the corner of the aforementioned salon, which is connected to the ginning machines by means of underground channels, and next to this building there is a 90-metre long and 30-metre wide spinning salon, which has the capacity to install nine thousand spindles.

In the interior of the wall around all the salons, sufficient water pipes have been installed for firefighting purposes, and channels for electrical cables have been dug throughout the aforementioned salons.

In order to ensure the comfort of the employees, another salon with a length of 90 metres and a width of 5 metres has been built, which has 500 small lockers for each worker, and in front of this salon, an area equal to 154 square metres has been built for the workers' cafe and restaurant, and three wickets of the shop, selling all kinds of food and drinks.

Machinery

According to the order of Mr Ali Gheissarieh, who is one of the founders and important partners of this company, the spinning machines were purchased from the German Richard Hartmann Factory, and consist of two cotton ginning machines connected to each other, eighteen carding machines, eight six-ply machines, six half-ply machines, twelve full-ply machines, and one four-ply machine, two double-ply machines, twelve coiling machines, one carding machine, three machines for making rollers, a special sanding machine and a complete trial and testing device.

The aforementioned machines have four-thousand six-hundred and eight single-layer spinning spindles and seven-hundred and twenty double-layer spinning spindles. These machines are among the latest and newest common systems in the industry. Yarn from grade six to grade 40 can be prepared with them.

The amount of cotton used by the factory in ten hours is one thousand and one hundred kilos. About nine-hundred kilos of spun yarn will be obtained from this amount, and one hundred and twenty kilos of the cotton will be wasted and unusable. The driving force of the machines is a six-cylinder diesel engine (380 hp) purchased from a German company (MAN). Another engine, like this one, was purchased, which arrived at Iranian customs last week, and is about to be transported and installed in the factory.

The power of this current engine alone is enough to run all the spinning machines and the new engine is a spare. The electrical equipment, generator and electric motor of this factory were all purchased from Siemens Schuckert. The generator has a power of 280 kilowatts and has an alternating current of 220 and 380 and rotates 375 times per minute.

Two iron tankers with a capacity of 75 cubic metres each have been purchased and installed for water and diesel. In order to ensure the health of the employees and prevent the cotton from drying out in the hot summer weather, six humidifiers (Wissner) were purchased from Germany, and installed at a height of 5 metres in the salon, and with special pumps, water enters these machines. The length of each of the machines is 21 metres.

Other matters related to the factory

From 26 Khordad 1316 (16 June 1937), six German experts started installing machines and on the fourth of Azar (25 November) of the same year, all machines have been technically tested. As a result of several years of experience of European and Iranian experts, all equipment and working tools of the factory are arranged in such a way that both improves the work and makes the factory employees comfortable in the performance of their duties. Around five hundred workers have been employed so far.

Another common benefit of this factory is the construction of a water reservoir with a capacity of 1,500 cubic metres, which will always be filled with clear fresh water, and, in order to be used by passers-by and travellers, a separate external door has been placed on the street and everyone can use it at all times.

The factory also provides a school for the elderly employees of the factory, which they benefit from every day for free. Moreover, the factory carefully considers the health issues of the employees, and always has one nurse with effective and simple equipment available to the employees, and regulations are applied that, in case of illness, they are treated at the expense of the factory by a special doctor. Considering that the distance between the factory and the city is about three kilometres, a bus takes the workers from the city to the factory and back every day.

Current capital of the company

2,163,751 rials – the price of the factory land and building expenses
2,638,178 rials – the price of all machines and their expenses
245,500 rials – the expenses of installing machinery and miscellaneous
5,047,430 rials – Total

Appendix 2

(Selections)

'Urban News: Increase of Work', *Ostovar*, 14 Mehr 1317 (6 October 1938), 1.

The working hours of the factory as of 9 Mehr 1317 (1 October 1938) have been changed from ten hours to twenty hours, with two groups of workers working ten hours a day and ten hours a night.

'City Lights', *Ostovar*, 16 Khordad 1319 (6 June 1940), 1.

The power of this factory is more than 6,000 volts, which comes to the city through a 35 x 3 cable and is converted to 220 x 380 volts in the pressure conversion station (transformer), and is then distributed through the wires.

'Helping Workers', *Ostovar*, 11 Esfand 1320 (2 March 1942), 2.

According to the information obtained from the Qom Risbaf Factory, in accordance with the order of the company's managers, from the point of view of the welfare and comfort of the factory workers, who are more than 400 people, the company management have opened a bakery shop in the factory and give them bread at the price of 3 kilos for 4 rials.

12

The private sector during the post-war era:

The destiny of an entrepreneurial family

Ali Asghar Saeidi

Introduction

In the post-war era, the private sector played an integral role in the development of Iran's economy. In addition, most large-scale companies expanded their economic activities within the framework of familial relationships. The objective of this chapter is to analyse Iran's economic development through the highs and lows experienced by an entrepreneurial family, that is, the Ladjevardis and Ladjevardians (see Figure 12.1).[1] The chapter argues that the economic life of this family was a reflection of a society in which people were raised with traditional ethical values and family members respected their elders and followed their advice. However, this family also pursued new ways of fostering industrial growth and development within political and economic contexts. The chapter shows how this family grew their companies, produced new products and expanded the distribution network by means of vertical and horizontal integration. Lastly, this chapter reviews the events that led to the decline of this family's fortunes and a new phase in the private sector of the Iranian economy.

In Iran, family and kinship have played an integral role in society. Many peaks and troughs are typically experienced within the average family. Yet when a family conducts itself not only in terms of social relationships among its members but also business dealings, involving strategy, risk-taking and accountability, we are no longer dealing with an ordinary family but with an entrepreneurial family.[2] This chapter is about such a family, one that played an active role in the social and economic development of Iran's private sector for more than a century (i.e. about 110 years) by being bold, courageous and willing to take risks,[3] while experiencing highs and lows.

The Behshahr Industrial Group, one of Iran's main conglomerates, had its origins in commerce and trade of the late nineteenth century and expanded its activities over four generations under the ownership and management of the Ladjevardis and Ladjevardians. Their range of commercial activities and achievements grew to include: the production of vegetable oils, soaps, detergents and packaging; the manufacturing of velvet, other textiles and clothing, as well as polyester and acrylic fibres; a bank and an insurance company;[4] and businesses in the construction sector, including prefabricated buildings and warehouses.[5] Thus, by 1979, this family had created more than 13,500 jobs directly and about the same number indirectly.[6] But what can explain this family's range of achievements and its role in the development of Iran's private sector, especially over the course of thirty years, from 1948 to 1978?

From the local bazaar to the international market

Seyyed Mohammad (known as *nil forush* or indigo seller), a first-generation member of the family, was one of the more enlightened, forward-thinking businessmen of Kashan around the time of the 1905 Constitutional Revolution. A self-made man, Seyyed Mohammad began from virtually nothing, first working for a cloth trader in the bazaar in Kashan. He then became an apprentice in a shop owned by Haj Morteza. By 1895, he had saved enough to start a business, marking the beginning of the commercial activities of this family.[7] His *hojreh* (chamber) was in the *timcheh* (small arcaded courtyard) of Haj Seyyed Hossein Sabbagh, in the upper part of the Kashan bazaar. During the reign of Nasser al-Din Shah, Seyyed Mohammad traded mainly with India, especially in imported indigo powder (*nil* or *lājevard*), which he distributed in Iran.[8] According to his son, Akbar Ladjevardian:

> At first, my father had worked as an apprentice at a small trading company in Kashan. After that, he established his own family business with his brother. After the death of his brother, he decided to get married. My father then started importing indigo from Isfahan to Kashan and distributed it among the dyers of Kashan . . . and for this reason, he was known as Seyyed Mohammad Nilforush. Later, my father expanded his business by exporting textiles from Kashan to Tehran . . . at that time, my father opened an office in Tehran, and appointed a person by the name of Mirza Abol Qasem to manage the office . . . to promote the activities of this office, he sent my elder brother, Seyyed Mahmoud, aged 16, who had volunteered to go to Tehran to help Mirza Abol Qasem.[9]

In 1911, Seyyed Mahmoud, who had learned about trade from his father, was sent to Tehran to manage his father's business in the Tehran Bazaar, as well as to expand the activities of the Ladjevardian & Partners Trading Company. He started his career in a rented *hojreh* in the *timcheh* of Amin Aqdas.[10] Within a few decades, with the support of his younger brother, Akbar Ladjevardian, and sons, Ahmad, Ghassem and Habib, Haj Seyyed Mahmoud Ladjevardi had established one of the largest industrial groups in Iran and the Middle East.[11]

After the First World War, in 1922, Haj Seyyed Mahmoud Ladjevardi travelled to the Soviet Union and Germany to learn about international trade and began to think about setting up a trading company.[12] Then, after the Second World War, the growing consumer demand for imported goods led to an increase in local sales agents of foreign companies seeking to sell their products in Iran. Thus, the Haj Seyyed Mahmoud Ladjevardi and Partners Company received licences to act as the sales agents for Golf

Star and the Coleman Company, both based in the United States. They also became representatives of Golden Brothers and Yorkshire Insurance, American and British firms.[13] At the same time, the Iranian textile market was particularly buoyant after the war. Hence, in order to take advantage of commercial opportunities, the Ladjevardi and Ladjevardian families established Javid Trading Company and Arien Trading Company, with ownership shared equally among the family members. This was the first step in forming a family business, based on the lessons that Haj Seyyed Mahmoud had learned from the unsuccessful experience of working with his father.[14] Their sales agent status for Golden Brothers and Yorkshire Insurance helped these trading companies significantly expand their turnover. Moreover, their private sector companies grew by opening offices overseas. By 1956, the family had set up offices in New York, Osaka and Hamburg. These offices enhanced the family's access to the international market.[15]

From commercial agriculture to the industrial sector

The Haj Seyyed Mahmoud Ladjevardi and Partners Company entered the world of industry through the cotton trade. The company would buy cotton from farmers around the Caspian coastal towns of Babol and Gorgan in northern Iran. The cotton would be exported to Europe and Japan in exchange for fabric. However, the company received complaints about impurities in the cotton from foreign buyers and had to pay compensation. As a result, Haj Seyyed Mahmoud decided to buy the cotton bolls from the farmers for local refining. The limited domestic capacity for cotton ginning, on the one hand, and the growing overseas demand for cotton, on the other, led him to consider setting up a cotton-ginning plant – a costly and difficult proposition in those days.

Thus, as soon as the Ministry of Commerce had given its approval, the company built the Behshahr cotton-ginning plant in 1949 and started its operations in 1952.[16]

Figure 12.1 Left to right: Haj Seyyed Mohammad Ladjevardian, *c.* 1940; Ahmad Ladjevardi, Haj Seyyed Akbar Ladjevardian, Ghassem and Habib Ladjevardi, *c.* 2005; Haj Seyyed Mahmoud Ladjevardi, *c.* 1975. Courtesy Masoud Ladjevardian's family album.

This was the first stage of the transition from the raw cotton export trade to the cotton-ginning industry.[17] As Akbar Ladjevardian explained:

> We would first refine the cotton to ensure that there would not be any dirt, seeds or twigs in the cotton. In the beginning, cotton-ginning plants were owned exclusively by the government, and permission would not be given for the building of new plants by the private sector. However, we knew both the Minister of Commerce and the director-general personally. We met and told them about our problems with low-quality raw cotton exports. The Ministry of Commerce [then] gave the private sector permission to build a cotton-ginning plant. The licence for the Behshahr cotton-ginning plant was issued in 1949. Ahmad, the eldest son of Haj Seyyed Mahmoud Ladjevardi, led the effort to build the plant. At this time, his second son, Ghassem, was in the United States. Within a year, the Behshahr cotton-ginning plant was built, and became operational in 1952.[18]

To meet the growing demand of cotton farmers, a further four cotton-ginning plants were built in Gorgan, Neka, Gonbad and Behshahr. At the same time, in order to help farmers, a company was formed to promote cotton cultivation, an initiative that should have been led by the Ministry of Agriculture.[19]

Vertical integration in the vegetable oil industry

The Behshahr cotton-ginning plant was the first step towards the development of the Behshahr Industrial Group. In addition to cotton ginning, the family built a cottonseed extraction plant in Behshahr. Over time, the family began to make changes to its business model. Initially, some of the cottonseed was sold to the Gol Vegetable Oil Company, managed by Habib Elghanian.[20] But Gol had limited processing capacity, leaving a large surplus of unsold cottonseed with no other buyers, prompting the family to build its own cottonseed oil extraction unit in Behshahr.[21]

In the coming years, the family continued to invest in the country under difficult economic, social and political conditions, among the very few willing to do so. Economically, Iran lacked enough basic infrastructure, such as paved roads, electricity, water and telephones. Only a few years had passed since the Allied occupation during (and after) the Second World War. Moreover, since 1945, the country had been plagued by disruptive labour movements.[22] Hence, there was no political stability. The oil nationalization of 1951 also led to foreign economic sanctions. At the same time, socially, the country was fragmented, with 70 per cent of the population consisting of villagers, tribespeople and nomads. Against this backdrop, the risk of investment was particularly high. Anyone prepared to make productive investments would have to be driven by nationalist motives and/or hold a particularly optimistic view of the future.

When the Behshahr extraction plant began its operations, the cottonseed oil had a high acid content. As a result, its only customers were small-scale soap producers, a cottage industry centred in Tehran. But as soap production began to exceed demand, prices and profits declined, and before long, most soapmakers went out of business.

At this point, seeking a new market for its surplus cottonseed oil, the family decided to build a vegetable oil production facility in Tehran.[23] In order to implement this project, Ahmad Ladjevardi travelled to the United States to learn about the edible oil industry. The result of his fact-finding mission was to set up a production plant to make shortening, using a mix of hydrogenated vegetable oil imported from the United States and locally produced cottonseed oil. The development of an oil hydrogenation facility was postponed to a later stage.[24] In the beginning, it was discovered that when the imported solid hydrogenated oil was combined with the domestic liquid cottonseed oil, the mixture would begin to separate as temperatures rose. The liquid oil would float to the top, and the solid oil would stay on the bottom. Consequently, customers turned away. Until the hydrogenation unit was built, the low-quality shortening was sold under the Gol Ladan (Nasturtium) brand name.[25]

As product quality improved with hydrogenation, a new vegetable oil called Shahpasand (King's Choice) was launched in 1956, supported by an extensive advertising campaign. It became a popular brand among Iranians, even as competition began to intensify.[26] Over time, Shahpasand and its principal competitor Ghoo (Swan) gained the largest share of the Iranian shortening market.[27] Other producers suffered losses but still managed to retain their market shares with the support of government subsidies.[28] As a result of market competition, 'from the time we started producing vegetable oil in the 1950s until the Revolution in 1979, its price did not increase by more than 1.5 per cent per year, that is, inflation was no more than 1.5 per cent', Akbar Ladjevardian pointed out.[29] The production and distribution of Shahpasand increased rapidly, with its capacity reaching 60 tonnes per day and was expected to rise to over 100 tonnes a day. In the 1960s, the family also launched Bahar (Spring) vegetable oil, which had the taste and aroma of Kermanshahi ghee.

Soap, detergent and related industries

'In the process of producing vegetable oil', Akbar Ladjevardian noted:

> About 20 per cent would go to waste as fatty acids. We first hired a local expert dealer, Mohammad Tafsiri,[30] to sell this by-product to soapmakers. He also did this job well. However, local soapmakers could not absorb all of the fatty acids and its price went down day by day. The soapmakers competed with each other and most of them went bankrupt. So we decided to build a soap-making plant to use the fatty acid by-product ourselves.[31]

Around 8.5 per cent of the weight of soap consisted of glycerine. At the time, however, all glycerine was imported. Having realized that the returns from glycerine production would cover its costs within three years, the Behshahr Industrial Group added glycerine to their portfolio. Its use in medicine helped the pharmaceutical industry, and its role in making gunpowder meant that it could also be used by the army.

Soap production led them to think about making another product: laundry detergent. Until then, only Tide, made by Procter & Gamble, was available on the domestic market.

The Ladjevardi and Ladjevardian family partnered with Hossein Mokhtari, who had contracted the Italians to build a detergent manufacturing plant, but was having trouble financing his project. Mokhtari had wanted to build such a factory with a business partner about fifty-five years ago but had problems raising funds and working capital. Thus, he called on the family circa 1961. They treated him very fairly: he transferred 70 per cent of the shares to them and kept 30 per cent for himself and his partner. He said, 'the project required a great deal of capital, and if they had not become our partner, we certainly could not have continued, and would have gone bankrupt. Meeting this family was perhaps the luckiest moment in my life.'[32] The family then increased the capacity of the plant to 750 kilograms of detergent per hour, and after the machinery was installed, it was ready to begin operations.[33] Prime Minister Hassan Ali Mansour inaugurated the factory.[34] According to Mokhtari, 'newspapers published full-page advertisements for Snow detergent every day. The company used to draw lots among consumers of Snow: the top prize was a Pontiac car. The plant grew to become the largest manufacturer of detergents in Iran and the Middle East.'[35] Farhad Hormozi, an advertising executive, led its media campaign. Fifteen days prior to its product launch, he had published an ad in all the newspapers announcing, 'Be ready for the most exciting news of the year!'[36] This enhanced publicity for Snow plus its low price led the competition to reduce their prices, benefiting consumers. Then, the family built a plant to produce sodium sulphate from the salt marshes of Qom. Sodium sulphate, an ingredient for laundry detergent, could now be sourced locally, rather than imported from abroad.

In the process of expanding their companies and manufacturing new products, which was similar to the process of vertical integration,[37] the family also began to produce cans, cardboard and cartons as well as oxygen for factories and hospitals while acquiring vessels to transport raw materials from abroad, building docking facilities in the southern ports and constructing industrial water treatment plants. Akbar Ladjevardian stressed that 'we launched these additional ventures because they were effectively forced upon us. For example, there were no manufacturers of cartons and cans in Iran. We entered these industries one after another, in a series, simply because we needed them. At the time, there was only one carton-manufacturing plant in the entire country and all of Iran depended on it.'[38] Thus, he told Dr Alinaghi Alikhani, the Minister of the Economy,[39] that Iran's newly established plants could not rely on one carton producer, supposing, 'what would happen if the only carton maker caught fire? Alikhani then said that the government would immediately allow us to establish our own carton-making unit.'

Thus, through the process of horizontal integration, the family moved away from traditional channels of distribution by developing their own modern distribution network to help stabilize the prices of their products across the country.[40] Moreover, a new company was formed for the direct distribution of products to 12,000 retail stores in Tehran and its sales representatives in the provinces. These sales representatives were given regular training by the company. As the Behshahr Industrial Group expanded with a growing variety of products, it needed to address the management issues arising from the steady increase in the size and complexity of its activities. Accordingly, it developed an organizational structure for each manufacturing unit. By 1978, the Group had twelve manufacturing companies.[41]

Entering the textile industry

As part of their trade with Japan, the family imported velvet. By the time it arrived in Iran, however, the fabric's raised patterns had fallen flat, leading to customer complaints and demands for compensation from local merchants. To solve this problem, Akbar Ladjevardian visited the velvet-weaving plant in Japan, located near Osaka. During the tour, it crossed his mind that Kashan had been the centre of velvet production at one time, and he began to think about setting up a plant there. Having seen that 'velvet-making was not a complicated task', he wrote a letter while in Osaka to his brother Seyyed Mahmoud and Haj Hassan Tafazzoli, 'proposing to manufacture velvet in Kashan and to avoid losses arising from velvet imports'.[42] They immediately agreed with his proposal. Thus, they acquired ten velvet-weaving machines for the plant's establishment with $200,000 of capital. They also signed contracts with two technical experts. In July 1955, the machinery and technicians arrived in Kashan. The velvet plant was set up with the help of Tafazzoli, the best carpet maker in Kashan. After two and a half to three years, the first batch of velvet was produced, marking the renaissance of Kashan's velvet industry.

Following the velvet industry's establishment, the family added related products. As Akbar Ladjevardian explained:

> When I went on a pilgrimage to Mecca, after the Hajj rituals, I found out that the most popular souvenir was prayer rugs, which pilgrims would bring home as gifts. As the prayer rugs resembled velvet, and we made velvet in Kashan, I thought of producing prayer rugs in Iran and exporting them to Mecca. On returning to Iran, we acquired equipment to weave prayer rugs at the velvet plant in Kashan. These prayer rugs were so popular in Iran that all of our production was sold domestically. Following the success of the prayer rugs, we produced larger carpets, and gradually moved to large-scale production of machine-made carpets.[43]

Iranian customers wanted large prayer rugs with a thicker pile for picnics in the countryside. Using starch to inflate the yarn, the family made prayer rugs with an enhanced pile. As they perfected the technique, there was more product demand in the market. Eventually, the rugs resembled carpets. But the machines were designed for making prayer rugs, not carpets. Thus, their production method did not stand the test of time. With wear and tear and washing, the starch would separate from the yarn and the rugs would lose their thick pile. When asked about weaving equipment for machine-made carpets, the manufacturer explained that the family needed a different type of machine. Hence, as soon as the government gave permission, they established the first machine-made carpet factory in Iran and invited Dr Banijamali, an extremely capable and detail-orientated person, to take on the management of the new venture.[44]

At the same time, Akbar Ladjevardian reached out to the Tehran Polytechnic (Amirkabir University of Technology) students directly and offered them scholarships.[45] The Behshahr Industrial Group also hired a large number of graduates in textile engineering. Thus, according to Managing Director Akbar Hosseinzadeh, 'As new units came on stream, such as the machine-made carpet plant in Ravand, the

Iran Knitting Factory in Qazvin, or the thread-producing plants in Arak, the Group would employ more textile engineers.'[46] He added, 'most of the Tehran Polytechnic College's graduates were employed by the Behshahr Industrial Group. I dare say that Mr. Ladjevardian revived its textile engineering department, either by hiring graduates or by providing financial assistance and purchasing equipment to train textile engineers.'

Although the Kashan Velvet Plant had 10,000 shuttles that produced all other types of thread, the fine 'no. 40' gauge used in the weaving of cotton velvet had to be imported. Therefore, the family decided to establish a new facility in Arak, with a capacity of 20,000 shuttles for the production of this thread.[47] However, a large amount of waste thread was produced in the velvet and carpet units of Kashan and Arak after the shearing process. Then, they discovered that by combining 80 per cent of this textile waste with 20 per cent synthetic fibre, they could manufacture non-woven carpeting – which was used to cover the floors of low-cost apartments. Consequently, they built another factory in Arak with a capacity of 19 million feet of non-woven carpeting per year.

Thus far, the family had acquired considerable know-how in silk weaving, spinning, carpet weaving and cotton ginning but not in the production of interlocking yarn loops for knitted fabric. The Tehran plant wove fustian using ordinary machinery. This thick, coarse cotton fabric was then shipped to other firms to be dyed or printed with patterns. However, the process was cumbersome and disorganized with high production costs – in contrast to competitors, whose prices were lower because all such equipment was integrated under one roof. Given that the family wanted their products to compete in the market, the addition of knitting, dyeing and printing equipment became a priority. While their knitting factory was successfully established in Tehran, it coincided with a jump in oil prices during the early 1970s. As Iran's oil revenues increased, customs duties on imports were eliminated or significantly reduced in order to prevent rising inflation. However, this policy encouraged the importation of cheap fabrics from Southeast Asia. Under these circumstances, Iranian textile manufacturers were forced to export their surplus production to neighbouring countries. The shortage of workers also grew worse, affecting all textile factories in Iran. Although there was an abundance of cheap labour from Pakistan and India, the family concluded that it would be in their best interests to hire skilled workers from South Korea.[48] Despite these challenges, the knitting, dyeing and printing complex in Tehran was transferred to Alborz Industrial District in Qazvin and became known as 'Iran Knitting'.

Meanwhile, the Iran Textile Company was established in order to distribute the Behshahr Industrial Group's textile products throughout the country and abroad. The director of Behpush (Wear It), Lily Ladjevardian, explained the benefit of mechanization for mass-market fashion:

> At that time, we were thinking of making low-priced, attractive and well-made clothing for the society . . . using modern methods that simplified the manufacturing process. Machine-made clothing was only beginning as the country became more industrialized. There was a great deal of potential, especially in men's shirts. Modern sewing was quite different from traditional ways of making clothes. Our

work lowered the price of clothes, making clothing accessible to everyone, and made the general public [*tudeh-ye mardom*] look much better.[49]

Synthetics for the country

The production of synthetic fibres was another step in the continuous expansion of the manufacturing activities of not only the Behshahr Industrial Group but the country. In 1974, polyester fibre, a key raw material for Iran Knitting and Kashan Industries, become increasingly scarce around the world. Previously, Japanese and German fibre producers would sell their surplus products to Iran and the Middle East below cost, to maintain domestic prices.[50]

In 1972, Mr Oya, the CEO of the Teijin Company of Japan, visited Iran. During a dinner party, Mr Ladjevardian asked him why they did not give a higher share of their fibre products to Iranian buyers. Mr Oya replied that Teijin was committed to meeting the demands of Japanese buyers. Then he suggested, 'Why don't you establish a fibre-producing facility in Iran?'[51] A week later, a delegation of Teijin executives came to Iran to carry out a feasibility study. They concluded that a polyester filament plant with a capacity of 5,000 tonnes would be appropriate for Iran.[52] They prepared a project plan and submitted it to the Ministry of Industry. However, ministry officials did not approve the proposal. They responded: 'Due to the increase in oil prices, this project is too small for Iran. It should be expanded. In addition to polyester filament, Iran needs acrylic filament. The manufacture of acrylic filament should be added to their project.' The Ministry of Industry believed that a plant with a total capacity of 20,000 tonnes was needed, in order to make 10,000 tonnes each of acrylic and polyester fibres.[53]

As the Ministry of Industry officials continued their research, their views on the capacity of the plant changed. It was decided that the plant should have a capacity of 25,000 tonnes each of polyester and acrylic. Akbar Ladjevardian explained that he had sent a four-member delegation, including Dr Shirsavar, Engineer Moravej, Engineer Tehrani and headed by Dr Banijamali, to Europe, the United States and Japan to carry out research on acrylic and polyester fibre manufacturers and to obtain prices for building and operating the proposed project. Following their six months of research, the American firm DuPont was selected because it was ready to invest 40 per cent in a joint venture, whereas the others were not interested in making an equity investment.[54] DuPont insisted on retaining 40 per cent of the shares, which, of course, was the best guarantee for the success of the project. Conversely, DuPont allowed for 99 per cent of the plant and equipment to be sourced by international tender and only 1 per cent, representing their proprietary technology, to be provided at the full price. Additionally, it was agreed that if their technology were to advance, they would provide the same technology to the plant in Iran.

On 13 March 1973, the company's founders and DuPont signed an agreement in Tehran to set up a major industrial unit for manufacturing synthetic fibre, polyester and acrylic. This unit would be called the Polyacryl Iran Corporation. At the time of signing, DuPont stated that it expected to earn 20 per cent of its profits from investments outside the United States. The Behshahr Group advised the Iranian government to accept DuPont's proposal, provided that three conditions were met. First, the product manufactured in Iran had to be identical in all respects to that made by DuPont in the United States. Second, the product had to be delivered to the market within thirty months and without any price increase. Third, three months after starting operations, the plant had to operate with 97 per cent efficiency and only 2 per cent waste.[55]

On 26 April 1978, the day stipulated in the contract, the plant produced the first sample of a fibre product. Three independent user firms certified that the product was better than that produced by Hoechst of Germany and Teijin of Japan and was as good as the American-made product of the DuPont Company. The plant achieved 97 per cent efficiency, and a high-quality product had been supplied to the market on schedule.[56] According to Akbar Ladjevardian, 'At that time, the Polyacrylic plant was the largest in the Middle East. Turkey, for example, had a 5,000-ton polyester plant at the time. We had a 50,000-ton polyester and acrylic facility.'[57]

During this period, fifty DuPont experts and their families lived in Iran, and 220 Iranian engineers, who had graduated from American and Iranian universities, were trained at DuPont's facilities in the United States for two years. Many of these engineers later worked in Iran's textile industry. Akbar Ladjevardian mentioned that about 140 engineers were needed, selected from among the graduates of American and Iranian universities.[58] DuPont's training was very thorough and every ten engineers had one dedicated full-time instructor. The management predicted that their trained engineers would be in high demand, and some would be lured away by other firms. For this reason, they trained 30 to 40 per cent more engineers than were needed. Their training went very well and within two years they returned to Iran and started working.

It was clear from the beginning, as Masoud Ladjevardian explained, that this was an advanced technological plan for Iran:

> In 1973, my father, who had come to Wilmington, Delaware to negotiate with DuPont for the Isfahan Polyacryl plant, came to Boston to visit me and my brother. He showed us with great enthusiasm the company's twenty-year financial forecast. My brother was concerned. He told my father that this joint-venture would take five years to build and then would have losses for a further ten years. It would only start making a profit in 1988. How could such an investment be justified? Were we not placing the family's capital at risk? My father replied that this investment was not for the family, but for Iran, and the only group that could make Iran self-sufficient from imported fibres for the textile industry was the Behshahr Industrial Group.[59]

By this point, the Behshahr Industrial Group had built manufacturing facilities in many parts of Iran, including Tehran, Kashan, Ravand-e-Kashan, Behshahr, Gorgan, Gonbad-e-Kavus, Neka, Qazvin, Arak, Kermanshah, Mashhad, Amol, Rasht, Nowshahr and Khorramshahr.

Industrialization of construction

In Tehran, in addition to the production of vegetable oil and a variety of soaps and detergents, prefabricated buildings were built by Souliran under licence from the Soulé

Company of the United States. All of these activities were under the management of Ahmad Ladjevardi. The prefabricated buildings saw high demand in the 1960s, as many industrial plants and warehouses were built in Iran. Starting in about 1972, as the commercial and residential building market began to expand rapidly, Ahmad Ladjevardi, with his experience in setting up and managing the Souliran Company, entered the construction sector. He launched the Akam Industries Group to provide integrated construction service for contractors. By 1979, the Akam Group had completed major commercial and residential building projects throughout the country.[60]

Welfare of employees

The managers of Behshahr Industrial Group knew that without considering the welfare of employees, one could not expect increases in productivity and efficiency. So, they provided various benefits for employees and their families, ranging from the sale of company shares to home mortgages, family welfare, private medical insurance and recreational facilities. For example, administrator Ahmad Ghaznavi noted, 'One of the good things that Mr. Ladjevardi did was to build company housing jointly with Sepanta and Arj for the benefit of factory workers.'[61] Another employee, Ebrahim Samani-Nejad, added, 'I was given shares in the company. Their value was no more than 100 tomans. But the shares would earn bonus shares, and as the company became more profitable, the value of the shares gradually increased. I then sold the stock and was able to buy a house for 75,000 tomans.'[62] Messenger Davud Aghili also mentioned, 'We had health insurance. The Group had a contract with Shahram Hospital and all our family members went there for free. We had a housing cooperative and many of the tenants eventually became homeowners.'[63] As Mohammad Hossein Keyhan Falsafi explained:

> Almost all the benefits we needed were available: home mortgages, emergency loans and private medical insurance . . . We paid a small amount of our salary for medical insurance, but then we could take ourselves and our family to the best private hospital. At a time when most industrial groups did not provide social welfare and insurance for their employees, the Behshahr Industrial Group stood out by providing all its employees with such benefits.[64]

Samani-Nejad also said, 'All members of this family treated us well. Employees' salaries were paid on time. They increased our salaries twice a year, in September and March.'[65] Likewise, another administrator, Ahmad Nahid, mentioned, 'Salaries and employee benefits were higher than other companies. Maybe our salaries were no less than oil company salaries. I think the staff were content and would avoid changing their place of work. However, people who resigned . . . were hired with higher salaries when they went to smaller companies because of their work experience at the Behshahr Industrial Group.'[66] According to financial manager Mohammad Reza Maashouri, 'Many people are aware of the high standing of the Abadan Institute of Technology and its role in educating engineers for the oil industry. Yet these graduate engineers preferred to be hired by the Behshahr Industrial Group rather than the Iranian National Oil Company.'[67] Thus, he concluded, 'What could be a stronger endorsement of the management and policies of the Behshahr Industrial Group?'

Social responsibility

In 1962, by establishing the Ladjevardi Foundation, the family started conducting charitable activities, such as building and supporting primary schools as well as technical and vocational schools, building dormitories, restoring historic sites and providing support for other educational and cultural causes. To this end, 15 per cent of the annual income from the Group's companies was allocated to the Ladjevardi Foundation. The creation of this foundation and its source of funding had been proposed by Haj Seyyed Mahmoud Ladjevardi. According to his brother, Akbar Ladjevardian, 'My father used to say that the Iranian nation's misery was due to illiteracy. At that time . . . there were no places to teach. My father invited someone named Mr. Zia to come to our house to teach all my sisters. Yet he was not satisfied with educating only the women in his family.'[68] Therefore, 'He opened a night school in Kashan and invited people to come to study for free. After four months, the turnout was still low. He then started serving tea and sweets to encourage attendance. He considered ignorance and illiteracy of the people to be the cause of their misery.' For this reason, the Ladjevardi Foundation built about sixty schools in and around Kashan. Hence, the Ladjevardi Foundation effectively continued what he had begun, the promotion of literacy and raising of the level of knowledge of the people of Iran.

Intellectuals and modern advertising

Another innovation of this family was the use of modern advertising to market their products. They signed a contract with the Facopa Advertising Agency, headed by Farhad Hormozi. Thanks in part to an extensive advertising campaign, the entire daily production capacity of 20 tonnes of Shahpasand shortening and vegetable oil were effectively sold in one day. The brand name of the new vegetable oil was chosen by the public through a promotional campaign and customer survey. An awards ceremony was then held to introduce the selected name, 'Shahpasand', as the new brand of vegetable oil.

In the 1960s, Habib Ladjevardi, who was in charge of administrative affairs, set up an advertising department within the Behshahr Industrial Group. He reorganized the market research and sales departments. The advertising department became directly responsible for producing advertisements and packaging designs. The market research department, besides providing statistics about the market share of products sold through grocery stores, conducted consumer surveys. In a laboratory of the head office, this department tested and compared their own products with those of competitors, from the viewpoint of consumers. Moreover, like their competitors, the company hired and trained travelling salesmen, who were responsible for taking orders from their representatives in the cities and provinces.

Habib Ladjevardi also invited artists, theatre and film directors, writers, poets and intellectuals, such as Siavash Kasraei, Kamran Shirdel, Mohammad Ali Sepanlou and Ahmad Reza Ahmadi, to work with the Behshahr Industrial Group in such areas as design, poetry composition, screenwriting and filmmaking to support the marketing effort. Nasser Shahinpar, who was responsible for advertising and exports, pointed out that 'Habib Ladjevardi wanted well-educated and open-minded professionals to join the company'.[69] Such employees even included Hassan Zia Zarifi, 'who turned out to be a member of "the Bijan Jazani organization" [Organization of Iranian People's Fedai Guerrillas or Sazman-e Cherikha-ye Fadayi-ye Khalq-e Iran] . . . One day the authorities showed up to search his office. He was later arrested elsewhere and executed.' Shahinpar added, 'The presence of such a creative group of people sent a positive message to the wider community about the possibilities of working in the Group. My experience in collaborating with such people enhanced my own career. Although I had met many of them previously, my friendship with [the poet and novelist] Siavash Kasraei started here.'[70]

In the past, advertising had been conducted in a completely traditional manner. There was no professional ad agency to develop suitable advertising material that would reflect the needs of consumers and support the sales networks. Marketing analyst Mohammad Hossein Keyhan Falsafi explained:

> We went to the bazaar (or market) in the towns and villages. There was another objective behind the advertising effort, which was not just to increase sales. Of course, the aim of marketing is to boost sales, but we thought, why is the annual consumption of toothpaste in the country only one gram per person? Why is the consumption of health products so low? Why is the annual consumption of laundry detergent only 500 grams per capita? Even the lowest amount in Europe was three and a half kilograms or more. We saw that the country's population was at a good level, but demand for such products was simply too low. The idea was that we should help promote the health of the country. Effectively, the main goal was to put ourselves in the place of the Ministry of Health.[71]

Business ethics

The family always placed ethics at the forefront of their business activities. They followed the advice of Haj Seyyed Mahmoud Ladjevardi, who advised them to be honest, sincere and amicable in business dealings and to respect business ethics by honouring their commitments. He reminded family members that their objective should be to create jobs for the society. Shahinpar recalled that, one day, Haj Seyyed Mahmoud saw him, a stranger, at a board meeting.[72] He asked why he was there. Habib Ladjevardi told his father that he had prepared a large and profitable proposal for the soap-making plants. After glancing at the papers, Haj Seyyed Mahmoud asked

Shahinpar to give him a brief summary of his project. He then said to him in a sincere, fatherly way,

> We are not sitting here to find ways to force people from their businesses. About 5,000 people all over Iran produce soap in their homes, dry them on the roofs of houses, and then take them to the neighborhood public baths for sale. If we were to implement your project, they would all go bankrupt, and would be unable to feed their families.

Shahinpar concluded, 'As I emerged from that board meeting, I realized that I, as a young leftist graduate, had thought they were profit-seekers, but instead, they declined my proposal in a most humane way.'

The fourth generation

As the Behshahr Industrial Group expanded and its Iran Center for Management Studies trained professional managers, the fourth generation of the family gradually came to work, in order to succeed their fathers. Despite their university studies in the United States, they began their careers as entry-level interns to train in various parts of the Group's industries. Lily Ladjevardian said, 'In 1974, I was the first female from the fourth generation of the family to return to Iran, after graduating in economics in the United States. I asked my father if he had a job for me. He told me to go to one of the textile companies and start work.'[73] Masoud Ladjevardian also mentioned,

> My father wanted us to start work as soon as possible. Our education was important to him. But he did not want us to waste our summers. Until 1979, the year of the revolution, when I was twenty-one years old, I spent seven summers working at different companies of the Behshahr Industrial Group. During the first summer, I worked under the guidance of Mr Zarandi in the Tehran Bazaar to learn how he carried out purchasing.[74]

Lily Ladjevardian added, 'In our family, there was no discrimination among boys and girls, and the family cared about sports as well as education. My aunts were quite veiled, but they worked and had financial responsibilities.'[75]

Political unrest and nationalization

In 1978, as political unrest began to spread, workers made various demands, including wage increases. But the government did not allow industry owners to raise prices.[76] In the first months of the 1979 Revolution, leftist groups exerted a significant influence on workers, inciting them to strike and seize control of factories and workplaces. They also pressured the provisional government of Prime Minister Mehdi Bazargan to take control of industries by nationalization. Against this backdrop, leading business owners met with Ayatollah Khomeini to try to hold on to their positions. Some members of the Chamber of Commerce also went to see Abol Hassan Bani Sadr, who was known as 'the economic theorist of the revolution'.[77] Akbar Ladjevardian said:

> We met with Mr. Khomeini twice: in Tehran and Qom. In Qom, we introduced ourselves and said that we were businessmen. He said, 'We have no intention of taking over your industries.' He told us to go and carry on with our work. Later, Mr. Matin [a member of the Chamber of Commerce] suggested that we meet with Mr. Bani Sadr. We met him at his sister's house. Mr. Bani Sadr told us that Iranian factories were low-value assembly units and should be destroyed. I asked, 'Have you seen any Iranian factories so far?' He said that he had studied Iranian industries in France. I asked, 'Are Iran's textile industries assembly units?' He said, 'Yes, they even import dyes from overseas.' I told him that dyes and colouring account for only 4 per cent of the total price of fabric. I added, 'If I were you, I would spend twenty days visiting plants, and then express my opinion.' He then left the meeting.[78]

During the period of instability in the early days of the revolution, arbitrary groups threatened leading businessmen. For example, one such group occupied the house of Haj Seyyed Mahmoud Ladjevardi, claiming that it was too big for him, and that one floor was sufficient. Others tried to occupy the house of Akbar Ladjevardian.[79] On one such day, when Mr Ladjevardian was no longer going to his office, he received a letter from the Revolutionary Prosecutor's Office with a summons to answer questions. After several questions, the revolutionary prosecutor finally asked, 'How did you become so wealthy?' Mr Ladjevardian responded by saying: 'You can also become wealthy. There are only three conditions. The first condition is to have patience. The second condition is to have perseverance. The third condition is to have average intelligence.' He added, 'My paternal uncle started the family business in 1868. Then, my father continued the business. My elder brother, my nephews and I were managing the family business. By 1979, we had spent one hundred and ten years developing our business.'[80]

But the pressure on the private sector increased to such levels that, in June 1979, the provisional government nationalized private sector banks, and the following month, large industrial and business conglomerates, including the Behshahr Industrial Group, were nationalized under the Industrial Protection Law.[81] In response to these extreme measures, Akbar Ladjevardian met with Prime Minister Bazargan's adviser, Dr Sahabi, who had known Dr Banijamali from his student days. During this meeting, as he recalled, 'We asked him why the companies had been nationalized. Dr. Sahabi had known us since before the revolution.' However, the latter replied, 'You are right. In a revolution, saints and sinners suffer alike. I am aware of your achievements, but this is a revolution.' Mr. Ladjevardian then told him, 'now that the businesses have been nationalized, at least we should be told what we had done wrong.'[82]

Concerning the consequences of this law, Nasser Shahinpar has expressed the view that:

> Nationalization completely stopped the growth of the industrial sector in Iran. Contrary to many leftists' claims that Iran's industries were low-value assembly operations and dependent on imported parts, there were in fact emerging industries that were growing rapidly. Even if a plant depended on imported machinery and raw materials, the share of domestic content was actually increasing at a fast rate. For example, in the textile sector, the family set up Polyacryl, the polyester and acrylic fibre-making plant, which was among the largest and technologically most advanced manufacturing facilities at the time. As Polyacryl's fibre production reduced the need for imported fibre, it effectively increased the local content for the textile industry as a whole.[83]

Yet the leftist forces were not satisfied with the confiscation of personal property and the nationalization of private industries. They also wanted to eliminate the country's industrial entrepreneurs. In such an environment, on the morning of 8 August 1979, Ahmad Ladjevardi was wounded in an assassination attempt by the Forqan Group. The *Financial Times* of London wrote that this assassination attempt had completely discouraged investors from working further in Iran. Although the attack had been carried out by the Forqan Group, which followed Dr Ali Shariati's ideas,[84] the targeting of entrepreneurs had started a few years earlier, when Bijan Jazani, one of the leaders of the Fedai Organization, had written the pamphlet *Armed Struggle*. Its first victim was Mohammad Fateh Yazdi, a well-known businessman, in August 1974.[85]

By the 1990s, after the end of the eight-year Iran-Iraq War, Iranian economic officials would try to bring back former leading entrepreneurs to invest in Iran. At meetings overseas, the officials were often asked what guarantee they could give to protect the life and limb of a returning entrepreneur. It was clear that the assassination attempt on Ahmad Ladjevardi had left an enduring impression on Iranian expatriate businesspeople. According to the Industrial Protection Law of July 1979, in addition to confiscating the property and assets of many business families, the possibility of their return to economic activity in Iran was prohibited. As a result, these families, like other entrepreneurs, moved to the highly competitive environment of Western countries and, despite the challenges, achieved notable successes in business and industry.

The nationalization of industries caused irreparable damage to the national economy. A number of manufacturing companies ceased operations and were closed. However, the Behshahr Industrial Group continued to operate, and even during the coronavirus pandemic that began in 2020, the Group's companies manufactured healthcare products, thanks to the infrastructure that this family had built for these industries. But if the Group's management had remained in their hands, it would have had the opportunity to gain access to more markets within the region and beyond. The managers of the Group were at their peak in terms of maturity and experience. They also had trained several layers of professional managers. They exported products to the Persian Gulf region and neighbouring countries and could have easily expanded the reach of their exports further afield. Some even believe that the Group could have had a manufacturing presence in other countries. Thus, just as the Behshahr Industrial Group would act as a sales agent in Iran for a foreign company, firms in other countries could have acted as sales agents for the Group.[86]

Notes

1 I am grateful for the editing of an earlier text of this chapter, which was prepared firstly for a family documentary by Saeid Ladjevardi. I also wish to thank Dr Hassan Jamali-Nik and Fereydon Shirinkam, who kindly assisted me, and Dr Mary Yoshinari for reading the manuscript and providing excellent editing, which has improved the chapter's structure. But I alone am responsible for the views expressed here.

2 Ramona K. Zachary, 'The Importance of the Family System in Family Business', *Journal of Family Business Management* 1, no. 1 (2011): 26–36, passim.

3 For more on merchant ethics, see Purnama Putra and Tjiptohadi Sawarjuwono, 'Traditional Market Merchant Attitudes in the Perspective of Islamic Business Ethics', *Opción: Revista de Ciencias Humanas y Sociales* 35, no. 20 (2019): 1471–87.

4 Established in 1959, the International Bank of Iran and Japan was the only such financial institution in which a family was its largest shareholder. See 'The International Bank of Iran and Japan' (*A World Financial Survey*), *The Economist* (14 December 1974): 94. For more on Hafez Insurance Company, see *Ettelaat*, no. 14537 (28 Mehr 1353/20 October 1974): 8.

5 *Mahnameh-ye Goruh-ye Sanati-ye Behshahr*, various issues (1348–1354/1969–1975); Ali A. Saeidi and Fereydoun Shirinkam, *Mowqeiyyat-e Tojjar va Saheban-e Sanaye dar Iran-e Asr-e Pahlavi: Sarmayehdari-ye Khanevadegi-ye Khandan-e Lajevardi va Lajevardian* (Tehran: Gam-e No, 1395/2016), 139–70; 'The Behshahr Industrial Group', *The Times* (22 May 1973): 1.

6 Haj Seyyed Akbar Ladjevardian (Co-Founder, Behshahr Industrial Group, 1944–79), interview by Ali Asghar Saeidi, April 2015, Houston, USA.

7 For more on the structure of the bazaars and social roles of bazaaris, see W. M. Floor, 'The Merchants (*tujjar*) in Qajar Iran', *Zeitschrift der Deutschen Morgenlandischen Gesellschaft* 126, no. 1 (1976): 105; W. M. Floor, 'The Guilds in Iran – an Overview from the Earliest Beginnings till 1972', *Zeitschrift der Deutschen Morgenlandischen Gesellschaft* 125, no. one (1975): 99–116, passim. For their political role, see Gad G. Gilbar, 'The Big Merchants (tujjar) and the Persian Constitutional Revolution of 1906', *Asian and African Studies* 11, no. 3 (1977): 275–303, passim.

8 Manouchehr Farhang, *Zendegi-ye Haj Seyyed Mahmud Lajevardi* (Tehran: n.p., 1353 (1974)), 12–25.

9 Haj Seyyed Akbar Ladjevardian, interview.

10 Farhang, *Zendegi*, 44–5.

11 Ibid., 30–5.

12 Ibid., 50–56.

13 Institute for Iranian Contemporary Historical Studies, L-117-3-78, 'Asnad-e Khosusi-ye Lajevardi'.

14 Farhang, *Zendegi*, 1–40.

15 Ahmad Ladjevardi, 'Memoirs of Ahmad Ladjevardi' (unpublished manuscript, October 2003), 53–5. For more on the role of foreign offices' access to international markets, see Henry Wai-Chung Yeung, Jessie Poon and Martin Perry, 'Towards a Regional Strategy: The Role of Regional Headquarters of Foreign Firms in Singapore', *Urban Studies* 38, no. 1 (2001): 157–83, passim.

16 Ladjevardi, 'Memoirs', 53–5; Farhang, *Zendegi*, 66–8.

17 For more on shifting from trade to industry, see James A. Brander, 'Rationales for Strategic Trade and Industrial Policy', in *Strategic Trade Policy and the New*

International Economics, ed. Paul R. Krugman (Cambridge, MA: MIT Press, 1986), 23–45, passim.

18 Haj Seyyed Akbar Ladjevardian, interview; Akbar Ladjevardian, *Sad o Dah Sal: Peydayesh va Gostaresh-e Goruh-ye Sanati-ye Behshahr, Khatirat-e Akbar Lajevardian* (Tehran: Lohe Fekr, 1396/2017), 129–33.

19 Ladjevardi, 'Memoirs', 53.

20 For more on Habib Elghanian, see Abbas Milani, *Eminent Persians: The Men and Women Who Made Modern Iran, 1941–1979*, vol. 2 (Syracuse: Syracuse University Press, 2008), 615–21.

21 Ladjevardian, *Sad o Dah Sal*, 169.

22 Concerning the labour movement's impact on the private sector, see Habib Ladjevardi, *Labor Unions and Autocracy in Iran* (Syracuse: Syracuse University Press, 1985), passim.

23 Ladjevardian, *Sad o Dah Sal*, 170.

24 Ladjevardi, 'Memoirs', 54.

25 Ladjevardian, *Sad o Dah Sal*, 171. See also *Ettelaat*, no. 9199 (29 Azar 1335/20 December 1956): 12. Customers voted 16,733 in favour of Shahpasand versus 4,204 for Gol Ladan.

26 Regarding the vegetable oil factories, see National Library and Archives of Iran (NLAI), 'Gozaresh va Pishnahad-e Modir-e Amel beh Heyat-e Amel: Sherkat-e Sahami-ye Khass-e Sanati-ye Behshahr', no. 956 (Tehran: Bank-e Towseeh-ye Sanati va Madani-ye Iran, 1356/1977), 16, http://opac.nlai.ir/opac-prod/bibliographic/2473933. Facopa Advertising Company, managed by Farhad Hormozi, carried out these ad campaigns. See also Ladjevardian, *Sad o Dah Sal*, 171; *Ettelaat*, no. 9187 (15 Azar 1335/6 December 1956): 2; *Ettelaat*, no. 9189 (18 Azar 1335/9 December 1956): 4; *Ettelaat*, no. 10379 (16 Azar 1339/7 December 1960): 20.

27 The competition between Behshahr and Pars, who produced Shahpasand and Ghoo, reached its peak in late 1959. Their controversial newspaper ads criticized each other's products. These ad campaigns evidently took up much of their managers' time. See *Ettelaat*, no. 10095 (1 Dey 1338/23 December 1959): 1, 18; *Ettelaat*, no. 10096 (2 Dey 1338/24 December 1959): 14, 16, 18.

28 For more on the vegetable oil factories' market share, see NLAI, 'Gozaresh va Pishnahad-e Modir-e Amel beh Heyat-e Amel', 16.

29 Haj Seyyed Akbar Ladjevardian, interview.

30 Mohammad Tafsiri, interview by Ali Asghar Saeidi, April 2002, Tehran, Iran. He was then promoted to CEO of Behpakhsh Co. Ltd.

31 Haj Seyyed Akbar Ladjevardian, interview.

32 Hossein Mokhtari (Co-Founder, Paxan Corporation, 1961–79), interview by Ali Asghar Saeidi, April 2001 and August 2016, Los Angeles, USA.

33 Ladjevardian, *Sad o Dah Sal*, 186.

34 *Ettelaat*, no. 11366 (31 Farvardin 1343/20 April 1964): 1, 12 and 20.

35 Hossein Mokhtari, interview. For more on Hormozi, see Najibeh Rahmani and Sara Sadeghinia, 'Tahlil-e Karkard-e Fan-e Eqna dar Karzarha-ye Tablighati-ye Fakopa', *Majalleh-ye Jahani-ye Resaneh* 15, no. 30 (1399/2020): 79–105, passim. On advertising, see also *Ettelaat*, no. 11385 (23 Ordibehesht 1343/ 13 May 1964): 8.

36 For more on Hormozi's ideas, see Philip H. Dougherty, 'Advertising: Unlocking the Key to Hormozi', *The New York Times* (4 March 1970): 72.

37 For more on this topic, see Martin K. Perry, 'Vertical Integration: Determinants and Effects', in *Handbook of Industrial Organization*, vol. 1, ed. Richard Schmalensee and Robert Willig (Amsterdam: North Holland, 1989), 183–255, passim.

38 Haj Seyyed Akbar Ladjevardian, interview.
39 For more on the Ministry of Economy, see Vali Nasr, 'Politics within the Late-Pahlavi State: The Ministry of Economy and Industrial Policy, 1963–69', *International Journal of Middle East Studies* 32, no. 1 (2000): 97–122, passim.
40 Magdiel Pérez-Lara et al., 'Vertical and Horizontal Integration Systems in Industry 4.0', *Wireless Networks* 26, no. 7 (2020): 4767–75, passim.
41 Ladjevardian, *Sad o Dah Sal*, 297; G. C. Bricault, *Major Companies of Iran, 1978/1979* (London: Graham & Trotman, 1978), 26, 79, 91 and 110.
42 Haj Seyyed Akbar Ladjevardian, interview. See also *Financial Times* (21 July 1977): 28.
43 Haj Seyyed Akbar Ladjevardian, interview.
44 Ladjevardian, *Sad o Dah Sal*, 224.
45 Akbar Hosseinzadeh (Managing Director, Kashan Velvet and Rayon Mills Ltd., 1963–79), interview by Ali Asghar Saeidi, July 2017, Los Angeles, USA.
46 Ibid.
47 Ehsan Anoushahr (Managing Director, Arak Industries Corp., 1967–79), interview by Ali Asghar Saeidi, November 2017, Tehran, Iran.
48 Ladjevardian, *Sad o Dah Sal*, 228.
49 Lily Ladjevardian (Director, Behpush Co. Ltd., 1975–79), interview by Ali Asghar Saeidi, April 2015, Houston, USA.
50 'Polyacryl Iran Corporation', *The Economist* (8 October 1977): 59; 'Tasis-e Vahed-e Azim-e Sanati: Tahiyyeh-ye Alyaf-e Masnui', *Ettelaat*, no. 14360 (29 Esfand 1352/20 March 1974): 1.
51 Ladjevardian, *Sad o Dah Sal*, 232.
52 Ibid.
53 Ibid., 233.
54 Haj Seyyed Akbar Ladjevardian, interview.
55 Our Own Correspondent, 'Work Starting on Iran's First Fibre Plant', *Financial Times* (16 August 1974): 4; Eric Pace, 'Cost of Joint Effort Held at Half Billion', *The New York Times* (6 September 1975): 27.
56 For more on this project, see Daneshjuyan-e Mosalman-e Perow-ye Khatt-e Emam, *Asnad-e Laneh-ye Jasusi: Dekhalatha-ye Amerika dar Iran*, vol. 1 (Tehran: Markaz-e Neshar-e Asnad-e Laneh-ye Jasusi-ye Amerika, 1366/1987), 243–5; Regina Lee Blaszczyk, 'Synthetics for the Shah: DuPont and the Challenges to Multinationals in 1970s Iran', *Enterprise & Society* 9, no. 4 (2008): 675.
57 Haj Seyyed Akbar Ladjevardian, interview.
58 Ibid.
59 Massoud Ladjevardian (CEO, Novo Industries, Houston, 1988–97), interview by Ali Asghar Saeidi, April 2015, Houston, USA.
60 Ali Ladjevardi (Managing Director, Iran Steel Buildings Corp., 1974–79), interview by Ali Asghar Saeidi, September 2014, Tehran, Iran, and 1998, London, UK.
61 Ahmad Ghaznavi (Head of Administration, Tehran Works, Behshahr Industrial Co. Ltd., 1964–83), interview by Ali Asghar Saeidi, November 2017, Tehran, Iran.
62 Ebrahim Samani-Nejad (Employee, Distribution Group, Behpakhsh Co. Ltd., 1975–94), interview by Ali Asghar Saeidi, November 2017, Tehran, Iran.
63 Davud Aghili (Messenger, Behshahr Industrial Co. Ltd., 1971–80), interview by Ali Asghar Saeidi, November 2017, Tehran, Iran.
64 Mohammad Hossein Keyhan Falsafi (Marketing Analyst, Paxan Corp., 1968–83), interview by Ali Asghar Saeidi, September 2014, Tehran, Iran.
65 Ebrahim Samani-Nejad, interview.

66 Ahmad Nahid (Head of Administration, Behshahr Industrial Group, 1974–85), interview by Ali Asghar Saeidi, September 2014, Tehran, Iran.
67 Mohammad Reza Maashouri, Finance Manager, Behpakhsh Co. Ltd. 1968–76, Tehran, September 2014.
68 Haj Seyyed Akbar Ladjevardian, interview.
69 Nasser Shahinpar (Head of Advertising & Export Planning, Behshahr Industrial Group, 1964–79), interview by Ali Asghar Saeidi, July 2017, Los Angeles, USA.
70 Hassan Bassak, Soghra Moradiyan and Esmaeil Hoseynpoor, 'Tahlil-e Armangerayi-ye Melli-Siyasi va Nasiyonalism-e Enqelabi dar Ashar-e Siavash Kasrayi ba Takid bar Moallefehha-ye Maktab-e Romantism-e Ejtemaei', *Pazhuheshnameh-ye Maktabha-ye Adabi* 3, no. 5 (2019): 111–28; *Kamyar Abedi,* 'Kasrai, Siavash', in *Encyclopaedia Iranica Online*, accessed 21 September 2023, https://iranicaonline.org/articles/kasrai-siavash-marxist-poet.
71 Mohammad Hossein Keyhan Falsafi, interview.
72 Nasser Shahinpar, interview.
73 Lily Ladjevardian, interview.
74 Massoud Ladjevardian, interview.
75 Lily Ladjevardian, interview.
76 Ladjevardian, *Sad o Dah Sal*, 251–2; *Tehran Ekonomist*, no. 1188 (13 April 1977): 39–40. Ghassem Ladjevardi, elected to the Senate in 1975, had criticized state policies on taxation, price control and the unilateral freezing of workers' wages in the 1977 budget proposal.
77 Ladjevardian, *Sad o Dah Sal*, 256.
78 Haj Seyyed Akbar Ladjevardian, interview.
79 Ibid.
80 Ibid. See also 'Behshahr Industrial Group', *The Times* (6 May 1977): 5.
81 *Keyhan*, no. 10751 (16 Tir 1358/7 July 1979): 1; *Ayandegan*, no. 3394 (16 Tir 1358/7 July 1979): 1–2.
82 Haj Seyyed Akbar Ladjevardian, interview.
83 Nasser Shahinpar, interview.
84 Ali Kordi, *Goruh-ye Forqan* (Tehran: Markaz-e Asnad-e Enqelab-e Eslami, 1387/2008), 35–6.
85 Peyman Vahabzadeh, *A Guerrilla Odyssey: Modernization, Secularism, Democracy, and the Fadai Period of National Liberation in Iran, 1971–1979* (Syracuse: Syracuse University Press, 2010), 10.
86 After the nationalization of the Behshahr Industrial Group and the confiscation of his property and assets, Haj Seyyed Mahmoud Ladjevardi remained in Iran until September 1984. He then went to the United States for cancer treatment, where he died in 1985. After trying to regain the Behshahr Group, Haj Seyyed Akbar Ladjevardian went to the United States in 1980, where he led the turnaround of Intamix Corp and founded Novo Industries. He died in Houston in 2023, aged ninety-nine. Ahmad Ladjevardi travelled to the United States to continue medical treatment after being severely injured in the Forqan Group's assassination attempt in August 1979. He died in Canada in 2009, at the age of eighty-nine. After emigrating to the United States, Ghassem Ladjevardi continued his civic activities as founder and board member of several Iranian community associations. He died there in 2011, at the age of eighty-nine. After receiving his doctorate from the University of Oxford, Habib Ladjevardi initiated and led the Iranian Oral History Project at Harvard University, beginning in 1981. Over the next twelve years, he and his team interviewed 132

political, economic, diplomatic and cultural figures who had played important roles in Iran during the 1920s–70s. The interviews can be accessed on the Iranian Oral History Project website. He died in the United States in 2021, at the age of eighty-three.

Bibliography

Archives and libraries

Institute for Iranian Contemporary Historical Studies, Tehran
Iranian Oral History Project, Harvard University
National Library and Archives of Iran, Tehran

Periodicals

Āyandegān
Ettelā ʿāt
Financial Times
Keyhān
Māhnāmeh-ye Goruh-ye San ʿati-ye Behshahr
Tehrān Ekonomist
The Economist
The New York Times
The Times

Secondary sources

Azimi, Fakhreddin. *Iran: The Crisis of Democracy, 1941–1953*. London: I.B. Tauris, 1989.
Bassak, Hassan, Soghra Moradiyan and Esmaeil Hoseynpoor. 'Tahlil-e Ārmāngerāyi-ye Melli-Siyāsi va Nāsiyonālism-e Enqelābi dar Ash ʿār-e Siāvash Kasrāyi ba Tākid bar Moallefehhā-ye Maktab-e Romāntism-e Ejtemā ʿi'. *Pazhuheshnameh-ye Maktabha-ye Adabi* 3, no. 5 (1398/2019): 111–28.
Blaszczyk, Regina Lee. 'Synthetics for the Shah: DuPont and the Challenges to Multinationals in 1970s Iran'. *Enterprise & Society* 9, no. 4 (2008): 670–723.
Brander, James A. 'Rationales for Strategic Trade and Industrial Policy'. In *Strategic Trade Policy and the New International Economics*, edited by Paul R. Krugman, 23–45. Cambridge, MA: MIT Press, 1986.
Bricault, G. C. *Major Companies of Iran, 1978/1979*. London: Graham & Trotman, 1978.
Daneshjuyan-e Mosalman-e Perow-ye Khatt-e Emam. *Asnād-e Lāneh-ye Jāsusi: Dekhālathā-ye Āmerikā dar Irān*. Vol. 1. Tehran: Markaz-e Neshar-e Asnad-e Laneh-ye Jasusi-ye Amerika, 1366 (1987).
Farhang, Manouchehr. *Zendegi-ye Hāj Seyyed Mahmud Lājevardi*. Tehran: n.p., 1353 (1974).
Floor, W. M. 'The Guilds in Iran – an Overview from the Earliest Beginnings till 1972'. *Zeitschrift der Deutschen Morgenländischen Gesellschaft* 125, no. 1 (1975): 99–116.
Floor, W. M. 'The Merchants (*tujjār*) in Qājār Iran'. *Zeitschrift der Deutschen Morgenländischen Gesellschaft* 126, no. 1 (1976): 101–35.

Gilbar, Gad G. 'The Big Merchants (*tujjār*) and the Persian Constitutional Revolution of 1906'. *Asian and African Studies* 11, no. 3 (1977): 275–303.
Kordi, Ali. *Goruh-ye Forqān*. Tehran: Markaz-e Asnad-e Enqelab-e Eslami, 1387 (2008).
Ladjevardi, Habib. *Labor Unions and Autocracy in Iran*. Syracuse: Syracuse University Press, 1985.
Ladjevardian, Akbar. *Sad o Dah Sāl: Peydāyesh va Gostaresh-e Goruh-ye San'ati-ye Behshahr, Khātirāt-e Akbar Lājevardiān*. Tehran: Lohe Fekr, 1396 (2017).
Milani, Abbas. *Eminent Persians: The Men and Women Who Made Modern Iran, 1941–1979*. Vol. 2. Syracuse: Syracuse University Press, 2008.
Nasr, Vali. 'Politics within the Late-Pahlavi State: The Ministry of Economy and Industrial Policy, 1963–69'. *International Journal of Middle East Studies* 32, no. 1 (2000): 97–122.
Pérez-Lara, Magdiel, Jania Astrid Saucedo-Martínez, José Antonio Marmolejo-Saucedo, Tomás Eloy Salais-Fierro and Pandian Vasant. 'Vertical and Horizontal Integration Systems in Industry 4.0'. *Wireless Networks* 26, no. 7 (2020): 4767–75.
Perry, Martin K. 'Vertical Integration: Determinants and Effects'. In *Handbook of Industrial Organization*, edited by Richard Schmalensee and Robert Willig, 183–255. Vol. 1. Amsterdam: North Holland, 1989.
Putra, Purnama and Tjiptohadi Sawarjuwono. 'Traditional Market Merchant Attitudes in the Perspective of Islamic Business Ethics'. *Opción: Revista de Ciencias Humanas y Sociales* 35, no. 20 (2019): 1471–87.
Rahmani, Najibeh and Sara Sadeghinia. 'Tahlil-e Kārkard-e Fan-e 'Eqnā' dar Kārzārhā-ye Tablighāti-ye Fākopā'. *Majalleh-ye Jahani-ye Resaneh* 15, no. 30 (1399/2020): 79–105.
Saeidi, Ali A. and Fereydoun Shirinkam. *Mowqe'iyyat-e Tojjār va Sāhebān-e Sanāye' dar Irān-e 'Asr-e Pahlavi: Sarmāyehdāri-ye Khānevādegi-ye Khāndān-e Lājevardi va Lājevardiān*. Tehran: Gam-e No, 1395 (2016).
Vahabzadeh, Peyman. *A Guerrilla Odyssey: Modernization, Secularism, Democracy, and the Fadai Period of National Liberation in Iran, 1971–1979*. Syracuse: Syracuse University Press, 2010.
Yeung, Henry Wai-Chung, Jessie Poon and Martin Perry. 'Towards a Regional Strategy: The Role of Regional Headquarters of Foreign Firms in Singapore'. *Urban Studies* 38, no. 1 (2001): 157–83.
Zachary, Ramona K. 'The Importance of the Family System in Family Business'. *Journal of Family Business Management* 1, no. 1 (2011): 26–36.

13

A pious lumbermill worker in Rasht and the impact of labour laws, 1920s–70s

Majid Saeli Kordehdeh

Preface

In this chapter,[1] I attempt to examine labour laws passed before the establishment of the Islamic Republic in Iran, while considering the working conditions of my father, Hassan Saeli Kordehdeh (hereafter, referred to as Hassan). Hassan was born in 1925, the same year that Reza Khan came to power and declared the Pahlavi dynasty in Iran, marking the end of the Qajar era. Interestingly, they both resided in the Caspian region at different points in time, although they were on opposite ends of the socio-economic ladder. Hence, Hassan grew up during a time of rapid economic modernization, which included the major urban centres of northern Iran, such as Rasht. A few decades later, he reached adulthood during the Allied occupation of the Second World War and began working in the prime of his life from the wartime period onwards until the post-revolutionary years. Rather than being displaced from his traditional agricultural lifestyle by economic modernization, this man lost his inherited property due to a family rivalry in his birthplace, Maragheh. Left without resources, he migrated to Rasht as a young man and married a Gilaki woman. Thus, he became a worker in the new tea and lumber industries of Gilan province.

History of labour laws in Iran

In Iran, at the same time as the advent of the new era, and beginning of industrialization during the reign of Reza Shah, the long-standing relations between the worker and the employer underwent fundamental changes. The private aspect of this relationship decreased and the public aspect and the government's involvement in regulating this relationship increased. Labour, social and political movements, Mohammad Reza Shah and 'the People's Revolution' (i.e. the White Revolution or Enqelab-e Sefid) and the growth of collective consciousness and wisdom of Iranians have had many effects on the formation of labour laws in Iran.

It was after the impressive development of modern factories and industrial enterprises in the 1930s that the issue of labour rights and the protection of workers' rights was raised against employers and industrial owners, who had a lot of economic power. It should be said that the approval of the initial labour law and its subsequent changes have had many ups and downs, which were directly related to labour movements and economic and social development in Iran. The occupation of Iran by the Allied powers in August 1941 had a lot of negative effects on the welfare and economic situation of workers, which had not yet been stabilized, and created a critical and unstable period in the relations between worker and employer, which continued until 1946.

When the Allies invaded Iran, my father was a sixteen-year-old teenager, who was shepherding in a village called Kordehdeh, located on Mount Sahand, near Maragheh, East Azerbaijan Province. My father explained that Soviet soldiers used to come and go to his village, and he even once looked into the distance and at the surrounding mountains with a Russian soldier's military camera, which surprised him, because he could see all the distant mountains and valleys as if they were near him.

Many economic, civil and construction activities were stopped or greatly reduced during this period. Hence, many workers became unemployed and were looking for jobs. Therefore, employers could easily and simply impose their terms and conditions on workers. In order not to be fired from their jobs, workers endured every cruel and unfair situation. Terrible and unprecedented inflation had started in Iran, but employers did not increase the wages of their workers. The majority of employers also did not bother to raise workers' awareness of their fundamental rights.

Due to the exile of Reza Shah in 1941, an open and free political space had been created. Marxist and other leftist parties and groups used this historical opportunity and strongly increased their activities and encouraged and incited workers to strike and protest. There were widespread strikes and protests in some areas of Iran, such as Isfahan, Khuzestan, Mazandaran, Yazd, Shiraz, Qom and Qazvin, some of which were bloody. Many of the founders of Iran's Tudeh Party were from Rasht and Gilan, as well. However, I do not know if the Tudeh Party or any other leftist groups were able to mobilize workers in Rasht.

Therefore, in order to establish political stability and order, the government was forced to create stability in the relations between workers and employers and regulate their relationship. In short, it can be said that in November 1944, an independent department, the General Department of Labour (Edareh-ye Kol-e Kar), was established in the Ministry of Commerce, Trades and Crafts (Vezarat-e Bazargani va Pisheh va Honar) and was assigned to deal with complaints and settle disputes between workers and employers. This general department dealt with disputes in factories, mining, shipping and construction institutions.

In order to formulate the first labour law, a commission composed of government experts and representatives of the Central United Council of Workers and Toilers' Unions (Showra-ye Mottahedeh-ye Markazi-ye Ettehadiyyehha-ye Kargaran va Zahmatkeshan) of Iran, affiliated with Marxists, other leftists and the Tudeh Party (Hezb-e Tudeh) of Iran, was formed. According to the political and social conditions, and inspired by the conference of the International Labour Organization in 1945, the aforesaid commission prepared a draft of the labour bill and presented it to the

Fourteenth National Consultative Assembly (Majles-e Showra-ye Melli or Iranian Parliament). Before this bill could be approved, the term of the Fourteenth Majles ended, and the interregnum until the election of the Fifteenth Majles lasted from 12 March 1946 to 29 July 1947. However, due to social pressures caused by frequent labour strikes and protests, the Council of Ministers (Cabinet) approved the labour law bill with amendments on 18 May 1946.[2]

In such a critical domestic situation, Hassan left his small rural world and migrated to a big urban hub when he was nineteen years old. He was neither literate, nor did he know the Persian or Gilaki languages, nor did he have any information or knowledge about the social and political situation of the country and the labour movements. The only thing he knew was that Reza Shah was gone and his son Mohammad Reza had become the Shah of Iran. At that time, there were no large industrial factories in Gilan and Rasht due to the vastness of the forest, large rice fields and tea gardens. Most of the economic enterprises and workplaces were small. Perhaps for this reason, there did not appear to be any labour unions and labour movements active in Rasht between 1941 and 1946, and in this sense, Rasht was a relatively peaceful city, where employers faced fewer obstacles in violating workers' rights.

The General Department of Labour was unable to fully implement the 1946 Labour Law, and, on 4 August 1946, it was separated from the Ministry of Commerce, Trades and Crafts, becoming the Ministry of Labour and Publicity. This new ministry, in cooperation with the International Labour Organization's office in Iran, submitted a bill updating the labour law to the Parliament. After being reviewed by its Trades, Crafts and Commerce Commission, the Parliament finally approved this bill on 7 June 1949.[3] However, the 1949 Labour Law did not meet the expectations of the labour movement's leadership, since it did not protect the rights of workers against employers. Therefore, it had to be amended again. The Iranian government, in cooperation with the International Labour Organization's experts, proposed a new bill, which was eventually approved by a joint commission of the Parliament and the Senate on 17 March 1959.[4] The 1959 Labour Law was valid for thirty-two years, that is, until 5 March 1991.

My father's character and views

My father started working a few years before the 1953 coup d'état. Sometimes he told us about Mohammad Mossadegh, which was very interesting! I can remember what he said about him: 'The Iranian people are unfaithful. Before noon, they chanted greetings to Mossadegh, and in the afternoon, they said "death to Mossadegh".' It is very interesting that his working years spanned three different governments in Iran. If he had been literate and read books and newspapers, he would have understood the conditions of his time better and could have even written his own memoirs. He was working in the lumbermill during the war in the 1980s. He always criticized the Iran-Iraq War and said that eventually the two countries would make peace, so it was better that they made peace as soon as possible. He also said to my older brother, who wanted to go to the battlefield: 'as long as there is Islam, there is war'.

Basically, he was not a traveller. He did not like travelling very much. As far as I know, he only went to Mashhad twice to visit Imam Reza's shrine in 1966 and 1985. Maybe the reason was that he had already left Maragheh and came to Rasht. He also did not change his job at the lumbermill and was unwilling to take risks to improve his economic situation. For this reason, he did not complain to his boss or the government about his working conditions, and he never joined a union. So, he always enjoyed a calm life. He used to go to the local mosque and listen to the ulema's lectures a lot. He used to say, 'I eat a plate of cooked rice, and the Shah also eats a plate of cooked rice. So, there is no difference between me and him.' Of course, he did not mean that he and the Shah were equals. He meant that they ate the same amount of food. So, he did not try to improve his economic situation. He did not know anything about the economy, but he liked to have enough money in his pocket. He was never afraid of the future because, at that time, the economy and prices were relatively stable. So, he did not need to know more about the economy, and his views were influenced by the stability of prices – which was a benefit of the Second Pahlavi period. This benefitted people's religious beliefs, too. In other words, they believed that God was providing a stable life for them.

Others read books, played sports, joined clubs, went to concerts and so on, but my father devoted his spare time to the local mosque. He did not even buy sandwiches for himself or us because he thought that they may contain pork. He considered all of these things forbidden (*harām*) during the Shah's period. We can say that his mentality and thoughts were shaped by communal religious life. He was so religious, and I have never heard that he complained to his boss or the government, or about his economic situation – his poverty and living conditions. He was a traditional religious person who firmly believed in divine destiny. He always told us the stories of the divine prophets and their patience. Marxists say that religion is the product of capitalism, but this is wrong because my father was poor but very religious. In Iran, the poor are more religious than the rich. In a sense, he was socially and politically conservative. He did not even allow my mother to buy a television, so she had to buy a black and white one secretly in 1971. Of course, she was punished by him for doing this. But later, he watched television, especially the news, more than any of us. I must add that he objected to the television for religious, not economic reasons.

He never passionately reacted to major domestic political events. He was not a political activist. For example, he did not participate in the demonstration against the Shah. One reason may have been that he had seen the experience of Mossadegh. He had an inner conflict. He had contradictory attitudes towards the Revolution. His conservative spirit did not allow him to play a role in the Islamic Revolution, but his religious sentiments agreed with its Islamic aspect. Although he was not active in the Revolution, he had a strong religious feeling and loved its Islamic leaders, especially Imam Khomeini.

The question that comes to mind is whether the Revolution brought any further material benefits to my father. I can say 'no, not at all'. In general, although our family was active in the Islamic Revolution, we did not benefit from it because we believed that God would reward us. We made the Revolution for the sake of God, not for material and economic gain and reward. After the victory of the Revolution, many houses and lands of great employers and capitalists in Rasht were confiscated. The Revolution officials even offered to give my father one of these plots of land or houses because he had been oppressed by the capitalists. But he did not accept their offer, and he said, 'these are usurped lands and houses, and my prayers and religious bathing in those houses and lands are void.' In conclusion, my father's ethics and views were largely based on his understanding of Islam, and he established definite political, economic and religious views – even without a formal education.

In terms of a work ethic, my father had a strong motivation for working. He loved to help his family, be useful to society and not be lazy. We can say that my father's 'work ethic' was influenced by his past losses, namely he tried to regain a stable economic position, like the one he had been born into. In general, he was looking for economic stability in his life. Economic stability was more important to him than the amount of salary he received or the wealth he had. That is why he never took a risk to increase his salary or accumulate more wealth. He preferred economic stability to making more money by taking risks. In this sense, he was quite conservative and not an entrepreneur at all.

My father's attitude towards work was based on his idea of what his family role should be, as well. He loved his wife and always advised her to be calm in life and protected her from dangers and threats. He valued work intrinsically. He always said that work is the essence of man: 'Man must work.' Of course, his religious views certainly had an influence on the formation of such a view towards work. Because in Islam, working, especially working for the family, is emphasized a lot, and he was a religious person. That said, he had started working when he was single. Also, he enjoyed his work and interactions with his co-workers but only in the workplace or outside the home, near the lumbermill. I think that he enjoyed this work and interactions with his co-workers. But his culture and religious values imposed some limitations on his relationships with his friends and colleagues. For example, he used to go to the mosque and listen to the sermons of the clerics, unlike his friends. I never saw him visit his friends' houses or invite them to his home for lunch or dinner. He did not smoke, drink alcohol or go to parties, but his friends and other co-workers did such things. Some of his friends made fun of him, saying 'You have deprived yourself of these pleasures, why were you born?'

My father never went to the seaside for fun because there were women wearing bathing suits without the hijab there. Also, he never went to the cinema, theatre, disco or cabaret, either. I never saw him dancing, and he never listened to songs or music. But he knew all kinds of whistles, more than ten types of whistling. With a small square piece of cloth that he used to dry his sweat, he made a puppet, for example, a rabbit. In this sense, he was an artist and I am always upset with myself that I did not learn this craft from him. He called it '*dowshan*' which means rabbit in the Azerbaijani language, and while moving this origami rabbit, he said: 'Gagushga, gagushga!!!' to make us happy. Sometimes he used to tell us traditional Azerbaijani stories or parables and sayings or the history of the prophets. He also spoke short words of wisdom from the corners of his life. He spoke Turkish fluently and eloquently. He was an exceptional man who was different in many ways from other people.

My father's work history

I think my father did not come to Rasht to establish a new family and circle of friends. Rather, he did not like his own village, and he saw his cousin's invitation to work in

Figure 13.1 Left to right: Hassan Saeli Kordehdeh with his co-workers, *c.* 1965. Family album.

Rasht as a good opportunity. At that time, Gilan province, and especially, Rasht, was one of the regions accepting migrants due to its favourable climatic, geographical and economic conditions, and many people came to Rasht permanently or temporarily to work because of the region's economic prosperity. A short time after migrating to Rasht, he started working in a tea factory, located in a village called Lakan, just south of the city.

At that time, a tea broker had many dealings with that factory. That is, he negotiated with the tea farmers and pre-purchased their products and then hired some workers to pick the tea leaves and take them to the tea factory for drying, the same factory where my father worked. After drying the teas, he sold or pre-sold them. It was in this factory that my father met the tea dealer. He was an entrepreneur and advocate of free enterprise who wanted to increase his profits. After my father had worked in the tea-drying factory for one year, the Labour Law of 1946 was approved. Then, three years later, in 1949, the second labour law was approved.

It is said that, in 1950, the tea dealer rented a large piece of land in Rasht's Naftanbar neighbourhood and invited six workers to saw wood. These workers were paid on a daily basis (*ruzmozd*) at the end of the working day or week. They were not paid on the days that the lumbermill was closed or were sick and could not come to work. One of those workers was my father. They cut the trunks of the trees into equal pieces, for example, 2 metres long, with big hand saws, and then cut these pieces lengthwise. Each of these pieces of timber was called lumber (*lambeh*). It was as if they were cutting cheese into portions of the same size. The work was very hard and laborious, especially in the hot and humid summers of Rasht. My father worked with other workers using a big hand saw until the employer became richer

Figure 13.2 Hassan Saeli Kordehdeh, *c.* 1965. Family album.

and bought the rented land in 1953, and shortly afterwards, some big bandsaw and surface planer machines.

His attention to job security

My father was always afraid of his employer firing him. In his mind, the employer was a great and imposing person. So, he always referred to him as 'lord' (*arbāb*). This word reminded me of feudalism and the unfair and unequal relationship between lords and vassals. He did not feel that he had any job security. Therefore, he did not risk looking for a new job with a higher income. He never protested to improve his working

Figure 13.3 Left: Hassan Saeli Kordehdeh working late in the lumbermill, *c.* 1965. Family album.

conditions. He was very cautious, and he did not want his job position and the welfare of his family to be jeopardized. The fear of loneliness and lack of money did not allow him to be rebellious and take risks.

He was separated from his family and his small village and had migrated to a big coastal city, where the culture, language and behaviour of its people were completely different from his hometown. His language was Turkish, and the language of the people of Rasht was a dialect of Persian, which was different from the Persian language of the people of Tehran, the capital. He did not know Persian – not to mention the Gilaki language! He had come from a rural, mountainous and simple culture, but Rasht was a relatively large, modern and historical city, bustling with economic and commercial activity.

Theft at the lumbermill

In 1973, there was a theft at the lumbermill. It happened when one of the most famous television series, 'Khaneh beh Dush' (Vagabond), was aired on Iranian national television at 9 pm. When this series was broadcast, almost all people went to their homes or neighbours who had televisions and watched this series together. In those years, people and neighbours were very kind and friendly to each other. They used to go to each other's houses to watch television or use the phone. Sometimes they went for lunch and dinner and even slept there for two or three nights. My father sometimes brought poor people home to have lunch, bathe and rest, especially at night, when they had no place to sleep, and my mother washed their dirty clothes. My father was accused of theft because only he and his family were on the premises that night.

They took my father to the intelligence department (police office). My father told us that 'the police wanted to fingerprint me. So, I was very scared, and that's why I decided to run away from the police station. Because I thought fingerprinting meant cutting off fingers. But after realizing that fingerprinting was a very easy task, I decided not to run away.' After filing the initial case, he was taken to court to be arraigned on a burglary charge. In the court, with his wife present, my father defended himself and said that he was a simple worker: 'At night, I went to bed early and fell into a deep sleep because of the fatigue caused by a lot of work. I only lived at the lumbermill, but I was not responsible for its property.' The judge accepted my father's defence. Because he realized that he was an honest and pious person and did not say anything other than the truth. Finally, after a few days, the thief was found. He was a relative of the employer. Hence, my father's truth was proven and the employer was ashamed of accusing him of theft. This story illustrates that my father was a pious man.

Buying a new house

In 1957, the employer had given Hassan and his family two rooms for living quarters in a small house on the lumbermill's premises. Gradually, as the children grew older and got to know new people, lifestyles and environments, especially my older sister, who was studying at the army nursing school in Tehran, they asked my parents to move out of these lodgings. But my father was against the idea of buying a new house. My father believed that, by living on the lumbermill's premises, we could reduce the cost of living. As mentioned, generally speaking, he was not a person open to development, progress and change. But my mother, who was a person of change and progress, considered these lodgings to be a form of humiliation for herself and her family and unworthy of our family's dignity and self-respect. So, finally, my father agreed to buy a new house. That is why my mother bought a new house in 1977 with the help of my older sister by going to work. The area of the house was about 75 square metres. It is an interesting coincidence that major life events, such as the birth of my father and purchase of our home, happened at about the same time as major political events in Iran.

Applying labour laws to my father's working conditions

Being an uneducated and unskilled worker, my father was unaware of the labour laws and the rights they imparted to workers. He also never tried to become literate or learn about these laws. Labour relations were mostly private and personal rather than public and national. The employer did not treat the workers, including my father, in accordance with the labour laws and always paid him less than the wages stipulated in them. In 1959, the third and most important labour law was approved by the Parliament. But the employer did not pay attention to this law, either. Rather, he tried his best to give the workers the minimum privileges and salaries envisioned in the labour law. However, the government gradually expanded its involvement in dealing with small private enterprises because it was the main engine of development in Iran. Development was not possible without political and social stability, and the stability of the society depended on the improvement of working conditions. Furthermore, the government did not want the workers to develop leftist tendencies, and thus increase the Soviet Union's influence in Iran, and, likewise, the activities of human rights organizations, especially the International Labour Organization, had increasingly drawn the international community's attention to human rights issues and workers' rights. Hence, the Labour Ministry's inspectors regularly visited the lumbermill between 1966 and 1970 to check and inspect its compliance with the 1959 Labour Law's regulations and standards.

Working hours and overtime work

According to Article 4 of the 1946 law, forty-eight working hours was the maximum per week, which meant eight hours a day. The employer did not have the right to ask for overtime work on Fridays and official holidays without the worker's consent. If the worker agreed, the employer was to pay 35 per cent more than the normal wage. In any case, the total was not to exceed twelve hours of work a day, including eight hours per night, between 10 pm and 6 am. The second article of the 1949 law contained the same provisions, except that the overtime wages were to be at least 25 per cent more than the normal wages. The eleventh article of the 1959 law had the same provisions, but it reinstated the overtime rate of 35 per cent on top of normal wages. Unlike the 1946 law, the 1949 and 1959 laws did not consider rest and meal times to be working hours, which disadvantaged the worker. In this way, the employer could increase his bargaining power and give the worker less pay.

It seems unlikely that these regulations were followed while my father was working in the tea factory, especially since the amount of work increased during the tea-picking season. It is possible that the employer gave additional money to the workers as a 'tip', but this was not in accordance with the labour laws. On the other hand, the lumbermill employer did not comply with any of the provisions of Article 11. My father worked eleven hours per day, from 7 am to 6 pm. But the employer did not pay him overtime wages. Sometimes there was so much work that my father had to stay until after midnight, but this 'night work' was not considered to be overtime.

Holidays

According to Article 6 of the 1946 Law, every worker had the right to one day of rest per week, which was Friday. Article 7 also stipulated that workers receive wages on six public holidays: Feast of Nowruz (New Year, 21 March), Ashura Day, twenty-first of Ramazan, Constitutional Day (6 August), Feast of Ghadir and Labour Day (1 May). According to Article 3 of the 1949 law, the worker was to rest every Friday with salary; those working on Friday would be given a weekday off instead. Article 4 also recognized paid public holidays, while adding 13 Farvardin (Sizdah Bedar Festival, 2 April) to the list. Article 14 of the 1959 law also declared Friday as a day off with wages, although it could be changed with the agreement of the worker and the employer. According to Article 15, official holidays were increased to ten days, including the aforementioned days and Feast of Qorban,

Birthday of Mohammad Reza Shah (26 October), Death of the Prophet Muhammad and Martyrdom of Imam Hassan.

Since my father was young and inexperienced and did not have any job security when the first two laws were approved, and worked on Fridays and official holidays in subsequent years, it seems unlikely that the above-mentioned regulations were observed in the tea factory, particularly when there was a heavy workload. According to the law, the factory was supposed to be closed on Fridays and official holidays. However, the employer was more concerned about the production level of the factory. Because the city of Rasht, like other Iranian cities, was developing and the population of Iran was increasing, so the society's need for tea products was increasing day by day. Therefore, the employer resisted the pressure of Labour Department and Ministry officials and even gave them bribes so that the factory stayed open on holidays.

On the other hand, unofficial reports prompted the Labour Ministry to pay more attention to the lumbermill. Before 1970, it was operating in the morning and afternoon on Fridays. But after 1970, it was only open on Friday mornings, and after a while, it was usually closed on Fridays and official holidays. The employer did not want to lose business and wanted to increase his profits. But he realized that it would be better to follow the labour law's regulations, because the bandsaw and surface planer machines were damaged later and the workers could be more productive with a rest on Fridays and public holidays. The employer viewed his relationship with the workers in those years as a private one, and he regarded them as daily wage labourers, much like the previous period when he was a tea dealer and hired temporary workers to pick tea.

While the lumbermill was closed during Nowruz for three days, it was only closed in the afternoon on other public holidays. The employer was more careful about closing the lumbermill on official religious holidays that had a mourning aspect, such as Ashura, twenty-first of Ramazan, Death of the Prophet Muhammad and Martyrdom of Imam Hassan, because he wanted to maintain his relations with the clergy, who were an important social and political force. These relations with the ruling clerics even increased after the 1978–9 Revolution. Conversely, he did not close the lumbermill on official religious holidays that had a celebratory aspect (*ʿeyd*), such as Feast of Fetr, Feast of Qorban and Feast of Ghadir.

Generally, my father worked a lot, from early morning to late afternoon and evening, even after midnight. He worked on Thursdays and even on Fridays and holidays. I cannot remember that he had holidays, such as Nowruz. My mother took us outside with our close relatives for Sizdah Bedar, but I never saw my father by our side. He was not interested in such leisure activities.

Social security

Before the 1946 Labour Law, most workers did not have job security, health insurance or pensions. Employers fired workers easily without paying compensation, pension insurance or medical expenses. When a worker was fired from the workplace, his or her relationship with that employer was terminated. Articles 17–20 of the 1946 law had addressed the worker's unemployment and financial compensation from the Cooperative Fund (Sanduq-e Taavon) in the workplace (Articles 35–43) for unemployed workers. But this was not a pension. Also, regulations regarding the formation of the

Cooperative Fund and the Health Fund (Sanduq-e Behdasht) were outlined. Expenses were paid from the Health Fund for the treatment of non-work-related diseases and from the Cooperative Fund for the treatment of work-related diseases and donations related to marriage, family, pregnancy and childbirth, retirement, disability and burial. These two funds were under the supervision of the Workplace Council (Showra-ye Kargah).

In order to provide the capital for these two funds, an insurance premium equal to 3 per cent of workers' salaries was paid to the Cooperative and Health Funds. One per cent was the worker's share and 2 per cent was the employer's share. However, these funds were unsuccessful because workers' salaries were low and 3 per cent was not enough to provide all the anticipated financial assistance. Employers were also reluctant to pay their share to the two funds because they did not consider the government's decision to be the law.

Likewise, workers did not have any job security according to the 1949 Labour Law's conditions for their dismissal. This law did not guarantee their job security nor did it consider the matter of pension insurance. Although there was a greater focus on regulations related to workers' insurance and minor reforms, this did not have much effect on improving their welfare. According to Article 16, it was decided that, from the date of this law's approval, the Workers' Cooperative and Insurance Fund (Sanduq-e Taavon va Bimeh-ye Kargaran) would be created to treat and pay compensation and assistance to workers for the following cases:

- Accidents and diseases caused by work.
- Accidents and diseases not caused by work.
- Accidents and illnesses of the worker's immediate family members.
- Senility, retirement and disability of the worker.
- Marriage, pregnancy, family, childbirth, funeral and burial expenses and helping the legal survivors of workers in cases of hardship and desperation.

According to this article, the insurance premium was increased to 6 per cent, 2 per cent of which was to be paid by the worker and the remaining 4 per cent by the employer. Moreover, Article 8, which dealt with the conditions for dismissal or leaving work, stipulated the payment of seven days' wages for each year of service from the Workers' Cooperative and Insurance Fund for the social security of dismissed workers.

The 1946 Labour Law did not contain any regulations regarding workers' social security insurance because a bill for the Workers' Social Insurance Law had been approved for the first time in February 1953, during Prime Minister Mossadegh's tenure,[5] and according to it, an independent institution, the Workers' Social Insurance Organization (Sazman-e Bimehha-ye Ejtemaei-ye Kargaran), was established. Then, on 11 May 1960, the Workers' Social Insurance Law was finally passed, and the Council of Ministers approved the renamed Social Insurance Organization (Sazman-e Bimehha-ye Ejtemaei) on 13 April 1963, which was to operate under the supervision of the Ministry of Labour and Social Affairs. This Cabinet decision was eventually ratified by the Twenty-Second Majles and the Senate in February 1969.

Another important development was the formation of the Ministry of Social Welfare in 1974. This ministry covered almost all matters related to medical insurance and the welfare of various sections of society. Meanwhile, the passing of the Social Security Law in July 1975 and the formation of the Social Security Organization marked the beginning of a new era in the country's social welfare system. In 1976, with the approval of a new law that led to the dissolution of the Ministry of Welfare and the establishment of the Ministry of Public Health and Social Welfare (Vezarat-e Behdari va Behzisti), the Social Security Organization was renamed the Social Security Fund, and its obligations and treatment facilities were assigned to the aforementioned ministry. However, this change did not last long with the approval of a bill in the Council of the Islamic Revolution (Showra-ye Enqelab-e Eslami) in 1979, reviving the Social Security Organization.

During the six years that my father worked in the tea factory and the forty years that he worked in the lumbermill, except for the last two years, my father was never insured and did not take advantage of insurance benefits, such as free or discounted medicine and treatment. This means that my father paid all the costs of medicine and treatment for those forty-six years. For example, one of my older sisters needed an important and expensive operation in 1975, when she was fourteen years old. However, since the employer had not insured my father, all the expenses of the doctor's visit, hospital, surgery, medicines and travel from Rasht to Tehran were borne by my parents. The brain scan and surgery cost 15,000 and 60,000 rials. My father borrowed the latter amount from his employer, which he later paid back.

Whenever the Labour Ministry's inspectors came to the lumbermill, the employer hid the workers so as not to provide them with the correct and true information and, thus, to avoid paying the workers' insurance premiums. The workers did not protest for fear of being fired. Later, under the Labour Ministry's pressure, the employer agreed to include all the workers in social security insurance. Apparently, in 1968, he agreed to insure the workers, telling them to have a personal photo taken. But when he saw that the number of workers and their families was large (e.g. at that time, my father had a family of six), he got angry and said that he wouldn't insure them. Because he did not want to pay a lot of insurance premiums, he abandoned the idea and, in the same year, he burned all the personnel files and documents of the workers so that the Labour Ministry could not force him to pay the workers' insurance premiums, based on those files and documents.

The employer had made arrangements with 'Nejat Pharmacy' in Rasht so that the workers, including my father, and their families, could get medicine for free. But the cost of a doctor's visit was borne by the workers themselves. Even the delivery expenses for a midwife were my father's responsibility, and he did not receive any financial assistance from the Social Security Organization. For this reason, my mother gave birth to her last two children, my brother and me, in the lumbermill's small two-story house with the help of a traditional midwife. Finally, after being pressured again by the Labour Ministry, the employer was forced to insure five of his workers, including my father, two years before the Islamic Revolution, that is, in 1977.

When my father reached the age of sixty-five, he should have retired. But there was a dispute between him and the employer about the number of years he had worked.

Based on the testimony of the employer's secretary, the Labour Ministry's Dispute Settlement Council calculated that my father had worked for thirty years. According to the regulations, the court allowed the employer fifteen days' right of objection. Using this opportunity, the employer was able to subtract one year, seven months and twenty-six days from my father's working years, and finally, the Labour and Employer Dispute Settlement Council announced that the start date of my father's insurance was 22 March 1959. In this way, the employer prevented my father (and mother) from receiving their full pension during the subsequent seventeen years of his retirement. This was a clear example of the employer's exploitation of the workers, including my father.

Leaves

Article 6 of the 1946 Law stipulated that the worker was entitled to one week's leave for six consecutive months of work and fifteen days' leave for one consecutive year of work. The employer had to pay the worker's salary while she/he was on leave. Of course, this law gave the employer a free hand to put pressure on the worker so that the number of such leaves could be reduced by paying the worker on Fridays and other official holidays. However, Article 4 of the 1949 Law reduced the number of leaves to five days and ten days, respectively. Conversely, Article 15 of the 1959 Law increased the annual leave to twelve days, and the requirement of six months of work was also removed. As far as I know, my father never used any of his annual leaves and only

Figure 13.4 Centre: Hassan Saeli Kordehdeh, visiting his former co-workers, *c.* 1991. Family album.

travelled to Mashhad twice in his entire life in 1966 and 1985. But I do not know if he was paid for the days that he was on leave.

Labour contract

Article 14 of the 1946 Law and Article 7 of the 1949 Law both referred to the labour contract between the worker and the employer individually or collectively. The important point was that this contract had to be in writing. However, neither the owners of the tea factory nor the lumbermill had signed a written labour contract with my father, and this issue seriously jeopardized my father's job security. That is why my father never protested or criticized his working conditions and salary, that is, so that he would not be fired. Also, the employer never signed any labour contract with my father so that he could distort his work records and not pay insurance premiums, and, as a result, my father could not prove his actual years of work to the Labour Office, based on such a contract, in order to receive his full pension.

The 1959 law dealt with the labour contract and its provisions in more detail. According to Article 30, the labour contract was a written or oral contract whereby the worker agreed to perform work for the employer during a certain or unlimited period in exchange for wages. In this article, the influence of traditional Islamic jurisprudence can be seen in relation to the validity of the oral contract. This article also referred to the private aspect of employee-employer rights. That said, this article's recognition of oral labour contracts was a doubtful advantage because it was difficult to prove when such a contract had been concluded between the worker and the employer, especially in the case of a dispute between the two parties.

My father encountered the same problem. He accepted the employer's offer to start working in the lumbermill in 1950, which could be considered an oral labour contract. However, the employer always avoided stating the actual date of this contract's conclusion and finally convinced the authorities that my father started working in 1959, and registered him with twenty-eight years of work experience, which considerably decreased his pension. If this contract had been concluded in writing, such an injustice would not have happened to my father. Of course, perhaps he could have proven the exact date he started working in the lumbermill by referring to other administrative and financial documents related to his work records. However, one day, the employer burned all the documents, files and other written evidence of my father and other workers. One of the workers even took a half-burnt sheet of paper from those destroyed records to the Labour Ministry to prove his actual years of work in the lumbermill, which was rejected because it did not contain any definite information.

Even now, oral contracts are very common in Iran because, on the one hand, Iranians usually prefer the ease of informal agreements, and, on the other hand, they consider a written contract to be a sign of distrust between the parties and an affront to one's honour. For this reason, they accept verbal obligations. For example, no written contract is concluded between a tradesman (e.g. a painter, builder, electrician, plasterer, cabinetmaker, parquet installer, carpenter, tailor, etc.) and the employer, even though disputes sometimes arise between the two parties. Likewise, at that time, relationships were considered to be more private than public in nature. Therefore, the employer resisted the government's pressure to disclose his relationship with the workers as much as possible. At the same time, my father's employer valued personal profit above all else.

Inspection of the workplace

All three laws acknowledged labour inspection procedures. However, as mentioned, employers often bribed labour inspectors to prepare favourable reports. Normally, the Labour Ministry's inspectors came to the lumbermill, but the employer hid the workers, and his bribes were usually accepted.

Settlement of disputes between workers and employers

Articles 27–33 of the 1946 Law explained how to resolve disputes between workers and employers. According to the law, the Workplace Council had the authority to handle disputes and issue decisions. In some instances, the Arbitration Board and the Dispute Resolution Board also had the right to hear cases and issue rulings. Although this law did not mention which institution was the executive authority of these verdicts, it is obvious that the execution of the decisions of legal institutions was the responsibility of the courts of justice. Articles 13 and 14 also were related to resolving labour disputes, and the Reconciliation Commission, the Agreement Council and the Dispute Resolution Board were all mentioned in the law.

Moreover, Articles 37–46 of the 1959 Law dealt with the resolution of labour disputes. According to this law, the Workplace Council was the first authority for hearing disputes and issuing decisions. In its absence, the Labour Ministry had the duty to hear disputes and issue rulings. In other cases, the Ministry of Labour and the Dispute Resolution Board, consisting of representatives of the government, workers and employers, heard disputes and issued verdicts. The courts of justice were the executors of the decisions of these institutions.

During the forty years that my father worked at the lumbermill, he never had a legal dispute with the employer. In general, in that period, complaining or filing a lawsuit in court was considered antithetical to one's moral code of honour. Also, my father never filed a complaint against the employer with the authorities (i.e. the courts) for fear of being fired, even though he was not paid the full salary stipulated in the labour laws.

Wages

According to Article 24 of the 1946 Law, the worker's wages were to be paid weekly or once every fifteen days at the workplace on weekdays, unless otherwise mutually agreed. The minimum wage of a worker had to be such that it covered the cost of living for his family. The main problem with this article was that the worker and his family had a different perception of the cost of living versus the employer, who usually underestimated this cost. As a famous saying goes, the employer gave the worker an 'eat and don't die salary' (*hoquq-e bokhor va namir*). Thus, my father and his family had to live hand-to-mouth, barely making ends meet on the edge of poverty.

Article 10 of the 1949 law had the same provisions as Article 24 of the 1946 law, with the difference that it stated the minimum wage of an unskilled worker should be determined in such a way as to provide for his living expenses and those of a wife and two children. This article made the method of determining the worker's minimum wage more complicated because if he had more than one wife or two children, their living expenses would not be taken into account, and they would become poorer. Article 21 of the 1959 law contained the same provisions.

My father used to get paid every week, but later, it became once every two weeks. The salary that the employer gave my father was insufficient for a family of eight people, so my mother had to work. She started her job in 1970. Obviously, the employer did not pay attention to the aforementioned legal articles. Also, he never gave my father a tip, bonus or extra salary. Until 1970–1, when my mother was working and I was born, my family had a very poor and difficult life. My father received little salary because he was a simple unskilled worker, and the employer believed that the worker must be hungry to work. Therefore, my father did not receive the salary he deserved. However, when my mother started working, our standard of living gradually improved, in terms of food, clothing and consumer goods.

In September 1969, my mother was employed by a private bank called 'Pars' as a daily wage worker. She was paid 70 rials a day. Because she was a daily wage earner, she was not insured, which meant that this bank did not pay her insurance premiums. In other words, she had no job security, and she had to pay all the costs of doctor's visits, treatment and medicine herself. However, two years before the Islamic Revolution, her employment situation improved and she became a contract employee. That is, the bank signed a one-year contract with her every year. Apparently, it was at this time that the bank also began to pay its share of her insurance premiums to the Social Security Organization, so my mother was insured.

The Islamic Revolution was considered to be a revolution in favour of the workers and low-income sections of society. Therefore, if my mother had continued working in the bank, her employment status would have definitely improved and would have become official and stable. By this time, she also would have had a pension. Even though many bank employees advised her not to resign, and it was not the right time to do so, especially since she had been working in this bank for ten years, and the new revolutionary government also supported the low-income sections of society, she resigned from the bank due to personal reasons. This is something that she always remembers with sadness and regret. She even participated in adult literacy classes to advance her career and improve her work situation and to do office work. But because there was no one to take care of her youngest children, she could not continue attending those classes. At the time of her resignation, she was receiving a monthly salary of 25,000 rials.

But, in general, my mother was very careful about our nutrition, clothing and education, and we were very happy and content in this sense. Especially, since my older sister had started working and helping my mother financially during my childhood. In addition, we received free milk, bread and Dutch cheese in the elementary schools where we studied during the time of the Shah, in 1977 and 1978. In terms of food, clothing and consumer goods while we were growing up, I can say that our standard of living was not as good as a rich person or a government or bank employee or a skilled worker in a large state or private factory. But my mother was trying not to make us feel deprived, especially when I was a child, and by the time our family's economic situation had improved because my father, mother and older sister were all working.

My brother and I were so happy, having fun and playing outside a lot and in the lumbermill that we really did not need any toys. We always had the most fun with the least expense. In terms of our personalities, we did not pay that much attention to toys. I never asked my mother or anyone else to buy me toys. My brother and I were known to have a stoic attitude. Of course, my mother and my elder sister bought some toys for us from time to time, like a toy dog that moved by turning its key, a bicycle and a harmonica.

Technical protection and occupational health

For the preservation of the country's human and material resources, all workplaces were required to observe government regulations in order to prevent job-related illnesses, protect the worker's health and maintain safety for all work environments, employers, workers and apprentices. The legislator also paid special attention to this issue. Article 15 of the 1946 law obliged violators of workplace health and safety regulations and bylaws to pay a fine. Also, Article 16 required the employer to implement the Workers' Insurance Law and the necessary technical regulations in the relevant bylaws for the workers' protection from possible risks. Similarly, Article 9 of the 1949 Law obliged the employer to implement regulations related to the workers' health and safety in the workplace, and difficult and dangerous work, which would be approved by the Supreme Council on Work. Technical protection and occupational health regulations were further developed in the 1959 law, and Articles 47–51 were dedicated to this matter. Moreover, the Supreme Council on Technical Protection was established to maintain occupational health, protect workers and prevent accidents in the workplace.

It must be said that none of the regulations related to technical protection and occupational health were observed in the workplaces where my father worked. For example, although there was a lot of dust from dried tea leaves and sawdust in his workplaces, my father had never been given any mask or special uniform. Likewise, periodic check-ups were not performed to assess the health of his lungs, heart and blood vessels. Sometimes my father tied a piece of cloth to his mouth and nose to prevent dust and particles from entering his lungs. I always noticed that he coughed a lot, and it was only when he retired that he stopped coughing.

Conclusion

The employer did not fulfil any of the provisions of the labour laws that were to his detriment and to the benefit of the worker. Labour laws were not yet fully established, and employer-employee relations were more private and personal. If the employer was a kind, honest, just and humane person, he would act in accordance with the economic and welfare status of the worker. But if he was a greedy, cruel, merciless and money-loving person, he would extract a lot of labour from the workers and give them less than their rightful wages.

Generally speaking, I think that the labour laws of this period did not have a considerable impact on my father's working conditions because they had just been approved and, therefore, had not yet been widely propagated and established. Employers, especially those in small establishments like the one where my father worked, were accustomed to private relationships with their workers. Moreover, the employer considered this relationship to be much like one where a person hires a carpenter to make a chair for him, so it was not public or national. The relationship between the employer and the worker was more influenced by the personality characteristics of the employer, and to a lesser extent, the worker, than labour laws. My father's employer shirked the obligations imposed by the labour laws and exploited his workers in order to increase his profits. Of course, sometimes he helped his workers and lent them money. But overall, he viewed them as slaves. That being said, fortunately, the women of our family, especially my mother and older sister, played an important role in elevating our economic situation and living conditions.

Appendix

Father's work and life chronology
Date of birth: 29 April 1925 (9 Ordibehesht 1304)
Place of birth: Maragheh, East Azerbaijan Province
Year of immigration to Rasht, Gilan: 1944 (1323 AH); at age nineteen
His driver and motivation to immigrate: his cousin
His introduction to work in tea factory: his cousin
Year started working in tea factory: 1944 (1323 AH)
First labour law approved: 18 May 1946 (28 Ordibehesht 1325)
Father's age when 1946 law approved: twenty-one years old
Duration of work in tea factory: six years
Second labour law approved: 7 June 1949 (17 Khordad 1328)
Father's age when 1949 law approved: twenty-four years old
Year started working in lumbermill: 1950 (1329 AH)
Father's age when he started working in lumbermill: twenty-five years old
Date of marriage to my mother: 1 January 1955 (11 Dey 1333); at age twenty-nine
Third labour law approved: 17 March 1959 (26 Esfand 1337)
Father's age when 1959 law approved: thirty-three years old
Date of insurance in Social Security Organization: 22 March 1959 (1 Farvardin 1338; twenty-eight years, four months and four days in total)
Retirement date: 30 May 1990 (9 Khordad 1369); at age sixty-five
Duration of work in lumbermill: forty years (1950–1990)

Date of death: 26 January 2008 (6 Bahman 1386); seventeen years after retirement
Father's age at death: eighty-three years old
Place of death: Rasht
Cause of death: kidney failure

Notes

1 I would like to thank Dr Mary Yoshinari for her encouragement, guidance and cooperation at each step of writing this chapter. Her questions for each section have been very helpful, and the resultant text has come together successfully.
2 *Majmueh-ye Qavanin-e Sal-e 1325: Moshtamel bar Qavanin–Tasvibnamehha–Ayinnamehha va Bakhshnamehha-ye Chap Shodeh dar Ruznameh-ye Rasmi-ye Keshvar, Chap-e Dovvom* (Tehran: Ruznameh-ye Rasmi-ye Keshvar-e Shahanshahi-ye Iran, 1328/1949), 83–93.
3 *Majmueh-ye Saliyaneh-ye Sal-e 1328: Moshtamel bar Qavanin, Tasvibnamehha, Ayinnamehha va Bakhshnamehha-ye Chap Shodeh dar Ruznameh-ye Rasmi-ye Keshvar* (Tehran: Chapkhaneh-ye Majles, 1328/1949), 95–110. See 'Qanun-e Ejazeh-ye Ejra-ye Gozaresh-e Komisiyun-e Pisheh va Honar va Bazargani Marbut beh Kargaran va Karfarmayan'.
4 *Majmueh-ye Qavanin-e Sal-e 1337: Moshtamel bar Qavanin–Tasvibnamehha–Ayinnamehha* (Tehran: Ruznameh-ye Rasmi-ye Keshvar-e Shahanshahi-ye Iran, 1337/1958), 710–24; *Majmueh-ye Qavanin va Mosavvabat-e Dowreh-ye Nuzdahom-e Qanungozari-ye Majles-e Showra-ye Melli*, Vol. 4 (Tehran: Chapkhaneh-ye Majles, 1337/1958), 2250–68.
5 *Majmueh-ye Saliyaneh-ye Sal-e 1331: Moshtamel bar Qavanin va Lavayeh-ye Qanuni va Tasvibnamehha va Ayinnamehha-ye Chap Shodeh dar Ruznameh-ye Rasmi-ye Keshvar-e Shahanshahi-ye Iran* (Tehran: Chapkhaneh-ye Majles, 1331/1952), 52–87. In particular, see Article 94 on page 86.

Bibliography

Archives and libraries

Library, Museum and Document Center of the Iranian Parliament, Tehran

Primary sources

Majmu'eh-ye Qavānin-e Sāl-e 1325: Moshtamel bar Qavānin–Tasvibnāmehhā–Āyinnāmehhā va Bakhshnāmehhā-ye Chāp Shodeh dar Ruznāmeh-ye Rasmi-ye Keshvar, Chāp-e Dovvom. Tehran: Ruznameh-ye Rasmi-ye Keshvar-e Shahanshahi-ye Iran, 1328 (1949).
Majmu'eh-ye Qavānin-e Sāl-e 1337: Moshtamel bar Qavānin–Tasvibnāmehhā–Āyinnāmehhā. Tehran: Ruznameh-ye Rasmi-ye Keshvar-e Shahanshahi-ye Iran, 1337 (1958).
Majmu'eh-ye Qavānin va Mosavvabāt-e Dowreh-ye Nuzdahom-e Qānungozāri-ye Majles-e Showrā-ye Melli. Vol. 4. Tehran: Chapkhaneh-ye Majles, 1337 (1958).

Majmu'eh-ye Sāliyāneh-ye Sāl-e 1328: Moshtamel bar Qavānin, Tasvibnāmehhā, Āyinnāmehhā va Bakhshnāmehhā-ye Chāp Shodeh dar Ruznāmeh-ye Rasmi-ye Keshvar. Tehran: Chapkhaneh-ye Majles, 1328 (1949).
Majmu'eh-ye Sāliyāneh-ye Sāl-e 1331: Moshtamel bar Qavānin va Lavāyeh-ye Qānuni va Tasvibnāmehhā va Āyinnāmehhā-ye Chāp Shodeh dar Ruznāmeh-ye Rasmi-ye Keshvar-e Shāhanshāhi-ye Irān. Tehran: Chapkhaneh-ye Majles, 1331 (1952).

Secondary sources

Hashemi, Seyyed Mohammad. *Tārikhcheh va Seyr-e Tahavvol-e Hoquq-e Kār bā Ākherin Eslāhāt.* Tehran: Moasseseh-ye Kar va Tamin-e Ejtemaei, 1385 (2006).
Iravani, Mohammad Kazem. *Hoquq-e Kār dar Irān.* Tehran: Ofset-e Golshan, 1353 (1974).
Mehr, Farhang. *Hoquq-e Kār.* Tehran: Chap-e Rasti, 1350 (1971).
Mehr, Farhang. *Hoquq-e Kār va Bimehhā-ye Ejtemā'i.* Tehran: Moasseseh-ye Ali-ye Hesabdari, 1345 (1966).
Moein, Mohammad Reza and Abbas Zeraat. *Hoquq-e Kār.* Vol. 1. Tehran: Entesharat-e Andishehha-ye Hoquqi, 1389 (2010).
Motamedi, Fatollah. *Tārikh va Hoquq-e Kār va Tāmin-e Ejtemā'i dar Irān az Dowrān-e Safaviyyeh tā Zamān-e Hāzer.* Tehran: Vezarat-e Kar, 1354 (1975).
Tafazzoli, Abolqasem. *Majmu'eh-ye Qānun-e Kār beh Enzemām-e Qavānin–Āyinnāmehhā– Tasvibnāmehhā–Bakhshnāmehhā-ye Marbut beh Qānun-e Kār va Gerdāvari va Moqaddameh va Tārikhcheh.* Tehran: Amir Kabir, 1341 (1962).

Index

Abadan 17, 168, 187, 190, 233
Abadan Institute of Technology 233–4
Abdullaev, Zakir Zul'fugarovich 12, 162
Abrahamian, Ervand 10, 14–16, 118, 123, 129
Afacan, Serhan 20, 27 n.51
agricultural sector 10–11, 55–8, 61–3, 76, 96, 97, 103, 123, 125, 132 n.46, 143, 154, 161, 162, 169, 181–8, 211, 225–6, 245
Ahvaz 102, 110 n.99, 123, 187, 188
Akhavan, Ahmad 201, 202, 214 n.3, 220
Akhgar 82–3
Alamdar, Abdolreza 21
Al-e Ahmad, Jalal 7, 167–8, 175–6 n.59
Alikhani, Alinaghi 228
Allied occupation 22, 93, 95, 97, 99, 102, 103, 108 n.48, 118, 137, 165, 169, 172, 181, 226, 245, 246
American College of Tehran (Alborz High School) 216 n.10
Amin al-Zarb
  Haj Mohammad Hossein 40, 60
  Mirza Hassan 56
Amini, Ali 122–3, 206
Amir Kabir (Mirza Taqi Khan Farahani) 71
Amol 149, 232
archives 4, 6, 15, 17, 23–4
army 39–40, 42–4, 47–9, 76, 82–4, 115–16, 121, 122, 138, 165, 166, 183, 227, 253
Arsanjani, Hassan 123, 132 n.46
Ashraf, Ahmad 10–11, 22
  and Ali Banuazizi 121
Atabaki, Touraj 15, 17–20, 25–6 n.16
  and Lana Ravandi-Fadai 26 n.17
Avanesiyan, Ardashes (Ardeshir) 14, 15
Azimi, Fakhreddin 22
Babol 149, 225
Bahar, Mohammad Taqi (Malek al-Shoara) 44, 46, 47, 52 nn.49, 72, 74
Baharestan Square 41, 44, 48
Bakhtiyaris 187, 188
Baku 11, 59–60, 94, 105 n.6
Bani Sadr, Abol Hassan 237
banks
  Bank of Agriculture and Industry 95–7, 102, 105, 107 nn.37–8, 108 n.47, 109 n.80
  Bank of Industry and Mining 97, 104, 140, 141
  Construction Bank 145
  Discount and Loans Bank of Persia (Bank-e Esteqrazi) 56, 95, 162
  Mortgage Bank 97, 108 n.47, 139
  National Bank of Iran (Bank-e Melli) 62, 76, 95–7, 100, 101, 103, 106 n.21, 107 n.31, 109 n.80, 139–43, 145, 156 n.27, 189–90
  Pars Bank 261
  Ruspersbank 65, 99, 139, 143 (*see also* Rusiranbank)
  Sepah Bank 97, 108 n.47, 138 (*see also* Pahlavi Bank)
Bayat, Asef 21–2
bazaaris 39, 40, 44, 45, 48, 56, 119, 191, 193, 224, 239 n.7, *see also* merchants
Bazargan, Mehdi 152–3, 236, 237
Behshahr Industrial Group
  Arak Industries 230, 232
  Banijamali, Dr. 229, 231, 237
  Behpush Company 5, 230–1
  building construction 224, 232–3
  business ethics 235–6, 239 n.3
  capital 228, 229, 232

collaboration with artists, intellectuals 235
cotton-ginning 225–6, 230
DuPont 231–2
entrepreneurial family 4, 6, 223–4, 239 n.4
foreign skilled workers 230
glycerine 227
Hafez Insurance Company 239 n.4
Haj Seyyed Mahmoud Ladjevardi and Partners Company 224–5
healthcare products for pandemic 238
horizontal integration 223, 228
International Bank of Iran and Japan 153, 223, 239 n.4
international markets 225, 238
Iran Center for Management Studies 236
Iran Knitting Factory 230, 231
Iran Textile Company 230
Javid and Arien Trading Companies 225
Kashan Velvet Plant 6, 223, 229–30, 232
marketing and advertising 227, 228, 234–5, 240 nn.26, 35
Mokhtari, Hossein 228
Mr Oya, Teijin Company of Japan 231
Osaka 225, 229
Polyacryl Iran Corporation 231–2, 238
Ravand Carpet Plant 229, 232
risk-taking 223, 226, 232
Shahinpar, Nasser 235–8
soap and detergent 227–8, 235
social responsibility 6, 234
state control of industries 236–8
vegetable oil 223, 226–7, 232, 234, 240 nn.26, 28
vertical integration 223, 225–8, 240 n.37
welfare of employees 233–4

Biglari, Mattin 20
Bolshevism 37
Braun, Rudolf 74
bread 72, 84, 108 n.48, 165, 195 n.33, 196 n.40, 222, 261
Bullard, Reader 103, 110 n.104
bureaucracy 115, 121, 128, 130, 138, 212
Bushehr 100

cabinet (Council of Ministers) 39–42, 44–6, 49, 102, 107 n.30, 116–20, 165, 175–6 n.59, 247, 257
capital 55–7, 62, 71, 75, 76, 86 n.15, 95–9, 103–5, 106 n.8, 107 n.31, 108 n.47, 109 nn.64, 80, 111 n.113, 124, 138, 139, 152–3, 163, 170, 184–5, 193–4, 256
capitalism 6, 10, 12, 13, 16, 45, 49, 60, 61, 74, 77, 143, 154, 184, 186, 188, 248
Caspian region 76, 106 n.23, 225, 245
Caucasus 9, 11, 64
centralization 50, 103, 105, 119–21, 125–8, 172, 181
Chalus 102
Chamber of Commerce 64, 65, 104, 140, 148, 202, 214 n.3, 219, 237
Chaqueri, Cosroe 23–4
charities 115, 116, 119, 122, 124, 126, 130, 132–3 n.62, 148, 154, 234
chervonets 65, 69 n.58
class
bourgeoisie 14, 38, 94, 163
conflict 12, 13, 118
elites 81, 119, 129, 181, 191
middle 16, 119, 148–9, 154–5
working 6, 11–14, 17–25, 38, 50, 84, 94, 121, 172, 181, 186
clergy 6, 15, 22, 46, 48, 63, 66, 82, 85, 150, 202–3, 215 n.9, 248, 249, 255, *see also* ulema
Behbahani, Seyyed Mohammad (Javad) 215 n.9
Esfahani
Haj (Sheikh) Aqa Nurollah 63, 82
Seyyed Abol Hassan 48
Haeri Yazdi, Ayatollah Abdol Karim (Haj Sheikh) 48, 202–3, 214 n.2, 215 n.9
Khoei, Haj Mirza Yahya (Emam Jomeh) 215–16 n.10
Khomeini, Ayatollah Ruhollah 237, 248
Modarres, Seyyed Hassan 43–8, 52 n.55

coal mines
  concessions 163, 173–4 nn.19, 20
  Gajereh 163–4, 171
  Lalun 163–4
  Shemshak 109 n.79, 163–4, 167
  Zirab 163, 167–8
Comintern 13–15
Commercial Bank of Iran
  articles of association 141
  board of directors 140–2, 151
  branches 141–5, 147–50, 152, 154
  cultural activities 146
  employee welfare measures 151–2
  establishment 138–43, 146, 148, 151, 153–4
  financial reports 145–8, 152, 155 n.6
  foreign exchange transactions 141, 146, 148
  German and British private banks 139, 146–7
  investment 141–2, 145, 148, 150, 151, 154
  London and Hamburg branches 147–8
  lottery 149–50
  merger 152–3
  new banking services 149–50, 154
  new building 5, 143–5
  new technologies 146–7
  opening 140–2, 144–5
  other commercial activities 150–1, 154
  personnel 141, 143, 145–7, 151–3
  public confidence 139, 143, 145, 153–4
  social responsibility 148–9, 154–5
  Trade Bank (Bank-e Tejarat) 141, 153
companies, *see* corporations, firms
  domestic advocacy 62, 84
  interwar growth 76, 93, 97–100, 104–5, 105 n.6, 106 n.20, 108 n.46, 110 n.108, 111 n.113
  post-war growth 122, 150–2, 170, 171, 223–4, 228
confiscation of private property 6, 153, 236–8, 242 n.86, 248–9
constitution 39–43, 48, 72, 78, 123, 254
Constitutional
  era 48, 117, 129
  Movement 13, 56, 57, 215 n.9
  Revolution (1905–9) 3, 9–10, 13, 15, 20, 38, 50, 56, 57, 59–61, 72, 75, 224, 239 n.7
constitutionalism 10, 13, 35, 43, 47, 72, 86 n.15, 129
construction sector 81, 96, 99, 101, 115, 118–20, 122, 123, 149–52, 154, 162, 169, 205, 210, 219, 224, 226, 228, 232–4, 246
copper mines
  Abbasabad 166–7
  Anarak 164, 166–7
  Qajar period 3, 162, 245
  Sarcheshmeh 21
copper smelting plant (Ghaniabad) 164
Council of Commerce 71
coup d'état
  1921 10
  1953 10, 121, 166, 168–9, 172
Czechoslovakia 95, 103–4

Davar, (Mirza) Ali Akbar (Khan) 104–5
Dehesh, Mirza Fazlollah Khan (Ata al-Molk) 81–2, 205
Dehgan, Seyyed Mohammad 35–6, 50 n.5
Department of Mines 163–4
development (economic and social) 246, 253, 254, 257
development plans
  First (1948–55) 120, 138, 169
  Second (1955–62) 122
  Third (1962–68) 123–4, 129
  Fourth (1968–73) 124, 129
  Fifth (1973–78) 124–5
  Six (1978–82) 128, 130
Dezful 187, 188
domestic manufacturing
  bricks 102, 190
  canneries 102, 150
  cardboard 102, 228
  carpets 49, 56, 58, 61, 62, 186, 191–2, 229–30
  cement 100–2, 104, 109 n.79, 110 n.106, 162
  cotton 99, 100, 102, 110 n.88, 201, 204, 216 n.11, 220, 221, 225–6, 230

glass 5, 100–2
matches 76, 95, 100–2
rice 100, 102, 110 n.96, 162
soap and detergent 76, 100, 102, 226–8, 235–6
sodium bicarbonate 102
subsidies 76, 77, 82, 100, 109 n.71, 181, 227
sugar 61, 76, 95, 100–4, 109 n.81, 110 n.92, 150, 162, 216 n.11
tea 76, 100, 102, 245, 247, 250, 254, 255
textile industry 6, 20, 36, 61, 71–3, 75–7, 79, 81–5, 99, 100, 102, 163, 182, 183, 194, 229–32, 237–8
textiles
artificial flowers 100
brocade 79
burlap (gunnysacks) and twine 102, 163
camel hair (*barak*) 82–3
canvas (*karbās*) 80–1
chintz 102, 163
cotton batting 102
fustian (cotton fabric) 230
jersey (*keshbāf*) 80
knits 86 n.15, 102, 230, 231
linen 102
polyester-acrylic 223, 231–2, 238
silk 55, 57, 62, 80, 100–2, 230
socks and knitwear 100, 102
thread and yarn 71, 100, 102, 201, 204, 205, 214 n.4, 220, 221, 230
velvet 6, 223, 229–30
wool 100, 102
tobacco 81, 100, 101, 109 n.80, 162, 189, 190 (*see also* cigarettes)
vegetable oil 102, 223, 226–7, 234, 240 nn.25–8
wood 189, 245, 250, 255
Dowlatabadi, Yahya 47, 48

Ebtehaj, Abol Hassan 6, 97, 118, 139, 142
Economic Council 49, 118
economic modernization 3, 6–7, 10, 103–5, 162, 172, 245
Economy Movement, *see also* merchants
formation 60–1, 65–6
impact on other cities 61–2, 66
leadership 60, 63
League of Merchants' Union 57, 60–1, 63–4, 66, 68 n.27
results and government response 64–6
those for and against 63–4, 66
education 5, 37, 115, 117–25, 128, 129, 149, 187–8, 234, 261–2
Ehsani, Kaveh 17, 19–20
electrification 6, 100, 109 n.79, 162, 201, 203, 208–9, 221, 222, 226
Elghanian, Habib 226, 240 n.20
employers
bargaining power 121, 164, 188, 189, 192, 195 n.25, 246, 251–2, 254
bribes 84, 194, 255, 260
exploitation of workers 6, 36, 79, 166, 167, 181, 184, 186, 188–90, 193, 253–5, 257–63
feudalism 38, 185, 192, 251–2, 263
paternalism 84, 192
rent capitalism 6, 184–6, 191–2, 194
employment statistics 182–4, 186, 188, 190
enterprises 5, 77, 100, 102, 150, 163, 171, 182–4, 192, 246, 247, 254
entrepreneurs
family business 84, 100, 102, 123, 191, 197 n.71, 224–5, 236–8
generational turn 203, 224, 236
partnerships 81–2, 97, 201–3, 214 nn.2–3, 220, 224, 225, 228, 231–2
women 100–1, 230–1, 236
Eqtesad-e Iran 37, 42–4
Eshghi, Mirzadeh 38, 146
Eskandari, Prince Soleiman Mirza 6, 39, 44–6, 49
Ettefaq-e Kargaran 35, 50 n.3
Europe 3, 39, 46, 57, 59, 72, 75, 76, 103, 139, 140, 147, 181, 225, 231, 235
Exposition of Iranian Products in Tehran (1936) 100

Facopa Advertising Agency 234, 240 n.26
family 5, 7, 22, 81, 119, 121–3, 126, 127, 150, 166–8, 171, 182, 189–91, 194, 196 n.52, 201, 203, 213, 223, 233, 236, 256, 257, 260
famines
  1918/19 35
  1942 108 n.48, 110 nn.100, 104, 165
farmers 38, 41, 63, 66, 104, 119–21, 225–6, 250
Farrokhi Yazdi, Mohammad 39–41, 47
Financial Times 238
Floor, Willem 11–12, 15–17, 162
foreign trade
  anti-import campaigns 63, 77, 85, 87 n.28
  balance 58, 60, 65, 93–4, 110 n.103
  barter and clearing agreements 95, 96
  customs duties 12, 55–6, 57, 58, 59–60, 65, 67 n.4, 76, 86 n.15, 94, 100, 115, 123, 163, 230 (*see also* tariffs)
  exports
    cotton 55–9, 62, 94, 225
    dried fruit and nuts 55, 58, 65, 94
    fisheries 99, 102, 162
    hides and leather 56, 58, 94
    rice 55, 56, 58, 65, 94
    silk 55, 57, 62
    wool 56, 62, 94
  foreign goods 49, 56, 60, 62, 63, 73, 75, 78, 85, 86 n.15, 94
  free trade 59, 62, 63
  import duties 12, 76, 86 n.15, 100, 115, 163, 230
  import substitution 75–6, 95, 100
  imports 55, 57–8, 60–2, 65, 94–7, 99, 100, 102, 105, 107 n.25, 108 n.48, 110 n.104
  tariff autonomy 76, 94
  third countries 94, 95, 103–4
  trade protectionism 75
  trade surplus 94
Forqan Group 238, 242 n.86
Forughi, Mohammad Ali (Zoka al-Molk) 105, 107 n.31
free enterprise 250
General Department of Labour 246, 247
  factory inspections 254, 257, 260
Germany 3, 77, 94, 95, 99, 103–4, 110 n.108, 122, 139, 140, 146–7, 193, 201, 205, 221, 224, 231, 232
Ghassemi, Farhang 15–16
Gheissari
  Ahmad 202
  Forough al-Zaman (Semsarzadeh) 215 n.7
  Morteza 201, 206, 215 n.9
Gheissarieh, Haj Mirza Ali 6, 201–5, 213, 214–17 nn.5, 7–10, 15
  Aliabad Gheissarieh (Qarchak, Varamin) 215 n.8
  Dowlatabad Gheissarieh (Shahr-e Rey) 215 n.8
Gilan 59, 63, 245–7, 249–50, 263
girls 5, 37, 79, 182, 193, 257
Gladstone, William Ewart 44
global context 3–6, 9, 10, 12, 13, 17–20, 24, 78, 103, 110 n.108, 117, 129, 147–8, 169, 225, 254
Golshan 48
Gonbad-e Kavus 226, 232
Gorgan 58, 225, 226, 232, *see also* Astarabad
government intervention 75, 172, 174 n.21, 181, 192
Great Britain
  Anglo-Persian Oil Company (APOC) 20, 187, 189
    Anglo-Iranian Oil Company (AIOC) 6, 96–7, 99
  British New East Bank 138
  embargo on Iranian oil 169, 172
  foreign trade 56, 67 n.5, 77, 93–4
  Imperial Bank of Persia 5, 96, 99, 105 n.2, 107 n.31, 139, 143–5
    British Bank of Iran and the Middle East 143
  imperialism 9, 16, 38–9, 42, 44, 93, 103
  observers 102, 108 n.51, 111 n.110, 165, 175 n.39
  wartime control 95, 103, 110 nn.100, 104, 165
Great Depression (1929–33) 76, 96
guilds

bazaar closures 39, 44, 45, 48
economic activism 46, 49, 63, 78–9, 81, 83, 104
historiography 11
labour movement 35, 37, 38, 41, 42
leadership 38–40, 42, 44, 45, 48–50, 52 nn.55, 74
petty shopkeepers and traders 61, 62, 63, 66, 73, 78, 81 (*see also* cigarette sellers)
political activism 6, 39, 41, 45, 46, 78
shoemakers 36, 46, 49, 78–9
subordination to state 47–50

Habl al-Matin 63, 64
Hakimian, Hassan 11–12
Hamadan 61, 79, 186
Haqiqat 4, 35, 36, 38–42, 45
Harvard Advisory Group 123, 129, 169
Hedayat, Mehdi Qoli Khan (Mokhber al-Saltaneh) 81
Hekmat (Shirazi), (Mirza) Ali Asghar (Khan) 165
Hobsbawm, Eric 74
Hormozi, Farhad 228, 234, 240 nn.26, 35–6
Hoveyda, Amir Abbas 125–8

India 11, 19–20, 187, 189, 224, 230
industrial sector 238
cottage industries 74, 77, 100, 189, 191, 193, 197 n.64, 226 (*see also* workshops)
factory system 6, 74, 75, 77, 81, 84, 85, 101–2, 104, 162, 219, 246
large-scale industries 72–7, 81, 84–5, 86 n.15, 100, 103, 229
manufacturing 74–5, 82, 100, 102, 122, 146, 163, 182–3, 223, 228, 230–2, 238
industrialization 6, 9, 12, 61, 71–7, 79, 81, 84–5, 95, 96, 100, 115, 130, 181, 194, 232–3, 245
infrastructure 3, 6, 61, 63, 72, 76, 78, 81, 103, 117, 120, 139, 162, 169, 201, 203, 207–10, 220–222, 226, 228, 238
intellectuals 7, 16, 38, 41, 42, 47, 63, 72, 85, 118, 119, 149, 155, 167, 176 n.59, 235
International Institute of Social History (IISH) 18–20
International Labour Organization (ILO) 117, 129, 246, 247, 254
interwar period 5, 93, 95, 103
Iranian economy
annual budget deficit 138
budgets 96, 100, 138, 163, 164, 166, 169, 242 n.76
capital flight 95, 96
cost of living 5, 16, 38, 108 n.48, 118, 124, 137–8, 189–90, 196 n.41, 253, 260–1
economic crisis 58–9, 61, 65–6
exchange rate stabilization 96
foreign exchange 95–6, 101, 107 nn.41–2, 109 n.81
grain 97, 100, 102, 110 nn.99–100, 104, 165, 166, 185 (*see also* wheat, barley)
growth 93, 97–102, 104–5, 110 n.108
hoarding 110 n.104, 143, 165
inflation 35, 97, 105, 108 n.48, 124, 138, 165, 189, 227, 230, 246
inflationary stagnation 122
military expenditures 96, 116, 119, 121, 163, 164
price stability 227, 228, 230–1, 248
purchasing power 118, 123, 248
revenue 95–7, 101–2, 106 n.7, 108 n.46
silver *vs.* gold standard 96, 107 n.35
staple goods 101, 110 n.104
stock exchange 105, 109 n.66
taxation 49, 95–7, 100, 108 n.51
Iranian National Oil Company 234
Iranian Oral History Project, Harvard University 242–3 n.86
Iranian Revolution (1978–9) 10, 11, 14–15, 19, 21–4, 151–3, 194, 212, 227, 236–8, 248, 255, 257, 258, 261, *see also* Islamic Revolution
iron ore mines (Bafq, Mesgarabad) 164, 171
Isfahan 58, 61–3, 73, 77, 80–4, 100, 102, 111 n.113, 118, 123, 143, 145, 164, 166, 182, 187, 189, 193, 195

n.33, 202–3, 205, 215–17 nn.9, 10, 13, 224, 232, 246
Islam
banking 6, 149–50, 153, 202
ethics 44–5, 48, 239 n.3, 247–9
Hajj 149–50, 229
holidays 254–5
Islamiyeh Company 62, 63, 82
law 184, 259
maktabhā 187
marjaiyyat 203, 215–16 n.9
mosques
Jameh Mosque, Tehran 44
local mosque, Rasht 248, 249
Qazvin Shah Mosque 61
Shah (Soltani) Mosque, Tehran 46, 140
Sheikh Abdol Hossein Mosque, Tehran 37–8
production and consumerism 63, 71–2, 229
Qom Seminary 202, 214 n.2
religious gatherings 37–8, 44, 46, 212, 248
Issawi, Charles 162, 173 nn.3, 5, 8
Italy 94, 228

Jafari, Peyman 19, 23
Jangali Movement 38, 59
Japan 95, 193, 225, 229, 231, 232
Jazani, Bijan 235, 238
Jefroudi, Maral 19

Kahrizak 101, 102
Kar 46
Karaj 101, 102, 164, 193, 216 n.10
Kashan 6, 58, 77, 80, 82, 102, 210, 224, 229–32, 234
Kasraei, Siavash 235
Kazemi, Farhad 10
Kazeruni
Haj Mohammad Hossein 81–2, 84, 205
Mirza Jafar 84, 102
Kerman 21, 82, 102
Kermanshah 46, 102, 165, 175 n.39, 232
Keyvani, Mehdi 11
Khameneh, Haj Mohammad Jafar Tajer 57
Khatunabad 186–8
Khorasan 61, 62, 64, 150, 162, 186, 190
Khorramshahr 106 n.23, 143, 145, 232
Khuzestan 150, 187, 246
Knowledge Corps 123
Kuznetsova, N. A. 11

labour history
new *vs.* old 6, 17, 18, 21, 24
Soviet historians 11–12
Stalinist perspective 12, 15
labour movement
armed resistence 167–8
collective action 6, 19, 23, 35, 77, 166
identity and influences 14–16, 35, 37–9, 44–5, 50, 192, 236
impact of activism 5, 22, 50, 118–19, 122, 166, 169, 172, 193–4, 226, 236, 240 n.22, 245–7
International Workers' Day 41
organized *vs.* unorganized labour 14–18, 20, 24, 197 n.66
petitions 12, 15, 20, 46, 73–4, 77–85, 87 n.29, 166–7, 172
protests 28 n.55, 35, 37, 41, 46, 49, 82, 119, 121, 122, 152, 166, 167, 176 n.59, 193–4, 246–7
state suppression 3–4, 19, 50, 77, 121, 167–8, 192
strikes 7, 17, 35–6, 39, 42, 46, 50 n.3, 84, 166–8, 190–2, 196 nn.35, 41, 236, 246–7
Ladjevardi
Ahmad 225–7, 233, 238, 242 n.86
Foundation 234
Ghassem 224–6, 242 nn.76, 86
Habib 4, 15, 225, 234–5, 242–3 n.86
Haj Seyyed Mahmoud 224, 226, 235, 237
Ladjevardian
Haj Seyyed Akbar 224–32, 234, 237, 242 n.86
Haj Seyyed Mohammad (Nilforush) 224
Lily 5, 230, 237
Masoud 232, 236
and Partners Trading Company 224
Lambton, Ann 10
landlord 6, 38, 63, 66, 118–19, 121, 123, 170, 173 n.19, 184–5, 188,

191–2, 194, *see also arbāb*, landowner

laws
- Banking Affairs (1979) 152–3
- Coal Mine Concessions (1930; 1932) 163, 173–4 nn.19, 20
- Commerce (1925; 1932) 76, 97, 138, 142, 155 n.6
- Commercial Trademarks and Inventions (1931) 100, 109 n.77
- Conscription (1925) 116
- Factory Act (1936) 77
- Foreign Exchange Transactions (1936) 96, 107 n.42
- Foreign Trade Monopoly (1931) 65, 76, 94–5, 100, 106 n.20, 174 n.21
- Formation of Municipalities and Association of Cities and Towns (1949) 119
  - Municipal Law (1952) 120
- Importation of Machinery (1925; 1931) 76, 86 n.15, 100, 109 n.78
- Industrial Protection (1979) 237–8
- labour
  - First (1946) 119, 129, 169, 171, 246–7, 250, 254–6, 258–63
  - Second (1949) 120, 247, 250, 254–6, 258–63
  - Third (1959) 189, 192–4, 247, 253–5, 259–63
- Land Reform (1963) 121, 184
- Loans for Domestic Factories (1934) 107 n.37
- Mines/Mine Exploration/Mining Code Legislation (1939) 164
- National Employment (1922) 116
- Northern and Western Provincial Roads (1926) 107 n.29
- Uniform Dress Code (1928) 76, 79–84
- Use of National Clothes (1923) 76–81
- Villagers' Social Insurance (1969) 121
- Workers' Social Insurance (1953; 1960) 120, 129, 171, 256–7

League of Nations 46, 105 n.1

leftists 5–7, 22, 42, 43, 115, 118, 176 n.59, 235–8, 246

Lindenblatt, Kurt 139

Litvinov, Maksim 103, 110 n.103

Lockman, Zachary 18, 27 n.42

Loraine, Sir Percy 47

low-value assembly 237–8

lutis 185, 188

Mahmoudi, Jalil and Nasser Saeidi 15

Majles *see* Iranian Parliament, National Consultative Assembly
- First, Second and Third 13, 35, 57, 72, 86 n.15
- Fourth 6, 39–45, 78, 86 n.15, 93, 105 n.1, 116
- Fifth 45, 47–9, 52 n.72, 96
- general trends (1915–1954) 117, 138
- Sixth 49, 61–2, 64, 79, 94, 96, 139, 163
- Seventh 79, 83
- Eighth 81, 82, 94–7, 163
- Ninth 96, 101, 109 n.83
- Tenth 107 n.42
- Eleventh 164, 219
- Twelfth 99
- Fourteenth and Fifteenth 95, 118, 166–7, 247
- Seventeenth 120
- Eighteenth and Nineteenth 140, 247, 253
- Twenty-Second 121, 257
- Twenty-Third 125–7
- Twenty-Fourth 127

Maljoo, Mohammad 24

Mani, Shokrollah 14, 36, 37, 45

Maragheh (Eastern Azerbaijan) 245, 246, 248, 263

Markov, Nikolai 210, 216 n.10

Marvdasht 101, 102

Marx-Engels-Lenin Institute 24

Marxist perspectives 13–16, 38, 94

Marxists 14, 16, 246, 248

Mashhad 62, 64, 82, 102, 111 n.113, 123, 163, 173 n.19, 193, 215 n.9, 232, 248, 259

Masjed Soleyman 190, 196 n.35

Mazandaran 58, 149, 167–8, 171, 246

merchants

Association of Merchants' Representatives 56–7
Caucasian 64
Gilan 60, 61, 64
Hamadan Merchants' Union 61, 79
Iranian 4, 6, 11, 40, 41, 47–9, 55–60, 65–6, 72, 78, 85, 94, 99, 100, 104, 105 n.5, 106 n.8, 118, 181, 229
Isfahan 61, 62, 188
Kashan 224
Khorasan 61–2, 64
Malek al-Tojjar (Shiraz) 62
protests 59, 66
Qazvin 61, 63
Qom 202, 220
Russian 56, 57
Shiraz 61, 62
Tabriz 61, 62
Tehran 57, 61–2, 201–2, 219–20
Messkoub, Mahmood 116, 117
Miandoab 101, 102, 104
Middle East 10, 78, 137, 168, 224, 228, 231, 232
middlemen 186, 189, 193
Millspaugh, Arthur Chester 95, 97, 103, 108 nn.48, 51, 110 n.104, 163
Mines Council 169–70
mining licences 170–1
ministries
Agriculture, Commerce and Public Works 79, 163
Agriculture 123, 226
Commerce 62, 140, 225–6
Commerce, Trades and Crafts 246, 247
Education 82, 117
Finance 95, 99, 101, 102, 104, 108 n.51, 116, 170
Health 126–8, 235
Public Health and Social Welfare 127–8, 257
Industry 162, 231
Labour 121, 167, 168, 192, 194, 197 n.64, 247, 260
Labour and Social Affairs 121, 126, 193, 257
Labour and Social Services 121, 190
Labour and Trades and Crafts 164, 167
National Economy 100, 164
Economy 132–3 n.62, 228, 241 n.39
Social Welfare 125–8, 130, 132–3 n.62, 257
War 43–4, 47
Mir Fendereski, Abolqasem 11
Moein al-Tojjar Bushehri, Haj Mirza Mohammad 40, 86 n.15
Moghadam, Valentine 21, 28 n.55
Moghissi, Haideh and Saeed Rahnema 23
monopolization 59, 65, 76, 94–6, 99–101, 103, 104, 106 nn.20–1, 109 nn.64, 80, 163
Moscow 24, 36, 60, 65
Moshaver al-Mamalek (Ansari, Ali Qoli Khan) 59
Mossadegh, Mohammad 6, 47, 48, 119, 120, 129, 144, 145, 169, 171, 172, 247, 248, 256
Mostowfi al-Mamalek (Ashtiani), Mirza Hassan Khan 45–8, 107 n.30, 139
Motamed al-Tojjar, Mirza Mohsen 43, 52 n.49
Muhammad Ali Pasha 72

Nain 80
Naini, Mirza Hossein 48
nation 9–10, 12, 38–41, 44, 47, 74, 103, 115, 122, 128–30, 167
National Association for the Protection of Children 120
National Front 119, 132 n.45
nationalism 5, 14, 60, 72, 79, 84–5, 104, 155, 169, 226
nationalization
forests (1963) 123
oil (1951) 20, 119, 120, 144, 169, 172, 226
private sector (1979) 6, 152–3, 236–8, 242 n.86
The New York Times 122
Nikpour, Abdol Hossein 201–2, 213–14 nn.2–3, 219–20
Nishapur 58, 173 n.3

Nosratian, Mohammad Ali 201, 220
Novo Industries 242 n.86

oil
embargo 169, 172, 226 (*see also* sanctions)
industry 4, 10, 17–20, 84, 103, 169–70, 172, 183, 187, 189, 196 n.35, 233–4
prices 124, 230, 231
refineries 17, 123, 168
revenues 6, 96, 101, 115, 120, 121, 127, 129, 130, 163, 169, 230

Pahlavi
Ashraf 120
dynasty 3, 10, 15, 50, 66, 115, 152, 245
Farah 124–5, 133 n.62
Foundation 122
Imperial (Royal) Court 64, 116–17, 121, 122, 130, 132–3 n.62, 145, 165
Mohammad Reza Shah 4, 120, 121, 123, 125, 145, 147, 165, 168, 172, 181, 185, 192, 245, 247, 248, 255, 262
Princess Fawzia 116
Reza Shah 3, 20, 50, 61, 63, 64, 71, 72, 73, 74–7, 81, 83, 84, 93, 104, 111 n.110, 115, 117–18, 128–9, 138, 139, 162, 165, 166, 172, 181, 219, 245, 246, 247 (*see also* Reza Khan)
Reza Khan 3, 14, 38, 39–40, 41–4, 46–9, 50, 82, 245 (*see also* Sardar-e Sepah)
Second period (1953–79) 152, 248
peasants 6, 10, 21, 38, 121, 184–6, 192
Persian Gulf 76, 106 n.23, 238
Pirnia (Moshir al-Dowleh), Mirza Hassan Khan 39, 41–2, 46–8
Pishevari, Seyyed Jafar 38, 40
police 4, 40, 61, 63, 84, 122, 183, 253
political parties 4, 15, 16, 22, 24, 45, 52 n.72, 118, 120, 129, 132 n.42, 167, 246
Communist Party of Iran (CPI) 13–15, 37–8, 50
First Congress (1920) 38, 50
Social Democratic Party 13, 25 n.15 (*see also* Democrat Party of Iran)
Socialist Party 45–8
Tajaddod Party 48
Tudeh Party 14, 118, 119, 123, 129, 132 nn.44–45, 166, 176 n.59, 192, 246 (*see also* CPI)
Workers' Party 50
population 11, 49, 57, 71, 129, 161, 172 n.1, 181–3, 186–8, 226, 235, 255
ports 59, 60, 96, 103, 123, 169, 228
post-revolutionary period 10–11, 22, 23, 245
post-war period 4–6, 22, 105, 166, 169, 194, 223, 225
private sector 5, 6, 76, 100, 105, 139, 140, 148, 163, 170, 172, 223–6, 237–8, 240 n.22
Procter & Gamble 227
production
capital-intensive 75, 228
domestic 37, 75, 101, 108 n.48, 163
labour-intensive 75
productivity 183, 184, 193–4, 233, 255
Profintern 36
proletariat 45, 194
provinces 5, 11, 43, 44, 47, 48, 50, 57, 61, 97, 99, 104, 107 n.29, 118, 127, 153, 183, 186, 192, 228, 235
public health and sanitation
medical facilities 117–18, 181
mobile hospitals and doctors 118–19
mortality rate of children 118
poor patients 119–20
public and rural clinics 118, 122
sewage and piped water 117, 120
wartime conditions 165

Qajar
Ahmad Shah 39, 46, 48
dynasty 3, 9, 66, 103, 245
Nasser al-Din Shah 56, 71, 224
Qavam (al-Saltaneh), Ahmad 39, 42, 44–6, 95, 105, 118–19, 129, 132 nn.44, 46
Qazvin 58, 61, 63, 183, 230, 232, 246
Qazvini, Aref 38

Qom 6, 48, 58, 201–3, 205, 207–11, 213, 215–16 nn.9–10, 217 n.15, 219–20, 228, 237, 246

Rashid-Yasemi, Gholam Reza 214–15 n.5, 217 n.13
Rasht 64, 82, 100, 102, 142, 232, 245–50, 252, 255, 257, 263–4
Red Lion and Sun Society 118, 125, 126, 148
regional disparity 124, 183, 202–3
republicanism 47–50
revolutionaries 10, 22, 50, 72, 213, 236–8
Revolutionary Prosecutor's Office 237
Rey 102, 104, 164, 215 n.8
Risbaf (Carding) Complex
  Arbab Hassan 207, 211
  architecture 203–5, 209–11, 216–17 nn.10, 13, 220–1
  capital 6, 201, 202, 220, 222
  carding 201–2, 219–21
  cotton 201, 204, 216 n.11, 220–1
  electricity for factory and Qom 6, 201, 203, 208–9, 222
  Habib Aqa 208
  machinery 201, 203, 205, 209, 213, 219–22
  Qaderi, Habibollah 212–13
  Qom-Kashan Road 208–10
  Siemens generators 201, 203, 208–9, 221
  water reservoir 207, 210, 220, 222
  workers 4–5, 201, 205–7, 209–10, 221–2
roads 11, 35, 55, 56, 78, 96, 103, 107 n.29, 123, 163, 169, 203, 206, 210, 226
Russia 3, 9, 11–13, 17, 56–9, 67 n.5, 76, 78, 93, 95, 103, 105 n.2, *see also* Soviet Union
Russian (October) Revolution (1917) 11, 13, 17, 35, 49–50, 58–60, 65

Saeidvaziri, Manuchehr 121–2
Saeli Kordehdeh, Hassan
  character 247–9, 251–3, 255, 259
  early life 245, 246, 252, 263
  family 245, 248–9, 253, 255, 257, 261–3
  insurance 257–8, 263
  lumbermill 247–55, 257–60, 262, 263
  migration 245, 247, 249–50, 252, 263
  moral principles 248–9, 253, 260
  religious beliefs 247–8
  retirement 258–9, 263–4
  salary 253–4, 259, 261
  tea factory 250, 254, 255, 257, 259, 263
  women 5, 249, 253, 255, 257–8, 261–3
  work ethic 249, 255
  working conditions 250–5, 259, 262–3
Safavid Empire 9, 11
sanctuary 39–41, 49
sarkārgar 189
Sazman-e Ettelaat va Amniyat-e Keshvar (SAVAK) 121, 168
Schacht, Hjalmar 147
Schünemann, Max Otto 205, 216 n.10
Second International of Socialist and Labour Parties (1889–1916) 13
Semnan 58, 167, 182
Semsarzadeh, Haj Abol Qasem 201, 220
Senate 140, 152, 242 n.76, 247, 257
Shahi 101, 102, 104, 163
Shariati, Ali 176 n.59, 238
Sheikholeslamzadeh, Shojaeddin 127–8
Shiraz 61, 62, 77, 82, 85 n.1, 102, 110 n.99, 246
Shushtar 187, 188
social insurance
  accidents and illnesses 116, 119, 121, 127, 171, 256
  disability 116, 119, 121, 124, 126–7, 171, 256
  employer avoidance 189, 196 n.41, 255–61
  pensions and retirement 116, 122, 127, 138, 171, 256, 261
  unemployment 118–19, 127, 171, 256
social insurance organizations
  Public Administration and Recruitment Organization 122
  Social Insurance Organization 126, 127, 257
  Social Security Organization 127, 257, 261, 263

Villagers' Social Insurance Organization 121–2, 126, 127
Workers' Social Insurance Organization 120, 129, 256
Social Services Association 120, 125–6, *see also* Imperial Social Services Organization
social standing 185, 188
Social Welfare Agency 119
social welfare funds
Construction and Cooperative Fund 119
Cooperative Fund 256
Health Fund 256
other funds 121–2
Road and Railway Workers' Provident Fund 116
Rural Cooperative Fund 119
Village, Rural District and Regional Development and Cooperation Fund 119
Villagers' Cooperative Fund 129
Workers' Cooperative and Insurance Fund 119, 256
Soviet Union
embassy 39–41, 59
foreign trade 6, 59–66, 68 n.20, 69 n.58, 93–5, 99–100, 103, 105 nn.5–6, 106 nn.7–9, 108 n.46, 110 n.103, 224
influence 3, 41, 47, 64, 93–4, 110 n.100, 122, 129, 132 n.42, 165, 169, 254
observers 94, 96, 100, 102, 105, 106 n.9, 107 n.41, 109 n.71
Treaty of Friendship (1921) 93, 95, 103, 105 nn.1–2
troops in Iran 97, 110 n.100, 165, 246
Sultanzadeh (Mikhailian), Avetis 13–14, 35, 39, 49
Supreme Council of Social Welfare 124–6, 130
Supreme Economic Council 118, 140, 169
Supreme Labour Council 118–19
Supreme Trade Council 65

Tabatabaei, Seyyed Zia al-Din 38–9, 46, 51 n.20
Tabriz 22, 28 n.55, 43, 50, 61–2, 77, 100, 102, 111 n.113, 123, 163
Tadayon, Seyyed Mohammad 48
Tafazzoli, Haj Hassan 229
Tajaddod, Mostafa
career experience 6, 140–1, 146–7, 150, 152, 154
political participation 140, 152, 154
Taqizadeh, Seyyed Hassan 48, 86 n.15
Tehran 17, 22, 35–6, 40, 41, 43–50, 57, 59, 61, 62, 76, 79, 80, 82, 97–102, 104, 105, 109 n.79, 110 n.99, 127, 128, 138, 140, 143, 145, 147, 150, 152, 164–7, 182–3, 186–8, 190, 191, 193, 195 n.25, 196 n.41, 203, 208, 212, 214 n.5, 215–16 nn.8–10, 219, 224, 226–8, 230–3, 237, 252, 253, 257
Tehran Bazaar 39, 40, 44, 45, 48, 105, 224, 236
Tehran Central Post Office 216 n.10
Tehran Polytechnic (Amirkabir University of Technology) 229–30
Teymurtash, Abdol Hossein (Sardar Moazzam Khorasani) 39, 96, 104
Thompson, E. P. 14, 16–17
Trans-Iranian Railway 61, 76, 95, 96, 101, 103, 104, 106 n.23, 115, 116, 123, 169, 190, 203, 219
Treaty of Golestan (1813) 9, 55–6, 76
Treaty of Turkmenchay (1828) 9, 55–6, 76
tribespeople and nomads 129, 143, 161, 187, 188, 226
Tufan 39, 40, 47
Turkey 3, 10, 11, 13, 14, 72, 94, 232, *see also* Ottoman Empire

unions *see* labour movement
Central Council of Labour Unions 168
Central United Council of Workers and Toilers' Unions 246
Construction Workers' Union 37, 46
General Council of United Workers of Tehran 36–8, 44, 45, 50

Government Departments' Union 37
Ministry of Post and Telegraph Employees Union 37
Municipal Workers' Union 37
Pharmaceutical Workers' Union 37, 45
Printing Workers' Union 36, 49
Teachers' Union 37, 39
Typesetters' Association 35
Union of Printing and Textile Workers 42
United Council of Workers 36
Weaving Workers' Union 36
United Nations International Children's Fund (UNICEF) 120
United States
advisory role 95–6, 103, 107 n.25, 122, 123, 129, 169, 192–3
economic relations 42, 94, 103, 107 n.34, 122, 147, 224–5, 231–3
knowledge transfer 147, 227, 231, 232, 236, 242–3 n.86
political intervention 5, 169, 172
products 49, 227, 228, 232
University of Tehran 186–8
urbanization 5, 13, 17, 24, 59, 78, 84, 104, 120, 121, 123, 124, 143, 148, 154–5, 161, 172 n.1, 181–4, 186–92, 194, 222, 245, 247, 255

Van der Linden, Marcel 17
Varamin 101, 102, 104, 215 n.8, 216 n.10
Vatan Factory 27 n.51, 73, 77, 81–4, 88 n.49, 102, 205, 216–17 nn.10, 13
villages 18, 119, 121–2, 149, 152, 184–6, 188, 192, 226, 235, 246, 249–50, 252

war
First World War (1914–18) 10, 13, 19, 35, 49, 57, 58, 60, 66, 115, 162, 224
Iran-Iraq War (1980–88) 23, 213, 238, 247
Second World War (1939–45) 14, 15, 22, 97, 102, 117, 118, 137, 143, 153, 165, 169, 172, 181, 224, 226, 245
welfare policies
homeless elderly 119
orphaned and destitute children 118–19
poor 118–20, 128
standard of living 118, 121, 127
Welfare Services Organization 127
White Revolution (1963–79) 123, 184, 245
women 5, 62, 116, 165, 167, 169, 189, 190, 196 n.40, 234, 236, 248, 249, 253, 255, 257, 258, 261–3
women's suffrage 118
workers
age 169, 182, 186–7, 190
Ahvaz 187–9
artisans 11, 36, 37, 61, 63, 72–5, 77, 80, 84, 104
bakers 36, 42, 188, 190
brick kiln workers 17, 186–8, 190, 193, 196 nn.40–1
carpet weavers 75, 79, 168, 182, 186, 189, 191–2
casual labour force 183–4, 188–9, 192, 193, 250, 254, 255
cloth weavers 36, 71, 74, 79–80, 82–3
construction workers 11, 35, 37, 46, 162, 166, 168, 183–4
craftsmen 6, 11, 20, 36, 37, 39, 41, 42, 45, 46, 49–50, 72–5, 77–85, 104, 120, 183, 188
endogamy 188
ethnicity 17, 18, 186–8, 190, 245, 249, 252
factory workers 100, 162, 182, 183, 233, 236, 250, 254, 255, 257, 259, 263
grievances 20, 73, 79, 83–5, 166, 167, 181
identity 17–19, 21, 188, 252
industrial workers 11, 12, 28 n.55, 121, 162, 183, 186–7
labouring poor 11, 17, 22–4, 49, 79, 81, 83, 118, 120, 165–7, 184, 187, 189–90, 248, 260–1
literacy 5, 7, 39, 45, 116, 149, 154, 187–8, 222, 234, 235, 247, 249, 253, 261

migration 11–12, 17, 19, 78, 121, 181–2, 184, 186–8, 230, 245, 247, 249–50, 252
mineworkers 7, 11, 21, 116, 161–2, 164–5, 166–9, 171–2 (*see also* miners)
oil workers 11, 17–20, 168, 183, 187, 189, 190, 196 n.35, 233–4
silk fabric makers 80
skills 84, 116, 184, 187, 188, 193, 230, 262
tāyefeh 188
textile workers 36, 42, 84, 162, 168, 189, 201, 205–6, 210, 221, 222, 230
training 115, 116, 120, 121, 129, 146, 147, 172, 193, 228, 230, 232–6, 238
unemployment 61, 78, 81, 83, 182–4, 193, 246
unskilled workers 124, 184, 187–90, 230, 253, 261
women and children 17, 21, 74, 75, 79, 165, 169, 171, 182, 189, 190, 196 n.40, 253, 261–2

working conditions
disputes with employers 17, 167–8, 172, 190, 192–4, 196 nn.35, 41, 246, 258–60
fatalities and casualties 167–8, 171
food 152, 162, 165, 166, 184, 189–90, 195 nn.33–4, 210, 221, 222
health and safety 119, 151, 164, 171, 184, 193–4, 220–2, 256, 262
holidays 41, 254–5, 258–9
hours 35, 169, 184, 189–90, 201, 222, 252, 254, 255
housing 162, 164, 184, 233, 253
lack of labour standards 75, 77, 119, 166, 171, 189–90, 192–4, 196 nn.40–1, 197 n.64, 253–63
medical care 151, 164, 222, 233, 256, 257
profit-sharing 121, 123, 190, 194, 233
relations with employers 121, 151–2, 164, 167–8, 172, 184–6, 188–9, 192–4, 195 n.25, 196 n.52, 197 n.71, 206–7, 233–4, 245–8, 250–63
unpaid labour 21, 182, 196 n.40
wages and salaries 24, 36, 39, 42, 75, 79, 116, 118–20, 127, 138, 151, 162, 166–7, 171, 181, 182, 184, 186, 188–90, 196 nn.35, 41, 203, 233, 236, 242 n.76, 246, 249, 250, 252–6, 258–61, 263

World Economic Crisis (1908) 57

Yazd 77, 79–80, 82–3, 150, 164, 166, 246
Yazdi
Haj Mohammad Hossein 201–3, 214 n.2, 220
Mohammad Fateh 238

Zabol 186–7
Zahedi, Ali 164
Zanjan 102, 166, 182
Zarkesh, Ali Asghar 201, 220
Zia Zarifi, Hassan 235

www.ingramcontent.com/pod-product-compliance
Ingram Content Group UK Ltd.
Pitfield, Milton Keynes, MK11 3LW, UK
UKHW020220041026
15470UKWH00012B/753

9 780755 65259